MANAGING INEQUALITY

Managing Inequality

Northern Racial Liberalism in Interwar Detroit

Karen R. Miller

NEW YORK UNIVERSITY PRESS
New York and London

NEW YORK UNIVERSITY PRESS
New York and London
www.nyupress.org

First published in paperback in 2017

LIBRARY OF CONGRESS CATALOGING-IN-PUBLICATION DATA
Miller, Karen R.
Managing inequality : Northern racial liberalism in interwar Detroit / Karen R. Miller.
pages cm
Includes bibliographical references and index.
ISBN 978-1-4798-8009-6 (cloth : acid-free paper)
ISBN 978-1-4798-4920-8 (paperback)
1. Detroit (Mich.)--Race relations--History--20th century. 2. Detroit (Mich.)--Politics and government--20th century. 3. African Americans--Civil rights--Michigan--Detroit--History--20th century. 4. African Americans--Michigan--Detroit--Social conditions--20th century. 5. Liberalism--Michigan--Detroit--History--20th century. 6. Equality--Government policy--Michigan--Detroit--History--20th century. 7. Detroit (Mich.)--Economic conditions--20th century. I. Title.
F574.D49A25 2014
308.896'07307743409042--dc23
2014024575

New York University Press books are printed on acid-free paper, and their binding materials are chosen for strength and durability. We strive to use environmentally responsible suppliers and materials to the greatest extent possible in publishing our books.

Manufactured in the United States of America

10 9 8 7 6 5 4 3 2 1

Also available as an ebook

CONTENTS

ACKNOWLEDGMENTS

This project has been a long time in the making. It began in the Shaker Heights, Ohio, of my childhood in the 1970s and 1980s. A self-consciously liberal, affluent, and integrated inner-ring suburb, Shaker Heights was known for its good schools, winding streets, and anti–white flight programs: low-interest loans designed to integrate neighborhoods, robust busing, and ordinances against blockbusting. But the city's liberalism and its pro-integration policies did not eliminate segregation or stratification, even locally. In spite of busing, elementary schools in the city's wealthiest neighborhoods were majority white, and those that sat next to Cleveland were almost all black. By high school, tracking by race and class was intense.

Available explanations felt inadequate: we were taught that racism was a relic left over from slavery, rooted in the American South, mostly a problem of the past, and something that was already fading away. Or, it was a failing of individuals who had absorbed toxic ideas and needed them purged. Shaker Heights was certainly more integrated than neighboring towns, and as I came to understand later in life, its racial progressivism and limited residential integration were quite rare for suburban America. But contradictions remained between the racial liberalism it espoused and the persistence of inequalities in wealth and schooling, even very locally. This book is my effort to understand why.

Archivists and staff members at the Bentley Historical Library at the University of Michigan, the Walter P. Reuther Library of Labor and Urban Affairs at Wayne State University, the Burton Historical Collection at the Detroit Public Library, the Library of Congress, and the Schomburg Center for Research in Black Culture at the New York Public Library went out of their way to help me find materials relevant to my interests. I am indebted to Debbie Gershenowitz, who acquired the book for NYU Press, and to Clara Platter and Constance Grady, who saw it through production. I am grateful for two incisive reviews that helped me reshape and strengthen the manuscript from Kevin Boyle and a reviewer who remains anonymous. Richard Thomas generously allowed me to use a map he dug out of his files, and I am thankful for that act of kindness. I would also like to thank Gianluca Vassallo for letting me use a photograph, part of his "Free Portrait" project, as my author photo.

I began to write about the history of Detroit as an undergraduate at the University of Michigan. I was incredibly fortunate to have Elsa Barkely Brown and Robin D. G. Kelley guide me through my undergraduate thesis and shape my thinking about the city and its racial dynamics. Graduate school faculty, including my adviser, Terry McDonald, and a committee that included Matthew Countryman, Earl Lewis, Hannah Rosen, and Heather Thompson, provided me with models of engaged and careful scholarship after which I modeled my own. Each of them helped sharpen the questions I was asking and the book that ultimately emerged. Friends and faculty in Ann Arbor, whom I met through the university, through activism, and through local networks, also contributed to my thinking and provided me with invaluable support and camaraderie. Thanks go to Chris Cassell, Leland Davis, Angela Dillard, Clara Kawanishi, Sarah Jessup, Tamara Joseph, Christine Kelley, Kate Masur, Regina Morantz-Sanchez, Alyssa Picard, and Nick Syrett. In 1997, I moved to Detroit and was fortunate to meet people who introduced me to the city and became my friends and comrades. Glen Bessemer, Dianne Feeley, Jessica LaBumbard, Peter Landon, Kristin Palm, Jenny Schmidt, Dave Schroeder, Matt Siegfriend, Jane Slaughter, and especially Jana Cephas, Mark Dilley, and Lori Stark helped me navigate Detroit and understand its many geographies.

In 2003, I moved to New York. A welcoming group of old and new friends and colleagues help me rethink and refine this project. David Kazanjian generously read an early draft of the manuscript and offered helpful advice about how to proceed. Both formal and informal writing groups with colleagues at the City University of New York were an essential part of the revision process. Carolina Bank Munoz, Stephen Steinberg, Celina Su, Saadia Toor, and Nicole Trujillo-Pagan all offered invaluable feedback. I am grateful to the many friends, colleagues, and comrades in New York and elsewhere who have listened to me work through my ideas over dinner, coffee, work dates, and playdates, as well as those who have provided a respite from thinking about this project: Kelly Anderson, Moustafa Bayoumi, Padmini Biswas, Shelley Curnow, Kristen Gallagher, Mary Greenfield, Alyssa Katz, Robin Kietlinski, Emily Kohner, Jude Koski, Allison Miller, Sarah Miller, Charlie Post, Deb Reichman, Kirsten Scheid, Brooke Smith, and Chloe Tribich.

Phyllis van Slyck has fed my son, Oscar, and me countless delicious Sunday dinners and whisked us away to the beach. She, Laura Tanenbaum, and Arianna Martinez have helped me feel at home at LaGuardia Community College. Michelle Billies, another CUNY colleague and friend, has been encouraging and interested in my work. I have known Liza Featherstone since I was an undergraduate, and we have been talking about these questions since we first met. Doug Henwood has whipped up fabulous delicacies over which we complain about politics and the Left. My cousin Sarah Miller wrote her senior thesis about Detroit as well; she served as an invaluable research assistant when I was finishing graduate school. Rebeca Carrion was Oscar's caregiver for two years, and I am indebted to her for her enthusiasm and generosity. Mary LuAllen has made this project possible by helping me analyze and understand my relationship to its content and production. I have also been honored to have had excellent students at LaGuardia Community College ask me provocative questions about cities, race, and history and push me to clarify my claims. One of them, Anthony Salcedo, worked as my research assistant. I look forward to reading his scholarship in the near future.

I feel very lucky and deeply grateful to have a full-time academic job that provides me with a living wage, summers off, job security, and a day job that is related to my intellectual pursuits. Other funding has also been crucial. Grants from CUNY's Faculty Fellowships Publications Program, the Center for Place, Culture, and Politics at the CUNY Graduate Center, and the PSC-CUNY Research Award Program have released me from teaching and allowed me to focus on my writing. I finished a major round of revisions when I was on sabbatical and in residence at the Eisenberg Institute for Historical Studies at the University of Michigan. Funding from the Educational Development Initiative Team's Professional Development Grant Program at LaGuardia

Community College and the National Endowment for the Humanities have also helped me carve out the space and time to write and travel.

A generous team of close readers, who are also close friends, helped me tighten and sharpen the manuscript. Prudence Cumberbatch has read many versions of various chapters and has provided me with vital intellectual and emotional support. Libby Garland has been reading drafts of my work, providing me with detailed and incisive feedback, and making me laugh since we met in graduate school. Aimee von Bokel's generosity, her close attention to nuance, and her enthusiasm for talking through ideas all improved the manuscript.

Jeanne Theoharis has always believed in the importance of this project and has provided me with more than two decades of loyal friendship. Her last-minute help tightening the manuscript improved and strengthened the book. In the last year of revisions, Chris Schmidt worked alongside me for countless hours and adopted my deadline as his own. Our conversations and his careful feedback, as well as his generosity and companionship, were crucial for helping me get through the revision process. Colleen Woods read an early draft of the manuscript from beginning to end, as well as countless versions of revised sentences, paragraphs, and sections. Her support, willingness to talk through ideas, and belief in this project have been invaluable.

My parents and my sister have also been incredibly generous with their love, support, and time. They have taught me to believe in social justice, to challenge inequality, to value analysis and careful scholarship, and to question and complicate received wisdom. They have also taught me that real love reaches well beyond immediate families and insular, narrowly defined communities. Analyzing and understanding how inequality and exploitation function, valuing alternatives, and imagining other possibilities are essential for imagining a more just and more equal future. I am grateful for their pride in my work and accomplishments.

Oscar Miller has made me happier since he came into my life as an eight-pound bundle of joy and distraction. For him, at six, my "working" means staring at a screen with disappointing graphics and tapping randomly at letters on a keyboard. Communicating with him as his analytic capacities develop has served to reinforce my commitment to clear prose and carefully explained logic. I still can't believe that I met

Emily Drabinski on the Internet, since our friends, interests, and lives overlap and complement each other so seamlessly. Her belief that this project is worthwhile and that I should "keep going," and her willingness to read every word have helped me meet deadlines, sidestep gaping emotional potholes, and take new pleasure in my ideas. Because of her, and the joys, challenges, and pleasures of the life we are building together and with Oscar, the last few years have been the best of my life.

This manuscript has benefited handsomely from these myriad connections, and I am deeply grateful.

Introduction

On September 9, 1935, the Detroit Housing Commission began tearing down condemned buildings in the heart of the city's largest black neighborhood. The fifteen square blocks, which were 95 percent African American in a city that was only 7 percent black, had the highest proportion of black residents in Detroit. Before the clearance began, the city held a "Demolition Ceremony" and invited Eleanor Roosevelt to be the principal speaker. Between 10,000 and 20,000 spectators, a mix of white and black Detroiters, listened to the First Lady deliver a five-minute speech in front of the vacated home of Mrs. Rosella Jackson.[1] Roosevelt declared that the Depression had piqued Americans' interest in poverty and inspired magnanimous public efforts like this one. The crowd cheered and applauded for the First Lady. A group of African American children from the Brewster Community Center performed a dance. Five-year-old Geraldine Walker, whose home was going to be torn down in the slum clearance, presented Roosevelt with a marigold. At ceremony's end, Roosevelt waved her handkerchief, signaling the destruction of the first condemned house on the fifteen-block site.[2]

Three years later, after the condemned buildings had been cleared and the Brewster Homes, Detroit's first public housing project, stood in their place, a crowd of African Americans convened in front of the new buildings, this time as protesters. These demonstrators were pushing city officials to hire an all-black staff for the new, segregated facility. Brewster Homes would accept only black tenants, but the city had hired white staff to work at the complex and allowed white business owners to set up shops in its storefronts. Across town, the Parkside Homes, which would open the same day, were entirely white. Black staff would not be hired, and black proprietors would not be permitted to open businesses in its storefronts. The Afro-American Institute, a black protest

Geraldine Walker hands a marigold to Eleanor Roosevelt at the opening of the Detroit slum clearance project, September 9, 1935. Courtesy of Corbis Images.

organization, had attempted to negotiate with local authorities to hire only black workers and restrict businesses to black ownership. When negotiations reached a stalemate, the institute collected hundreds of signatures on a petition and called for daily protests. Facing considerable pressure from the African American activists, the city's mayor, Richard Reading, endorsed the plan to hire an all-black staff to work at Brewster. However, Detroit's city council vetoed the proposal. Black residents continued to fight for an all-black staff and guarantees that black merchants would have priority for Brewster's storefronts.[3]

Roosevelt's demolition ceremony promoted white liberal leaders' understanding of the promises of the New Deal for African Americans. The Afro-American Institute's protests three years later illustrate the limits of liberal sympathy and good intentions in the face of ingrained social structures and material inequality. The first illustrates that northern white liberals imagined themselves as generous and magnanimous in relation to African Americans, who they saw as passive, if deserving. The widely circulated photograph of Geraldine Walker and Eleanor Roosevelt captures this well-intentioned but ultimately problematic dynamic. It portrayed a young, small Geraldine Walker holding Roosevelt's hands and listening intently to the First Lady. Roosevelt, who had bowed down to Walker's level, seemed to be imparting kind advice to the young girl. In this image, Walker was cast as defenseless, sweet, innocent, and inactive—someone who absolutely deserved help and would graciously accept support. Although she was handing Roosevelt a marigold, her gesture was lost in an image that emphasized Roosevelt's activity and generosity, and Walker's passive gratitude.

The implicit message in this staged photograph was that white liberal leaders and African Americans should sustain a clearly imbalanced relationship whereby white leaders provided vulnerable African Americans with the resources they needed and African Americans were grateful recipients. This image erased the protest that African Americans had been waging for years as they fought to get the city to address their needs. Black Detroiters were not receiving these resources simply because white liberals intuitively recognized and acted on social need. Instead, their victories were a product of black political power, built over years of struggle against persistent, state-supported inequality that pushed white liberals to these positions.

While the first of these two events portrayed white liberal leaders' perspective, the second showed how black activists interrupted that widely accepted narrative. By protesting the inequities at Brewster Homes, black activists exposed the limitations of liberal policies that were ostensibly guided by the logic of magnanimity. Instead of accepting resources as passive recipients, they recast themselves as political participants with a self-conscious project aimed at building a racially egalitarian city. Black activists presented this alternate image to passersby by holding picket signs and petitions as they fought to reconfigure their relationship to white liberals and their place within the urban political sphere. These African American protesters were challenging the unequal distribution of resources at the same time that they were calling into question the basic assumptions upon which that allocation was premised—northern racial liberalism.

Northern Racial Liberalism and "Colorblind" Racism

Managing Inequality examines the formulation, uses, and growing political importance of northern racial liberalism. Northern racial liberalism is the notion that all Americans, regardless of race, should be politically equal, but that the state cannot and indeed should not enforce racial equality by interfering with existing social or economic relations. This idea became popular among Detroit's white liberal leaders during and immediately after the First World War and came to be consistently embraced by the majority of mainstream white politicians by the end of the 1920s. This occurred alongside the spectacular expansion of the city's population, economy, physical size, and municipal government. By the 1930s, as city leaders responded to the Great Depression and began to build the local New Deal infrastructure, northern racial liberalism had already come to shape their ideas, define their policies, and characterize their practices.

White proponents of northern racial liberalism did not always embrace the discourse of racial equality for the same reasons. Indeed, their understanding of its implications and their motivations for accepting its tenets were manifold and changed over time. In the early twentieth century through the First World War, white northern racial liberals were likely to define political racial equality narrowly. A legacy of northern sectional politics from the Civil War and postbellum eras, northern racial liberalism helped white urban leaders explain why they opposed racist violence in favor of urban order. But few of them saw social, economic, or residential integration as desirable goals. Fewer still believed that African Americans' critiques of the prevailing racial and economic order were valid or required their attention. Indeed, northern racial liberals in this period rarely believed in racial justice. These men and women used the rhetoric of northern racial liberalism to conceal their support for existing forms of subordination.

By the 1930s, though still a minority, a far larger proportion of white liberals believed in the tenets of urban racial equality and saw it as inherently socially, politically, and morally good. For them, a more racially equal city would be a better city, one in which everyone would benefit from a commitment to justice and racial equality. Members of this group worked most closely with African Americans, were most inclined to link racial inequality to economic stratification, and were most likely to work in coalition with the Left. They disagreed about how far they could push established political institutions to respond to the dictates of racial equality. Many believed that a conservative backlash would undermine their political power if their commitment to racial equality was too explicit or if their policies directly challenged social, residential, or occupational segregation. They were also constrained by their belief that racism was a moral problem of individual sentiment and did not need to be addressed institutionally.

These positions sat on two ends of a spectrum. They represent white leaders' main motivations for embracing northern racial liberalism and political racial equality, but they were rarely distinct from each other. The majority of Detroit's white liberals believed in some aspects of each of these tenets. Some were far more committed to the expansion of racial equality, while others saw the maintenance of urban order as their principle interest and maintained a scant degree of concern about racial injustice. This tension among white proponents of northern racial liberalism also represented the paradox that stood at its heart. White northern leaders came to embrace racial equality in the political realm. They saw the North as a place where modern forms of racial democracy could be and were already being practiced, in contrast to the backward and violent application of segregation in the Jim Crow South.[4] At the same time, they supported and implemented policies that promoted racial inequality. Although this may seem like an internal contradiction, it was not. Northern racial liberals certainly wanted to ease the political and economic consequences of racial stratification, but for many, their higher priority was to manage racial discord with an eye toward sustaining urban peace.

This made northern racial liberalism a double-edged sword for African Americans. A range of black activists, from middle-class reformers to supporters of mass action, capitalized on the language of equality that white leaders increasingly embraced and as a consequence won new resources and concessions from city officials. At the same time, though, many white city leaders who embraced northern racial liberalism were not interested in acknowledging or confronting the underlying racism that already structured urban life. Instead, their racial liberal ideology helped to reinforce and mask the enduring power of existing hierarchies and to contain African Americans' growing demands for citizenship and equality. At its worst, rather than undermining racial inequalities, northern racial liberalism could and did function as an instrument for subduing the aspirations of the growing African American population and for casting their demands for equality as irrelevant and disruptive.

This paradox should sound familiar because it sits at the heart of early twenty-first-century American racial politics. Indeed, northern racial liberalism is the basis for what contemporary critics call "colorblind racism"—the idea that the United States is no longer racially unequal because overtly racist speech is no longer an acceptable element of mainstream political or social discourse.[5] This study shows that our current racial system—where race-neutral language coincides with extreme racial inequalities that appear natural rather than political—has a history that is deeply embedded in contemporary governmental systems and political economies. It challenges the commonsense notion that these inequalities are the direct legacy of southern slavery and will fade away with time as we move further away from slavery. It shows instead that racism survives because it is also a modern creation, emerging out of discourses and policies that came to be codified alongside the expansion of municipal governance and the welfare state in the early twentieth century. As such, understanding this history continues to have contemporary relevance in a broad array of local and regional political economies, including the urban North.

Contemporary proponents of colorblind racism maintain that the successes of the civil rights movement—the dismantling of Jim Crow, alongside the antidiscrimination legislation and judicial decisions of the 1950s and 1960s—effectively eliminated racism in American institutions and marginalized the shrinking minority of whites who continued to articulate racist ideas. Racism, they assert, is dead. It no longer shapes American institutions, government practices, or social behaviors. Accordingly, colorblind racists castigate civil rights leaders, whom they characterize as opportunistic and self-serving, for producing racial divisiveness by inventing false specters of inequality. They see these claims as misplaced resentment on the part of people of color toward whites. Rather than a measure of the durability of discrimination, colorblind racists see persistent racial inequality as evidence that communities of color foster negative, dysfunctional, and defeatist "cultures of poverty" that hold their members back from success. This idea is widely accepted in popular cultural discourse about race and used as a tool to argue against affirmative action and other policies oriented toward remedying racial inequality.[6] Even critics of colorblind racism accept the idea that it developed as a reaction against the civil rights movement. They rarely see its much longer history back into the early twentieth century or examine the suppleness of urban governing ideology in thwarting African American claims that racial hierarchies shaped northern cities.[7] Northern racial liberalism married the same two components that colorblind racism does today: an extension and affirmation of racial inequality alongside a commitment to the language of interracial understanding and race neutrality.

Political Economy, Northern Racial Stratification, and Urban Peace

Northern racial liberalism had its roots in progressivism and the political and economic relations that shaped the First Great Migration. Northerners developed and intensified their own systems of segregation between the 1890s and the beginning of the First World War at the same time that they drew on Michigan's Reconstruction-era tradition of legal race neutrality. Northern white progressives, like their southern counterparts, saw segregation as a tool for suppressing social discord and reducing urban conflict. Unlike southerners, however, they held fast to the idea that their practices would lead to fuller racial equality, even though they also easily accepted the racial inequities that segregation amplified.[8]

During the First Great Migration, white progressives in northern cities drew a sharp distinction between their strategies for managing race relations and white southerners' racial practices. They cast their relationships to African Americans as fundamentally better than southern whites'—more modern, more progressive, and more just. Even as they built racially segregated institutions that separated European immigrants from African Americans, most white progressives downplayed the idea that white supremacy or discrimination shaped systems of power in northern cities. Instead, they blamed African Americans' exceptional difficulties on black deficiencies.[9] Thus, white progressives cast their racial practices in opposition to their flattened understanding of southern culture at the same time that they sustained condescending assumptions about African Americans.

Understanding that southern racial practices depended on Jim Crow's continuing utility, rather than southern whites' sentimental attachment to slavery, helps provide a model for seeing how racism in the urban North was linked to its own regional political economy. The culture of southern segregation was a distinctly modern response to rapid economic and cultural changes, including emancipation, the introduction of consumer culture, and the need to sustain a large-scale, agriculturally based political economy.[10] Similarly, northern racial ideologies should be understood as linked to the political economy of the North and understood in relation to shifting ideas about the productive economy and about the role of workers within that economy. Detroit was an important location for the production of this ideology. The introduction of the automated assembly line and its counterpart, an aggressive Americanization program among workers by the beginning of World War I, assumed that the infinite replaceability of workers was their most important asset. The economic and political elite thought of workers as interchangeable cogs—indistinguishable pieces of a modern machine. This ideology, informed by the needs of capital, helped support the rhetoric of racial equality, since it assumed that individual workers should not be differentiated from each other based on their non-work-related identities.[11] However, while corporate leaders aggressively integrated their workforces by ethnicity in the 1910s as a strategy for undermining ethnic alliances and disrupting workers' potential for union organizing, most sustained an equally passionate commitment to racial segregation, excluding black workers and pushing them into the worst jobs and into segregated areas of factories.

Racial stratification in the urban North was considerably more elastic than southern practices and policies. African Americans represented a far smaller portion of the population in the North and were permitted more social and cultural latitude as they moved through northern cities. Nonetheless, significant formal and informal dictates upheld occupational and residential segregation, shutting black residents out of the vast majority of well-paying jobs and white neighborhoods. African

Americans were not always denied access to city resources, and most public spaces, such as schools, sidewalks, and streetcars, were officially integrated. However, informal segregation was regularly practiced. For example, city parks frequented by both black and white residents were seldom marked with placards announcing segregation, but they usually maintained separate areas for black and white patrons, and African Americans could face significant consequences if they crossed over these invisible boundaries.[12]

This study returns the city government to debates about urban racial geographies. It demonstrates that local politicians and city managers sustained a common interest in upholding order and maintaining the racial status quo even when they made an explicit claim that they were committed to racial justice. Elected and nonelected city officials often shared the belief that challenges to the racial status quo would disrupt their ability to manage an orderly city and support its continued growth. A chief function of interwar urban government was thus to regulate race relations and avoid racial conflicts in the name of urban peace. This priority came into direct conflict with activists' struggles to promote racial justice in cities like Detroit, whose administrations positioned themselves as racially progressive, but worked to uphold existing racial relations of power as part of their effort to keep the city operating as smoothly as possible.[13]

"The Value of Some Adequate Plan of Segregation"

A private communication from March 1935 between Detroit's mayor Frank Couzens and the secretary of the city's planning commission, Herbert Russell, baldly outlined the central ideological components of northern racial liberalism as well as its regional biases. Carl Storm, a local white attorney, had written to the mayor suggesting that the municipal government should take full advantage of the federal money that had become available for "useful projects" by implementing a citywide program of residential segregation. This program, he argued, would "add stability to real Estate values . . . and give more desirability to the City generally." Storm believed the city should use zoning ordinances, condemnation proceedings, and the sale or exchange of properties to eject all African Americans from predominantly white areas and encourage whites to leave majority-black districts. The plan, Storm projected, would cost the city less than $5 million, and he was confident it would succeed. "Almost without exception," he explained, "segregation [has been] effective in the South." Finally, Storm closed his letter with a request: "Please do not assume that I have any prejudice against the people of the negro race, for that is not the case. I have the greatest of sympathy for them."[14]

Mayor Couzens appealed to Herbert Russell for guidance about how to reply to Storm.[15] In response, Russell lamented the city's inability to implement the kind of segregation plan Storm had outlined. Legal restrictions made laws and zoning ordinances ineffective. Furthermore, the southern model, which Storm found so compelling, was unlikely to work in Detroit. "Almost without exception," Russell explained, "the so-called effective colored segregation in the South is accomplished by means of arbitrary domination, rather than by legal procedure." Russell argued instead that there was a "real need of an intensive educational program, which will prove to our colored people the value of some adequate plan of segregation." Indeed, he claimed, some of the "leaders of the race" already agreed that segregation was beneficial to African Americans, even though they disagreed about "how [it] might be accomplished." To be most constructive, he explained, "any proposed plan should be prompted by an earnest desire to aid and assist our colored race to something better for them, rather than simply ejecting them from their chosen home sites."[16] By positioning himself against southern forms of racial domination, Russell cast himself as both modern and rational—an urban leader who would resist prejudice in favor of sound governance.

Russell opened his letter to Mayor Couzens with a reference to Abraham Lincoln, who had devised a plan for segregation at the end of the Civil War that would have been implemented had he not been tragically assassinated. Russell used Lincoln as well as his connections with African American elites to justify his support for segregation as morally and politically appropriate. At the same time, he rejected southern strategies designed to achieve this goal as inappropriate and inapplicable for the urban North. Rather than implementing a version of the South's extralegal and "arbitrary" domination of African Americans, he claimed an "earnest desire" to help black Detroiters. His plan was to educate

African Americans to accept their appropriate roles in northern cities—as members of a segregated minority.

Northern racial liberalism was thus marked by a desire to maintain racial hierarchies while rejecting the arbitrary dominance of African Americans characteristic of the South. Russell used social science discourse to cast himself as an objective proponent of modern urban management and rational, unbiased efficiency. He claimed that segregation was not always linked to discrimination, denying its connection to white supremacy or to the sustenance of racial hierarchy. For him, segregation was a natural outgrowth of difference, and he cited "sociological studies" that had indicated that African Americans "show a definite tendency to centralize and colonize in their own race districts" in order to justify this claim.[17] Ultimately, Russell used the language of northern racial liberalism to disguise the second-class quality of the citizenship he imagined for Detroit's black residents and to deny the white supremacy inherent in his vision of how race should work in the urban North. Russell described himself as someone who was committed to producing the greatest good for the greatest number. If African Americans were left out of that aggregate calculation, it was not the result of anything so primitive, backward, or southern as racism.

The slum clearance and low-cost housing projects that Eleanor Roosevelt helped celebrate are also excellent examples of this dynamic. Brewster Homes, developed by liberal white city planners and housing commissioners, upheld and formalized residential segregation in Detroit. Black residents from the cleared neighborhood would only be relocated to other majority-black areas, and the Brewster Homes—with 100 percent African American occupancy—would be even more segregated than the neighborhood it replaced. In the face of African Americans' clearly articulated complaints that segregation promoted inequality, white liberal leaders provided two responses. First, they claimed, the maintenance of segregation was a concession to conservatives who would otherwise block the projects. Second, they argued that the resources African Americans were receiving, and the community benefit those resources conferred, far outweighed any potentially negative effects of segregation. African Americans fought for and won unprecedented benefits from the state during the New Deal. They consistently claimed that they should sustain equal and unfettered access to the city's resources as well as full urban citizenship. However, the northern architects of the welfare state designed programs that helped codify, rather than undermine, social and geographic stratification based on race.[18]

Tolerance

During the interwar years, the liberal political idea that the state should use its resources to promote social welfare became increasingly popular in Detroit. Self-identified liberals, like Detroit's mayor Frank Murphy, were the architects and most enthusiastic proponents of these kinds of governmental systems. In the mayoral race of 1930, for example, Murphy promised to use city resources to address massive unemployment, while other candidates attempted to convince voters that it was inappropriate to dip into city coffers to support the "downtrodden."[19] However, Detroit's white liberals did not believe they should use the state in a similar manner to address racial inequality. By the interwar years, they generally accepted the notion that racial differentiation was limited to physical characteristics. Following prominent social scientists like Franz Boas, they believed that variations between racial and ethnic groups were cultural rather than biological.[20] Thus, white liberals promoted what Murphy called "tolerance and good temper" in response to the "races question." They argued that governments should function in a race-neutral manner and that racial difference should not matter in the administration of justice or state resources. But they rejected the idea that racism was lodged in social, political, or economic structures and shied away from state policies designed to reduce racial stratification. Racist practices, they claimed, were neither rooted in the productive economy, nor did they benefit whites as a group. It was individual hearts, rather than municipal institutions, that needed to be changed. City residents should try their best to get along with each other across racial and ethnic lines.[21] Despite these professions, Detroit's northern liberal leaders were more likely to accept the racial hierarchies of Detroit's workplaces, neighborhoods, sites of leisure, public institutions, and private settings than to challenge segregation or the unequal distribution of resources that ran through the city's schools, housing stock, political institutions, and job market.

White northern liberals embraced a model of racial equality in the interwar years that presumed equality of opportunity, but it was neither politically nor economically redistributive. White liberals believed that society and the marketplace were imperfect institutions that needed to be regulated. However, they did not imagine that political power or economic resources should be fundamentally reallocated, or that the capitalist system that created these inequalities should be overturned or significantly challenged. Instead, northern urban liberals embraced a modern form of regulatory liberalism, inviting the affluent and privileged to share their expertise with those social actors who had failed, as yet, to achieve economic success. Their early twentieth-century liberalism was tied to the growing power of corporate capitalism. They saw themselves as defenders of just and fair municipal systems at the same time that they believed that the economic dominance of corporations was a public good that produced and spread wealth. Detroit's liberals reconciled this contradiction by casting the capitalist asymmetries of power and limits to democracy as natural. Their tolerance and even support for the structures upon which economic inequalities were built allowed for and encouraged their acceptance of racial inequality and their sense that it was natural.[22] Ultimately, Detroit's white political leaders helped protect existing racial hierarchies without boldly denigrating African Americans. In other words, they contributed to the production of a system whose discourse was racially neutral, but whose effect was to protect segregation and ensure African American inequality.

African American Political Engagement

Managing Inequality uses a political economic approach to demonstrate that the changing position of African Americans in the labor force in the urban North during the First Great Migration was a crucial moment of racial formation out of which northern racial liberalism emerged. It examines how black civil rights liberalism and urban policy informed each other by placing an analysis of black political engagement into close dialogue with white city residents' changing ideas about race and African Americans.

During the interwar years, as Detroit's black population grew, African Americans fought to build an ideal city within which they could sustain full access to space and resources, as well as occupational, social, cultural, and economic equality. They imagined a future where blackness would not limit their opportunities. This ideal—an urban terrain, within which racial discrimination, segregation, and animosity would be eradicated—provided black Detroiters with a vision toward which they could work together in spite of class and ideological differences. Between the beginning of the First Great Migration and the end of the 1930s, African Americans' ideas about how to best work toward a more just world changed. Early in this period, the most prominent political tactics for addressing this goal were black leaders' appeals to white paternalism for jobs and aid. By the end, the most high-profile black activists were building more mass-based organizations and appealing to white leaders' sense of justice about the enormous gaps between liberal promises—that all urban residents were equal—and the realities of living in Detroit. African American activists, across a range of political orientations, used civil rights liberalism as a strategy to push for more robust access to full local citizenship. They fought to expose the gap between the promises of northern racial liberal ideology and the realities of black urban experiences. Because these activists were most involved in negotiations with white leaders about the meanings of racial equality in the interwar years, this study focuses on their work rather than offering a comprehensive look at black urban life.[23]

Even though activists' victories were partial, and sometimes frustratingly small, the demands that black residents placed on white leaders and the state shaped the resources they received, shaped the meanings of race in the city, and helped push questions about racial justice into the political sphere. Furthermore, African Americans accepted all of the concessions that they won, but they never agreed to settle for second-class citizenship in exchange for resources. Rather than inducing complacency, partial victories inspired activists with a range of political commitments to continue fighting for full access to material goods as well as equality and citizenship. This second goal remained important, even when resources were difficult to win.

Black activists pushed liberals toward a facial commitment to racial equality in the interwar years and thereby helped shape the meanings of urban liberalism. Indeed, white northern liberals borrowed language about formal racial equality from black activists and scholars. They embraced the notion that in an ideal society, race would become politically irrelevant. However, they did not include black activists' commitment to disrupting the balance of power between white "haves" and black "have-nots." Instead, they developed strategies to manage and contain African Americans' demands for equal access to city resources. They helped support rather than overturn black political and economic subordination. The discourse that African Americans used as a rallying call for freedom and a critique of structural discrimination was taken up by some white racial liberals to obscure the existence of racism and segregation and justify their continuation. Struggles over public as well as private housing, residential geography, leisure, segregation, work, welfare, and political representation were all venues within which these questions were debated and within which ideas about race and racial difference were formulated.

In spite of its severe limitations, the growing popularity of northern racial liberalism among white city leaders had important consequences for black activism. White liberal leaders' embrace of the languages of racial equality and neutrality helped foster an emerging civil rights community.[24] Beginning in the 1920s, black activists used these promises to expose the gap between the ideology of northern racial liberalism and the realities that black Detroiters faced. This new generation of activists was less concerned about alienating white leaders than their predecessors had been, more closely aligned with labor activists and unions in the city, and more interested in using black electoral strength to disrupt the balance of power between whites and blacks. Many of them sustained a fundamental faith that change within the system was both possible and desirable, even if that change needed to be quite dramatic.

The Origins of Colorblind Racism and the Myth of Regional Exceptionalism

This study illustrates that, since the beginning of twentieth century, architects of modern urban governance promoted the language of race neutrality at the same time that they built racially unequal urban geographies. It shows that the bureaucratic, legalistic, institutional mode of governance that characterized early twentieth-century cities had as its conceit that the state's project was to make urban life possible by managing residents' conflicting needs, preventing gross abuses of power, and functioning as if each legitimate resident was equal, regardless of her identity. This ideal helped mask the state's other goal, which was to conform the city to the needs of corporate capitalism and the rule of law, each of which was built on clear hierarchies—including racial hierarchies—between different kinds of city residents.[25]

Urban historians interested in the historical origins of colorblind discourse, such as David Freund, Thomas Sugrue, and Daniel Martinez HoSang, tend to focus on the post–World War II world when they explore the production of these modern ideas about race, consider the historical antecedents of today's racial geographies, and examine colorblind practices.[26] This choice implies that racial hierarchies came to shape the urban North from the start of the Second Great Migration in the 1940s. This study, conversely, shows that prewar northern white leaders helped produce seemingly nonracial narratives about clearly racial projects, including residential and occupational segregation and the unequal distribution of public and private resources. It thus illustrates that modern urban governance, from its inception, extended the racial and economic hierarchies that already shaped modern cities. It shows that African Americans moving into postwar northern cities confronted a complex racial system, rooted in the contradictions of northern racial liberalism, which preceded their arrival.[27] Some scholars who are critical of liberals' use of colorblind discourse in the postwar world leave unexamined northern white leaders' representations of themselves in the prewar period as architects of urban systems designed to promote some forms of racial equality. This lack of interest in the complexity of prewar racial systems helps reproduce the idea that the modern urban state was race neutral at its inception and then corrupted by backlash against the high volume of black migrants who arrived during and after the Second World War.[28]

This study also challenges the notion that contemporary racism is an outdated legacy of southern slavery. It illustrates instead that the origins of colorblind racist discourse are northern, urban, and modern. It thus fits within a growing literature that debunks the myth of northern racial exceptionalism—the misplaced belief that white supremacy and racism structured institutions and social relations in the American South but not the North. This idea, that the South is uniquely racist and conservative, has distorted Americans' historical imagination and limited their ability to understand racial politics. It has thus obscured the link between racism and contemporaneous regional systems of political and economic power.[29] This study illustrates that northern racial liberals rejected the idea that discrimination was embedded in the fabric of modern economic, political, and social institutions in the North before the Second World War began. They identified the North as a place where modern forms of racial democracy could be and were being practiced, in contrast to the backward and violent application of segregation in the Jim Crow South, even when, as in the case of Herbert Russell, they sympathized with white southerners' approach.[30] They used this regional comparison to justify their racial practices and to undermine black claims to equality. This study demonstrates that northern racial liberals promoted the idea that racism was illogical, backward, and southern since the beginning of the twentieth century. It illustrates that white northern elites and political leaders constructed a regional identity rooted in the belief that their flexible racial system was both distinct from and superior to southern practices before mass suburbanization, the Cold War, or the mainstream southern civil rights movement got under way.

A corollary to the myth of northern racial exceptionalism is the idea that southern legislators pushed racism into northern states by insisting that New Deal policies include racial stratification. Jill Quadagno has argued that southern Democrats used their disproportionate power in Congress during the 1930s to ensure that seemingly race-blind federal programs would have racially unequal effects. Scholars such as Ira Katznelson and Robert Lieberman, interested in how the New Deal helped extend racial inequalities, have accepted Quadagno's claim.[31] Historian Mary Poole, however, has demonstrated that this claim is empirically incorrect. She shows that white policy makers from Wisconsin, the architects of the Social Security Act, spearheaded and subsequently insisted upon the exclusion of black workers from social insurance coverage because they wanted to protect "the political and economic value of whiteness."[32] *Managing Inequality* takes on this idea from another angle. By examining the local germination and urban origins of northern white liberals' participation in the building of a racially inegalitarian state, it shows how the progenitors of New Deal inequality got their start at the local level. It helps expose how white liberals' representations of themselves as hindered by southerners' and conservatives' racism, rather than their own prejudices and ideologies, masked a lack of political will.

Finally, understanding race-blind language as a primarily postwar project leaves intact one of its central myths—the myth of racial progress. This myth is the popular cultural idea that racism is becoming less potent as we move further away from slavery, that "race relations" are improving, and that the nation is moving toward more, not less, racial equality. It flattens our understanding of past unequal racial systems, suggesting that past racisms were consistently overt, uncontested, and accepted by whites without ambivalence. Indeed, contemporary proponents of colorblindness, from its theorists to white defenders of segregation who used market-based language to explain their decision making, implicitly cast themselves in opposition to a more racist and less enlightened prewar period. Understanding that expressions of racism before the civil rights movement took more subtle forms than contemporary critics would have us believe illustrates that racial systems have, like northern racial liberalism and colorblind racism, always been laden with contradictions.[33] Indeed, this study helps debunk the idea that racism used to be obvious and straightforward, not the slippery, confusing, coded, and elusive animal that it has become today. Furthermore, it illustrates that different systems of racial inequality and disfranchisement are born out of different economic needs and political realities and thus require different ideological frames.

Rethinking Urban Liberalism and Urban Conservatism

Scholars of racial formation in postwar northern cities, such as Arnold Hirsh, June Manning Thomas, and Robert Self, have shown that local governments and business elites used aggressive measures to implement segregation, excluding African Americans from downtown and all-white residential areas since at least the 1940s.[34] Historians have also demonstrated that working- and middle-class white residents, especially homeowners, fought to hold onto racial privilege in their workplaces and residential exclusivity in their neighborhoods. These white women and men came to equate liberalism with blind allegiance to racial equality and indifference to whites' concerns. As Thomas Sugrue illustrates, economically stable white Detroit homeowners "defended" their neighborhoods against black homebuyers and through these struggles came to ally themselves with the city's conservatives and Republicans, rejecting the interracial vision and political priorities of their unions.[35] Republican leaders successfully capitalized on these racial divisions as they built political power in northern metropolitan areas, especially majority-white suburbs.[36]

Managing Inequality challenges the clarity of the political divide these scholars describe. It shows that metropolitan segregation was not the exclusive province of political conservatives. Liberals were ambivalent defenders of racial integration, and clear lines did not exist between the actions and attitudes of racists and the intentions of northern liberals. Overly clear political distinctions obfuscate rather than clarify our understanding of northern racial geographies. Conservatives cast liberals as dyed-in-the-wool defenders of racial equality, radical integrationists, and promoters of mongrelization in order to undermine their opponents' popularity and promote their own agendas. This representation, while politically effective, was grossly inaccurate. White liberals often consciously rejected models for instituting racial equality that they believed would redistribute resources away from whites. They also upheld segregation as part of their gradualist vision for change—African Americans, they suggested, were not ready for integration. Integrationist and inclusive models, developed by African American thinkers, were available to white liberals and policy makers who often worked in coalition with African Americans and even belonged to moderate civil rights organizations like the National Association for the Advancement of Colored People. But white liberals publicly rejected ideas as politically implausible that they privately deemed undesirable. Looking closely at liberals' practices rather than focusing on their policies and pronouncements helps expose these dynamics.

Studies of grassroots mobilizations against integration have implicitly cast white workers as the upholders of segregation and let the local liberal state officials off the hook for promulgating racial inequality. White working-class Detroiters, these studies show, fought openly to exclude African Americans from their neighborhoods and institutions, joining conservative political coalitions to protect their whiteness and their interests. Municipal administrators and liberal as well as conservative elected officials, however, oversaw the organization and development of urban geography on the scale of the city itself. While their political commitments ranged across the mainstream spectrum, their ideas about how and whether to integrate the growing African American population into the fabric of daily life were remarkably consistent: almost all of them believed that segregation helped secure interracial urban peace. Conservatives used racist language to explain their commitments. Liberals, conversely, promoted racial tolerance but simultaneously embraced the language of gradualism. They argued that the city's white population was not ready for integration. They suggested that African Americans needed to evolve culturally, socially, and politically in order to take on full citizenship and become integrated into the life of the city. And they asserted that black migrants needed state assistance and self-help to accustom themselves to the practices of the modern city, and equality would flow from there. This language of gradualism, tolerance, and peace developed into the northern explanation for segregation as a necessary tool for managing un-conflicted interracial urban spaces. It was developed by liberals but became commonsense knowledge about the urban north.

Why Detroit?

Detroit occupies an important place in the political imagination of the United States as an extreme example of the fortunes and failures of northern industrial cities.[37] This portrait has always had a racial cast. When the city was largely white, its working class was celebrated for its affluence; now that Detroit is majority-black, its population is maligned for its impoverishment. In the 1910s, when this story starts, Detroit boasted an extremely powerful and well-organized class of industrialists and property owners. This elite, almost all of whom were connected to automobile manufacturing, ran what many have identified as the world's largest antiunion "open shop" town. Because Detroit was dominated by a single industry, its corporate elite were remarkably unified. Their economic and political visions overlapped more consistently than the interests of other large cities' diverse merchant and industrial classes would allow. The local bourgeoisie were thus comparatively successful in both shaping and sustaining control over Detroit's political agenda. They aligned themselves with progressive reform, an ideological and political program that complemented their dedication to robust antiunion welfare capitalism. Detroit's ethnic working-class political institutions, both unions and party machines, remained relatively weak in the face of this corporate unity. Furthermore, the northern industrial labor regime relied on the illusion that all workers, even black workers, were essentially free agents. Overt southern segregation, as the clear legacy of slavery in the eyes of Americans, was a poor fit in the urban North because it undermined the underpinnings of free labor ideology.

Detroit is also famous for becoming the heart of the industrial union movement in the 1930s, which proclaimed its commitment to interracial organizing. Furthermore, Detroit produced a number of prominent white and black liberal leaders, many of whom went on to become important national figures. Frank Murphy, for example, served as the mayor of Detroit in the early 1930s, accepted an appointment from Franklin D. Roosevelt to be the governor-general of the Philippines in the middle of the decade, became the governor of Michigan in the late 1930s, went on to serve as attorney general under FDR, and finally was appointed to the U.S. Supreme Court. Murphy was perhaps most famous for his dissent in the *Korematsu* case, where he harshly criticized the majority for upholding Japanese internment during the Second World War, arguing that internment was based on "disinformation" and "racial and economic prejudices" and "falls into the ugly abyss of racism."[38] This decision reflected the ideological commitment to racial equality Murphy had sustained for decades. Murphy sincerely criticized the racially unequal status quo, even though he had neither devised nor implemented state policies to undermine it. He thus represents the central paradox of northern racial liberalism—his strident ethical rejection of explicitly racist practices coexisted alongside his role as an upholder of elements of racial stratification. African Americans active in Detroit's struggles for racial equality also moved on to national prominence. Gloster Current, for example, a leader of Detroit's youth branch of the National Association for the Advancement of Colored People, went on to become the director of branches for the national organization in 1946, a position he held for decades.[39]

If Detroit's destiny represents the fate of northern industrial cities, those cities have come to represent the fate of liberalism itself. In the popular historical imagination, the postwar growth of American cities overlapped with an era of liberal ascendancy. Liberalism prospered, this narrative goes, as these cities prospered. As these cities lost jobs, were abandoned by their white, prosperous, and middle-class populations, and turned into majority-black enclaves, political power shifted to the ever-expanding, lily-white, and conservative suburbs. In this popular story, the destruction of the New Deal liberal alliance was a product of racial tensions that emerged in the 1960s and the limits of liberal social welfare for addressing cultural and structural divides. This popular narrative is seductive in its simplicity.[40]

In reality, black and white city residents and politicians fought over how to understand racial difference and define its political consequences in the urban North between 1916 and 1940. Struggles between African American and white residents over access to resources and over the relationship between race and citizenship had been shaping northern cities since well before the Second World War. By 1940, race and racial conflict were already central components of northern, urban, social and political culture.[41]

This study is arranged both chronologically and thematically. The first three chapters focus on the years between the beginning of the First Great Migration and the end of the 1920s. They show how struggles over African American access to local resources framed public discussions about identity, entitlement, and city politics among both white and black residents in diverse class settings. They examine the increasing assertiveness of black protest alongside the emergence of the discourse and practice of northern racial liberalism. These chapters demonstrate that colorblind political language came to be adopted and used by politicians and activists who sustained a broad range of ideas about black equality, segregation, and racial stratification. Finally, these chapters explore the evolution and ascendancy of the seemingly neutral but ultimately racially differential assumptions of northern racial liberalism.

The four remaining chapters consider how these dynamics helped shape politics in Depression-era Detroit and how they helped define the local management of New Deal programs. These chapters explore how discourses about welfare, dependency, and state resources, produced by local government officials, as well as by members of the city's white and black elite, helped shape ideas about citizenship in Detroit and helped link those ideas to race. Two figures emerged out of this debate: the "freeloader," understood to be black, who was stuck in a state of chronic dependence, and the "taxpayer," understood to be white, who represented the entitled and deserving recipient of city resources. Indeed, northern racial liberals contributed to the evolution of a popular discourse that linked African Americans to indigence and transience, and whites to full, taxpaying citizenship. Among African Americans, the Great Depression contributed to a shift in the reigning political discourse that was already under way—from a voluntarist politics of patronage and uplift to a more confrontational politics informed by liberalism. These dynamics developed along similar lines in the city's labor unions, where white and black activists adopted interracial organizing as a strategy to mobilize power. Finally, northern racial liberal supporters of New Deal housing programs connected urban "improvement" to the removal of African Americans from the city's downtown district. White liberals attempted to build a New Deal city and a New Deal coalition that included blacks as recipients of resources, but in actuality, their plans created perpetually second-class citizens. Meanwhile, black leaders and most black residents embraced the federal government's claim that "better housing makes better citizens" and fought for full access to both of these promises.

This study historicizes current debates about the persistence of racial inequality and white privilege in contemporary America. In other words, it uses a historical lens to examine a contemporary paradox: if explicit expressions of racism are no longer acceptable within the public sphere, and if civil rights legislation prevents conscious acts of discrimination, then why have racial stratification and segregation proved so durable? As African Americans struggling for social, economic, and political equality in Detroit during the interwar years made clear, liberal promises that racial equality would emerge as a result of good intentions were insufficient. Ultimately, white liberal leaders failed to remedy or even significantly tackle the problems that their new ideology was ostensibly designed to address.

1

African American Migration and the Emerging Discourse of Northern Racial Liberalism

In May 1918, Detroit police officers began to stop African American travelers arriving at the Michigan Central Railroad station to inspect their bodies for smallpox vaccination scars. If no scars were found, the new arrivals were lined up, taken into a common room, and required to submit to a vaccination shot. The Board of Health had instituted these shots to prevent an epidemic but targeted only African American travelers as carriers of disease.[1] White male police officers inspected black migrants in a room "where both sexes [were] present" and in a manner that intimidated and humiliated them. One woman protested that despite her objections, "the upper part of her body was exposed in an embarrassing manner with men present." The vaccination program thus relayed a strong symbolic message: black newcomers should expect city officials and institutions in Detroit to treat them with suspicion. At the same time, the Board of Health did not disrupt the flow of African American travelers into the city; black migrants were crucial to the local labor market from the beginning of the First World War through the 1920s. Some of the new arrivals were detained for a few hours, but none was turned away.[2] The vaccination program promoted race-based distinctions between white and black migrants that shaped the social, political, economic, and occupational terrains of Detroit.

Public health workers found as many cases of smallpox among whites in Detroit as they did among blacks, but they did not target white migrants as carriers of disease. Indeed, the Board of Health's belief that black migrants were likely carriers and its simultaneous disinterest in white travelers illustrate that it understood public health concerns through a racial lens. The smallpox vaccination program reflected white leaders' more general worry that the presence of black migrants in Detroit posed a threat to the city's social, political, and economic order. Rather than casting all African Americans as inherently inferior because they were black, northern white leaders targeted black migrants as carriers of pathogens. This move was both racially specific (directed only toward black migrants) and racially ambiguous (ostensibly directed at them because of their potential for illness rather than their race itself). This approach to black newcomers was a central lexicon for how northern racialization would work in Detroit and other northern cities. Concern about black migrants' potential to threaten public health was a double-edged sword, since it brought some resources to African Americans at the same time that it helped vilify them. For example, beginning in 1917, the board worked with the Detroit Urban League (DUL), a social service agency for African Americans, to improve sanitation among blacks to prevent the spread of smallpox. The board paid for DUL social workers to visit recent migrants, give them advice about diet and clothing, and encourage them to be vaccinated.[3]

During the First Great Migration, Detroit's white leaders increasingly and self-consciously defined the city against popular conceptions of the American South, characterizing their racial practices as more flexible and less harsh than the systemic racism and vigilante violence so prevalent in the South. However, the treatment of black migrants at the train station reveals a deep gap between the idea that race would play a negligible role in shaping Detroit's economic and political geographies, and the reality of the racially disparate treatment and deeply unequal conditions of northern life. It contradicted the implicit northern promise that blackness would be an insignificant barrier to full urban equality, especially compared with the South. Indeed, it confirmed for African American travelers that racially based differentiation, exclusion, and discrimination would shape their lives in the urban North as well. The quality of the racial systems in these two regions would be different, as would white explanations for the persistence of deep racial inequalities, yet racial inequality would play a central role in shaping Detroit's economic, social, and political terrains. Ultimately, the promise that the North would be the land of racial freedom reflected the ideology of northern racial liberalism rather than the reality of life in the region.

Detroit's white leaders overplayed the differences between their racial practices and those of southerners', but their interest in confirming that their regional system was fairer meant that they did accommodate some black challenges to inequality. They made these concessions on their own terms, however, without acknowledging that racism in the North was systemic and without disclosing that their decisions were effected by black protest. For example, white leaders initially ignored African American migrants' complaints about the vaccination program and about police officers' invasive behavior at the train station. However, after a committee of middle-class black leaders from the local branch of the National Association for the Advancement of Colored People (NAACP) approached the city's commissioner of health, Dr. James Inches, the vaccination program was terminated. Inches did not acknowledge that this meeting affected his decision. Instead, he claimed the program was ending because it was ineffective, thereby avoiding responsibility for having implemented a racially discriminatory policy. By not mentioning race, or recognizing that it had played a role in the vaccination program, Inches cast himself and his department as immune from prejudice.[4]

Ultimately, the formation of northern racial liberalism and of black responses to this new racial ideology was the product of a number of contemporaneous changes in Detroit and the nation. First, it emerged alongside the beginning of the First Great Migration of African Americans from the South to the urban North, a demographic shift tied to black workers' new role in the local labor market. Second, it developed as migration reshaped the city's housing market and racial geography during which struggles over racial boundaries became more pronounced. Third, it coincided with a significant change in the city's white leadership and in the municipal government more broadly, characterized by the growing power and popularity of urban reform. Urban reformers provided a language for explaining stratification and developed institutions for managing urban populations that white leaders then used, both ideologically and practically, to handle the influx of black newcomers. Finally, northern racial liberalism emerged as a response to an increasingly vocal and politically organized African American minority that was actively debating the meanings of full racial justice and challenging the racial hierarchies of the North. In order to comprehend the city's treatment of African American people at the train station, it is important to consider several intertwined historical developments: migration, racially based labor market segmentation, urban reform, and black political activism. Developments in each of these crucial areas set the stage for white leaders' political engagement with African Americans and contributed to new ideas about race in Detroit and the urban North more generally.

The Political Tradition of Race Neutrality

The posture that characterized northern racial liberalism—a discourse of race neutrality, an ambivalent stance against racial violence, and a belief that African American equality would emerge gradually as black people progressed and assimilated middle-class norms—evolved out of existing political discourses and practices. Michigan's mainstream white political leaders had passed laws banning racial discrimination and mandating integration well before the beginning of the First Great Migration. Indeed, the state had been a haven for fugitive slaves through the antebellum era and was more welcoming of African Americans than its neighbors into the late nineteenth century. The Republican-dominated state legislature passed a handful of laws during Reconstruction, the two decades immediately following the Civil War, that integrated the state's public schools, overturned prohibitions on interracial marriage, and banned discrimination in the administration of life insurance, the selection of juries, and public places of accommodation, recreation, and amusement. These laws illustrate that the majority of Michigan's Republican lawmakers believed in and supported the idea of legal racial egalitarianism in the 1860s, 1870s, and into the 1880s.[5]

Michigan's Republicans supported race-neutral laws and antidiscrimination statutes because these positions stood in line with their political economic vision. Founded to oppose the expansion of slavery, encourage industrial development, and foster the "free market," Michigan's Republican Party stood for free labor ideology, the antebellum notion that white workers' economic independence was the foundation for republicanism and civic virtue, both of which were fatally encumbered by slavery.[6] This ideal—that white workers should be able to sell their labor freely—did not preclude virulent racism against African

Americans. However, for white northerners, support for race-neutral laws helped amplify the distinctions they drew between their legal system, which promoted the free market, and the racially hierarchical legal system upon which slavery was built. After the Civil War, Republicans continued to support legal race neutrality, position themselves against the brutal racism of the South, and distance their racial practices from white southerners' efforts to sustain control over populations of former slaves. New laws marked a decisive rejection of efforts to legally exclude African Americans from public spaces and institutions and provided avenues for challenging race-based exclusion. However, Republicans' commitment to legal race neutrality should not be mistaken for an effort to integrate Michigan's small African American population into the state on an equal footing with whites. Few Michigan Republicans expressed an interest in altering the material effects of existing race-based structural inequalities. The new laws remained difficult to enforce and included few consequences for the businesses or individuals who broke them.

Despite their support for the legal theory of race neutrality, white Republicans only occasionally achieved substantive victories for black equality. Detroit and Wayne County were both majority Democrat during and after the Civil War. Democratic city and county leaders rarely prosecuted violators of the Republican-sponsored state laws and frequently resisted those laws' mandates. The city's school board, for example, refused to implement the 1867 statute calling for school integration and supported white teachers who turned black students away from their classes. Joseph Workman, whose son had been excluded from a nearby school, took the case to court with support from the African American Second Baptist Church and the financial backing of John Bagley, a white Republican financier and tobacco manufacturer who later became Michigan's governor. In 1869, the state supreme court overruled the city's school board, mandating integration.[7] In the 1870s and 1880s, a handful of well-connected African Americans won political offices and appointments through the Republican Party machine of Michigan, but Republicans' power in Detroit, home to the vast majority of the state's black residents, was limited. While African Americans won the struggle for school integration, they were unable to enforce other newly passed laws against black exclusion. Like their twentieth-century counterparts, few white Republicans moved beyond proclamations about their belief in equal protection under the law, fewer still mounted challenges to existing hierarchies, and many subscribed, self-consciously or unself-consciously, to contemporary ideas about race that justified the inequalities their laws were aimed at undermining.[8]

By the 1890s, Detroit, like the rest of the state, had become a Republican stronghold, but by then, white Republicans had become even weaker political allies to African Americans. Former abolitionists and Civil War officers thinned out of the ranks of active white Republicans, and the party moved away from its Civil War identity. For example, the reform measures introduced by Hazen Pingree, Detroit's Republican mayor through most of the 1890s, and Michigan's governor through 1900, undermined black access to public office. Civil service measures undercut patronage appointments, and direct primaries meant that political parties lost the power to unilaterally forward candidates to run in general elections. Reformers expressed no remorse about their new policies' effects on African American political representation or access to public jobs, but they did use race-neutral language to dismiss black complaints—claiming that their reforms were about efficiency and fairness, not race. By the beginning of the twentieth century, African Americans were shut out of public office in Detroit, and civil rights legislation had fallen off the agendas of white leaders across the mainstream political spectrum.[9] While white politicians made no effort to overturn legal racial equality, Reconstruction-era laws remained on the books but provided scant protection to black Detroiters.

Between 1890 and the 1920s, northern whites expanded their own segregationist practices while quietly watching the institutionalization of legalized Jim Crow and vigilante violence in the American South.[10] Beginning in the mid-1890s, white employers began to replace black workers with white men and women in some of the most visible service jobs in the city. African Americans lost positions as barbers, coachmen, butlers, and maids in both private homes and hotels that had previously employed many of the most well-off blacks. In response, a group of black community leaders formed a committee to place African Americans in industrial jobs. While the organization successfully pressured the Detroit Street Railway to hire a number of black motormen, African Americans continued to be largely excluded from industrial employment.[11]

The Springfield Riots

Mainstream white city leaders continued to position themselves against explicit expressions of racist violence in the first decade of the twentieth century, even as African Americans faced increased residential segregation, growing exclusion from jobs over which they once held practical monopolies, and decreasing access to public employment. The *Detroit News*'s coverage of the Springfield, Illinois, race riots of 1908, the event that precipitated the organization of the NAACP, reflected a practical consensus among the city's white leaders about the need to reject violence against African Americans as unacceptable because of the urban disorder it caused. The newspaper lauded the Illinois governor, C. S. Deneen, for calling out the National Guard and declaring the violence "intolerable" and "inexcusable."[12] The paper thus condemned the white rioters and positioned itself on the side of peace. However, its editors did not question the basic premise that white rioters used to explain their actions—that black male violence against white women was at the root of the racist hysteria.

For the *Detroit News*, lynching was unacceptable because it was extralegal, and rioting was deplorable because it caused urban mayhem and hurt innocent bystanders, including African Americans. But, like the vast majority of white Americans, the paper was not willing to consider either lynching or rioting as tools for enforcing systemic inequality, even though this analysis, generated by African American crusaders against extralegal racial violence, was available and relatively well publicized. Instead, the *News* suggested that whites and blacks shared responsibility for the bloodshed, even though white rioters perpetrated nearly all of the attacks and directed their animosity almost exclusively against African Americans and their allies. While *News* reporters deplored the racist rampage, they also shared white rioters' concern that black male violence against white women was a chronic and dangerous social problem.[13] For example, alongside news of the Springfield riots, the *News* reported soberly that "great excitement prevaile[d] at

Pensacola," Florida, because a black man accused of assaulting a white woman would almost certainly "be lynched and perhaps burned" that evening.[14] Two other stories about black male violence against white women appeared farther up on the same page. One reported on a thwarted lynch mob in Virginia, and another covered the suicide of a black man accused of assaulting two white women. A third story reported that African American men who had fled from Springfield were "looking for trouble," attempting to "arouse the people of their own race" to go back with them and fight.[15] Taken together, these stories implicitly confirmed white rioters' justification for their animosity, even while the newspaper explicitly condemned their extralegal behavior.

On the same page, the *News* ran a story announcing that a "Negro Minister," the Reverend Henry W. Jameson, blamed the Springfield riots on the interracial association between the "undesirable of both classes mixing freely with each other." Jameson expressed the same sentiment the newspaper communicated—that violence against African Americans was deplorable but understandable as a defense of racial purity, something that respectable African Americans could also defend. Publishing these sentiments voiced by a black reverend whom the paper identified as respectable and patriotic—Jameson led an African American military regiment in Cuba during the Spanish-American War of 1898—helped the paper legitimize its position against white *and* black violence without appearing to discriminate.[16] The *News*'s coverage of the Springfield riots reflects white city elites' interest in positioning themselves against extralegal racial violence but simultaneously confirming existing racial hierarchies.

Eight years later, white city officials' responses to the film *The Birth of a Nation* in Detroit and elsewhere in Michigan reflected a similar practice of condemning racial prejudice for its potential to lead to disorder without simultaneously challenging existing urban racial hierarchies. *The Birth of a Nation* opened in cities across the country in February 1915 to widespread acclaim and popularity. That month, President Woodrow Wilson screened it in the White House, applauding the film for what he saw as its accurate rendering of black political and sexual aggression toward innocent white southerners during Reconstruction, and the Ku Klux Klan's heroic defense of order and white womanhood. The movie was wildly successful in New York, where men on horses dressed in Klan regalia and road through the streets of Times Square as part of the opening spectacle. *The Birth of a Nation*, which showed to large crowds across the country, helped spark the Klan's reemergence.[17] Even before the film was finished, the NAACP organized protests aimed at banning it across the country. In Boston, in April, clashes between more than 500 black protesters and hundreds of white moviegoers escalated into a riot. After the riots in Boston and a series of other racial clashes that followed screenings of the film, the NAACP won victories in some cities, including Denver, Minneapolis, Pittsburgh, and St. Louis, where local officials banned it.[18]

Although the national NAACP had been vocal about its opposition to *The Birth of a Nation*, Detroit's NAACP failed to organize a visible response to its local premiere.[19] However, a significant number of white city leaders expressed concerns about the racial violence the film had spurred elsewhere. Together, they pushed Detroit's mayor, Oscar Marx, to restrict its showing and edit its content. The mayor called for the "eliminat[ion of] specially objectionable features" that were "calculated to arouse racial prejudice" and might "stir up racial feelings," and he forbade the movie's "performance to children."[20] Editors of the city's daily papers applauded these actions, as did Michigan's governor, who lamented his inability to ban the film statewide.[21]

From across the political spectrum, Detroit's white political leaders expressed their support for banning *The Birth of a Nation*. Woodbridge Ferris, who had campaigned heavily for Democrat Woodrow Wilson, expressed sentiments similar to those of Oscar Marx, an active Republican. White leaders in Detroit and other cities in Michigan who wanted to ban the film agreed with the national NAACP's argument that its screening threatened public safety by inciting racial violence. However, they were not invested in protecting African Americans from the discrimination that they faced *in Detroit*, or in undermining segregation in *local* workplaces, neighborhoods, or public facilities. Rather, they wanted to keep an orderly city that was not threatened by racially motivated clashes.

Between the 1890s and the First Great Migration, Michigan's white leaders made less effort to distinguish the racial dynamics of the North from southern racial practices than they had during Reconstruction. During this period of the African American "nadir," rather than amplifying regional differences, whites pointed to the similarities between northern and southern racial attitudes. In an editorial about the Springfield riots, for example, the *Detroit News* suggested that race riots could happen anywhere given that "passionate explosions of public sentiment take place regardless of geographical location."[22] Mayor Marx and Governor Ferris demonstrated a similar disinterest in marking *The Birth of a Nation* as a particularly southern expression of racial ideas or their opposition to it as particularly northern. Yet, once Detroit began to absorb large numbers of black migrants, regional differentiation came to animate white leaders' sense of their commitment to race neutrality.

Migration

Between 1910 and 1920, Detroit's population more than doubled, moving it from America's ninth-largest to its fourth-largest city. Southern migrants, black and white, began to arrive in Detroit in unprecedented numbers in the fall of 1915; 85 percent of these migrants were white. The First World War brought new jobs into the already booming industrial sector and simultaneously cut the flow of European immigration to a trickle. Boats full of immigrant workers could no longer cross the Atlantic Ocean during the hostilities, forestalling the influx of cheap labor upon which Detroit's manufacturers had relied since the 1880s. African Americans, who had accounted for a little more than 3 percent of Detroit's residents in 1860, represented only 1 percent by 1910, fewer than 6,000 residents. The First Great Migration reversed this trend.[23] In 1916 and 1917, approximately 25,000 African Americans—mostly men traveling alone—came to Detroit. Even in 1918, as wartime manufacturing wound down and migration decelerated, hundreds of black travelers continued to arrive in Detroit each week. Although African Americans represented a minority of arrivals, between 10 and 15 percent any given week, Detroit's black population saw the largest proportional increase among the nation's twenty biggest cities. By 1920, Detroit's 40,000 African Americans represented more than 4 percent of the total population.[24]

In 1918, black migrants arrived at Detroit's train station cautiously optimistic about racial equality in the urban North. Most would have heard stories about the city before they arrived from friends and relatives who had already moved or read articles in black dailies like the *Chicago Defender*, which circulated among African Americans in the South and were famously read aloud among neighbors and friends. Most letters and newspapers compared life up north favorably to conditions in the South, especially when it came to new kinds of racial freedoms. A letter from a black migrant to Philadelphia captured the excitement that many migrants relayed about their new lives. Writing to his former doctor, he reported his happiness at escaping the surveillance and abuse of the South:

> [I] don[']t have to mister every little white boy [that] comes along[.] I havent heard a white man call a colored nigger you [k]no[w] now—since I been in the state of Pa. I can ride in the electric street and steam cars any where I get a seat . . . and if you are first in a place here shop[p]ing you don[']t have to wait until the white folks get thro[ugh] tradeing.[25]

These often upbeat accounts also captured their authors' uncertainty about northern life and their frustrations with the limits of racial freedom. In the same letter, for example, the author suggested that he had to maintain his hyperawareness about social interactions across racial lines, explaining that he was "not crazy about being with white folks." Ultimately, he implied, real equality was still out of reach for African Americans up North. "I don[']t want to worry you[,] but read between lines." Northern newspapers also presented a mixed picture of race relations in the region. While articles directed at migrants were often celebratory, newspapers also covered struggles to overcome discrimination and racial exclusion, illustrating the persistence of inequality in the North.[26]

Although black migration continued after World War I, its character shifted in 1918. That year, women and children constituted a far higher proportion of black migrants than during the three previous years of the First Great Migration. In 1920, many more black men than women lived in the city, with a ratio of 137 men to 100 women; by 1925, that ratio had fallen to 113 men for every 100 women. Anecdotal evidence suggests that the ratio peaked in 1918 and evened out quickly in the early 1920s.[27] Many of these new migrants moved to Detroit to join husbands, fathers, and brothers who had already made the trip. Other women came independently, with or without children. The arrival in 1918 of unprecedented numbers of black women and children meant that the destination itself took on new significance. Rather than merely a place of work where they would essentially live in exile, incoming African Americans saw Detroit as their new home.

This demographic shift concerned city leaders. Since the beginning of the First Great Migration, city leaders had made a point of discouraging single black migrants from imagining that Detroit would become their permanent residence, consistently treating migrants as temporary residents meant to fill wartime labor shortages. For example, white philanthropists involved in funding the Detroit Urban League discouraged migrants from sending for their families and refused to fund efforts to help migrants find housing, communicating that they did not want black workers to become permanent residents.[28] For municipal officials, reunited families intending to settle in Detroit posed a more serious threat to the racial status quo than the single black men who had preceded them. Their decision to stay meant that the city was on its way to becoming interracial rather than simply multiethnic.

Labor Segmentation and the Material Foundations of Northern Racial Liberalism

The changing position of African Americans in the labor force during the First Great Migration was a crucial moment for both racial formation and the ideology of northern racial liberalism. Black men benefited from their expanded access to wage labor in northern industries, opportunities that were most often out of reach for African Americans down south. Black women, the majority of whom worked in private homes, also made more money in northern cities. However, these material gains, albeit extremely significant to African Americans' comparative quality of life, do not tell the whole story. African Americans' access to more lucrative opportunities in the North was both inconsistent and unreliable. Black men entered into a fiercely segregated industrial labor market. Last to be hired and first to be fired, they became Detroit's reserve labor force during the First World War. In other words, when jobs were plentiful, they had a relatively easy time accessing employment, but when production contracted, they were the first workers to be laid off. Furthermore, they almost always were paid lower wages than their white coworkers and tended to work in segregated, more dangerous jobs, especially in larger plants.

Historians have demonstrated that before World War I the majority of northern whites understood racial stratification as a natural and just form of social organization based on the inherent moral, cultural, and biological superiority of whites and inferiority of blacks. This ideology of "scientific racism" was built on an evolutionary notion of race that cast Anglo-Saxon Protestants as the most evolved racial group, with other races arranged hierarchically below them.[29] Forrester Washington, head of the Detroit Urban League between 1916 and 1918, argued that these ideas about race had had a profound impact on the policies embraced by Detroit's white leaders since the nineteenth century.[30] However, during the First Great Migration, whites began to replace their explicitly racialized hierarchical language with the idea that African Americans, as a population and not a race, were deeply disadvantaged because of the historical, social, and environmental challenges they faced. Thus, during the First Great Migration, white leaders began to devise a distinct language for talking about African Americans that rejected the idea that they were inherently *biologically* inferior to whites but continued to represent them as socially inferior. Whites suggested that African Americans, stunted by their deep disadvantage, should remain subordinate to whites and should be excluded from full municipal citizenship.[31]

By 1920, the sheer size of the black population had changed African Americans' relationship to white city leaders and residents. Yet, the increase in population was not the only dynamic that affected black residents' experiences in Detroit or shaped how race was understood. The reorganization of Detroit's labor market and the role of African Americans within that market were catalysts for shifts in how white leaders approached African Americans and for changes in how African Americans fought for their rights. White leaders' newfound adoption of the racially neutral ideologies of northern racial liberalism by the early 1920s can be understood, in part, as a response to profound changes in the organization of industrial work. African Americans' struggles to attain full local citizenship also changed in response to shifts in ideas about race. Two elements embedded in these shifts were particularly important for the formation of northern racial liberalism. The first were new corporate strategies for dealing with labor and for organizing production that had become increasingly popular before the First Great Migration. The second was black male workers' new role at the visible bottom of the city's industrial labor market. Together, these changes contributed to the development of a self-consciously northern sensibility about race and racial difference among white leaders who began to distinguish their ideas from those of their southern counterparts.

In order to attract a large enough workforce, industrialists supported black migration and its promise of racial freedom at the same time that they continued to use segregation as a tool to organize factory production, undermine workers' power, and garner consent during the First World War and into the 1920s. Detroit's industrialists employed labor agents, who traveled into the American South to recruit black workers, promising them higher pay as well as the wages of racial freedom. They suggested that part of black migrants' remuneration would be access to new forms of equality. This promised equality, however, was not as consistent or clear-cut as recruiters suggested, even in the plants.

As Detroit's industrial sector expanded dramatically between 1880 and the beginning of the First World War, industrialists developed strategies for managing the huge influx of European immigrant workers that were designed to keep costs down, control workers' power over production, and minimize their ability to organize unions. In the 1880s, industry in the city was both diverse and comparatively small-scale. Less than 5 percent of the city's 900 manufacturing firms employed more than 100 workers, and Detroit had fewer than 120,000 residents. Although it had some light industry—cigar making, lumber, copper smelting—its economy depended primarily on commerce and trade. By 1920, however, Detroit had become the nation's fourth-largest city, with almost 1 million residents and the third-largest manufacturing sector in the country. It was the capital of the American automobile industry, housing the headquarters of most domestic car companies, as well as large numbers of parts and assembly plants. As the scale of production grew, fewer small firms were able to sustain viable businesses. Furthermore, the number of industrial owners shrank, and a relatively new managerial class emerged.[32] By the beginning of the war production boom that sparked the First Great Migration, large corporations, with extensive bureaucracies developed in response to the new scale of production, dominated Detroit's economy.

As factories grew larger and more bureaucratic, managers experimented with tactics for disciplining workers that were aimed at reducing the social importance of ethnic affiliations. Managers emphasized Americanization, encouraging European immigrants and their descendants to identify as white. African Americans were consistently excluded from Americanization programs. However, managers' and capitalists' interest in defining all unskilled industrial workers as fundamentally alike and infinitely interchangeable helped make room for the idea that racial differences were less essential than many had previously believed. Promoters of these "modern" ideas of management believed that ethnic segregation encouraged mutuality among workers, thereby fostering class consciousness and unionization. Larger companies thus took hiring power away from foremen, who had been likely to fill shifts with men from their own immigrant groups. Instead, these firms instituted personnel departments to hire workers from a range of European origins. These companies automated manufacturing, deskilled their blue-collar workforces, and hired an army of professional managers to administer production, distribution, sales, marketing, and each other. In 1900, for example, Ford automobiles were largely built by skilled tradespeople. By 1922, the majority of Ford workers were unskilled and easily replaceable: Henry Ford could boast that 85 percent of his workers needed less than two weeks of training. These innovations allowed for larger plants and took much of the control of the industrial process out of workers' hands, weakening the ability of workers to disrupt the production process. These changes also had important implications for the cohesion and interdependence of ethnic groups in Detroit, which tended to be less residentially segregated and sustained fewer ethnic institutions than the same groups in other industrial cities.[33]

By deskilling workers and unlinking ethnic identification from specific jobs or areas in factories, industrialists and labor managers relied on the idea that all European-descended factory workers were essentially the same: workers were interchangeable parts rather than members of ethnic clans. Automobile and other large companies went one step further, actively working to homogenize their workforces by requiring employees to learn English and participate in Americanization programs. Bosses were willing to pay higher wages if it meant more efficiency on the job and more control of workers' lives beyond the factory floor. Henry Ford, for example, famously introduced the five-dollar day in 1914, accessible only to workers willing to learn English, live clean lives, and attend church regularly. Industrialists cast these ideas as progressive and forward thinking, arguing that they would promote industrial order and prevent class conflict.[34] Although this idea about equality among laborers was limited almost exclusively to European-descended workers before the beginning of the First Great Migration, the notion that workers were interchangeable and thus functionally equal was the material groundwork on which northern racial liberalism was built in Detroit in the early twentieth century.[35]

The influx of African American male workers into the bottom rungs of industrial employment beginning in 1916 also contributed to the formation of northern racial liberalism. Because European immigration had slowed to a halt with the opening of World War I, white and black southerners became the newest source of workers in the city, but their experiences in the labor market were quite different. White southerners entered the existing white, working-class labor market with few challenges. African Americans, meanwhile, faced discrimination and employment segmentation immediately upon arrival.[36] African American men entered an industrial labor market that had, until World War I, excluded them almost entirely. However, during World War I, Detroit's industrialists, as well as other local employers, began to depend on black migrants as a reserve labor force, using them as the most disposable and exploitable workers in the city.

Employers came to see African Americans as an important and needed presence in Detroit: black migrants worked in the hardest, dirtiest, and most dangerous jobs. Indeed, Detroit's African American industrial workers were most often found in factories' foundries, where they operated heavy machinery and poured liquid steel into molds, often working in temperatures well over 100 degrees Fahrenheit. At the same time, they were the workers least likely to be promoted and most prone to layoffs. They also faced higher overall unemployment than any other group of workers in the city. The presence of African American men also helped employers sustain more control over all workers. Employers encouraged white men to see black men as threatening—always available to replace white workers if they went on strike, registered too many complaints, or misbehaved.[37]

African Americans' access to industrial work expanded dramatically. In 1910, just 400 black male Detroiters worked in manufacturing and mechanical jobs, less than 18 percent of the population of black male workers in the city. By 1920, almost 14,000 black men worked in the same job classification, representing 70 percent of all employed black men in Detroit. Black men in Detroit were much less likely than their counterparts elsewhere to work in nonindustrial jobs typically seen as "black": by 1920, Detroit had the lowest percentage of black male workers in the fields of "domestic and personal service" of any major northern industrial city. The same was not true for women: the portion of black women working in domestic and personal service in Detroit between 1910 and 1920 held steady at a little less than 80 percent. While a larger percentage of African American women held jobs in manufacturing, up from 8 to 12 percent, that number was still quite small.[38] Yet, even as black men became a crucial and visible segment of Detroit's industrial workforce, they were effectively sidelined from the opportunities available to their white counterparts. By 1920, only about 12 percent of black men who worked in factories held skilled jobs, another 19 percent worked in semiskilled jobs, and the remaining two-thirds worked in unskilled positions.[39] At the same time that European-descended workers came to be more occupationally integrated, African Americans' presence in segregated areas of factories grew. These factors had important implications for northern racial liberalism; they meant that even as workers were becoming increasingly interchangeable, race segregation prevailed.

This segmentation also meant that employers and white workers were likely to regard African Americans as subject to a different set of rules and customs than those that governed whites. World War I was a time of employment surpluses, when white and black men could find industrial jobs relatively easily. For the first half of the war, white leaders and residents expressed little resistance to black in-migration or to the presence of African Americans in industrial jobs. This relative tolerance of a black presence in Detroit eroded, however, as the war went on. In 1918, manufacturing slowed and the city sank into a recession. By the next year, the Urban League reported that "rents had gone sky high." This recession coincided with an upsurge in both labor militancy and racist violence.[40] Even though some African Americans participated in strikes on the side of the union, white workers often saw all blacks as antiunion and potential strikebreakers. Employers saw the divisive effect that segmenting their labor force by race had, and thus actively fostered it. According to African American economists Sterling Spero and Abram Harris, employers' logic at the time was that large outbreaks of racial violence during strikes would actually be beneficial, since the state would intervene to prevent rioting and simultaneously repress strikers.[41] Both white employers and workers saw it as crucial to their own interests to keep African American men at the bottom of the industrial system.

After World War I, white union resistance to black employment and employers' manipulation of white workers' racism increased. These dynamics helped to solidify black male workers' place on the bottom of Detroit's occupational scale as local unions remained bulwarks of white privilege. Furthermore, employers used black workers to manipulate and intimidate their majority-white workforces. In 1919, for example, a series of strikes shut down a number of factories across Detroit. One black replacement worker was killed when racial violence broke out at factory gates across the city. While the American Federation of Labor (AFL) claimed credit for preventing riots, Forrester Washington, head of the local Urban League, suggested that the "real credit" should go "to Negro strikers who went among the Negro 'scabs' and persuaded many of them to cease their anti-union activities."[42] Although the AFL approved a request by the National Urban League to make more serious efforts to organize black workers in 1917 and again in 1919, most of its locals continued to segregate and exclude blacks. Detroit's AFL branch had 1,227 black members, the vast majority of whom belonged to segregated locals. In an attempt to address the employment needs of its constituents, the Detroit Urban League, at different times, sided with the union and the employers. While it tried to claim credit for preventing racial unrest in the workplace, it also helped provide black strikebreakers to factories on more than one occasion. During a strike in the metal trades in 1921, the DUL furnished black workers to plants affected by the strike. On another occasion the Urban League's industrial secretary personally brought more than 150 black replacement workers to the Timkin Company, leading them across the picket lines himself. Despite these examples, African Americans' reputation among white workers as strikebreakers was a gross overstatement. It was invoked as a justification for excluding blacks from whites-only jobs much more often than it was used to describe a contemporary labor struggle. White workers' embrace of this idea illustrates their awareness that employers used racial divisiveness as a tool for undermining workers' bargaining position. However, it also shows that white workers were more likely to absorb the idea that black workers threatened their livelihood, and direct their hostility toward African Americans, than they were to reject racial divisiveness as disruptive and harmful to their interests.[43]

Finally, by the 1920s, as African Americans had taken on a more significant role in the local labor market as the city's most marginalized and vulnerable industrial workers, European-descended Detroiters were more likely to identify themselves as hyphenated Americans who shared similar concerns with others of European descent. Europeans' decreasing ethnic differentiation and industrial employers' interest in promoting Americanization helped popularize the idea that ethnic and national origin should be irrelevant markers of difference in public and occupational spaces. Liberals in the 1920s attempted to extend this idea to include African Americans. However, blacks' position at the bottom of the city's labor market and their consistent marginalization in other urban arenas limited the effectiveness of this appeal.

Urban Reform

The economic and geographic transformations that reshaped Detroit in the early twentieth century contributed to the expansion and popularity of movements for urban reform, the political ideology upon which northern racial liberalism was built. By 1916, the year that thousands of black migrants began to arrive in Detroit, native-born white city leaders had already adopted the language of reform to explain and naturalize newly emerging forms of social and economic stratification. Reform represented a departure from the scientific racism of an earlier age that ordered humans along a rigid hierarchy based on racial and ethnic heritage.[44] However, it used coded language about culture and modern ideas about how to take care of urban populations in order to justify urban stratification based on race and class. In their quest to undermine the political power of ethnic communities—widely seen as enabling deeply corrupt city governments—reformers mobilized a highly effective rhetoric of "efficiency" and "management" that sounded neutral and race and ethnicity blind even as it was not.

Urban reformers were a loose coalition of largely white, Protestant, and middle-class government officials and private citizens of both sexes who were interested in rationalizing and modernizing municipal government. As a group, reformers were interested in eliminating ward-based politics and professionalizing the administration of cities. They distrusted the uneducated masses who, they believed, made poorly informed choices about city governance and were vulnerable to manipulation by corrupt party "bosses." Instead, they favored putting authority into the hands of supposedly apolitical experts—women and men whom they identified as having proven ability—to run city programs and services. Reformers equated proven ability with either business success or appropriate formal training in one of the new administrative professions: urban planning, social work, public health, or public administration. Ultimately, reformers saw themselves as the appropriate class of people to deal with city governance because of their dual identities as representatives of corporations and as middle- and upper-class urban residents.[45]

Urban reformers supported changes in city government that would undermine ethnic and immigrant political power. At the same time, they promoted the erasure of explicit references to race and ethnicity in formal political discourse. Both of these dynamics would come to characterize northern racial liberalism. In the 1910s, reform-minded municipal activists celebrated city-run boards of health as modern institutions because they operated independently of cities' elected legislative bodies, and because they were managed and staffed by health care professionals rather than politicians.[46] These professionals imagined themselves as apolitical experts. For example, the smallpox vaccination policy of Detroit's Board of Health singled out black migrants not *as* black migrants per se but rather as a public health threat.

White leaders turned to reform ideology for guidance on how to manage the new urban black population and how to sustain urban peace in the face of dramatic inequality. Like earlier statements against racial unrest echoed by Detroit's newspapers and political leaders, their interest in building and maintaining ordered cities led them to reject the notion that vigilante violence against African Americans was an admissible part of the urban polity. However, this embrace of urban order simultaneously led them to deny the legitimacy of black struggles for access to municipal rights and resources. Therefore, even as a new group of white leaders began to see African Americans as an important and growing workforce in the city, this did not guarantee blacks' access to respect. In crafting modern political policy, racial liberals borrowed many of their tactics for thinking about African Americans and for managing black Detroiters from the discourse of urban reformers.

By the beginning of the First Great Migration, a professional class of white urban reformers had successfully allied itself with a political coalition drawn from both small and large business concerns. The interests of these two groups coincided in many significant ways. Both belonged to a national movement of urban reformers intent on rationalizing urban government *and* using the new public institutions they developed to manage and order cities and their residents. In 1912, Henry Leland, founder of the Cadillac Company, created the Good Citizens League, a political organization designed "for the uplift of our fellow men and for the civic and moral betterment of our city in general."[47] The Good Citizens League worked to break the power of "political machines" and fight "corruption" in urban government—terms it used to describe a party-based patronage system through which ethnic and working-class leaders had been able to mobilize support for their campaigns and win some political power. Leland, who had founded the antiunion Detroit Employers' Association in 1902, began his new political group with thirty-six members of the mainline congregation to which he belonged, the Westminster Presbyterian Church. The main preoccupation of the group was the "political reorganization" of local government from a state of "complex indirect organization to simple responsive administrative machine."[48]

The men who joined the Good Citizens League were Detroit's new corporate managers. They were wealthy, native-born, white Protestants. Unsatisfied with the municipal government, they believed the existing political structure to be hopelessly corrupt, inefficient, and incapable of handling the problems associated with the modern city. They were also distraught over what they saw as the negative consequences of industrial production—a set of social ills that they believed were rooted in the disorganization that characterized modern urban life. Members of the Good Citizens League identified their enemies as uneducated and power-hungry aldermen who used ward politics to curry favor from their constituents, sustain their political dominance, and serve their myopic interests at the expense of running the city effectively. Reformers argued that this was particularly problematic when it came to city administration because machine politicians would appoint their unqualified cronies, or people to whom they owed political favors, to municipal posts.[49]

By 1916, the Good Citizens League, alongside other white, native-born urban reformers, had mobilized significant political power in the city and was nearing the height of its success. Detroit reformers' interest in rationalizing and simplifying municipal government led them to fight to strengthen the authority of the mayor, eliminate ward-based voting, create nonpartisan city elections, and introduce civil service exams as a prerequisite for city employment. These changes marked a deliberate campaign to disrupt the party system and undercut ethnic political power. In 1918, working in a close alliance with the Detroit Employers' Association and the local Board of Commerce, the Good Citizens League won these reforms in a citywide referendum for a new city charter. The most immediate effect of this victory was to create a power vacuum in the organization of local political institutions that had relied on party politics. This void was quickly filled by organizations and individuals sympathetic to the needs of local corporations and the newly emergent Protestant elite. Indeed, reformers' push for reorganization in Detroit was particularly effective because political parties and the ward-based system were not as powerful as they were in cities with strong ethnic organizations like Chicago and New York.[50]

Reformers' enthusiasm for order and efficiency in municipal government was intertwined with their interests as members of industry's managerial elite. Large corporations depended on administrative predictability to manage their own finances and bureaucracies. Detroit's reformers thus pushed for what they saw as the rationalization and simplification of municipal government and cast themselves as protectors of the public purse against the profligate interests of the less well informed. Reformers also worked to eliminate unpredictability by more closely managing urban populations through new technical tools like urban planning, public health, social work, "improved" policing, and other elements of public administration. For example, in his book-length retrospective about the fight for a new charter, William P. Lovett argued that poorly educated, nonnative speakers of English had turned the local school board into a political organization, committed to the dispensation of party favors instead of public education. Lovett, who became executive secretary of the Good Citizens League in 1916, headed the campaign for a new municipal charter. He consistently portrayed working-class, immigrant politicians as inherently corrupt, untrustworthy, and self-promoting. "Predatory politicians and the ruthless, insolent, aggressiveness of the political 'gang,'" he maintained, used the city government as an important sector of their "operating circle."[51]

Urban reformers used discourses that northern racial liberals subsequently adopted about the political power of nondominant groups. They articulated cultural ideas about immigrants and the "lower races" through coded language about efficiency and education to help discredit the current government and reshape city politics. Lovett, for example, castigated city inspectors who "could not boast even a grammar school education" but were unashamed to face "their audiences with staccato speeches of ungrammatical lingo."[52] He thus portrayed working-class, immigrant politicians as inherently untrustworthy. When urban reformers spoke about the need for "Americanization," "education," "cleaning up slums and crime," and "efficiency," they were using neutral-sounding language as a code for talking about racial and ethnic minorities. They used the language of modernity rather than prejudice to explain a process that effectively limited nonelite participation in urban government. When they attacked poolrooms, dance halls, and saloons—working-class and immigrant cultural institutions that provided venues for political and labor organizing—they focused on corruption rather than ethnicity. Detroit's upper- and middle-class reformers suggested that they were developing a healthy parental relationship to the city's immigrants by shepherding an otherwise downtrodden working class toward enlightenment.

Urban reformers were so successful in their deployment of the language of modernity, anticorruption, and efficiency that they won over not only middle-class native white Americans but also large segments of the very ethnic communities whose influence they sought to undermine. Indeed, the Good Citizens League's rhetoric about clean government appealed to middle-class ethnic and African American leaders, many of whom endorsed the campaign for a new city charter. Local Jewish, Polish, German, Italian, and black newspapers all came out in favor of the plan, and many of them mimicked the logic promoted by the league.[53] The charter won with almost 90 percent of voters. In spite of their seemingly well-meaning justifications and the support they received, however, reformers' crusade against corruption undermined a structure that had allowed for ethnic, immigrant, and black participation in local politics. Their reform efforts ultimately helped to uphold and strengthen existing racial and ethnic inequalities in northern cities, undermining the power of immigrant communities in the city government.

African Americans arrived in Detroit in large numbers just as urban reformers won sweeping changes in the organization of local politics and the language of municipal governance. However, white city reformers were not the only group of people working to build a better city or thinking about the roles and rights of residents. As the black population grew, African Americans themselves developed more community spaces and institutions where they debated many of the same questions. The growth and increasing visibility of the black public sphere during the First Great Migration had a significant impact on white residents' and leaders' perceptions of black Detroiters and helped shaped their ideas about how to understand race in the city.

Housing and Racial Geography

Other elements of city life, including changes in residential geography and in the political activity of African Americans themselves, came to play an important role in shaping debates over northern racial liberalism in Detroit. In response to the demographic, political, and labor market shifts of the 1910s, white leaders developed new, seemingly nonracialized ways to justify and explain racial stratification that foreshadowed the popularity of northern racial liberalism and its racially neutral discourse in subsequent decades. The geography of race was shifting in Detroit during this era: just as workplaces were becoming more visibly stratified by race, residential patterns increasingly reflected a black-white racial divide.

It may seem like the story of the city's housing market—one of increasing residential racial segregation—contradicts the growing popularity of a modern, liberal, and explicitly northern discourse that white city leaders were developing to talk about the gradual flowering of racial equality in cities. However, white city leaders developed northern racial liberalism and racially neutral discourse as a tool for managing both black and white urban residents as the residential racial terrain of the city became increasingly segregated. They developed a political ideology designed to reduce racial conflict within an increasingly racially stratified city. Managing racial conflict, in the language of northern racial liberalism, was akin to impulses of progressive reform because it was directed toward maintaining urban peace and ensuring that the city ran smoothly. And like their earlier counterpart, these goals did not necessarily aid in developing a more just and racially equal city. Understanding the housing market—the political and economic reasons that it shifted as well as white individuals' growing interest in enforcing segregation—sheds light on the terrain that northern racial liberals were attempting to manage and the strategies they used to do so.

As manufacturers began to reorganize production, African Americans became a more visible and significant presence in the city. The simultaneous and dramatic expansion of industrial production and of the city itself contributed to the racial reorganization of residential space. Between 1880 and 1920, Detroit annexed huge tracts of land. Over these forty years, the city grew to four times its 1880 size. At the end of the nineteenth century, ethnicity (not class or race) was the most important social and geographic marker in the city. European American immigrants and native-born whites lived in ethnically homogeneous but economically diverse neighborhoods. Meanwhile, the small population of black Detroiters was spread thinly throughout ethnic-dominated sections of the city. By 1920, however, large-scale industrialization, combined with the massive in-migration of black and white workers and the arrival of corporate managers to create economic and race-based, rather than ethnic, segregation. Instead of moving into ethnic neighborhoods, newly arrived white workers began to settle down close to the factories where they worked, and the well-to-do of all ethnicities moved into suburb-like outlying areas of the city. African Americans were welcome only in three majority-black areas. At this point, white working-class immigrants were more likely to live in multiethnic, but exclusively white, working-class neighborhoods. This new geographic organization of space coincided with a dramatic decline in immigration due to the First World War.[54] As European migration slowed to a trickle, black migration soared.

The African American population followed the opposite trend. Black residents of all classes became more isolated and segregated from whites in the city. Between 1860 and 1900, about 80 percent of black Detroiters lived on the near east side, in and among recently arrived immigrants, most of whom were German. Most of the remaining 20 percent were scattered throughout the city, living in their employers' homes as domestic workers. By 1920, conversely, the far larger population of African Americans lived almost entirely in three majority-black areas.[55]

As European Americans became more geographically mixed in neighborhoods that were "white" rather than specifically Italian or Polish, black residents of all classes became more segregated from whites in the city. Urbanization and industrialization contributed to the creation of a class-based urban geography for white Detroiters and a racially segregated space for blacks. Middle-class whites of all ethnicities were more likely to live side by side than they had previously, although native-born whites with native-born parents dominated new middle-class neighborhoods on the city's periphery. The majority of northern industrial cities saw similar changes in their ethnic and racial geography, but Detroit's transformation was earlier and more complete than it was in cities like Chicago and New York, which sustained far more ethnic homogeneity by 1920.[56]

The chasm between what it meant to be white in Detroit and what it meant to be black was underlined by the physical quality of the housing available to different groups. Securing decent housing had already been a chronic problem for working-class residents, especially for black Detroiters, but the population explosion during World War I created a housing shortage that plagued the city for years to come. Between 1910 and 1920, construction did not keep pace with the high demand for housing; by 1920, finding any shelter at all became difficult. Only

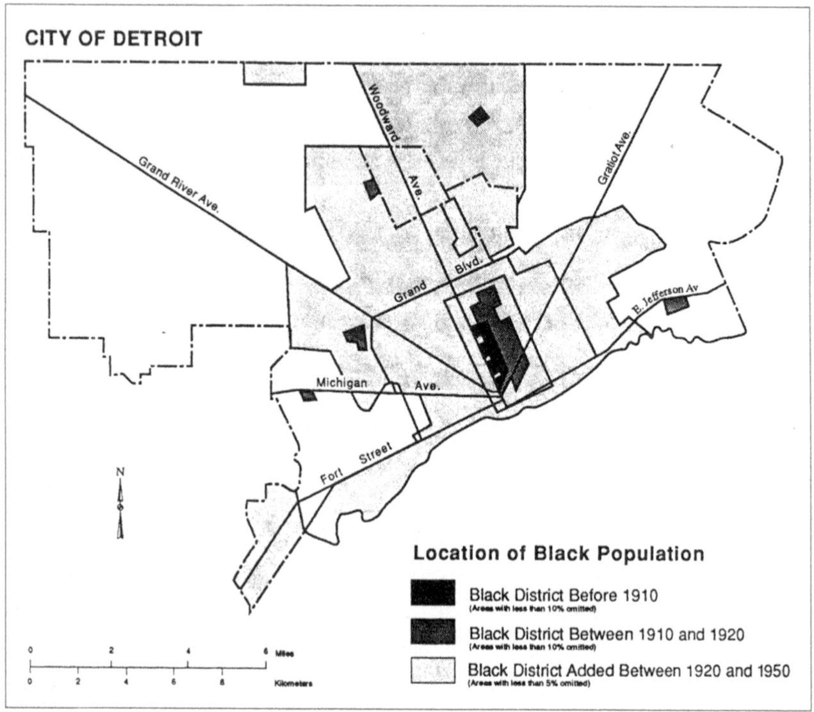

City of Detroit, location of black population, 1910–1950. Image courtesy of Richard Thomas.

87,000 new dwelling units were built, while the population increased by more than half a million.[57] While the African American population was expanding at a much faster rate than the white population, the areas of the city where blacks could live hardly grew at all during the war. Black Detroiters were restricted to four districts—two downtown neighborhoods and two smaller areas outside of downtown. These were Paradise Valley, the first and largest black neighborhood located on the near east side; the black west side, a newer area; Conant Gardens a black middle-class and largely owner-occupied neighborhood in the northeast; and the Eight Mile–Wyoming district on the northwestern border of the city.[58] Landlords and real estate brokers exploited this dearth of options, charging exorbitant rents to the captive population. In order to help defray the cost of rent, families often doubled up, took in lodgers, or moved in with relatives.[59] By 1919, the majority of African Americans lived "in such crowded conditions that three or four families in an apartment [was] the rule rather than the exception."[60]

Racial tensions were heightened by the housing shortage that plagued the city and disproportionately affected black Detroiters, who could not spread into adjacent areas because of white-imposed restrictions against expansion. The formalization of racial segregation in the country as a whole, and in the urban North in particular, dramatically curtailed residential mobility for black Detroiters. In 1917, the U.S. Supreme Court declared racially restrictive zoning laws unconstitutional. The elimination of these laws, which had been popular in southern cities, sparked the expansion of racially restrictive covenants in the North as well as the South—clauses in the deed of a home preventing its sale to nonwhites.[61] Following the Supreme Court ruling, white Detroiters turned toward restrictive covenants to enforce residential segregation.[62] Extralegal enforcement of this practice, including violence against African Americans and their property, discouraged black residents from moving into areas that were mostly white or from expanding the boundaries of congested black districts.

As the First Great Migration accelerated, some members of Detroit's black elite challenged residential segregation by moving into all-white neighborhoods. Over the course of the First World War, white responses to these move-ins changed from quiet toleration to outright hostility and physical violence. Before 1917, African American families that had moved into middle-class white neighborhoods remembered "[having] little trouble." For example, an African American family that moved into a white district in 1915 explained that they had "no difficulty" because "racial difficulty [was] not in the air at that time." According to a 1926 study, "White families knowingly bought property next to colored families" in "high class" neighborhoods before 1917, "apparently giving it little heed."[63]

Before the acceleration of the First Great Migration in 1917, white Detroiters saw the presence of one or two black families as isolated incidents rather than the beginning of an influx, so they did not mount organized resistance to their new black neighbors. One explained her tolerance for African Americans who lived on her block as provisional, based on their inconspicuous behavior and small numbers: "They don't try to associate with us [and] they give us no trouble." However, she emphasized, "We don't want any more moving in."[64] As black migration continued and the city became increasingly characterized by racial divisions, African Americans faced progressively more organized and violent responses to their arrival in white middle-class neighborhoods. Beginning in 1917, physical attacks on newly purchased, black-owned homes in these areas became commonplace. For example, "Dr. J——" explained that in 1917, when his family moved into their house in a white neighborhood, they "weren't wanted at first [and] there were several committee meetings to oust us." On August 23, 1917, a "mob of 200 whites" drove fifty African Americans out of a duplex located just north of Paradise Valley, in a largely white, "perceptibly run down" neighborhood. The house had been occupied by four white, southern families, but the landlord "decided to try colored tenants," probably because he would be able to extract more rent from them. He leased the entire house to Trigg, an African American man, who found families to fill the rooms. Led by William Koenig, a former city alderman, and John Van Dusan, a white mob stopped the new tenants from moving into the house, loaded their belongings onto trucks, and drove it back to Trigg's old house. At the time, an African American family lived only two doors away and had been there "for years." There were also several other black families living in the immediate vicinity. These changing responses point to white residents' mounting anxieties about African Americans, which developed as it became clear that the latter would be a permanent feature of city life.[65]

The coincidence of increasing black migration alongside the tight housing market helped white Detroiters make connections between the presence of African Americans in the city and urban problems more generally—a notion that stood at the core of northern racial liberalism. Housing became politically important in Detroit during World War I because it was an issue that captured what many whites felt about the dangers of an African American "invasion" of the city. Whites had already begun to see blacks as competitors in the workforce—even though they were segregated into the worst jobs, they remained an omnipresent threat. At the same time, they pointed to the ills of black neighborhoods as evidence that African Americans were unwelcome neighbors. The dilapidated and overcrowded houses of Paradise Valley, the largest residential concentration of African Americans, became a metaphor for white concerns about the negative effect black Detroiters had on city life. Shifts in the local labor market, urban reform discourse, and tensions over housing each contributed to the notion that African American Detroiters presented city leaders with a set of new social problems that needed to be managed and contained.

The Politics of African American Reform

In response to the mounting hostility directed toward them, African Americans produced a range of discourses about themselves that simultaneously complicated, challenged, and reinforced elements of these narratives. Black residents built and expanded a large number of political and social institutions during this period, reflecting their diverse experiences and philosophies. Many African Americans, for example, pushed hard to engage and refashion white perceptions of black residents—although in so doing, some embraced ideas about class and respectability that bolstered, rather than undermined, white justifications for racism. Elite African Americans often promoted the notion that poor black migrants were partly to blame for the surge in racist attacks because of their inadequately "respectable" comportment. Debates among black Detroiters as well as those between black and white city leaders are crucial for understanding northern racial liberalism. These debates responded to, and indeed helped create, white liberals' ideas about how to manage the newly interracial city. Some white city leaders, including industrialists, politicians, and social service providers, adopted ideas from African American leaders of black social service and civil rights groups. Others became acquainted with black demands for change because they were the objects of black protest. Ultimately, white leaders drew on African Americans' languages of equality and class difference to explain their own approaches to black Detroiters, even as the policies they promoted were not intended to rectify the racial inequalities that black residents were fighting to overturn. While the visibility of racial divisions in Detroit increased, racial liberalism hinged on the concept that municipal politics could and should be racially neutral. At the same time, African Americans across the class spectrum used race-specific language as they continued to fight to gain access to the full range of citizenship rights in Detroit.

Black responses to the vaccination inspection program at the Michigan Central Railway station illustrate the range of ideas that Detroit's African Americans sustained about the influx of black migrant families into the city and about white officials' efforts to contain and manage this population. African American travelers defended their dignity at the train station. They protested vocally, asserting that white perceptions of African Americans as potential contaminants were simply untrue. Some migrants used institutional strategies to confront the Board of Health, taking their complaints to the local branch of the National Association for the Advancement of Colored People.

The NAACP leaders' approach to the vaccination inspections reflected their political priorities as some of Detroit's best-educated and most financially stable African Americans. The NAACP sought to balance the pursuit of racial justice with a desire to maintain and enforce middle-class respectability, a tension that characterized its approach to civil rights issues at the time. The group also sought to protect black men and women from physical vulnerability and overexposure at the hands of white men. NAACP leaders were "pleased" with the health commissioner's decision to end the inspections, but middle-class black leaders were concerned about how the image of diseased African American migrants contributed to discrimination against the race as a whole, undermining their own positions in the city. Many black middle-class Detroiters saw southern migrants as unfit for city living and therefore unwelcome additions to their small community. Thus, although black leaders opposed the brutal and invasive administration of the Board of Health's program, they sympathized with the class-based concerns expressed by the board—that working-class and poor people (of all races) were potentially diseased and posed some hazard to established and respectable middle-class Detroiters.

The city's black elite and the groups they established were the most self-consciously engaged with white leaders. During this period, black elite leaders began to forge connections with white reformers and businesspeople and worked to build legitimacy for themselves as spokespeople for "the race." These black leaders, mostly professionals and entrepreneurs, shared some of the anxieties about African American migrants that inspired the board's policy. While they pushed white liberals to respond to their concerns about mounting segregation and persistent inequality, they also embraced those elements of reform discourse that confirmed their suspicion of black migrants, authorized their understanding of themselves as rightful leaders, and reinforced their class-bound sensibilities about the limits of racial justice. Members of the city's black elite saw themselves as natural "race leaders" and embraced elements of urban reform discourse in their organizational work. Like white reformers, they believed that leaders should be educated, financially stable, and morally upstanding. They consistently contrasted their own political work and social philosophies with the growing number of working-class and poor migrant leaders. For example, elite African Americans maligned storefront churches, "voodoo" medicines, and migrants' attire as components of backward, southern traditions that needed to be modernized or eradicated. In reports, studies, and court cases, they fought for racial justice, but they staked their claims to full citizenship on respectable middle-class cultural behavior such as appropriate comportment and good manners—behaviors they cast as modern and northern, as opposed to backward and southern.[66] Black reformers thus found support for their work among white leaders, as well as a provisional and limited legitimacy. At the same time, white city leaders began to use their relationships with black leaders and institutions to win support among black voters and to build a reputation for being racially fair-minded. While this strategy may have been calculated to help white leaders win elections, it was not exclusively cynical. White reformers sincerely believed in the racial liberalism they embraced and saw it as an important element of their vision.

The relationship between the Reverend R. L. Bradby and the Ford Motor Company exemplified these dynamics. Bradby was minister of the Second Baptist Church, the city's oldest and largest black congregation. He took an early interest in African American migrants and built a social service arm of his church designed to facilitate the assimilation of black southerners into northern life during the First World War. Bradby's church, like the Urban League and other reform organizations, emphasized respectability and middle-class comportment as the avenue to independence and equality.[67] In 1919, Bradby began to recruit and manage African American workers for the Ford Motor Company, which had just started hiring blacks in large numbers in a range of jobs and departments at the enormous River Rouge plant. Henry Ford's interest in hiring black workers lay in his hostility to bolshevism, which he associated with immigrant labor. He imagined that black southerners would be unreceptive to unionization. By offering African American men high wages, good benefits, and consistent employment, Ford aimed to sustain a more stable workforce. Indeed, black men at Ford were less likely to quit than were white men, who had many more options. The company was thus able to sustain a brutal pace of work at its integrated plants, relying on black men, who had few other places to turn for equally well-paying work, to set the standard.[68] Bradby worked with Donald Marshall, the African American personnel manager in charge of black workers at Ford's plants, sending members of his church whom he deemed "steady workers"—accommodating, dependable, and unmistakably antiunion. Bradby also helped mediate disputes involving black workers and patrolled the plants in order to resolve inter- and intraracial disagreements. Bradby's presence on the shop floor, ostensibly designed to encourage racial harmony, also meant that an extra set of eyes helped enforce the strict standards of behavior and comportment that complemented Ford's vision for shaping the morals of black workers. Bradby and other "Ford ministers" helped the company's Sociology Department monitor black workers, making sure that they attended church, were not alcoholics, and maintained traditional families, with a wife and mother at home taking care of the children.[69]

In 1916, Birney Smith, an African American realtor and a member of the city's small black elite, pulled together the first board of directors for the Detroit Urban League. As a national organization, the DUL encouraged members of the black professional and business classes to open branches in cities that were migration destinations. As a social service agency, the league helped assimilate recently arrived working-class African Americans into northern society.[70] From the beginning, the league sustained a class-bound perspective: its interracial board of directors included very wealthy white philanthropists alongside middle- and upper-class African Americans, while the league targeted the working-class and poor for its services. The DUL's class politics and its interest in migrant assimilation were typical of black reform organizations in Detroit and in the urban North more generally. The league drew most of its resources from the local Community Fund, an entity that raised money from wealthy donors and distributed it to social service agencies across the city. Of the forty-two agencies supported by the Community Fund in 1918, the Urban League and the Phyllis Wheatley Home, which provided housing services to African American women migrants, were the only two that served all-black clienteles.[71]

League leaders believed that black community success depended on being able to sustain positive relationships with the city's white businesspeople and government leaders. They saw the cultivation of these relationships as the best strategy for expanding black access to good jobs. For example, Forrester Washington, the organization's first director, worked with Boyd Fisher on a survey of black workers in factories across the city. Fisher, a white industrialist, was a member of the city's Board of Commerce and vice president of the Detroit Executive Club, a group of business executives. Furthermore, beginning in 1917, the Employers' Association of Detroit began to pay the salary of the DUL's employment secretary. One league report declared that the organization had "gone a longer ways [than any other group] toward mitigating the racial difficulties that have arisen by conferences with those of power and influence."[72] The report offered no details but clearly indicated that its authors believed they had found the best approach for addressing the concerns of African Americans. By the end of the First World War, more than half of the black workers employed in Detroit had been placed through the league's employment office. The DUL also helped employers by teaching black workers acceptable work behavior, "from proper clothing to suitable docility and anti-unionism."[73] League leaders did not explicitly address discrimination. Instead, they believed that their priorities—helping black migrants find industrial employment—offered the best strategy for assimilating blacks and for contributing to the creation of a peaceful interracial city.

The DUL's small black staff, most of whom were trained social workers and caseworkers, tended to be better educated and to have lived in the city for longer than the migrants to whom they provided services. Often sharing the class perspective of white employers, the league staffers worked with factory managers in Detroit to develop personnel policies and procedures to manage newly hired black workers. For example, league social workers suggested using the sociological components of Americanization programs to improve black workers' productivity and reduce those behaviors that may interfere with their work. They recommended that plants employ an "industrial welfare worker" for black employees, encouraging manufacturers to manage African American workers like they managed their immigrant employees.[74] The DUL recommended that black welfare workers provide many of the same services and practice similar levels of surveillance as Ford's sociologists. League literature suggested that industrial welfare workers show men how to invest their money in war bonds, "act as a go-between for the employment dep't and the men," and "talk to them on the value of regularity and thrift and at the same time urge them to stay on the job on all days directly following pay day."[75]

Established black residents of Detroit often blamed migrants for eliciting increased segregation and racism and for putting undue stress on shared resources, which led to regional and cultural explanations for class divisions. Birney Smith, for example, remembered that "the big problem was the influx of Southern colored people. Previous to that time . . . we went about our business and the neighbors had a friendly attitude." While Smith may have been romanticizing the premigration period, he did capture a sense of nostalgia that had already become popular among more established residents by the end of World War I. In a characteristic report from 1917, Forrester Washington compared long-time residents, whom he described as "high grade colored families, self-respecting, self-supporting moral, intelligent and comfortable," to the "touts, gamblers and other followers of the ponies [who] came to Detroit" in the early part of the decade.[76] In his 1918 study, George Haynes observed that "the coming of many of the less desirable type [produced] a gradual tending toward the segregation of all Negroes."[77] Washington suggested that the simultaneous arrival of a large group of racist white migrants from the South had contributed to the upswing in discrimination faced by all black residents. However, he explained, the "old Detroiters" among the African American population were blaming *black* migrants for this increase in segregation and racial discrimination, "and their resentment amounts to antipathy—if not to actual hate."[78]

Urban League leaders explicitly rejected the notion that highlighting discrimination or mounting an explicit campaign against racial prejudice would be effective strategies for black Detroiters interested in gaining more access to city resources, public space, jobs, decent education, and other elements of full citizenship. In a press release, the league explained approvingly that "Negroes of Detroit are not spending all of their time protesting against race prejudice and the persecutions heaped upon their race, nor trying to advance by favors from without, but that they are rather trying to accomplish real progress by improvement from within."[79] This notion, that community advancement required self-improvement rather than external social change, helped to legitimate the approach of white racial liberals. Ultimately, the idea that full citizenship should be accorded only to the most deserving elements of black society fit neatly within the most conservative strains of uplift in the 1910s.

This approach to black politics was not the only one endorsed by the city's black elite. At the same time that many members of the black elite sustained a paternalistic attitude toward migrants, even blaming them for discrimination itself, some participated in challenging discrimination and white racism from a liberal, civil rights perspective. These activists characterized antiblack discrimination as backward, illegal, unfair, and illiberal, and they called on white leaders' sense of justice to remedy these problems. For many black reformers and elites, these two approaches were not contradictory: as the activism of the NAACP demonstrates, many African Americans mixed the politics of uplift and respectability with the politics of civil rights.

The Detroit branch of the NAACP, founded in 1912, was the sixth branch in the nation, with forty-one charter members.[80] The NAACP was a membership organization supported by dues and run by a small cadre of volunteers. By 1918, it had doubled its membership but remained relatively inactive. That year, in response to the increasing discrimination and segregation that all black residents were facing in Detroit, the branch began to take on a more ambitious program intended to increase membership and challenge white hostility. NAACP leaders formed a series of committees designed to fight discrimination, alter popular perceptions of African Americans in the city, and develop and promote "race consciousness and race work" among black residents, especially the city's youth. These committees would work on organizing against discrimination in public places; they also would "conduct educational propaganda thru the press, an open forum, a circulating library of race literature, edit and manage a branch bulletin,

[and] conduct entertainments, concerts, bazaars, etc." NAACP activists understood their program as one that would build stronger collective resources for African Americans in the city.[81]

By 1918, African Americans saw the local NAACP as an organization they could turn to for help when they were fighting against discrimination. The association often won discrete victories by approaching white leaders in key political positions. For example, NAACP leaders helped black migrants win their fight against vaccination inspections at the railroad station by appealing to the city's commissioner of health. Irene Davis, a black clerk at a local post office, also turned to the NAACP for help. In May 1918, Davis lost her job when protests from white clerks prompted her manager to ask her to leave. She appealed to the assistant postmaster, who let the decision of her manager stand. Davis then turned to the NAACP, which sent a committee to the postmaster, and won Davis her job back.[82] These victories demonstrate the willingness of prominent white leaders to rectify specific instances of discrimination. This dynamic—white leaders' willingness to reverse isolated acts of prejudice—confirmed black leaders' sense that their approach was effective. It also demonstrated that whites in positions of power in the city were familiar with and thus positioned to be influenced by black strategies designed to fight against discrimination.

As the African American Detroiters of the NAACP fought for respect during and after World War I, they also recognized and denounced the increasing incidence of segregation and discrimination in the city. In 1918, the Detroit branch ran a petition campaign to press local newspapers to stop using race-specific descriptions when reporting on crimes committed by African Americans and to cover black Detroiters positively. NAACP members found that 80 percent of the references to African Americans in the city's white newspapers referred to blacks either as criminals or "in an uncomplimentary manner."[83] In a 1920 report for the NAACP branch bulletin, J. F. Johnson was "sorry to say that discrimination in public places seems to be on the increase in Detroit." He attributed this rise in discrimination to "the great number of southern whites who have come to our city along with our southern colored people," and explained that the Detroit branch was beginning to litigate more discrimination cases.[84] In September 1920, Johnson's concerns were confirmed when the Michigan Central Railway "began to jim-crow colored passengers" on the train from Detroit to Cincinnati. The NAACP sent a letter to the Passenger and Traffic Department, which agreed to investigate and ultimately rectify the situation, but the incident was part of a larger trend toward exclusion and segregation in the city and the region.[85]

Like the Urban League, the primarily middle-class NAACP asserted that African American respectability was an important component of claims for equality and integration. In its first bulletin, from September 1920, the editors explained that African American Detroiters must do "everything in our power . . . to prevent the increase of prejudice and to secure justice for our people." Thus, the bulletin recommended that parents and guardians should "see that [their] children's faces, necks and hands are washed clean." It also suggested that parents "not arrange children's hair in 'corn rows' [because] it makes her a laughing stock and object of ridicule" and that they ensure their child "does not neglect his school lessons and that he behaves in school. By him a race is being judged."[86] The branch pulled together two Parent-Teacher Associations among African Americans where "a majority of our people live." Members of the Parent-Teacher Associations sought to "adjust reported discrimination in the schools" by "visiting the schools where reports of bad deportment and uncleanliness [*sic*] of our children come from."[87] The NAACP shared the Urban League's ideological commitment to respectability and racial uplift, but the association's commitment to litigating specific discrimination claims meant that it attempted to fight discrimination on two somewhat ideologically contradictory fronts: self-help and the legal system. Discourses of respectability implied that unrespectable African Americans (and others) did not deserve the full rights of citizenship accorded to respectable Americans.

Conclusion

Early in the First Great Migration, northern and southern racial regimes had more in common than defenders of white racial practices in the North suggested. Indeed, the effect of the racial systems in both regions—to produce and maintain racially based inequalities—was actually quite similar, and some aspects of the northern racial regime were as overt as southern practices. African Americans in the North faced residential and workplace segregation, racial differentials in pay and job opportunities, very little access to mainstream political power, disrespect, episodic physical violence, disproportionate levels of poverty, and disproportionate levels of arrest and incarceration, among other insults.

During the First Great Migration, white city leaders positioned themselves as racial moderates, standing on the middle ground between what they characterized as the radical racism of the South and the radically disruptive equality that African Americans were fighting to attain. City officials aimed to keep Detroit peaceful, orderly, and prosperous by supporting business interests on the one hand, and using modern, administrative methods to manage the resources and daily workings of the city on the other. They designed policies based on the expertise of city planners, social workers, and health officials and downplayed the significance of racial differentiation and discrimination.

The growing power of urban reform, the increasing importance of black workers in the industrial labor market, and the growing visibility of African Americans in the city as the black population and black institutions expanded all laid the groundwork for northern racial liberalism in Detroit during and immediately after World War I. This change in white leaders' perceptions of African Americans foreshadowed incremental improvements in black access to city resources and equality. But it also pointed to shifts in white leaders' justifications for sustaining racial inequality and stratification. The race-based elements of their hostility toward African Americans were becoming more covert, an important component of the racially neutral discourse that characterized northern racial liberalism and white northern leaders' attitudes toward African Americans by 1920. The story that opens this chapter is a good illustration of these dynamics: Detroit's Board of Health explained its race-specific use of vaccination inspections as rooted in its interest in protecting all Detroiters from epidemics. African Americans as a population were cast as diseased and threatening, in contrast to earlier justifications for singling out African Americans based on the illiberal race-based prejudice of the South. White city leaders' rejection of scientific racism as an explanation for racial stratification was neither consistent nor complete by the 1920s, but it was a trend that set the stage for the emergence of northern racial liberalism. At the railroad station, white officers who implemented the Board of Health's vaccination inspections were certainly hostile toward black travelers. However, the official reasons for the inspections articulated by members of the Board of Health were about managing and controlling disease, regardless of race, not about suppressing or intimidating black travelers. This allowed white city leaders to continue to implement practices that had the effect of excluding, intimidating, or humiliating African Americans without expressing overt support for racial stratification, the dynamic that undergirded northern racial liberalism.

Both white and black reformers and media grafted some of their anxieties about the way the city was changing onto African Americans, specifically working-class black migrants. White reformers and journalists represented them as temporary Detroiters, necessary due to the wartime labor shortage but unwelcome as permanent residents. "Old" black middle-class residents also saw the newcomers as an unwelcome addition to their small community, blaming them for bringing segregation and racism with them in their move north and for putting undue stress on the resources of the community. While middle-class African Americans focused their anxieties on working-class newcomers, white reformers and media were less discerning about what the image of the black, male migrant represented. Instead of representing a portion of the black community, images of migrants produced by whites were designed to portray all African Americans in the city. These black residents were seen by many as workers with no rights or permanent attachment to the city. Over the next two decades, black residents and activists would both draw on and modify these tactics.

2

Protecting Urban Peace

Northern Racial Liberalism and the Limits of Racial Equality

It does not always do for any man to demand to its fullest the right which the law gives him.[1]
—Mayor John Smith, 1925

In April 1921, Walter White, an official at the National Association for the Advancement of Colored People, published an article titled "Reviving the Ku Klux Klan" in *Forum*, a liberal journal popular among politicians, social workers, and other self-styled progressives. The new Klan, according to White, had adopted its name from the white supremacist militias of the 1860s and was led by self-proclaimed "Imperial Wizard" Joseph Simmons of Atlanta, Georgia. It got its start in 1919, the same summer that race riots swept through American cities and the nation fell into a recession. By 1921, the Klan had gained considerable momentum. White was especially troubled by its growing popularity in the industrial urban North and West, where Klanspeople were working to drive African Americans "back to the land of lynching."[2]

White used Detroit as an example of these dynamics, suggesting that conditions "affecting the Negro" there were likely "due to Klan propaganda." In Detroit, acute unemployment caused by the postwar recession helped cultivate hostility toward African Americans. According to White, the local Employers' Association, a group of the city's largest employers and most prominent businesspeople, shared these Klan-inspired ideas and was considering a proposal to urge its members to stop hiring African Americans and to fire those they already employed, in an effort to ensure that needy whites received employment. Furthermore, he explained, in an effort to push African Americans out of Detroit, the city's Department of Public Welfare was refusing relief to black families and forcing them instead to accept railroad fare back to the South. Ultimately, White concluded, these conditions "show definitely how [Klan] propaganda can militate against the Negro in Northern industries with exceedingly vicious results."[3]

In his discussion of Detroit, White attacked the most mainstream elements of its white leadership for attempting to immiserate and expel black migrants from the city. He suggested that this Klan-like behavior was southern, premodern, and illiberal, qualities that many of Detroit's white leaders would identify as reprehensible. White pushed these men, who saw themselves and the North as forward thinking and modern, to change their approach and be more actively "northern" in their outlook and practices.

The NAACP circulated White's article widely, sending copies to supporters along with a fund-raising letter. The mayor of Detroit, James Couzens, himself a member of the NAACP, received the article in the mail. One of Detroit's most prominent proponents of urban reform and clean government, he was also one of the wealthiest residents of the city and an original investor in the Ford Motor Company, where he served as vice president and general manager until 1915. While at Ford, Couzens was widely celebrated, both locally and nationally, for his managerial acumen.[4] Like other reform leaders, Couzens was committed to creating a professional and well-run administration that could effectively meet the needs of business interests. He also saw himself as a friend of black Detroit. He viewed these commitments—to business and to African American progress—as complementary.

When Couzens received White's article from the NAACP, he responded with outrage and threatened to withdraw his membership from the association. White, Couzens claimed, was making unsubstantiated false accusations. Adopting an opposing position, he defended the city's employers and relief workers—its white leaders and city managers—and asserted that they were not practicing racial discrimination. The Employers' Association, he explained, had entertained no such recommendations from its members, and local relief agencies were not singling out black recipients. Instead, employers were uniformly tightening their belts and letting their most recent hires go, and relief workers were turning away *all* applicants who had lived in the city for six months or less, offering them carfare home instead of relief.[5]

While Detroit's employers and agency administrators did not say they were targeting the city's most recent arrivals because they were African American, their practices affected black workers and residents disproportionately. A far higher proportion of African Americans than European-descended residents were new migrants. Furthermore, as historian James Gregory points out, white southern migrants blended more easily than African Americans into existing social and occupational enclaves in the urban North. Even though these white migrants were disdained as backward "hillbillies," this condescending cultural dismissal had a far smaller impact on their access to jobs, housing, and other city resources than did African Americans' racial identity.[6] African Americans accounted for almost a quarter of the relief rolls in 1921, when they represented just 4 percent of the city's population.[7] Layoff decisions based on seniority had a similarly racially disparate effect. Job discrimination meant that African Americans were the last ones hired during a labor shortage, and the first fired when the economy soured.

Walter White and James Couzens exchanged eight letters over the course of the next two months, in which each man elaborated his understanding of racial politics in Detroit. Couzens unself-consciously defended the racially hierarchical status quo. By defending exclusions of the most recent hires and the most recent arrivals from jobs and the city, he suggested that longer-term residents, a group whiter than the city's population, had rightful ownership of Detroit. Furthermore, by casting employers' and administrators' intentions as racially neutral, he dismissed the most important element of White's critique—that their practices had racially discriminatory consequences. Couzens's defense of local businesspeople, relief workers, and his own administration captures white liberals' difficulty seeing how the policies they supported could help sustain racial stratification. By casting their practices as not deliberately discriminatory, and suggesting that their intent was more important than the consequences, his response helped mask as race-neutral policies that bore racist consequences.

Couzens suggested that by raising charges of racial discrimination, Walter White and his allies were disrupting the racial social peace that had to exist in order for black rights to be respected: "It is this sort of propaganda that is exciting your people more than anything that is being done by the whites even including the Ku Klux Klan."[8] Offended by White's suggestion that Detroit's white leaders were practicing Klan-style discrimination, he saw himself and his allies as enlightened people with the city's best interests at the top of their agendas. "I have worked hard to keep the relationship between the two peoples satisfactory here," he explained to White. "I have taken a lot of trouble to see that the blacks get their fair distribution of [city] work, and the records I think will show that they really have gotten more—because of the lack of other opportunities."[9] Couzens clearly recognized that inequalities shaped black experiences in Detroit. He saw himself as best positioned to judge whether fairness was being meted out, and best able to ensure that it was. At the same time, however, he instructed White to remain skeptical of accusations of racial discrimination and encouraged Detroit's black residents to do the same: "You must discontinue agitating the colored people by a lot of stories not substantiated by facts."[10] Couzens was willing to see extreme expressions of discrimination that were perpetuated by people he identified as racists, but he was unwilling to consider that his own policies or those of his close allies created racial inequality. He saw independent black activism, directed at securing resources and exposing racism, as disruptive of urban peace, rather than productive of more robust civic equality. Indeed, he cast it as the principle cause of discrimination.

Couzens's sense that black protest was a problem was shared by other prominent whites who lent their support to groups like the NAACP. In spite of his interest in helping African Americans, Henry Stevens, one of the city's high-profile white philanthropists, shared Couzens's concerns. Stevens, whose wealth came from western mining and land speculation, was a close associate of Mayor Couzens, an avid promoter of urban reform, and an important friend to black Detroit. He worked as vice president of the Associated Charities, the citywide organization that raised funds for private charitable and social work agencies. He also served as chairman of the board of directors for the Detroit Urban League, a social work agency whose staff and constituents were African American. Like Couzens, he was a member of the NAACP. Stevens sustained close relationships with middle-class black leaders, including Forrester Washington, the first executive secretary of the DUL, who was working as a director at the Associated Charities in 1921. Indeed,

Stevens had been the source of White's information about the Employers' Association proposal to whiten the city's workforce.

Although African Americans celebrated Stevens for his support of black causes, like Couzens, he was concerned that independent black activism was often based on false or overblown suspicions of racism that could be disruptive to the urban fabric.[11] For example, at the same time that White and Couzens were engaged in their dispute, Stevens had begun to express reservations about the NAACP holding its national convention in Detroit in June 1921. He was concerned that the NAACP had been "stirring-up" black Detroiters with "negative" words and "unfounded charges." Stevens pointed to a recent demonstration in Hamtramck, an incorporated village within the boundaries of Detroit, as evidence that growing black discontent had increased activism, which he believed had the potential to disrupt urban peace. Four hundred protesters, "most of whom were Negroes," accused the village of "not furnishing adequate relief during this period of unemployment and appealed to the prosecuting attorney of the county to aid them." They argued that the village should provide adequate aid to its citizens and that the county was ultimately accountable for making sure the village lived up to its responsibilities. For Stevens, this protest was foreboding, inspiring fear that the NAACP convention would "breed further discontent among Negroes."[12]

The dispute between James Couzens and Walter White and Henry Stevens's concerns about the NAACP provide clear illustrations of some of the contradictions embedded in northern racial liberalism. They afford an unusually frank portrait of white liberals' ambivalence about struggles for African American equality in Detroit. They demonstrate white leaders' simultaneous interest in casting themselves as the most effective defenders of the fair distribution of city resources *and* in avoiding black protest. Furthermore, this dispute exposes white leaders' keen interest in distinguishing white Detroiters' modern responses to black migrants and residents from premodern southern strategies aimed at controlling and suppressing African Americans. When African Americans mounted independent protests challenging overt racism or the maldistribution of resources, white leaders who considered themselves champions of black Detroiters critiqued black protest as disruptive and ultimately counterproductive.

Urban Peace

Attention to liberal white leaders' preoccupation with urban peace makes the seeming contradiction between their stated interest in black equality and their frequent failure to defend that position—as well as their intermittent efforts to undermine those struggles—comprehensible. Like Couzens and Stevens in 1921, when white liberal leaders believed that the push for racial equality would produce an intolerable or uncontainable level of conflict, they turned toward criticizing black protest and promoted the racially unequal status quo as the most sustainable urban form. Historians have celebrated northern white liberals' interest in race neutrality as an important step toward full equality. However, they have spent less time examining white leaders' reservations about the disruptive effects of black protest.[13]

White northern liberals saw peace as a prerequisite for racial equality. They believed it would only be possible to build a racially equal city once openly racist rhetoric was no longer an element of public debate *and* once African Americans stopped making claims about discrimination or demands for inclusion that disrupted the current order too much. Thus, for northern white urban liberals, sustaining urban peace meant celebrating the more expansive freedom African Americans could access in the North while tolerating existing stratification. White urban progressives in the early twentieth century, the predecessors of white racial liberals, had been willing to extend resources to African Americans "as long as the boundary lines of segregation remained firmly drawn."[14] Unlike their progressive forerunners, northern racial liberals were by the 1920s likely to oppose segregation on principle. However, when they believed that demands for integration proved too disruptive, they would resist black calls for equal access in favor of the existing racially hierarchical status quo. This chapter examines black activists' efforts to integrate exclusively white neighborhoods and the local government's push back against these incursions. It illustrates that white leaders' ideas about the meanings of peace certainly varied, but for most of them, their commitment to urban order defined the outer limits of their support for black equality.

Northern racial liberals argued that race should neither structure relations of power nor serve as the basis for inequality. For them, racial language should not be part of legitimate public discourse. The legal and administrative codification of racial neutrality, which characterized Michigan and Detroit lawmaking in the late nineteenth and early twentieth centuries, helped open avenues for black political engagement and struggle in the urban North. As I demonstrate in this chapter, African Americans capitalized on the implicit promise that the local government would oppose racially based hierarchies, using these openings to develop new forms of protest in the 1920s.

However, northern racial liberals also used their commitment to race neutrality in public discourse as a tool for dismissing complaints about racism as a structural problem. They were willing to see that racism pervaded white political and cultural institutions that were explicitly committed to the celebration of white supremacy and the outright demonization of African Americans. For example, Couzens criticized and distanced himself from the Ku Klux Klan. However, northern racial liberals frequently dismissed African Americans' complaints about the pervasiveness of race-based discrimination and cast black accusations that the job and housing markets were shaped by racial discrimination as misperceptions, as the White-Couzens dispute illustrates. For white liberals, existing occupational and residential segregation were not the result of hateful sentiment toward African Americans but natural outgrowths of an organization of work and space built on the availability, natural capacities, and time of in-migration of different groups of workers. By arguing that there was an absence of malicious intent in the racial organization of space, northern racial liberals dismissed the idea that city leaders were responsible for rectifying racial inequalities that already existed.

The Political Orientation of African American Liberal Protest in the 1920s

Rather than seeing northern racial liberalism as the exclusive product of white liberal goodwill, it should be understood as a response to demands made on the state by African Americans themselves. These included claims to rights in private settings, like the housing market, as well as direct appeals to government agencies to manage state resources fairly and adjudicate private conflicts without bias. Black protest was rooted in African Americans' unwillingness to accept second-class citizenship in Detroit. It was also part of a national "New Negro" movement that grew out of similar trends in industrial cities whose black populations were also rapidly expanding.[15]

The African American activists whom I examine in this chapter were race-conscious liberals who made a different set of claims about how to think about race and racism in northern cities than the majority of their white allies. They asserted that the city and its residents' lives were already shaped by racial inequalities. While they imagined a future in which race would no longer be linked to privilege or disadvantage, they believed that silence about prejudice helped foster the system of race-based stratification they were fighting against. They capitalized on liberals' interest in race neutrality and used the growing popularity of liberalism among urban whites to strengthen their contention that every citizen, regardless of race, fundamentally deserved equal rights and equal access to resources.

African American Detroiters often agreed with white liberals' representation of racism as a holdover from a previous time and a different place. Many celebrated greater access to forms of mobility and employment that were not available in the rural South. However, they criticized white leaders for using this contrast as a tool for undermining black criticisms of northern racial inequalities. Black activists, Walter White among them, drew increasing attention to the contradiction between white leaders' characterization of Detroit as more free than the South and the realities of discrimination that they regularly encountered in the city. They also critiqued the notion that equality would develop gradually, rejecting the idea that they should wait for freedom to emerge in the future, arguing instead that current relations of racial power in the North needed to be disrupted.

African Americans shared a variety of responses to the changing demographics of Detroit and to the hostility they faced from whites. As they moved to the city in large numbers, they joined, built, and developed a range of institutions, some of which appealed to poor and working-class migrants, and others of which sustained relatively exclusive memberships, appealing to the most well-off African Americans. Black Detroiters also engaged in activism designed to defend their collective or individual positions and expand their access to resources.

African Americans did not share a single vision of what urban equality meant or how to achieve it, but each person fought in her or his own way to challenge the racial status quo. African American cultural, social, and political visibility increased dramatically in Detroit during the First Great Migration as black people streamed into the city and participated in public life. Many whites saw African Americans' new visibility and their challenges to the existing racial order as disruptions to urban peace.

Many studies that examine black political life in the North in the first half of the 1920s focus on the enormous popularity of the Universal Negro Improvement Association (UNIA) and its charismatic leader, Marcus Garvey. Detroit's UNIA chapter boasted more than 4,000 members at its peak in early 1923, and could attract four times that many African Americans to its largest local marches, when the black population of the city hovered around 50,000.[16] These parades were regal affairs. They represented a rare opportunity for black Detroiters to comfortably and safely possess city space, reshaping their relationship to urban power for a celebratory day. The UNIA encouraged black Detroiters to build an African American community economy centered on black-owned businesses that could operate independently of the predominantly white city. While the vast majority of UNIA followers were employed by whites, the association's vision captured their imaginations and helped shape their relationship to urban politics. As Michael McGerr observes, the majority of black Americans had "little reason to place their faith in state power and little reason to believe they could gain it. Skepticism about the state . . . helps explain [their] emphasis on self-help and self-development."[17] Thus Garveyism functioned as a model for UNIA members' distance from urban political institutions from which they felt alienated. Leaders of the group positioned themselves explicitly against reform organizations that fought for integration, recognition from whites, or a greater piece of municipal resources. To them, groups like the NAACP and the Urban League were insufficiently independent of white society. Garveyites argued against those organizations' engagement with the city's white-led public and private institutions. John Charles Zampty, for example, an early and active member of the Detroit branch, suggested that these two groups were simply "asking for . . . handouts." He advocated instead for a turn away from the government and toward black-owned private businesses as the potential answer to African Americans' problems.[18]

Leaders of the Urban League and the NAACP certainly supported the expansion of independent black businesses alongside Garveyites, but they rejected the idea that building the black business sector could provide the answer to African Americans' myriad challenges. The Urban League was a social service agency with a small paid staff of three to five full-time caseworkers. The NAACP waged political campaigns, principally lobbying white leaders in both the public and private sectors to respect African Americans and provide them with equal access to city resources and city space. Organizing the black elite to participate in these efforts, it appealed to all black residents to become members by contributing at least fifty cents in annual dues. Rather than rejecting engagement with the white city, NAACP leaders saw participation in white-dominated institutions as the avenue through which black marginalization could be addressed.

Leaders of these groups, most of whom were members of the city's small black middle class, saw themselves as exemplary local citizens and positioned themselves as political leaders of the race. They believed that alliances with powerful whites would benefit African Americans, and they worked to garner the support of white liberals, recruiting prominent whites like Couzens and Stevens to sit on their boards of directors. Fifty percent of the members of the DUL's twenty-six-member board were white.[19] Over the 1920s, as the city government expanded and leaders became more consistently committed to reform, African American elites found that they had more official avenues through which they could express their concerns and develop access to conventionally recognized political power. This approach impacted the tone, course, and fervor of their protest, since their interest in state-oriented activism often meant that they identified with the needs and concerns of government leaders. White liberals were drawn to the Urban League and the NAACP because leaders of these groups welcomed them and believed that working within existing political systems would deliver an expansion of rights and resources to black Detroiters. While each of these groups pushed for greater racial equality, they were fundamentally reformist—committed to the belief that existing institutions needed to be changed, not fully reinvented. Like white liberals, these organizations criticized African American working-class comportment as a potential problem for full assimilation, suggesting that poor black migrants were compromised in the urban North because of their own deficiencies. Thus, the Urban League and the NAACP helped connect black elites to white city leaders around a set of shared concerns.

Although some NAACP activists were also members of nationalist groups, their nationalism per se did not play an important role when they turned toward the city government and its white leaders. In their struggles for equality, NAACP and the Urban League leaders argued that race should not serve as a valid grounds for distinguishing city residents from each other in the realms of politics, housing, or access to public resources. Drawing on the liberal language of equality, leaders of these institutions rejected the race-specific language of the Garvey movement and UNIA. Reform groups like the local NAACP and Urban League believed that African Americans should build their political power through their identities as citizens of Detroit—a geographically specific locality populated by both white and black residents. Garvey's UNIA did not engage politics on this scale. Instead, Garvey's nationalism engaged African Americans as members of all-black, separate, and independent communities across local, national, and international settings.

Rather than examining the broad range of black associational life in Detroit in the 1920s, this chapter focuses on African American liberals. It considers those individuals and groups that engaged white city leaders and residents in a push for fuller access to existing structures of power. These black liberals certainly challenged elements of the racially hierarchical status quo, as White's letter to Couzens illustrates. They capitalized on white leaders' increasing commitment to race neutrality, and on African Americans' slowly expanding access to state institutions. However, by primarily aligning themselves with liberal white leaders, whose vision of racial equality remained limited by concerns about urban disorder, they contributed to the production and legitimacy of northern racial liberalism. The modern racial liberal state, characterized by its leaders' disinterest in addressing structural racism, was thus engineered at the points of struggle and reconciliation between white and black liberal leaders.

Urban Liberalism and Racist Conservatism

Although elections in Detroit had been officially nonpartisan since 1918, the vast majority of the city's political elite were Republican in the 1920s, as were the majority of Detroit's voters, both white and black. Northern urban Republicans were generally pro-business, antiunion, and against the regulation of business, but they also contributed to the expansion of the local government and its public services in ways that may look surprising from the vantage point of the present. They built urban institutions and governmental systems oriented toward growth and effective city management, extending the legacy of early twentieth-century reform. For example, Detroit boasted the most expansive state-funded welfare system of cities its size in the 1920s.[20] The 1920s also saw the vast expansion of urban infrastructure, including the annexation of huge swaths of new land, the public platting of streets, and the enlargement of the city's water system, sewers, and electrical grid. Under Mayor Couzens, the city of Detroit built its own public street railway system and subsequently bought the operations of the privately owned Detroit United Railway Company. Borrowing extensively to pay for these massive improvements through the 1920s, the city faced crushing debt in the 1930s as a result of overexpansion.[21]

In the early 1920s, some progressives made inroads into Detroit's urban institutions and self-consciously built an alternative to pro-business conservatism. Judge Edward Jeffries, who joined the city's criminal court in the 1910s, was a pro-labor advocate who had defended members of the Industrial Workers of the World, attended meetings of the Socialist Party during the Red Scares of the late 1910s, and sent the secretary of the local Board of Commerce to jail for contempt of court. As a judge, he was a champion of defendants.[22] Jeffries was able to maintain his judgeship because elections were at-large and the top six vote getters won seats on the bench.

In 1923, a new daily paper, the *Detroit Times*, helped spearhead an expansion of liberal politicians' power. The paper campaigned to reelect Jeffries and unseat a group of four conservative judges who controlled the court. Frank Murphy, a young attorney who had been working as an assistant prosecutor in the federal district court, joined Jeffries on the ballot, alongside two other liberal candidates. Murphy, who had secured his federal appointment through his father's Democratic Party political connections, had made a name for himself prosecuting war profiteers. During the campaign, the *News* and the *Free Press* supported the conservative "Big Four" and attempted to exploit white, middle-class anxieties about African Americans and their supposed connections to the criminal "underworld" in attacks against Murphy, Jeffries, and the other candidates. Both papers, for example, accused Jerry H. Brock, a black "pawnbroker and gambler," of directing a campaign to deliver 20,000 votes to Murphy and Jeffries by "herding" blacks to the polls.[23] However, with the support of the *Detroit Times* and African American and immigrant voters, Murphy and Jeffries won seats on the bench, while two of the four conservative judges lost their positions.[24]

Conflicts outside of Detroit helped set the stage for white liberals' concerns about maintaining racial peace. In 1919, race riots broke out in more than twenty industrial cities, haunting Detroit's white and black residents. These riots claimed scores of lives and scared both white and black residents across the nation, stirring up concerns about the implications of migration. During the two largest conflicts in East St. Louis in 1917 and in Chicago in 1919, the fighting lasted for days, coming to a halt only after the cities' leaders called in troops to manage the conflict. Images of American cities occupied by military forces in response to racial conflict helped confirm both black and white anxieties about the fragility of racial peace. While no large-scale race riots broke out in Detroit in 1919, the city shared many of the same dynamics that sparked rioting in other places.[25]

The other candidates, Joseph Martin and John Smith, both campaigned against the Klan using the language of northern racial liberalism. Martin, favored by the business community and the city's upper classes, derided Bowles for sustaining a connection to the "un-American" KKK but spent little time defending the targets of the Klan's animosity. Smith, a member of the Common Council who served as interim mayor, won his principal support among Catholics, African Americans, and recently arrived immigrants. Smith was more aggressive in his attacks against Bowles and clearer about defending the groups that Klan members derided. Smith dismissed southern whites as "ignorant hillbillies," calling the Klan "an ugly monster from the South."

He thus connected the Klan's blatant racism to what he described as its backward southernness. He also appealed directly to black Detroiters for their votes. Before his stint on the Common Council, Smith had served as Detroit's postmaster and earned a reputation as a friend to African Americans by overseeing the hiring of "large number[s]" of black workers.[26] Ulysses Boykin, a black journalist and stalwart Republican, remembered Smith's campaign as having "marked the beginning of the rise of the Negro in Detroit as a political factor." Boykin argued that the election of 1924 "paved the way for a large scale registering of the Negro vote."[27] Like other northern racial liberals, Smith positioned himself against blatant expressions of racism, helped open new avenues to black public employment, and invited African Americans into his political coalition. At the same time, he remained extremely cautious about positions and actions that could be construed as attacks on the racial status quo.

The formation and popularity of the Klan in Detroit and other northern cities in the early 1920s grew out of the same anxieties that sparked these riots and emerged alongside increasingly visible struggles for equality on the part of African American residents. African American migration to the urban north during the 1910s and 1920s coincided with a dramatic decrease in European immigration, which was halted first by war and then by sweeping immigration exclusion policies. These shifting demographics left the majority of Detroit's white residents concerned about their ability to sustain their political and economic power and exclusivity. A large group of Detroiters, as well as whites in cities across the urban North, joined a resurgent Ku Klux Klan in the early 1920s. Detroit's klavern was founded in the summer of 1921, approximately a month after White and Couzens ended their dispute about whether Detroit's white leaders had been practicing Klan-like discrimination. By the fall, the organization boasted 3,000 local members but initially did little more than hold meetings. For example, when the group attempted to sponsor a Thanksgiving Day parade, it quickly called it off after city leaders, responding to African American complaints, threatened to arrest attendees. By 1923, Detroit's Klan garnered more serious local attention when its members staged a series of rallies and cross burnings near public buildings. By 1924, the group's membership peaked at 32,000. The mayoral elections of that year were the height of political power for the Klan in Detroit. That summer, after the sitting mayor stepped down from office because of illness, the city held open primaries for the mayoral race to determine which two candidates would make it onto the ballot in November. The Klan's candidate, Charles Bowles, came in third in the primaries and then stayed in the race as a write-in candidate. The Klan worked hard to promote Bowles's campaign for the November election, staging the largest meeting of the Klan in the city's history.[28] The night before the November election, 25,000 to 50,000 supporters converged on a field in Dearborn Township, just outside Detroit, for this Klan-sponsored Bowles rally.

Smith ultimately won the race, but he remained acutely aware of the power of the Klan in local politics. Indeed, Bowles would have won the election by close to 7,000 votes if the 17,000 ballots with his name misspelled had been included in the count.[29] Bowles and Martin split the white native-born Protestant vote, while Smith won with enormous margins in Catholic and black neighborhoods. This electoral geography indicates the wide popularity of Bowles, and thus the Klan, among the city's native-born Protestants. The results also demonstrate that the city's ruling elite—those men and women who had the power to certify or dismiss Bowles's supporters—sustained hostility toward the Klan, which they perceived as dangerously disruptive to urban order.

The Ossian Sweet Case

Less than a year after Smith defeated Bowles, a high-profile court case became a testing ground for northern racial liberal discourse and politics. By the mid-1920s, housing had become one of the most visible sites of struggle between African Americans fighting for fuller access to city space and white Detroiters' opposition to integration. Prior to 1915, the housing shortage was not an acute problem, but by 1920 decent housing was a scarce resource, and the dilapidated and overcrowded houses of Paradise Valley became a metaphor for concerns about African Americans. As it became easier to find housing after the intense wartime shortages abated, housing became an important site of struggle for white Detroiters working against integration. While the NAACP reported some instances of violence surrounding black move-ins to previously all-white neighborhoods through the early 1920s, these tensions peaked in 1925, when the national office was writing to local association leaders asking to be kept up to date on the "Detroit housing situation."[30] That summer, a number of middle-class black families faced violence and harassment from their white neighbors when they bought houses and moved into majority-white areas. Two heated skirmishes became prominent new stories. In both cases, black families were unable to stay in their homes because of pressure from white neighbors.[31] Finally, at the end of the summer, a high-profile case threw these issues onto the national stage.

On September 8, 1925, a black couple named Ossian and Gladys Sweet moved into a house in an all-white neighborhood on the east side of Detroit. The Sweets had postponed their move in order to wait for the publicity and animosity to die down from two other highly publicized move-ins. Anticipating problems, the Sweets left their infant daughter with friends. Ossian Sweet's two brothers, Otis and Henry, along with two family friends and the Sweets' chauffeur, helped the couple unload their furniture and their guns into the house, ready to defend themselves against their new neighbors. Organized by the Waterworks Improvement Association, formed in response to the Sweet move-in, an angry crowd of white protesters convened on the Sweets' front lawn and began to heckle the family. The mob dispersed by morning, but it reconvened later that day. Threats, vandalism, and harassment persisted into the evening while on-duty police officers stood idly by watching the scene. The crowd pelted the Sweets' house with rocks and attacked Otis Sweet when he returned that evening for dinner. Finally, a stone was thrown through the Sweets' window, and someone from inside the house shot into the crowd, killing one of the white protesters and wounding another. The Sweets, along with eight of their friends and relatives, were arrested and put on trial for murder.[32]

Three African American lawyers, all active members of the local NAACP, initially represented the Sweets and were confident they could win an acquittal based on self-defense. However, Ira Jayne, a white Detroit circuit court judge who sat on the executive board of the national NAACP, pushed association leaders to hire the most prominent white lawyer they could find to take the case. Jayne, as well as leaders from the national office, including Walter White, were concerned that racial tensions in the city, exacerbated by the Sweet shooting, would

The home of Gladys and Ossian Sweet. Image courtesy of the Walter P. Reuther Archives of Labor and Urban Affairs, Wayne State University.

make it impossible for black attorneys to prevail. The Sweets' black lawyers had already had trouble gaining access to their clients and the crime scene. Jayne and White imagined that a white lawyer would face fewer obstacles, would have more success managing white-dominated urban institutions, and ultimately would procure more sympathy from a majority-white jury. They cast their push for a white lawyer as a realpolitik effort to develop a winning strategy. Their decision reflected their concerns about alienating liberal white allies and their belief that white sympathy was ultimately limited.

Over the protests of the Sweets' black attorneys, the national NAACP approached and ultimately hired Clarence Darrow to represent the defendants. In choosing Darrow, the NAACP positioned itself and the Sweets' defense squarely in line with white northern liberals, a central part of its vision for how to promote African American rights in the urban North. Darrow had just finished representing John T. Scopes for teaching the theory of evolution, which he had cast as modern, scientific, and cosmopolitan, against the orthodoxy of creationism and backward southern conservatism. Darrow thus epitomized northern urban liberalism at the same time that he brought his fame and a record of success to the case.[33]

Darrow's approach and outlook were congruent with those of the black lawyers he replaced. Cecil L. Rowlette, Charles Mahoney, and Julian Perry were some of the highest-profile members of the city's black elite. They sustained close relationships with prominent white liberals and shared the belief that civil rights struggles should be fought in the courts and won with appeals to justice, equality, and civility. Mahoney, for example, had already served three years on the city's planning commission and was one of Mayor John Smith's "closer advisors."[34] However, once he decided to take the advice of Ira Jayne and push to replace the Sweets' black attorneys, Walter White began to cast the three black lawyers as incompetent opportunists who were more interested in collecting the sizable fee the association had raised for the Sweets' defense than they were in ensuring the Sweets' freedom.

After almost a year of proceedings, including one mistrial, Darrow convinced an all-white jury to acquit Henry Sweet, and charges were subsequently dropped against the other defendants. Essentially, the jury ruled that the hostility directed toward African Americans by whites had created a climate where it was reasonable for the people inside the house to take verbal aggression, vandalism, mob protest, and police neglect as threats to their lives. Although the defendants were afraid of a mob of northern whites congregated on a Detroit lawn, Darrow framed this issue in a manner that underlined southern racism. Darrow suggested that white northerners' concerns about integration were rooted in fears they had absorbed from southern whites and that Ossian Sweet saw the mob outside his house as menacing because he understood it through the lens of his childhood experiences in Florida. Sweet witnessed a ruthless lynching at a young age, as well as other acts of violence in his hometown. As a young man at Howard University, he also lived through the 1919 race riot in Washington, DC, and was terrorized by what he saw.

Sweet also described his knowledge of northern racist violence, including his awareness of recent attacks by white mobs on African American homebuyers in Detroit. However, he did not relay accounts of personal experiences with racism in the North, as either a victim or a witness. Instead, he learned of these assaults through newspapers, friends, and acquaintances.[35] The experiences that allowed Sweet to see the mob on Garland Avenue as threatening enough to justify violent self-defense were southern. In Darrow's closing argument, he reconfirmed his suggestion that northern racism was an outgrowth of southern hatred. Referring to his recent time in Tennessee during the Scopes trial, he explained that southern whites were "pretty raw" when it came to African Americans, whose "place," they believed, "was the place of a servant." Northern whites, he suggested, were "born with some of that psychology and some of that feeling," but they were not the same. When they acted similarly, it was the effect of southern mores.[36]

The Sweet case represented a change in the usual script of white mob violence because of the Sweets' armed self-defense and because of the response the violence provoked from the city government. While many "black pioneers" held out in the face of harassment, the Sweets' decision to arm themselves meant that they were mounting a new kind of protest against harassment. Furthermore, the NAACP turned the Sweet indictment into a test case that tried the legitimacy of armed self-defense as a response to white attacks.[37] Sweet, his family, and his friends came ready to turn their house into a veritable bunker in order to defend the sanctity of their new home and to police the boundary between their privacy and the public world of the white neighborhood.[38]

Both the Sweets and Clarence Darrow emphasized the respectability of the socially and economically successful black family as a strategy to underline their right to security in all parts of Detroit. Between the two trials, Gladys and Ossian Sweet traveled in the East and Midwest, sharing their stories and raising money among black residents of Baltimore, New York, and other cities. Often referring to his medical training in Europe, Dr. Sweet explained that his parents were tenant farmers in Florida, that he had supported himself all through school, and that he had traveled and studied in Europe, emphasizing a distinction and sophistication that few other black or white families could boast. By focusing on his social and class positions, Sweet connected the rights of privacy and home with his upwardly mobile middle-class family. Like Ossian Sweet, Darrow equated the black family's right to live where they pleased with their middle-class income, values, and nuclear family structure, calling the president of Wilberforce University, Sweet's alma mater, as a character witness to demonstrate the doctor's upstanding moral qualities.[39] He frequently called Dr. Sweet "doctor" in his arguments and questioning, further emphasizing Sweet's professional and well-respected occupation. In his closing argument, after emphasizing the ubiquity of "race prejudice," Darrow asked the jury, "What kind of man is Dr. Sweet? Out of these [ten defendants], half of them are at least college graduates, or attending college," and he compared the defendants favorably to the whites who lived near the Garland Avenue house.[40]

Gladys Sweet also stressed her social, economic, and familial positions as central to the defendants' understandings of dignity and respectability. In an interview with the *Pittsburgh Courier*, Gladys Sweet told reporters that she was not involved in the violence, for she was cooking a ham in the kitchen for the men. She was literally "making a home" in the most traditional way at the moment that white rioters attacked her house. By linking these two activities, her cooking and the assaults of white protesters, she underlined her own civility, respectability, and privacy in the face of the barbarity and incivility of the rioters.

While the Sweets, Clarence Darrow, black newspapers, and prominent African American leaders consistently emphasized the class position of the defendants by referring to the Sweets' education, Dr. Sweet's profession, and the middle-class domesticity of Mrs. Sweet, they also articulated the importance of the case as one that affected all blacks. Access to housing for the African American middle class would help open doors for all African Americans. The anecdote of Gladys Sweet's calm preparation of a ham as the ten men in the front rooms were arming themselves was repeated by Darrow and by the newspapers.[41]

On the first day of the trial, more than 500 black residents came to the courthouse eager to watch the case and to support the Sweets in their defense. When it became apparent that the bailiff was allowing more white than black spectators into the room, African American visitors protested by "becoming very loud and noisy."[42] One black woman shoved a white spectator in the hall outside of the courtroom.[43] Several hundred African American spectators religiously attended the court proceedings, remaining in the courthouse as the jury deliberated until the early morning on the day before Thanksgiving.[44] While these spectators may not have shared all aspects of the Sweets' understanding of their fight, the issues of the case clearly resonated with their sense of justice in the city.

The Sweet case swelled the ranks of the local NAACP further. The organization's membership jumped to more than 3,000 in 1926,[45] demonstrating wide support for a proactive stance in the larger fight for racial equality. This was an important turning point for the national NAACP, which used the case to build a permanent Legal Defense Fund for "cases as may arise involving the Negro's constitutional and citizenship rights."[46] Local Detroiters got involved in the Sweet case through the City Wide Committee for the Sweet Defense Fund, raising more than $1,200 in six weeks following the Sweets' arrests. The committee held a mass meeting in the fall of 1925 and received donations from a wide range of black organizations across the city, including the Knights of Ethiopia.[47]

The Sweet case also raised the profile of white racial liberals in the city. In 1926, when the Ossian Sweet case came to Detroit's criminal court, Judge Murphy, an ambitious young politician, was in charge of the docket and assigned the trial to himself. Clarence Darrow had come on the case, and it was clear that the trial would garner national attention. Murphy claimed that the other judges on the bench were afraid to touch it, but for him, hearing the case would be "the opportunity of a lifetime."[48] By providing a fair trial to the African American defendants in a high-profile case, Murphy believed that he could earn a reputation as a committed protector of justice and publicize his racial liberalism, boosting his political chances. As judge in the Sweet case, Murphy lived up to his commitment to fairness. He was roundly reviled by white segregationists for allowing Clarence Darrow latitude in dismissing admittedly racist jurors and for letting Darrow admit evidence about the deleterious impact of racial discrimination on defendants' lives. African Americans and white liberals in the city and across the country celebrated Murphy as an advocate of fairness and equality.[49]

Mayor John Smith and Urban Peace

While Judge Murphy used his courtroom to solidify his reputation as a racial liberal, the positions taken by John Smith, Detroit's mayor during the Sweet case, demonstrate the inherent contradictions of northern racial liberalism. Mayor Smith's response to the Sweet case illustrates how northern racial liberal leaders, even Smith, who garnered political support from African Americans, backed away from their support for black rights in the face of racial violence and urban discord. Although Mayor Smith was sympathetic to black concerns about white violence, his response to the shootings demonstrated that he would neither advocate for residential integration nor defend African Americans who faced violent mobs when they moved into white neighborhoods. In fact, he went to great lengths to demonstrate that his approach to the situation would neither disrupt the racial geography of the city nor disturb the power relationship between white and black residents of Detroit.

Smith quickly went on record publicizing his views about what he saw as the limited role government should play in managing racial tensions. He wrote two open letters—printed in full on the front page of the city's daily newspapers—to allay the concerns of white residents who, he imagined, would feel threatened by a government response to racial violence that recognized the rights of African Americans. He simultaneously condemned the Sweets for trying to move into a white neighborhood and cautioned African Americans against continuing to push for residential integration.[50]

In his first letter, published four days after the riots and addressed to the city's police commissioner Frank Croul, Smith had only harsh words for black pioneers. He suggested that these men and women were "incitant[s] of riot and murder," responsible for the violence against them. Their interest in moving into white neighborhoods, he claimed, was evidence of their arrogance, vanity, and "personal pride." Furthermore, while they cast themselves as community leaders, they should be seen as "enem[ies] of their race." In his letter, Smith acknowledged that the law guaranteed equal protection to all citizens, but he also clearly asserted that African Americans should refrain from claiming their rights. For him, black efforts to access equality were inappropriate. "It does not always do," Smith declared, "for any man to demand to its fullest the right which the law gives him." He suggested that only "a very few colored persons are unwilling to live in sections of the city where members of their race predominate," and he called on the "real leaders of the colored race" to dissipate the "murderous pride" that he believed caused the violence. He suggested that any effort on the part of middle-class black men and women to occupy a social position commensurate with their class position was presumptuous and potentially disrupted the urban social fabric.[51]

At the time of the Sweet incident, Smith was campaigning against Charles Bowles in upcoming mayoral elections. Smith had learned that there would be no primary runoff just two days after the Sweet incident; the other candidates had dropped out of the race.[52] Now, he was running only against Bowles, who would have defeated him in the last election. Smith worked hard to cast the Klan, which most city residents associated with Bowles, as responsible for the recent upsurge in racial tensions and violence. However, Smith did not criticize the group for promoting racism or supporting racist acts. Instead, he accused the Klan of cultivating and supporting black protest as a strategy for disrupting urban racial peace. He claimed that the Klan was "inducing negroes to move into white neighborhoods." He also claimed that Klan leaders were paying black people to spread rumors among African Americans that the city government was excluding black workers from public jobs and police protection. There was, he declared, a "constant procession" of black agitators "moving in and out of the headquarters of a candidate for mayor favored by the Ku Klux Klan." Smith thus cast black criticisms of the government as illegitimate and rooted in Klan-sponsored agitation.[53] He suggested that *any* kind of race-based claim—including black claims for civil inclusion and rights—should be blamed on the Klan and should always be seen as incendiary.

By eliding what he cast as two political extremes, Smith positioned himself as a promoter of peace, neither white supremacist nor supportive of black struggles for equality. He also turned to the liberal solution of governance as a tool for managing racial tensions. In a second open letter, Smith reinforced his assertion that extremists had caused the disturbances. He announced the creation of the Mayor's Interracial Committee (MIC) to study the problem—confident that "among the great majority of persons of each race a spirit of common sense and sensible co-operation can be utilized."[54]

The Mayor's Interracial Committee

Mayor John Smith's Interracial Committee represents a strategy for managing race in urban environments that was a model for liberal politicians in their effort to deal with racial conflict and black activism through the next decade. Smith built a public institution designed to address racial tensions and, in doing so, cast himself as interested in black equality and racial peace. At the same time, the Interracial Committee was an advisory body whose recommendations Smith largely ignored. By developing an urban institution with little real power, Smith exposed his disinterest in responding substantively to black demands or in designing strategies that would reallocate the racial distribution of resources or power in northern cities.

Northern racial liberal leaders began to build government institutions designed to help address racial conflict in the 1910s and 1920s. The commissions and committees they established were weak advisory bodies, set up to examine the causes of racial violence and make recommendations to mayors and city councils about how to calm discord and avoid future conflict. They had no legislative power, and their architects rarely acted on their often-extensive recommendations. However, for African Americans, they had important symbolic weight as the first state institutions designed to address black concerns. These committees and commissions strengthened elite African Americans' relationships with white liberal leaders and institutions, offered a handful of employment opportunities to black social scientists and social workers, and helped amplify the influence of African American–produced discourses about race relations. Finally, they became a repository for complaints about racism and discrimination. In so doing, they helped produce the sense among African Americans that their grievances had a new legitimacy in the eyes of the state. However, at the same time that these committees and commissions opened new doors for African Americans, they also helped isolate black residents' concerns about discrimination and racial violence from other aspects of city governance under the auspices that these issues were receiving special and more direct attention.

Many historians have used commission reports to examine the texture of black life in the urban North, but few have paid attention to these commissions' political function. Clearly, these bodies failed to eliminate racial violence in northern cities. They did help shape emerging liberal discourse about how to manage increasing racial diversity. Mayor Smith's committee, for example, represented a new strategy on the part of Detroit's liberal leaders because it was the first time that city leaders were willing to recognize racial conflict as a problem that the government could or should address. Like northern racial liberals in other cities, Smith established the committee to show white and black Detroiters that he was addressing a problem that everyone agreed had spun out of control. At the same time, by appointing an Interracial Committee with little power, he was limiting the role the state agreed to play in the resolution of racial conflict.

Smith drew on the model of other northern cities in establishing this committee. The first similar state-appointed commission to study race relations as a response to racial violence was formed in Chicago in 1919 after a catastrophic race riot. City and state leaders faced significant pressure from social and civic organizations, including many African American groups, to do something about the tensions that had led to days of violence. Illinois governor Frank Lowden appointed the Chicago Commission on Race Relations, an interracial group of thirteen prominent businesspeople, government officials, professionals, and clergy, to investigate the causes of the conflict and make recommendations about how to avoid future problems. The report, published as *The Negro in Chicago: A Study of Race Relations and a Race Riot*, listed fifty-nine recommendations for resolving racial tensions, including the razing of substandard housing, an increase in recreational centers for the city's black residents, the elimination of discrimination in public facilities, more schools in black areas, and better police protection for African Americans. These recommendations, most of which called for structural changes, included proposals that middle-class black activists had been promoting since the beginning of the First Great Migration.[55] Ultimately, few recommendations in the report, which was published three years after the riots, were taken up by the city or the state.

As riots and racial conflict hit other urban areas, government officials looked to Chicago as a model for establishing similar interracial commissions. These commissions relied on the developing field of race relations and drew on the expertise of black social scientists and social workers, whose priorities were reflected in the commissions' findings.[56] In Chicago, for example, commissioners appointed Charles S. Johnson to take charge of the research. Johnson, an African American sociologist who had received his PhD in 1917 from the University of Chicago, had served as the director of research for the Chicago Urban League.[57] Black sociologists thus helped shape the conclusions of these commissions, contributing to the production of northern racial liberalism as an ideology. Soon after the Chicago Commission disbanded, the national leadership of the NAACP and other national black leaders joined together to push President Warren G. Harding to form an interracial commission for the United States, but to no avail.[58]

These reports were quite similar to each other. For example, all of the studies examined the "conditions" of black neighborhoods as an avenue for understanding discrimination. The reports included strong denunciations of white efforts to enforce segregation, but they also took African Americans to task for activism that could be seen as disruptive to urban order. As black sociologists St. Clair Drake and Horace Cayton observed two decades later, these reports criticized African Americans for "thinking and talking too much in terms of race alone" and encouraged black residents to move away from a growing consciousness of race.[59] This argument reflected northern racial liberals' push toward an approach to race relations that was invested in muting both white hostility and black defense. It also reflected elite African Americans' willingness to shy away from protest that could be cast as disruptive of the urban order. Commissioners' findings also drew heavily on existing sociological literature on race relations and community formation. Most of the sociological interest in these issues came from black scholars already working to develop an understanding of race relations and black experiences more generally.

Mayor Smith adopted this approach in Detroit. One week after the Sweets were arrested, Smith appointed six white and six African American men to serve on the city's first interracial board. He charged the commissioners with studying racial violence and tensions in the city, explaining that "discussion and mutual understanding" would permit a solution to the problem of race-based civic disorder. Smith chose Tracy McGregor, a politically active supporter of urban reform and son of a wealthy auto manufacturer, to head the committee. McGregor was a prominent philanthropist who ran a relief institute that served the largest number of African American recipients of private relief in the city.[60]

Members of the Mayor's Interracial Committee had different ideas about the role of the state in resolving and managing racial conflict than Smith did. First, they took their role more seriously than Smith might have wanted. After a year studying the problem, committee members concluded that they had no "quick means of assuring harmony between the races." Instead, they offered suggestions about how the city government could help to build "mutual understanding and sympathy" between white and black residents. Their recommendations included forthright critiques of public institutions for neglecting African Americans and practicing discrimination, as well as suggestions for how the city government could begin to enforce politicians' stated commitment to equality. None of their recommendations was implemented, and the committee was disbanded soon after it submitted its report.[61]

Smith paid little attention to the findings of his Interracial Committee but found its existence politically useful. In the spring of 1926, a few months after the Ossian Sweet case drew to a close, he appointed a new Interracial Committee "with the purpose of helping to bring about more harmonious relations between colored and white people in the city."[62] Like the first group, this "semi-official inter-race committee" would make recommendations to the administration about how to handle racial problems and serve as a clearinghouse for complaints about discrimination.[63] This time, Smith appointed the Reverend Reinhold Niebuhr to head the group. Niebuhr, a liberal white pastor at the Bethel Evangelical Church, had gained local and national prominence for his criticisms of labor practices at the Ford Motor Company and concern about labor conditions for African Americans in Ford's foundries. Niebuhr would go on to become a nationally known social justice theologian.

Like the first group, the members of the new committee included prominent black and white businesspeople, government officials, and clergy.[64] Both groups had substantial political clout and connections, which seemed to evidence Smith's commitment to the endeavor. However, like the work of the first group, Smith and other city officials ultimately ignored the second group's recommendations. Smith's treatment of his interracial committees reveals the limited scope of northern liberal political commitment to African American equality to study rather than address racism in city government.

The Negro in Detroit

As the basis for their recommendations to the mayor, Detroit's Interracial Committee hired a team of black and white social workers and sociologists to conduct a comprehensive study of "racial conditions in Detroit."[65] Having received no funding from the mayor, they secured a grant from the Detroit Community Fund to pay for the study.[66] *The Negro in Detroit*, a 700-page volume, contained detailed statistics and vivid descriptions of Detroit's African American neighborhoods and residents. The report, like others of its kind, was shaped by contemporary social scientific discourse about black urban life. Social scientists in the mid-1920s tended to characterize African Americans in northern cities as "disorganized" but "ascribed [their] social problems to the social environment" rather than racially shared biological deficiencies.[67] This liberal analysis, which won prominence in the 1910s and 1920s, reflected a move away from the scientific racism that had characterized social scientific discourse and popular perceptions of black inferiority earlier in the century. It also represented the expanding influence of work by black social scientists whose small but growing numbers were helping to reshape academic racial knowledge and whose ideas reflected the commitments of Detroit's elite black civil rights activists.[68] Ultimately, social scientific language about black urban life came to be embraced by white liberal politicians, even as many of the same politicians demonstrated little interest in social scientists' often modest prescriptions for how the state should address persistent racial conflict.

The Negro in Detroit was based on interviews and surveys with 1,000 black families along with reports from agencies that served African Americans. It was split into eleven sections addressing population, industry, thrift and business, housing, health, recreation, education, crime, religion, community organization, and welfare. The two principal investigators were Forrester B. Washington, who had become executive secretary of Philadelphia's Urban League, and Robert T. Lansdale, a white sociologist from the University of Michigan. Other investigators included sociology and social work graduate students and faculty from universities across the state, as well as "25 colored field workers, all of whom had college or social work training."[69]

The Negro in Detroit exposed its researchers' ambivalence about where to place blame for black inequality. Researchers vacillated between claiming that racism structured black life and generated African American poverty and claiming that inequality was rooted in African Americans' inability and/or unwillingness to assimilate into northern urban culture. In some sections of the report, researchers emphasized the role that government and private institutions—like businesses, voluntary associations, and unions—played in producing segregation and supporting racism. In other sections, they reserved their ire for African Americans, whom they cast as authors of their own misery and "disorganization." Ultimately, the report suggested, both dynamics were at play in Detroit. This analysis had important implications for Interracial Committee prescriptions about how the local government should ensure urban racial peace, limiting its authors' calls for institutional changes and inviting strategies to correct black "disorganization" focused on educating African Americans to make appropriate choices.

Authors of *The Negro in Detroit*, like authors of other 1920s studies of black urban life produced for similar committees, were also torn about the origins of urban racial disorder. They often suggested that interracial violence was rooted in white enforcement of black inequality, an analysis that would call on the state to rectify, if not address, inequality itself. However, in some sections, the report put forth apolitical explanations for the origins of violence such as racial misunderstanding or fear, both of which could be easily divorced from the social, cultural, and economic contexts within which they emerged. If urban racial violence was not necessarily about the structural enforcement of black inequality, then prescriptions to change it did not need to focus on rectifying even gross racial disparities.

This ambivalence about the origins of racial violence reflected the Interracial Committee's political centrism, which it pronounced in the opening pages of its recommendations to the mayor. It was "improbable," the authors claimed, "that any recommendations of this Committee will meet the unqualified favor of extremists on either side."[70] Members of the committee were careful not to suggest too-radical alternatives or a too-fast pace for change because, they believed, white Detroiters' racism would stand in the way of more fundamental changes. "The final solution," committee members argued, "must wait upon the cultivation of better understanding and the diminution of prejudice in the public at large."[71] As long as racism was located in the minds of whites, this logic suggested, the city was limited in its ability to intervene: all the government could do was manage racial tensions, but it could neither address nor help to resolve discrimination because prejudice was rooted in the hearts and minds of individuals over whom the state had little control. Liberals thus acknowledged that racism existed in Detroit at the same time that they absolved both themselves and the growing state of responsibility for its elimination.

Indeed, the Interracial Committee's recommendations reflected its perception that its work required navigating a field of political landmines. In the face of anticipated opposition, the committee often opted to recognize the role of racism in shaping white perceptions of African Americans and the interracial city, but it pulled back from recommendations that would openly challenge these ideas. For example, in the section on housing, the committee dismissed claims that there was a "loss of real estate value" when African Americans moved into majority-white neighborhoods, suggesting that "in many cases the rentals and sale prices increased." However, the committee believed that its task was "to suggest solutions which, while not imperiling legal rights [of African Americans], will also not ignore the cultivated or instinctive race prejudices of large sections of the [white] community or the fear that race migrations may result in loss of real estate values, as real factors in the situation."[72] For the committee, racism was a problem the state could not directly address because government action would likely fuel the flames of white racist anxiety and reaction.

The reports' authors saw segregation as a strategy for cultivating racial harmony and described "this tendency" as "conducive to community peace."[73] The committee thus supported a separate-but-equal vision of residential segregation, falling back on the apolitical claim that city residents of *all* races had a "natural tendency" to live in their "own communities." Indeed, it argued, African Americans' principal interest in white neighborhoods was their desire to gain "equal civic facilities with whites." Rather than working toward integration, the committee suggested strategies for discouraging "this general tendency." City officials, committee members suggested, should work to ensure that African American neighborhoods were as desirable as white neighborhoods by cracking down on violence and educating African Americans about "the special desirability of keeping their houses painted and their yards in attractive condition." While the report made some structural suggestions, including improving city services to black neighborhoods, such as more policing, providing incentives for banks to extend loans to African Americans, and encouraging contractors to build housing in black areas, it emphasized African Americans' responsibility for keeping their neighborhoods clean and attractive. Ultimately, the report suggested, a permanent "committee of white and colored persons" would have "the responsibility for encouraging Negro groups in the proper care of their property and for exercising vigilance upon governmental agencies that flagrant neglect of Negro districts may be prevented."[74]

At the same time that the committee allowed for the possibility that residential segregation was necessary for urban peace, it also recognized that racism shaped African Americans' access to city resources and justice. In the second section titled "Crime and Police," the reports' authors claimed that it was "obvious" that "exact and even justice for the members of the minority race (in this case the Negroes) is still an unattained ideal." The report thus moved back and forth between a recognition that racism shaped African Americans' experiences in the city and the assertion that African Americans were themselves responsible for at least some, if not a majority, of the animosity directed toward them. While the report explained that "in many cases Negroes are treated with undue severity, not to say brutality, by the police," it still asserted that "the decrease in lawlessness in the Negro community must wait upon a completer adjustment of the newer migrant to the social conditions of the city," which would ostensibly discourage her or him from crime.[75]

The rest of the report continued on in this manner. In each section, the committee pointed to the inadequacy of city services and chronic prejudices directed toward black people while simultaneously pointing to black inadequacies to help explain the persistence of white prejudice. In every section, the committee reminded its readers that progress would be slow and that *both* white residents and African Americans would have to change. Ultimately, the Interracial Committee's recommendations demonstrate that northern racial liberalism, while sympathetic to the problems that black residents faced, simultaneously blamed working-class African Americans for their inability to overcome poverty or defeat racism.

Although *The Negro in Detroit* and the Interracial Committee did not propose radical changes, even the report's fairly modest suggestions fell on deaf ears. Mayor John Smith shared committee members' ambivalence about the causes of racism but showed little interest in addressing black concerns beyond his appointment of the Interracial Committee itself. The mayor allocated no money for its study, and *The Negro in Detroit* received a very limited distribution. The grant that the committee received covered the cost of the research but not the cost of the report's reproduction or dissemination. One anonymous donor financed the publishing, printed 100 copies, and "gave them about as he saw fit."[76] Even within the narrow purview of the Interracial Committee's mandate, the city's support for its work was limited and thus fulfilled Smith's limited vision of its role within the city government.

Conclusion

Under pressure from African Americans and in response to shifting northern racial ideologies, Detroit's white business and municipal leaders increasingly expressed disdain for acts of racial discrimination and support for a northern racial system that they saw as more just than the South's. However, as their actions in the 1920s illustrate, the maintenance of urban racial peace was a higher priority for them than enforcing racial equality. Instead of considering strategies for alleviating the discrepancies between the lives of black and white Detroiters, white liberal leaders sought a way to manage racial conflicts. Even though they saw themselves as allies of all urban residents, including African Americans, the ideological limits of liberalism gave them the tools to oversee rather than resolve structural inequalities. For example, Frank Couzens suggested that racial difference and stratification became political problems when groups like the Ku Klux Klan, or what he characterized as the overly defensive black activists of the NAACP, pushed these questions into the public sphere. Mollifying and dismissing these extremists was at the top of Couzens's agenda.

The groundwork for northern racial liberalism was laid in response to the changing urban landscape in Detroit during and after World War I. Residents agreed that the city was becoming interracial, but what that meant and how it shaped local politics and access to resources remained hotly contested. Debates over racial boundaries and the rights of African Americans became more magnified in Detroit in the 1920s. For African Americans, local conflicts between black and white men and women confirmed the importance of struggles for equality and full citizenship in the city. For white leaders, the crescendo of black-white racial conflict produced an urgent sense that they needed to create a language and a set of strategies that could help quell racially motivated violence and sustain urban peace. Liberal whites' commitment to urban peace, which they often cast as in tension with urban justice, shaped the limits of their solidarity with black struggles for equality.

Public debates about African Americans' roles in Detroit and about the meanings of racial boundaries were fought among black and white residents and subsequently managed by the city's white governing elite. While city leaders used northern racial liberalism as a tool to manage growing black dissent and white hostility toward African Americans, the language they used was distinctly different from that used by the resurgent Ku Klux Klan and other explicitly antiblack organizations that had gained popularity in the urban North early in the decade. However, these white leaders were ambivalent about black equality, and their policies reflected their hesitation. At the same time they rejected Klan-style expressions of antiblack hostility, they cast African Americans as less than deserving of full citizenship. White northern leaders made persistent, if often implicit, comparisons to the racial mores of the American South, deflecting racism onto a place that they characterized as backward. What was happening in Detroit, they consistently suggested, was not a problem that required fixing; the racial institutions that demanded challenge and repair could be found in Alabama, Mississippi, and Georgia.

3

Between Ossian Sweet and the Great Depression

Tolerance and Northern Racial Liberal Discourse in the Late 1920s

In March 1927, members of the Mayor's Interracial Committee delivered addresses at both African American and white YMCAs and churches across the city to discuss "race relationship[s] and race prejudice, [their] cause and cure." These lectures were part of the MIC's attempt to promote interracial tolerance among the city's residents. They were conducted a year and a half after Ossian and Gladys Sweet faced an angry mob of white rioters on their front lawn, and just eight months after all charges were dropped against the defendants for killing a white protestor. During their visits, representatives of the MIC administered surveys to listeners, asking attendees to report on their beliefs about African Americans, black rights, segregation, and discrimination. The Interracial Committee, formed in response to the Sweet affair, was also attempting to measure racial feeling in order to identify and quell potential conflict. The results of one survey, conducted at a men's Bible study class at a white church, capture white Detroiters' profound ambivalence about African American equality and racial integration.

While the MIC survey was limited by its small sample size—sixty men responded—the results point to white acceptance of the paradoxical logics of northern racial liberalism. The men answering the survey may have been more progressive than white Detroiters in general, since they attended a church that was willing to work with the Interracial Committee and since they agreed to respond to the MIC's questionnaire. At the same time, they were not racial radicals. As a group, they accepted mainstream ideas about African Americans, racial integration, and black equality; a majority expressed sympathy for black struggles but antipathy toward integration. Their answers illustrate that mainstream white ideas about race were varied and conflicted, characterized by a tension between tolerance and measured suspicion.

A majority of respondents claimed to embrace the principles that African Americans should not be confined to "labor and servant positions" (73 percent), were negatively affected by "a lack of opportunity due to physical, economic and political forces" (75 percent), and should have access to "equal educational opportunities" provided by the city and state (90 percent). These opinions suggest that Detroit's whites held a more sympathetic understanding of African Americans then they had earlier in the century, one that recognized that racism shaped African Americans' experiences and that black Detroiters deserved more access to state resources. Almost 50 percent agreed that newspapers gave "an exaggerated emphasis on the Negroes' connection with crime," and only 12 percent agreed with the notion that the "Ku Klux Klan has been a helpful influence in building a better citizenship." These responses suggest that white Detroiters had moved away from support for the segregationist politics that groups like the Klan represented and toward more liberal and tolerant sensibilities about race.

At the same time, however, a significant minority of the same respondents (40 percent) expressed their collective suspicion that African Americans lived in "slum conditions" because of their "shiftlessness." Indeed, only 32 percent disagreed with this claim. Majorities or significant minorities of the survey group subscribed to ideas about African Americans and segregation that betrayed their collective doubts about black Detroiters and integration. Fewer than half of all respondents disagreed with the statement that whites were "born mentally superior" to nonwhites, which means that more than half of the survey sample doubted the innate mental capacities of nonwhites. Respondents were also torn about segregation. More than two-thirds rejected the notion that segregation "aggravate[d] race friction," suggesting that they saw it as neutral or potentially positive for race relations. At the same time, a large majority of respondents (78 percent) believed that a "self-respecting Negro" would not want to be among white people "except where he is wanted." They thus believed that segregation had more to do with social preferences and comfort than the enforcement of inequality. Finally, in one of the most revealing questions, 60 percent of the group rejected the idea that "the Negro must be kept in his place—by force if necessary," a collective response that suggests that whites were more accepting of African Americans' presence in Detroit than they had been previously. However, a significant minority of respondents (39 percent) believed that the violent suppression of black challenges to existing racial hierarchies either was necessary or could be a tolerable political position. These answers were contained in the very same survey that concluded that African Americans were victims of racism and deserving of equal rights. Many respondents did not see such ideas as inconsistent. Indeed, such apparent contradictions shaped the terrain of white public opinion and political culture in Detroit in the late 1920s.[1] Ultimately, a majority of respondents believed that the city government should delegate resources in a more racially equitable manner, rejected the idea that African Americans were morally or ethically corrupt, and believed that black workers should not be locked into menial jobs. Majorities or significant minorities of the same group expressed serious doubts about whether the city's African Americans should or could be integrated into the urban polity alongside whites. In their simultaneous sympathy and blame, embrace for rights and support for segregation, the Detroiters responding to the MIC survey captured the tensions at the heart of northern racial liberalism, which in turn shaped the city's politics at every level.

Tolerance

Detroit's white politicians shared survey respondents' ambivalence about African American equality. Even white liberal politicians harbored concerns about the consequences of racial integration and growing black political power. They did not, however, express their reservations in explicitly racist terms. Instead, they saw their approach as a sharp departure from the antiblack sentiment that characterized white supremacist politics in the first half of the decade. Nevertheless, their move toward embracing interracial equality was still fraught with tensions. White liberals cast themselves as pragmatists and worried aloud about whether the city's white majority would withstand the pace of change that black activists pushed for. However, as a closer look at their ideas illustrates, their embrace of gradualism was also rooted in their often unself-conscious embrace of elements of the existing racially hierarchical order.[2]

Frank Murphy, an ambitious local judge, self-identified liberal, and future mayor, provides an important example of how white liberals' gradualism reflected these conflicting notions about race and African Americans. In a speech on the "races question" in the late 1920s, he celebrated tolerance as the first step toward building a more racially equal urban polity. Murphy had grown up in Harbor Beach, Michigan, a lakefront town about a hundred miles north of Detroit. He came from a comfortably middle-class, Irish Catholic family. His father, a lawyer, was active in Democratic state politics and had helped Murphy secure his first political appointment as a federal prosecutor in the early 1920s.[3] Murphy encouraged native-born whites to tolerate immigrant and African American Detroiters. At the same time, however, he suggested that some aspects of existing racial hierarchies were natural and acceptable. For example, invoking well-known eugenicist notions that biologically inferior immigrants were breeding too quickly and would thus lower the nation's racial quality, Murphy expressed concerns that the "natural and unobstructed reproductiveness" of "immigrant settlers" was outpacing the "normal fecundity" of the "native American element." Murphy's promotion of equality was thus equivocal—he persistently celebrated tolerance as a political and social approach to intergroup relations, even as he confirmed popular fears about the dangers posed by burgeoning immigrant populations.[4]

Murphy's perception of African Americans was similarly both sympathetic and condescending. He saw discrimination and segregation as potent and corrupt forces that kept African Americans poor and vulnerable to exploitation. However, he did not regard African Americans as agents who could capably address these issues. He suggested instead that they were inadequate to the task of helping themselves because of the "environmental" problems that had emerged as a consequence of their tireless mistreatment. In other words, poverty and discrimination had had a toxic effect on African Americans, whose lack of sophistication paralyzed their progress. Immigrant "newcomers" were experiencing "evolution and upward march . . . in every activity," but the only action he attributed to African Americans was their fall as "easy prey to schemes and exploiters."[5]

Murphy suggested that policy solutions from above were inadequate to the task of changing race relations because they would fail to change white attitudes, which he saw as central to the maintenance of inequality. He believed instead that the solution to the "races question" involved two distinct stages. During both stages, liberals would work to popularize their commitment to "tolerance and good temper" in the present, especially on the part of the "100 per centers." Teaching Protestant, native-born whites to endure and even accept immigrants' and African Americans' social and cultural practices would be a move toward equality. For the future, though, Murphy had separate visions for European-descended immigrants, who would assimilate, and African Americans, who would continue to be tolerated. For white immigrants, he saw intermarriage and Protestantism as centrally important. "When Abie of the [Jewish] Ghetto takes Rosie from Corktown [a working-class, Irish Catholic neighborhood] before the Methodist minister to plight their troth, the process of assimilation is far along." However, Murphy did not suggest that intermarriage between blacks and whites would be a marker of the successful resolution of the "races question." Unlike white immigrants, who should intermarry and assimilate, African Americans, in Murphy's view, could not blend into American society. Having been victimized by racism, they were not prepared to be effective political advocates for themselves. Instead, they should trust in white liberals' promotion of tolerance as the best possible strategy for addressing inequality. Their future was one in which they would be truly, rather than begrudgingly, tolerated.[6]

The principle of "tolerance" was both the beginning and the end of northern racial liberals' prescription for the problems of African Americans, suggesting only a gradual move toward acceptance and citizenship, each of which would be fulfilled in an undefined future. By the late 1920s, tolerance language had become the reigning, though contested, political discourse for public conversations about African Americans in Detroit, a development that both white liberals and African Americans celebrated. However, as political theorist Wendy Brown has shown, tolerance language is double-edged. It promises movement toward a more equal future for populations that need to be tolerated but also helps mark these populations as subject. Excluded by hatred and thus politically impotent, tolerated populations are victims rather than agents.

Unable to shape their own futures, they need to rely on powerful liberals to be their advocates, extend them resources, and ultimately, but gradually, pull them into the polity. Indeed, in order to maintain their status as tolerated, these populations cannot struggle for their own rights, since self-determined political mobilization makes them disruptive and thus unworthy.[7] The explosion of tolerance language about African Americans in Detroit in the 1910s and 1920s, as well as its importance to liberals as a template for achieving African American equality, can best be understood through Brown's insights. The liberal promotion of tolerance language failed to achieve its goal of producing a racially equitable city. Gaining currency at the end of the 1920s, these ideas about African Americans shaped urban political discourse in Detroit. This discourse, in turn, contributed to the deeply rooted inequalities upon which the local New Deal state would be built.

By the time Murphy delivered his speech on the "races question," the popularity of Detroit's Klan had waned considerably, and explicit celebrations of white supremacy had become less visible along the mainstream political spectrum than they had been early in the decade. Proponents of tolerance represented their project as a necessary first step on the long road toward racial inclusion. However, the popularity of this language among whites was neither a turn toward egalitarianism nor antiracism. Few of its white proponents offered clear proposals for how racial equality could be achieved in the present, and many did not even support that project, in theory or in practice.[8] Furthermore, many African Americans looked to the state to address and remedy racial discrimination, a project that required state officials to see prejudice as a real social, political, and structural force rather than viewing it as misunderstanding or a lack of tolerance. The Universal Negro Improvement Association and similar nationalist groups rejected the idea of tolerance as well. They believed that racially separate economic and civic organizations represented African Americans' best hope for raising their collective standard of living and mobilizing urban political power, not sympathy from white leaders.[9]

The language of tolerance that dominated urban political discourse in Detroit by the late 1920s was at the heart of northern white liberalism's racial contradictions and structured African Americans' responses to white politics. Northern racial liberalism promised a future that would look distinctly more equal than the racist order of southern society. At the same time, however, many of its subscribers helped reproduce aspects of the racially hierarchical social order that seemed natural to them. Tolerance shaped white liberals' political rhetoric but represented only part of the political story that their policies and practices would help produce.

Criminality, Tolerance, and Urban Geography

Frank Murphy's and other northern racial liberals' commitment to the language of tolerance obscured their unself-conscious embrace of aspects of the racially unequal status quo that they understood to be the products of sociological and cultural truths rather than political choices. Rather than invoke innate inferiority, northern racial liberals used the languages of culture, difference, and deprivation to explain the persistence of racial hierarchies. One important example of this trend was the connection they drew between black Detroiters, criminality, and dependence. Frank Murphy's record as a judge in the late 1920s captures this thinking. Murphy was first elected to the Recorder's Court, Detroit's municipal criminal court, in 1923. That year, he and three other liberal candidates ran against a bloc of four incumbent judges who were notoriously conservative, frequently charged with denying defendants their habeas corpus, and renowned for harsh sentencing, especially when it came to immigrants and African Americans. Murphy saw his own judicial practices as an antidote to the prejudices of his predecessors. For example, he saw presiding over the Ossian Sweet case as a chance to "demonstrate sincere liberalism and judicial integrity." He believed he was living in "a time when liberalism is coming into its own," and he saw his commitment to fairness for African Americans as the cutting edge of that larger trend.[10]

However, Murphy's racial liberalism was tempered by his tough stance toward suspected offenders. In 1926, for example, the year he was hearing the Sweet trial, Murphy had the highest overall conviction rate for felons among the ten judges sitting on the Recorder's Court; his was 64 percent, while the average conviction rate for the court was 45 percent.[11] Murphy was also reluctant to release suspects on bail.[12] This treatment of convicts meant that Murphy was far more likely to uphold the suspicions and prejudices of prosecutors and police officers than he was to be skeptical of their accusations. Although he prided himself on his commitment to racial equality, he did not interrogate the racialized assumptions that were built into the administration of the law.

While Detroit's white residents might not have been in the habit of questioning the racial bias behind the law's implementation, liberal public officials like Murphy had ready access to this critique. The authors of the 1926 report of the MIC, for example, used this paradigm to demonstrate that representatives of the state racialized crime in Detroit. "Legal authorities," they explained, "assume that the Negro is a bad man. . . . Officers of the Italian Squad . . . proceed on the principle that the Negro is essentially vicious."[13] The report observed that African Americans represented less than 7 percent of the population of the city in 1926, but 26 percent of the defendants charged with felonies in Recorder's Court. African Americans were thus 500 times more likely than whites to be convicted of felony charges. Some officials did take note. Judge Edward Jeffries Sr., the most politically progressive judge on the Recorder's Court and an early supporter and mentor of Murphy's, took these conclusions to heart. He believed that "judges and juries [were] unconsciously prejudiced against Negroes." Jeffries presided over the fewest black convictions of judges on the Recorder's Court. Only 31 percent of African American defendants who appeared before him were convicted, a significantly lower rate than for whites.[14] Even the city's police commissioner readily admitted that disproportionately high criminal rates among African Americans could be attributed "to the many unfair arrests." In a 1927 speech to an African American assembly, Commissioner William T. Rutledge argued that white southern officers were to blame for racial discrimination, displacing northern culpability onto southern racist backwardness. While Rutledge blamed urban racism on whites from the South, he still recognized the important role that discrimination played in policing.[15]

Murphy, however, was part of a larger group of white liberals who regarded the operation of the law—including their own role in it—as necessarily race blind. Murphy's conviction rates for African American and white suspects were about equivalent, but his overall conviction rate stood well above the court's average. Forty-nine percent of all African American defendants to appear in Recorder's Court that year were convicted; Murphy's court convicted 61 percent. Only two other judges presided over trials that convicted a higher proportion of African American defendants than Murphy, and both of their records were dramatically imbalanced against African Americans.[16] Although Murphy proclaimed himself committed to racial fairness, his faith in institutions like the police and the courts meant that his practices helped uphold their discriminatory conduct.

Murphy's approach to sentencing shows that he believed in the moral and social benefits of juridical race tolerance, but it also provides an illustration for how racially tolerant discourse helped obscure the racial disparities built into the practice of criminal justice in Detroit. Rather than try to confront the structural nature of racism in the application of the law, Murphy sought to bring scientific efficiency, "precision," and standardization to his legal work. These, he believed, would serve as a counterweight to any personal prejudice he or others involved in a case might hold. Murphy borrowed the tool of the "case history" from social workers, who used the format widely in social service settings by the 1920s. By collecting the details of a person's life, social workers believed, experts could design appropriate and scientifically sound courses of treatment for their clients.[17] Murphy saw his sentences similarly. They represented an opportunity for the benevolent state to care for and correct the behaviors of offenders through disciplinary control. While his sentences included punitive elements, like prison terms, they also required offenders to sustain state-appointed relationships with parole and probation officers, as well as social workers, whose paternalistic steering would lead convicts out of the life of crime. Indeed, it is likely that Murphy's conviction rates were so high because he saw his sentences as ultimately helpful for the individuals serving them and for the city.[18]

The format of the standardized case history, which Murphy used to determine the sentences he meted out, bore the appearance of evenhanded blindness to race but in fact perpetuated race-based inequities that Murphy apparently never thought to question. These case histories served to uphold existing relations of power in that they linked African Americans to criminality by interpreting crime as the product of poverty. Because African Americans were more likely than whites to experience poverty, this seemingly nonracial approach criminalized them disproportionately. Murphy developed an elaborate chart for recording convicts' case histories and made his decisions about sentencing based on this information. The chart included boxes for recording practically everything about convicts' lives, suggesting that these details could help explain criminal activity and thus contribute to a "scientifically" determined "treatment," which would most likely include jail time.[19] Murphy compelled convicts to share relatively intimate information about themselves with officers of the court, and all were required to undergo psychiatric evaluations. The guilty thus became subjects of intense scrutiny in an invasive and condescending process designed to diagnose an individual's problem and then offer a paternalistic, state-mandated solution to address it.

Murphy's chart suggests that he saw crime as rooted in a troubled family, one racked by infidelity, lax discipline, interfering relatives, undue friction, and harmful uses of leisure. In an article in the *Nation* praising Murphy for his "scientific" methods, J. A. Fellows reported that after looking over the case histories of 100 felons convicted in Murphy's court, he was struck by the large number who had been "left orphans at an early age, whose homes were broken up, or whose homes were listed as very poor."[20] The charts thus dramatically conveyed that an anemic family life—defined by its failure to provide children with two parents and a quiet, middle-class domestic space—breeds criminality. While this seemed, on the surface, to reflect objective observations about individual trajectories toward criminality, it in fact fit into larger ideas about race and class that animated social workers' and Murphy's concerns. Murphy saw that "the squalor of the cradle in the unlighted, unheated attic of the city slum is where we must begin our study of crime."[21] He cast poor families as virtual incubators for criminality, suggesting that they were inadequate to the task of breeding and raising good citizens. Incapable of producing future men and women equipped to contribute to society, these families were destined to rear children who would ultimately prey off of deserving citizens. Thus, the very categories and correlations the charts depicted were generated by deep notions of racial difference and, more particularly, of African American dysfunction and criminal tendencies.

Murphy's reference to the "slum" functioned, intentionally or not, as an allusion to African Americans. Many whites in the city struggled with financial instability in the 1920s, but no single white ethnic group or neighborhood was as visibly run-down or overcrowded as Black Bottom, the largest African American district. In fact, white ethnic neighborhoods, in general, were becoming less distinct, which meant that a geographic connection between a particular white ethnic group and slum conditions was far more difficult to read into the city's landscape than had been the case in the late nineteenth century. Large-scale industrialization, the massive in-migration of unskilled labor, and the exponential physical growth of the city all contributed to economic segregation but also to ethnic integration among whites in the first third of the century as workers began to populate neighborhoods close to factories and the well-to-do moved into outlying areas of the city. For blacks, however, the city was becoming more and more rigidly segregated.[22]

Black Bottom, which lay north and east of the city's downtown commercial district, had been identified as the city's most concentrated slum since well before it became majority black. In the late nineteenth and early twentieth centuries, it was the first destination for most southern and eastern European immigrants, many of whom moved out of the area once they could afford to. A combination of intense residential segregation by race and the huge in-migration of African Americans meant that black residents living in Black Bottom in the 1920s faced even more crowded conditions than white immigrants had earlier in the century, but they had fewer opportunities to move to other districts. In 1926, 66 percent of black residents lived in Black Bottom; the other 34 percent lived in a handful of smaller majority-black neighborhoods, most of which were also poor. A small number of middle-class African Americans had begun to move into these smaller, less crowded neighborhoods, but for most black residents, the cost of moving and the price of accommodations in these newer areas were prohibitive. Black Bottom also housed the city's largest red-light district, including most houses of prostitution, "numbers banks," and other illicit institutions.[23]

The increasingly segregated geography of the city allowed Murphy and other northern racial liberals to make claims about Detroiters living in slum areas that sounded like racially blind statements about the poor but that implicitly referred to African Americans. In the 1920s, well-publicized struggles over African American access to majority-white neighborhoods, like the Ossian Sweet skirmishes, persisted and received wide coverage. These clashes helped produce an understanding of space in Detroit that allowed geographic and spatial descriptors to became coded stand-ins for race. African Americans, this logic suggested, lived in slum conditions in poor neighborhoods and would bring poverty and chaos with them wherever they moved. Detroit residents who were not already familiar with the segregated racial geography of the city thus learned that Black Bottom, and a few other neighborhoods were African American, whereas the rest of the city was white. The name of the neighborhood, a reference to its rich soil, had been used since well before African Americans moved there, but it still helped reinforce the connection between African Americans and slums.

Racial Recognition and Black Struggles against Exclusion

The work of the Mayor's Interracial Committee reflected and furthered the centrality of residential segregation to contemporary debates about race in Detroit. While the committee functioned as a clearinghouse for complaints about discrimination of any sort, the vast majority of cases brought to its attention involved efforts to halt black migration into majority-white neighborhoods.[24] This emphasis on the difficulties faced by African Americans who could afford to buy homes in white areas stemmed from the concerns of the middle- and upper-class African Americans who were motivated to appeal to the committee—those who saw state institutions as potential allies. The tightly circumscribed range of concerns they brought to the committee also reflected their understanding of its limited power. Unlike white liberals, who embraced the fraught concept of tolerance, African Americans explained their right to move into majority-white districts as a fundamental aspect of urban fairness. They argued that the state should function in a racially neutral manner. At the same time, however, they pushed state actors to recognize how race shaped the urban terrain and to see that racial recognition was essential for remedying the problems of exclusion and inequality.

The Ossian Sweet case pushed struggles over residential segregation and racial conflict further into the public consciousness of white politicians and city residents. Interested white liberals and leftists helped this shift in consciousness along by paying more attention to black rights and working more closely with African Americans in the late 1920s. For

African Americans, however, the Sweet case did little to alter existing ideas about the meanings of race in the city or in organizational or individual approaches to struggles for racial justice. In the late 1920s, black Detroiters continued to fight against exclusion and work toward political integration at the same time that many maintained their enthusiasm for nationalist political and economic organizations.[25] As they had before, African Americans pushed white city leaders, especially liberals, to embrace race neutrality when it came to equal access, but when it came to remedying existing structures of discrimination, they called for racial recognition. They pushed white leaders to recognize that racial discrimination limited African Americans' opportunities and access to resources, and they fought for racially conscious solutions oriented toward reversing these trends. Furthermore, many African Americans remained skeptical of white leaders' embrace of the language of tolerance. They concluded that a gap persisted between white leaders' commitment to finding solutions for social ills and their minimal interest in attending to black concerns.

The relationship between African Americans and the Mayor's Interracial Committee, the state agency that emerged out of the Ossian Sweet incident, illustrates some of these dynamics. The MIC was first established to manage a large-scale study of African American Detroit and make recommendations to the mayor about how to avoid racial conflict in the future. The committee issued its report, *The Negro in Detroit*, in 1926, alongside a series of suggestions oriented toward the gradual integration of city agencies, the amelioration of living standards in black neighborhoods, and the management of residential racial tensions. Rather than following up on the recommendations himself, Mayor Smith charged the MIC with implementing its suggestions, although it had little political weight, a very small budget, and a tiny paid staff. The committee thus embodied the ambivalent tendencies of northern racial liberalism in a few ways. It was intended to signal that race relations constituted a serious issue for the city, and yet it was expected to operate with few public resources. It was the institutional expression of city leaders' belief that promoting the discourse of racial fairness while implementing gradual integration—rather than forceful head-on policy approaches to curb discrimination—was the best state approach for solving urban racial conflict, a cautious policy that foreclosed on the possibilities for implementing bold change in the city's racial landscape. At the same time, however, the MIC became a repository for black complaints about discrimination in the city, suggesting that, however conservative the racial politics behind the committee might be, it nevertheless provided an opening for a new kind of African American participation in civic affairs.

The members of the committee worked hard to reconcile the contradictions inherent in their mandate and to address questions of racial injustice. Without the ability to implement broad policy changes or enforce antidiscrimination laws, the MIC focused on integrating African Americans into city agencies and businesses on a case-by-case basis. These efforts illustrate that the MIC, which was made up of black and white political and religious leaders, saw the targeted expansion of opportunities for African Americans as a crucial element for black inclusion. Influenced by African Americans who called on city leaders to recognize that racial discrimination shaped black city life, the MIC saw African Americans' opportunities as severely limited by racism. Expanding the terrain of possibility could only happen by literally assigning more jobs to blacks. Within these parameters, the committee had some successes. It pressured the police department, which employed only fourteen African American officers, to accept eleven black recruits into its training school.[26] It also convinced two banks and two downtown stores to hire black workers and extend credit to African Americans.[27] Clearly, these victories did not have a significant effect on race relations or African Americans' collective fortunes, but they did mean that one small branch of the city government was working toward integration.

The existence of the MIC, alongside white leaders' celebration of their own racial liberalism, helped convince African Americans to approach the city government as a potential if not always willing ally in their fight for racial equality. After the Sweet case, middle-class African Americans were especially likely to turn to the MIC as part of their strategy to reverse the continued harassment they faced when they moved into majority-white neighborhoods. For example, Dewey and Annie Mae Adams, with the help of the NAACP, appealed to the MIC to stop white attacks on their new home in January 1928. The Adamses had bought a house one block south of the invisible line that divided a black district from an exclusively white residential area. In the month after they moved, hundreds of angry white protesters surrounded their home on two separate occasions, demanding that the couple leave. Police officers stood by and watched as protesters hurled "missiles" and fired shots at the house, breaking at least two windows. The Adamses were confronted with numerous threats to their lives and their property but actively chose to stand their ground and continue appealing to officials for help on the basis of race neutrality. The state, their actions suggested, needed to protect them and their house if it was truly committed to protecting all citizens and their property, regardless of race. African Americans continued to appeal to the MIC, but the group was extremely cautious in its responses to their complaints. The committee sustained its commitment to studying problems rather than pursuing avenues for intervention. For example, when Isabelle Johnson called on the MIC to help fend off white vandals after she moved into a majority-white neighborhood, the committee agreed only to "make a survey of the situation."[28]

At the same time that African Americans increased their appeals to the city government to protect their rights and property, those white Detroiters who were fighting to sustain segregation expected the state to support them as they worked to uphold racial exclusivity. Eighteen of Johnson's white neighbors, for example, posted a threatening note on her door, warning her that they would attack her and her property and take her to court if she moved into her new house.[29] Their signed threat indicated that white Detroiters believed they could attack black homeowners with impunity. They implied through their actions that enforcing segregation was a priority that city officials should favor over protecting the rights of African Americans. Johnson's neighbors took her to court. The presiding judge ruled that she had the right to own her property but not to live there. This decision was a total defeat for Johnson and the NAACP, both of which were fighting for residential integration, for Johnson's right to live in her new house, and for the state to actively embrace racial equality, even in the face of existing covenants.[30] Ultimately, the MIC was as reserved about taking action in the face of specific complaints of racial violence as it had been about recommending citywide, state-level solutions for racial conflict. As a state agency, it offered a new opening for black complaints to city leaders and governmental institutions, but it neither called on the police nor worked with other state agencies to implement integration on a city-wide scale.

African Americans also appealed to city leaders outside of the context of the MIC both to implement remedies for black exclusion based on racial recognition and to secure a commitment to race neutrality. In one case, these strategies butted up against each other. In the fall of 1928, two black men, Dr. J. W. Ames and Mr. Wheeler, convinced the civil service commissioner to offer a separate exam for African American "playleaders" in order to ensure that black workers would staff city programs for African American youths. In response to the public posting for the separate exam, an African American lawyer, Francis Dent, wrote to the mayor and the civil service commissioner expressing his concern that the segregated exams were both discriminatory and illegal.[31]

Most often, however, African American calls for racial recognition and race neutrality fit neatly together and did not produce these contradictions. Organizers' efforts to reform the city's police force, for example, deployed both strategies. African Americans called on the police commissioner to end racially discriminatory policing and to hire more black officers. They were thus pushing the department to promote neutrality in policing and to simultaneously implement targeted, racially conscious employment practices. In 1927, Commissioner Rutledge responded to black pressure for accountability by visiting two African American churches within two weeks. In front of large audiences—2,000 at the First Colored Presbyterian Church and 2,500 at St. John's Presbyterian—Rutledge blamed white southerners for discriminatory policing and defended his decision to maintain a force with only fourteen African American officers, just 1 percent of the total.[32]

Black listeners agreed that white southern officers were most likely to harass, intimidate, and mistreat them. Rather than absolving northern leaders of responsibility for this state of affairs, however, African American critics charged them with deliberately using southern white men to do the dirty work of controlling and suppressing African American residents. "The belief that has been prevalent here for some time," the *Pittsburgh Courier*, an African American weekly, reported, "was that southern white men were appointed in greater numbers to the police department because of their dislike for Negroes and because the authorities believed that southerners could by some means better hold the Negro under subjection."[33] In African Americans' minds, northern whites did more than just collude in southern whites' mistreatment of African Americans. They encouraged these abusive practices as a tool to manage black populations and simultaneously displace the blame for racial discrimination from themselves. Rutledge denied that police administrators used southern white men to "handle the colored people," but he did concede that southern whites were a majority on the force. He positioned himself against these officers, calling them "cowardly, lazy, and ill-bred," and he claimed that he was already working to replace them with "Michigan men."[34]

Snow Flake Grigsby had invited Rutledge to speak at St. John's Presbyterian as part of his "Let's Know the Negro in Detroit" speaker series, a program designed to bring white government officials and businesspeople in front of black audiences. Unlike the rhetoric of black nationalist organizations, which were popular among a broad range of African Americans, Grigsby's approach was to fight for the integration of black people into existing systems of power. However, he remained harshly critical of current institutions and city leaders for excluding African Americans, practicing discrimination, and helping to build a racially unequal city. For example, although he described his speaker series innocently enough, as an opportunity for "the Negro" to "see himself as others see him," Grigsby approached white leaders with heavy skepticism about their willingness to address African American concerns. The questions that he posed to Rutledge exposed his anger and frustration with ongoing police brutality and the small representation of African Americans on the police force. Grigsby asked Commissioner Rutledge to give "accurate information" about "the attitude of the department as a whole toward the Negro, number of Negroes killed by police officers in past year, numbers of Negroes on police force, how many appointed by present commissioner, attitude of department toward its appointments, if Southern men are given preference, and the percentage of crime committed by Negroes."[35] He thus pushed for integration into existing systems of power, but from a position of critique.

Grigsby's success in attracting speakers was rooted in the growing political and economic power of African Americans. This, in turn, allowed African Americans to harness the language of racial liberalism more effectively for their own political struggles. In some ways, this power went hand in hand with the city's strong tradition of racism. Segregation in Detroit in the mid-1920s was as prevalent as in southern cities. According to the African American intellectual and writer Kelly Miller, "The lives of the two races [in Detroit] are as separate in all social ways as one finds in Washington or Atlanta."[36] However, the rapidly expanding and geographically concentrated African American population had become a visible constituency in the realm of electoral politics. By the late 1920s, a broad range of white politicians visited African American institutions on their campaigns and during their time in office. Mayor Smith, for example, welcomed attendees to the annual convention of the Eastern and Western Colored Leagues in 1927. In a brief talk that captured the paradoxes and ironies of northern racial liberal discourse, he used the languages of interracial cooperation and African American "advancement" to celebrate the successes of the segregated leagues without mentioning the color line in professional baseball that excluded African American players from white teams. Baseball, he exclaimed, "attracted Americans of all kinds, without regard to race, creed, or color."[37] While Smith may have been an ambivalent ally, he nonetheless recognized the importance of sustaining good connections with black voters.

African American candidates also began to win small electoral victories in the late 1920s, pointing to their growing importance in the electoral realm. George H. Green, for example, won a spot on the primary ticket in the nonpartisan, citywide Common Council race in 1927. He ran seventh in a field of twenty-one candidates, eighteen of whom remained on the ballot for the general election.[38] Green failed to win a seat on the nine-person council, but his initial victory indicates the new terrain of possibility. African Americans did start winning election to office a few years later when, in 1930, African American lawyer Charles Roxborough won a state senate seat.[39] An unprecedented and increasing number of white politicians also aligned themselves closely with African Americans in the late 1920s. Councilperson John Kronk, for example, attended a banquet organized by African American supporters in his honor a month after he was elected to the council in 1927. Kronk thanked the audience for helping him secure his seat and described black support as "a decided factor" in his win. He promised to build on his record of addressing African American concerns, saying, "Remember that you now have a friend in the council, and if you need anything, come in and ask for it." Sheriff Edward Stein of Wayne County spoke at the same event, drawing attention to his support for and alliances with African Americans. "I have given you employment which after all is the real issue," he declared. Unlike city jobs, which required high scores on civil service exams, county employment continued to be political and often was distributed to supporters in exchange for their allegiance.[40] Unlike the majority of politicians in Detroit's municipal government, Kronk, like Stein, was a Democrat. County politics continued to be partisan, and Democrats had far more power on the county level than they did in the city. A small but growing number of African Americans in the urban North aligned themselves with the Democratic Party in the late 1920s, since they saw promise in northern Democrats' interest in expanding social programs, developing a more robust welfare state, and regulating more aspects of the economy. Some white northern Democrats, like Kronk and Stein, had also built interdependent political relationships with African American voters and positioned themselves as defenders of black access to resources and rights. This shift from the Republican to the Democratic Party was contested and comparatively slow in Detroit. Democrats were less powerful than they were elsewhere and had limited access to the spoils of partisan politics, and their efforts to align themselves with African Americans were foiled by African American workers' and city leaders' strong allegiance to the Ford Motor Company, which promoted political conservatism.[41]

African American activists thus found themselves working in a context of paradox and contradiction. Their growing importance in local politics and the commitment to tolerance expressed by white liberal politicians suggested that the time was ripe to push for redress within existing structures. Yet, the state's refusal to aggressively remedy persistent racial inequities worked against this possibility. Membership in the local NAACP branch had swelled significantly during and immediately after the Ossian Sweet case. The branch's 1926 membership drive yielded more contributions than any other local association's, but membership leveled off as the case faded from the headlines.[42] Local leaders failed to mount a sustained effort to keep membership up, and once the Sweet case ended, the association lost some of its visibility among

African Americans. Through the rest of the 1920s the branch maintained a legal defense committee, but it was not a membership-based organization. In other words, outside of paying dues, there was no real role for a branch member who did not assume an official leadership position. The work of the organization was primarily by and for elites, whose demands could be addressed through a race-neutral approach to resource distribution that would benefit the "right" kind of African American, one whose demands were limited and required no change to the existing order.

Between 1925 and 1927, the Reverend R. L. Bradby was president of the branch, and between 1928 and 1937, the presidents of Detroit's NAACP were executives at the Great Lakes Mutual Insurance Company—one of Detroit's most successful black businesses.[43] All these leaders were cautious and conservative in their outlooks; they preferred inactivity to alienating their white allies and often clashed with their more activist counterparts. For example, in 1927, the national office encouraged Bradby to respond to a series of police brutality cases by setting up "as imposing a committee as can be obtained of prominent white and colored citizens" to investigate and address the problem. While this proposal fit into Bradby's vision of interracial action to address civil rights problems, it meant that he would have to assert that African Americans suffered from systemic abuse at the hands of the police. He was unwilling to make this claim, and instead, the local NAACP did not pursue investigations or actions related to police brutality.[44] Instead, Grigsby took up the cause and used his church as a venue for organizing. Aside from its legal work, Detroit's NAACP functioned as a fund-raising organization for the national office and as a vehicle for local black elites to promote themselves as community leaders.[45] By the end of the 1920s, the branch provided legal assistance to a few African American defendants and investigated a handful of complaints about discrimination, although it only brought three cases to court in 1929, compared with fourteen in 1914.[46] Although African American activist strategies did not change considerably in the late 1920s, white responses to the Sweet case helped produce new political openings that contributed to the expansion of black political power in Detroit. In the years leading up to the Great Depression, African Americans won some small successes in the political realm and some victories over discrimination, although by the end of the decade they faced disproportionate economic contraction. African Americans were walking a difficult line. They were both using the opportunity that race-neutral language had offered to push white liberals to live up to their implicit promises but at the same time finding themselves hemmed in by white liberals, who were friendly but unwilling to prioritize black equality.

Urban Conservatism and the Language of Race Tolerance

In the years after the Sweet case, the language of racial tolerance came to be adopted not only by white liberal politicians but also by politicians across the political spectrum. This turn to racial liberalism was a result both of the growing power of African Americans and of liberal white leaders' efforts to effectively manage the increasingly interracial city. For white liberals, racial tolerance was a language that allowed them to straddle the contradictions between their limited support of civil rights and their embrace of aspects of the existing racial order. The language of racial tolerance served conservatives differently. For them, it was a cover for the ongoing promotion of racist ideals, couched now in racially coded language. For conservative white politicians, in other words, racial tolerance provided a rhetorical strategy that allowed them to appeal both to their traditional white constituencies, steeped in notions of white privilege and racial segregation, and to the slice of the urban electorate that was increasingly uncomfortable with overt racism.

The 1929 mayoral candidacy of Charles Bowles and the dynamics of the election that he won illustrate this strategic shift well. As the Great Depression was beginning to descend on the city, Bowles exploited white anxieties about the emerging political power of African Americans without ever using openly racist language. Bowles had been enthusiastically supported by the Ku Klux Klan in his losing bids for mayor against John Smith in both 1924 and 1925. For his 1929 campaign, however, Bowles disassociated himself from the Klan and stopped using explicitly anti–African American or anti-Catholic rhetoric. At the same time, he worked to maintain popularity among his former supporters, implicitly endorsing a "whisper campaign" that lent support to his candidacy.[47] Bowles ran on a platform full of promises to clean up the streets, cut taxes, and "bring the city government out of the morass of politics."[48] Despite his shift away from blatantly racist rhetoric, his campaign covertly connected black residents to city problems and suggested that growing black political power would spell the demise of white exclusivity if it was allowed to flourish unchecked. Bowles's effort to publicly distance himself from the Klan had few negative political consequences. Membership in the local group had fallen precipitously from its 1924 height, and the more tolerant political language of racial liberalism now characterized mainstream political discourse. To keep from sounding anachronistic, white conservatives needed to invoke this new language, but they did their best to use it to their own political ends.

Both Bowles and his opponent, John Smith, were Republicans in a city dominated by Republican politicians, although each one was connected to a different faction of the party. Smith, who had served as mayor from 1924 to 1927, was an outspoken opponent of Prohibition and had established a pro-labor record as deputy state labor commissioner. He was a liberal Catholic who had been in office during the Ossian Sweet trial and had established himself as a northern racial liberal through his management of the infamous case and his political alliances with African Americans. In his 1929 campaign, Smith sold himself on his record. Drawing attention to his commitments to good government and sound fiscal policy, he worked to amass support from business interests.[49] Smith, however, had more success among liberal city leaders, who enthusiastically supported his candidacy. Many of these men and women were Democrats, and they were beginning to organize themselves into a more self-conscious liberal and progressive political force in the city.

Like Murphy, Bowles served as a judge on the Recorder's Court in the late 1920s. During his tenure as judge, he earned a reputation as fair and evenhanded. "Klan or no Klan," one newspaper reporter explained, Bowles "strove to prove to the people that he would treat all alike." In fact, by the time he ran for mayor in 1929, a "sizable group" of Jewish, African American, and Catholic attorneys supported his campaign. Bowles was able to maintain this support thanks to the fact that he consistently avoided explicit language about race or religion in his speeches, public appearances, and official campaign literature. However, even as his campaign literature maintained a tone of racial respect, it also used carefully coded language about African Americans and Catholics as a strategy for garnering white votes. For example, a week and a half before the election, Bowles's campaign sent letters to Protestant ministers calling on them to distribute a pamphlet to their congregants. Only the "lower precincts of the east side" the pamphlet declared, had supported Smith in the primary; the "better citizens" had not. Bowles, the pamphlet continued, only wanted the support of these "better citizens" in his run for office.[50]

In this pamphlet, the lower east side came to serve as a stand-in for black and Catholic Detroiters—it contained the largest and poorest black neighborhoods in the city, as well as some of the poorest white neighborhoods, which were majority Catholic. The pamphlet implied that Smith's political successes could be attributed to the growing electoral power of black and working-class Catholic voters, a power that should be held in check. Bowles, conversely, pledged the "rigid enforcement of the law" and ridding the city of "the kidnaper [*sic*], racketeer and hold-up man." Thus, Bowles's pamphlet connected the black east side as well as working-class Catholic neighborhoods to the "criminal element" and to the underworld, linking the area's expanding political power to criminality.[51]

Bowles's campaign literature points to the ascendancy of colorblind political language within formal public discourse, even among racial conservatives, since it communicated ideas about African Americans and Catholics without mentioning these groups by name. Instead, its authors used geographic descriptions as stand-ins for urban populations, indicating their interest in masking the racially and ethnically specific nature of their concerns about criminality. Unlike liberals, Bowles did not claim to support black rights or take a stand against discrimination. However, as this pamphlet demonstrates, he also resisted overt allusions to the inferiority of African Americans, the dangers of racial integration, or fears of "mongrelization," language that had been current only a few years earlier but that had rapidly fallen out of favor as white liberals and African Americans pressed for social and political change.

Rather than using racist or anti-Catholic language himself, Bowles relied on volunteer campaign workers to stir up support among residents interested in specifically race-based appeals. Most contemporary observers agreed that his victory could be attributed to the well-organized, neighborhood-based canvass run by his supporters, the majority of whom were white women. The canvassers' goal was to remind voters that Bowles would protect white Protestants from the threats of Catholic and African American political power while Smith, by contrast, would encourage and even help expand these populations' access to municipal resources and power.[52] For example, two days before the election, canvassers printed and distributed 200,000 copies of an article originally printed in an African American newspaper, arguing that the "tremendous vote obtained by former Mayor John W. Smith in the primary election was piled up solely in the Negro districts of Detroit." African American voters, this ploy suggested, had handed Smith a win in the primaries and would expect to be thanked for their support.[53]

Bowles's canvassers focused their campaign on Brightmoor and Redford, two majority- white and Protestant neighborhoods that had been incorporated into Detroit in 1925.[54] Most of these neighborhoods' residents were middle-class homeowners and saw their own interests—the extension of municipal resources to newly developed areas—as antithetical to African Americans' concerns. While the area was far away from any significant black settlement, and thus unlikely to be attractive to African American homebuyers, Brightmoor and Redford residents worried about African American move-ins and attendant declines in property values. Bowles' campaign workers used African American support for Smith to steer white residents away from the former mayor, even though Smith's support for African Americans during his tenure had been ambivalent at best, as evidenced by how he handled the Sweet case. Furthermore, they criticized Smith for neglecting Brightmoor and Redford. While Smith defended his record, explaining that he encouraged the governor to veto a bill that would have forced area residents to pay more for city services than other Detroiters, his defense fell on deaf ears.[55] Brightmoor and Redford residents responded enthusiastically to Bowles's campaign appeals, and in some areas of the ward, Smith was beaten by four to one.[56] Race-baiting proved to be an effective tool in garnering white support even in those neighborhoods where black in-migration was *not* apparently imminent.

At the same time that Bowles quietly allowed volunteers to run this hate campaign in his name in white Protestant neighborhoods, he worked publicly to build support for his candidacy among a diverse group of Detroit residents, including Catholics, Jews, and even African Americans.[57] For example, in one day, a week before the election, Bowles visited Italian, Ukrainian, Swedish, Jewish, and German societies and dances.[58] His campaigners also worked to win over African American voters. At the same time that they were linking Smith's successes to black political power in white neighborhoods, they appealed to black Detroiters by attempting to expose Smith as a racist. Bowles's advocates distributed a political cartoon showing that Smith was a hypocrite: that he claimed to support black rights but was secretly against integration, racial equality, and African Americans. The cartoon, captioned "John Smith Gives Campaign Orders," showed a large Smith pointing at Ossian Sweet and Charles Diggs and saying, "You should not live in a white neighborhood." Sweet and Diggs were both holding "Smith for Mayor" placards and were standing in front of a small crowd of African Americans. Behind Smith stood a crowd of white onlookers led by a person in a Ku Klux Klan hood and robe with the letter "K" emblazoned on his lapel. The white crowd was saying, "You tell 'em John," indicating their support for Smith.

In this image, Ossian Sweet and Charles Diggs represented relatively affluent and politically powerful African Americans who were attempting to buy decent houses and move into middle-class white neighborhoods. Charles Diggs, who hailed from a well-established family, owned a lucrative funeral home on the black east side. He would go on to become a state senator eight years later, in 1937, but was already politically well connected in Detroit. The hooded Klan members represented the city's white racists and supporters of segregation, those with whom Smith, according to this cartoon, had cast his lot. Bowles thus ran a campaign that effectively exploited white anxieties about African American political power in the city at the same time that it played on black fears about white racism.

The prominent professionals and businesspeople who supported Bowles's campaign tended to remain quiet about his canvassers' tactics, neither openly supporting nor publicly denouncing their grassroots appeals to antiblack racism.[59] Detroit's conservative political establishment thus quietly consented to Bowles's campaign tactics. Carl Weideman, a well-established attorney and active member of the Wayne

County Republican Club, was one of Bowles's principal supporters, as was John Gillespie, who had made a fortune in real estate and insurance after he left public office as police commissioner in 1918.[60] Real estate developers and prominent Republicans Robert and Milton Oakman also poured thousands of dollars into Bowles's campaign.[61] All these men distanced themselves from the crass language of racism associated with Bowles's canvassers, focusing their criticism of Smith on his ties to organized labor, his opposition to Prohibition, and his rejection of pro-business reform. Weideman's, Gillespie's, and the Oakmans' enthusiastic support for Bowles suggested that his past support for the Klan did not cause them concern.[62]

Smith differentiated himself from his opponent by rejecting Bowles's "mud slinging," his "whisper crew," and his message of "prejudice." However, he was concerned about the effects that his support from African Americans might have on his white support, and he distanced himself from African Americans in front of white audiences. A campaign photograph of Smith at an integrated nursery school captures his support for, but ambivalence about, African Americans and integrated spaces. In the picture, which appeared in the *Detroit Free Press*, Smith sat on the far left of the frame with a small white girl leaning on his shoulder. Two smiling African American children stood on the other side of the frame, making no physical contact with Smith.[63] In all-black contexts, however, Smith openly embraced African American voters. A week before the election, he attended an African American costume party at the Graystone Ballroom and awarded prizes to the best-dressed attendees.[64] In the most densely populated black districts, Smith beat Bowles by nine to one in an election that attracted 60 percent of registered black voters to the polls. African Americans votes represented 7.6 percent of all votes cast in the November 1929 election.[65]

The mainstream press painstakingly resisted classifying either candidate as affiliated with a political party or ideology in the nonpartisan elections, but the candidates' different platforms clearly marked Bowles as conservative and Smith as a liberal. Bowles, who pledged to reduce taxes and cut city spending, endorsed a set of fiscal policies that appealed to Detroit's business community. Smith, who called himself a "progressive," consistently said that he was friendly to business interests, but he proposed state-sponsored initiatives to deal with the emerging unemployment problem and with the city's transit system, the Department of Street Railways (DSR). Smith argued that the city should proceed with necessary public improvements to provide work for people laid off from slowing-down factories. He also advocated public refinancing of the DSR, which was the largest municipally owned urban transportation system in the country.[66] Furthermore, even though John Smith was a Republican, Detroit's liberals and Democrats rallied to his cause in his campaign against Bowles in 1929 and were sorely disappointed when he lost.[67]

Bowles successfully brought together a diverse group of supporters by balancing their competing and even contradictory interests. His success demonstrates the political power of using neighborhood-based smear campaigns that connected liberal city leaders with African Americans as early as the 1920s. Bowles could thus build on the momentum of his supporters' "whisper campaign" without developing a public persona that included appeals to white Detroiters' racism. This was important because it allowed him to sustain a respectable, modern, and northern political persona. By the late 1920s, shifts in the political terrain had created an atmosphere within which these expressions were less tolerated within mainstream political discourse. This also means that in Detroit, in the realm of electoral politics, African Americans had already come to be associated with an activist government, a liberal set of urban policies, and a pro-union bent.

After Charles Bowles became mayor, he sustained the same caution about blatant racism that he had embraced as a candidate. He distanced himself from the canvassers who had worked on his behalf in the city's all-white neighborhoods, failing to show up at banquets held for him by campaign workers from the Twenty-Second Ward, both before and after his inauguration.[68] At the same time that he maintained his distance from overt racism and racists, Bowles kept African Americans at arm's length, showing little interest in their concerns and disinterest in their attempts to push the city government to address their needs. Bowles disbanded the Mayor's Interracial Committee, for example, closing down the only government agency designed to address interracial conflict. Thus, Bowles rejected overtly racist language in his own political speech at the same time that he rejected the notion that African Americans should be able to make official claims about inequality through state institutions—even though the institution in question had so little power. The MIC, which provided some recognition that racial discrimination and conflict were problems that the state should work to fix, contradicted his colorblind racial conservatism.

Charles Bowles's success, however, proved short-lived. His term as mayor lasted for only eight months and ended with a successful recall campaign. When Bowles took office in January 1930, the Great Depression had begun to grip the city with newfound force. Bowles faced the largest deficit ever held by the city and a growing unemployment problem. Tax delinquency and bonded debt had both shot up in 1928 and 1929. Construction had been contracting since 1926. Layoffs came with a vengeance in September and October 1929. In spite of the growing crisis, Bowles maintained his commitment to shrinking the city's budget and reducing taxes. Within his first week as mayor, he cut city jobs and proposed a two-cent increase for city-run buses and streetcars—from four to six cents. He also made it clear that he believed that unemployment was a problem to be addressed by industry, not government. Instead, he focused on crime.[69] "The first obligation of the public officers of this community," he said, "is to disarm the gunman."[70]

Bowles took little interest in welfare or unemployment except as these issues intersected with his ambitions. Thus, he did pay attention to related political appointments. For example, over the protests of social agencies and the Department of Public Welfare (DPW) he chose not to reappoint Minnie Jeffries, the wife of the progressive Recorder's Court judge Edward Jeffries, to a seat on the Public Welfare Commission. Instead, he appointed conservative welfare commissioners, including Alex Blain, who were interested in cutting relief benefits and shrinking eligibility.[71] Bowles also made cuts in city services and ignored the rapidly rising toll unemployment was taking on Detroit's residents. Over Bowles's term, the number of people applying for and receiving public relief jumped dramatically. The month he was elected, in September 1929, the DPW handled about 2,600 cases and spent a little more than $90,000 on "general family relief." Just six months later, in March 1930, the department's caseload hit 17,000, and it gave out $730,000 in direct aid. An investigation of the DPW conducted by a citizens' committee recommended increased staff and new administrative procedures to handle the exploding caseload, but Bowles rejected these proposals, and the relief agency languished under unmanageable administrative burdens.[72]

While he maintained the fiscally conservative stance he had struck in his campaign, Bowles failed to live up to the principles of "good government" and ultimately alienated his pro-business allies. He appointed a number of candidates to head city departments who had clear conflicts of interest, he failed to keep his law-and-order campaign promises, and he did nothing to stem the seemingly epidemic tide of vice in Detroit.[73] Instead, he used a "hands-off" policy, allowing gambling houses to flourish and undercutting the power of the police to crack down on vice. Finally, in May 1930, with Bowles out of town attending the Kentucky Derby, Police Commissioner Emmons raided and shut down gambling establishments all over the city. When Bowles returned, he fired Emmons and touched off a recall campaign. Many of Bowles's original supporters joined the recall effort, and Bowles lost the election with 58 percent voting against him.[74]

Building a Racially Liberal State

Charles Bowles's recall and the mayoral election it sparked reignited citywide debates about the deepening economic depression and the role the local government should (or should not) play in mitigating its effects. The Depression set in at the same time that the discourse of racial tolerance was becoming more widely accepted in Detroit. White liberals, the most vocal white proponents of this discourse, saw their political capital increase as city residents rejected Charles Bowles and sought public recognition for their economic hardships and state support for managing privation. The city's liberals, some of whom had been active in Democratic Party politics, capitalized on organizing they had done through the 1920s and on the coalitions they helped build between themselves, African Americans, ethnic Catholics, and the city's labor movement. When Frank Murphy won the mayoralty in 1930, it was clear that the discourses of racial tolerance and northern racial liberalism would help shape how local government leaders managed and addressed the economic crisis. Murphy's success indicates the growing power of northern racial liberalism as a contemporary discourse about race.

The same year that Bowles won his mayoral campaign, Frank Murphy was reelected to a seat on the Recorder's Court. Murphy was one of the few Democrats to win a race in the city's nonpartisan elections, and he saw himself as a committed liberal pioneer, a champion of the downtrodden, and an advocate for fairness. In 1928, he proclaimed that the city needed "a mass movement of liberal and progressive thought that will unfurl its banners on behalf of downtrodden peoples."[75] In fact, Murphy promoted a larger and more comprehensive city government that would expand its direct aid to citizens. He supported state-sponsored social programs like unemployment and old-age insurance. Once unemployment became widespread, Murphy started his own informal employment agency in his chambers and found jobs for hundreds of Detroiters during the winter of 1929–1930. He also worked on a citizens' committee "concerned with the problem of unemployment" that developed a fivefold plan, including calls for direct relief from the city government, a survey of the unemployment situation, city-sponsored public works projects, and the "rationalization of industry."[76] Murphy also saw racial liberalism as the cutting edge of his political commitments. Indeed, he believed that he could demonstrate his true commitment to liberal ideals by publicly demonstrating his commitment to *racial* fairness. Indeed, he was the most prominent white politician in the city identified with northern racial liberalism, and by the time he ran for reelection to the Recorder's Court in 1929, northern racial liberalism had become a central tenet of his politics.

Frank Murphy's mayoral victory in 1930 was a triumph for liberals and for Democrats in Detroit, and he brought his racial politics with him into office. He was the first Democrat to win the mayoralty since the city established nonpartisan elections in 1918, and he won with the support of the city's Catholics and African Americans. Murphy was elected in the "face of a vitriolic attack from the conservative press and the big-business elements of the city," who promoted President Herbert Hoover's lack of enthusiasm for state solutions for unemployment and promised to reorganize the city government on a "business basis." Murphy shaped his campaign around calls for government-sponsored unemployment insurance and old-age pensions. He promised a "no starvation era" in Detroit if he was mayor. "If conditions warranted such steps," he told an audience of African American supporters, he would open city-run soup kitchens and lodging houses. At the same time that Murphy was a champion of a more robust state response to the Depression, he was careful not to alienate the city's elite or to be identified with the Far Left. Murphy praised the belt-tightening recommendations of the Stone Committee on City Finances, an advisory board of bankers and prominent businessmen appointed by the Common Council in 1929 to provide guidance on the city's financial matters. He promised to maintain a tight economy in city government and to keep a balanced budget while in office.[77]

Throughout the 1920s, Murphy used his racial liberalism and inclusivity as electoral strategies. He recognized that his strength as a candidate lay in building a coalition of what he called "the minority groups" in the city. In a letter to the editor of Detroit's *Hungarian News*, he explained that he depended on his "friends in the minority" for support because of his "interest in the social and economic problems of the community." He also explained that his "intimacy with the minority groups" had effectively alienated him from many of the "more conservative groups in the city." Murphy concentrated a large proportion of his energy campaigning among white ethnic and African American communities. While he did not run for mayor until 1930, he maintained his popularity among African Americans for his role in the Sweet case. One black lawyer, Charles A. Roxborough, who would become a state senator in the same election, explained that many African American Detroiters were voting for Murphy because he "stands for a square deal for every one, the high or low, the poor or rich, the powerful or the friendless." Murphy was aware of this support and made a number of campaign stops in African American neighborhoods, visiting the Ebenezer African Methodist Episcopal Church at least twice. On September 5, four days before the election, he addressed eleven groups, one of which was Polish, one Hungarian, one Serbian, and six African American.[78]

Conclusion

By 1930, the language of racial liberalism was, to some extent, pushed to the forefront of political discourse by African American Detroiters. Nevertheless, white liberals turned that language to their own ends, using it as an electoral strategy and a way to signal their inherent commitment to fair-mindedness. White liberals helped proliferate and extend the languages of racial tolerance and African American inclusion in their political coalitions, campaigns, and offices. They embraced the idea that their promotion of racially tolerant discourse, alongside the gradual integration of African Americans into city institutions, could do the work of producing a more racially egalitarian urban terrain. However, as this chapter suggests and the next chapter illustrates, they did not reshape the stark racial imbalances that characterized either the local government or city space, even when they controlled the state. Clearly, they were constrained by the racial hierarchies built into the structures they inherited, but their inability to develop significant alternatives to the racial status quo reflected their political priorities and their understanding of racism as well. Self-identified pragmatists, the majority of Detroit's white liberals embraced a belief in capitalist urban development that required inequality. Their highest priority was to support business prosperity, which also meant the accumulation of wealth among elites. White liberals did work to mitigate some of the inequalities this system helped produce by supporting workers' interests and developing a local welfare state. Ultimately, however, they subscribed to its basic tenets and so could not fully consider proposals that would directly undermine racial inequalities, since the most embedded of those inequalities seemed natural and were thus difficult for white liberals to even see. Furthermore, because racial liberals persisted in their belief that racism was an individual characteristic, rather than a pervasive cultural and structural problem, they did not conceptualize or challenge the entrenched racism built into the institutions of Detroit's urban political sphere. Detroit's local welfare state, built before the advent of the New Deal, was seen as a laboratory for welfare programs that would come to be taken up by the Roosevelt administration.[79] The racial ideologies embedded in these programs, which were spearheaded by white liberal advocates of racial tolerance, represented the politics of the urban North and came to shape federal New Deal programs. The discourse of northern racial liberalism was forged, in part, in opposition to conservative politics.

4

"Living Happily at the Taxpayers' Expense"

City Managers, African American "Freeloaders," and White Taxpayers

In June 1931, a year and a half into the Great Depression, the city of Detroit was strapped for cash. The public outcry against its relatively generous welfare benefits was mounting. In response, the welfare commission started reducing city services for indigent residents, cutting cash assistance, and ordering the Department of Public Welfare to slash its relief rolls. In a move both cruel and symbolic, welfare commissioners attempted to eliminate all sixty-five beds and sixty-five bassinets on the maternity ward at Herman Kiefer Hospital, a downtown public hospital devoted to the treatment of "communicable diseases, tuberculosis and indigent maternity cases." Herman Kiefer was adjacent to the black east side, the city's largest African American neighborhood, and close to Hastings Street, its main thoroughfare. The welfare commissioners announced that they wanted to reorganize the city's obstetrical services "along more economical lines." African American women on relief, they decided, should deliver their babies at home. Executives at the hospital warned that this change would result in a dramatic rise in maternal and infant deaths. The mortality rate for deliveries in the hospital was one-third the rate for the city at large, and these beds were always full.[1]

Dr. Alex W. Blain, a member of the city's welfare commission, explained the commissioners' decision in terms that pitted African American mothers and their newborn babies against the needs of "white taxpayers." He condemned indigents for freeloading off of city hospitals and connected the fraudulent use of public resources to African Americans. "Being a city patient has gotten to be a racket," he explained, so "let's not worry so much about a few Hastings street pickaninnies and start worrying more about the white taxpayers." For Blain, higher maternal and infant mortality rates among African Americans were a reasonable price to pay in order to save white taxpayer money. He was a conservative politician who was deeply invested in the racial status quo. He sustained little interest in expanding local government or in building political alliances with African Americans. Charles Bowles, a mayor who had been identified with the Ku Klux Klan early in the decade, had appointed him to the welfare commission in 1929. In his role as commissioner, Blain consistently voted to slash the budget of the DPW and reduce city programs designed to help the indigent. Blain's comments are an example of an increasingly influential narrative about public scarcity, black freeloaders, and white taxpayers that was emerging in Detroit alongside efforts to manage city resources in the face of the Great Depression. Blain and his allies used racialized ideas about welfare, dependency, and local citizenship to justify their support for state policies that institutionalized discrimination, calcified existing manifestations of racial stratification, and produced new procedures to strengthen racial difference.[2]

As they would have in the past, African Americans responded to Blain's pronouncement with anger and protest. The city's sanitation workers, for example, whose membership was more than 90 percent black, sent a poignant, one-line telegram to Mayor Frank Murphy declaring that they "resent[ed]" Blain's statement.[3] Charles Roxborough, Michigan's only black state senator, called on Murphy to demand Blain's resignation.[4] The Reverend A. C. Williams, a black Baptist minister, complained to the mayor that Blain's disdain for African Americans was inappropriate.[5] Leonard Harris, infuriated by Blain's remarks, reminded the commissioner that African Americans had fought heroically in the Great War, only to return home to inequality. Black soldiers had sacrificed so that "you and yours might be able to continue to enjoy a white mans [*sic*] democracy in America, which is forbidden fruit for the Negro." "Remember," he added ominously, "the fact that you are white will not save you always."[6]

W. G. Bergman of the Department of Education, a white liberal supporter of Murphy, also registered concern about Blain's use of racist language. Recognizing that African Americans had been the targets of discriminatory invectives for years, he argued, "There is not the slightest occasion for adding insult to injury and offending a large section of the population of Detroit which has been too much offended in the past by such references." However, Bergman was more concerned about Murphy's reputation than he was about the consequences of eliminating the maternity program. "Entirely aside from the question of whether or not it is necessary to eliminate this service," he wrote in a letter to Murphy, "your official conduct, both as judge and as Mayor, has attracted widespread favorable attention on account of your fair-mindedness in dealing with the negro problem and I trust that the inconsiderate utterances of one of your holdover appointees will not be allowed to obscure this record in the public recollection."[7] Bergman thus cynically dismissed the welfare commission's proposed elimination of hospital services for African Americans as less important than Murphy's reputation as a defender of black rights.

Both African American and white observers trusted that Murphy would condemn Blain's use of racist language and defend African Americans as much as he could against discrimination. As Bergman noted, Murphy had established a name for himself as a defender of racial equality, first when he presided over the Ossian Sweet case in 1926 and subsequently in his political alliances with African American voters and black politicians. He was a member of the NAACP and a promoter of both tolerance and race neutrality. Indeed, in a gesture of support for African Americans who might use the hospital, Murphy did not approve the welfare commission's proposed elimination of the Herman Kiefer maternity ward.[8]

Blain and Murphy clearly disagreed about who needed support and protection from the state. For Blain, white taxpayers were the most beleaguered victims of the crisis, immiserated by the demands of the fraudulent and undeserving, including the African American poor. For Murphy, conversely, the "downtrodden," a racially inclusive group of unemployed or underemployed men and women, warranted the most care from the local government. Blain's racist invectives and his disdain for a more expansive welfare state captured one end of the spectrum out of which debates over welfare policies and practices emerged. Murphy stood at the opposite end of that divide. However, the clarity of their disagreement over how to represent African Americans obscures the ways that their ideas about welfare and the state also overlapped. Indeed, the effects of the policies they supported on both African Americans and urban racial stratification were more similar than their rhetoric suggested, and not only because Murphy was constrained by the conservatism of Blain and his political allies. While Blain stood for racial inequality and Murphy stood against it, these two men shared a belief that the city's capitalist political economy needed saving. They saw the social and political hierarchies upon which the city had been built as natural. Blain defended these hierarchies and the racial and class inequalities they produced whole cloth, although he denied he was racist. Murphy, in contrast, worked to mitigate the most egregious effects of inequality on the men, women, and children on the bottom rungs of the economic ladder. However, he simultaneously embraced the concerns about welfare defrauders and worries about municipal debt that made the reordering of these inequalities untenable.

By the early 1930s, northern racial liberalism had come to characterize most public discourse in the halls of the government. This meant that the kinds of expletives that Blain used to describe African American infants, even in the mouths of conservatives, were unlikely to be heard in formal public venues like a welfare commission meeting. Even Blain, in response to the criticism of Rev. Williams, denied that his interest in closing Kiefer's maternity ward was rooted in animosity toward African Americans. He proclaimed instead that a large part of his work as welfare commissioner "was for the uplifting of your people." Thus, he both denied that he had racist intent *and* used a language of care for African Americans to describe his actions. Blain insisted that his support for eliminating hospital beds was driven by his deep, abiding, and legitimate concern that the distribution of welfare had been profoundly hampered by widespread fraud. "Deserving" and "self-respecting Americans," he declared, had to be "turned back" from the welfare rolls because fraudulent claims had drained the DPW's coffers and were taking a heavy toll on its budget.[9] Although Blain was a conservative, in his role as welfare commissioner he was helping to manage city resources and services, both of which were expanding under the liberal leadership of Mayor Frank Murphy. Conservative opponents of public relief exploited anxieties about fraud to undermine popular support for expanding state programs. Indeed, the Herman Kiefer Hospital had been the object of attack and scrutiny the previous year when tabloid newspapers accused its administration of overspending, mismanagement, and embezzlement.[10]

Blain's defensive rhetoric points to the currency of racially neutral discourse across the political spectrum, even though his embrace of that neutrality was both ambivalent and disingenuous. Even as he attempted to shy away from the explicitly racist speech he used in the welfare commission meeting, he continued to link blackness to dependency and fraud in order to justify his larger claim that the city government should not provide services or support to indigent residents, especially African Americans. In other words, he blamed African Americans, not racism or inequality, for producing the racially unequal urban landscape. While white liberals actively defended race neutrality, they often drew similar ideological links between blackness and dependence as their conservative counterparts. Unlike conservatives, they were often willing to recognize that racism had shaped individual lives, but like conservatives, they were less interested in how racism shaped urban systems, or helped produce and reinforce inequality among Detroit's population. While conservatives used this language to argue against state support for indigents, liberals used it to explain the limits of the welfare state they were crafting and to defend themselves against the criticism that that state was either inadequate or unfair. While distinctions between liberals and conservatives were certainly important in the production of policy and the running of the state, white racial liberals were not providing as clear an alternative to racial conservatism as their rhetoric suggested.

The local government's response to mounting unemployment and diminishing tax revenues provides a window into these racial dynamics, another facet of which was the highly politicized construction of the "white taxpayer." Early on in the Depression, self-described "white taxpayers" pushed for a dramatic reduction in the welfare budget and helped achieve this goal in collaboration with the city's banks and financiers. Furthermore, their self-definition reinforced the popular discourse that linked African Americans to indigence, dependence, and corruption and whites to full, taxpaying citizenship. The administration of relief and welfare in Detroit in the early 1930s turned into a debate about northern, specifically urban, politics. When confronted with dramatic unemployment and public scarcity, white city leaders, including liberal supporters of the welfare state, implicitly denied black assertions that African Americans' *local* residency—their citizenship in a northern, urban locality—was legitimate and long-term. They thus rejected in practice, if not in theory, the idea that black Detroiters deserved the rights and resources conferred on legitimate local citizens.

The Sympathetic White Unemployed Man

Coverage of the worsening Depression in the city's newspapers reflected the political establishment's views on the relationship between race, unemployment, and who deserved state aid. In the beginning of the Depression, when the economic crisis seemed urgent but still possibly temporary, the city's newspapers, especially the more liberal ones, represented the most sympathetic unemployed person as a relatively passive white male victim of processes beyond his control. These men were depicted as down on their luck: struggling in vain to support their families, maintain their dignity, and preserve the last shreds of their masculinity. Those unemployed people who publicly protested their lot or asserted that jobs, wages, and welfare were rights they deserved fared far worse in the mainstream press. As the Depression deepened, representations of the unemployed were more likely to connect poverty and relief to moral weakness; African Americans were more likely to appear as some of the worst abusers of a potentially too-generous welfare system.

The Great Depression hit Detroit hard and early. Factory employment actually peaked for the decade in the spring and summer of 1929, but by September a steep decline set in. Unemployment skyrocketed, and by the next summer, employment fell below 1920 levels, even though the city's population had increased by 60 percent over the decade. A paralyzing drought also dealt a severe blow to Michigan's economy.[11] While some conservatives held the poor accountable for their indigence, shiftlessness, and irresponsibility, the shock of the October 1929 stock market crash and the explosion of unemployment blunted the power of their accusations. Before the crash, newspapers mostly covered unemployment in the business section as a set of statistics, with few references to actual unemployed people. After the crash, unemployed white men became sympathetic subjects of news stories.

A January 1930 profile of Pat Richards in the *Detroit Free Press* captured this attitude, providing an early-Depression allegory about "good" and "bad" kinds of poverty. Richards, a nineteen-year-old white man, had hit a dead end. After losing the odd jobs that were keeping him afloat, he was evicted from his boardinghouse. He pulled a fire alarm in an attempt to get arrested so he could find "warmth and a pillow" in jail. Richards had long resisted attempts to corrupt his life—the boys in his neighborhood, his cellmate in jail, the men and women who participated in vice and illicit sexuality. His sad tale was so moving that the judge suspended his sentence, and he was back on the street the next day. He was a young man who was worth saving. His portrait implied that many casualties of the current crisis could be saved by an expanded welfare state.[12]

Conversely, mainstream journalists had less sympathy for unemployed people who were organizing against the systems that had produced the economic crisis. A mere two months after the *Free Press* profiled Richards, the unemployed returned to the news, but this time they were cast as protesting, disruptive, and angry. On March 6, 1930, between 75,000 and 100,000 Detroiters rallied outside of City Hall to demonstrate against unemployment and to demand "work or wages." Police violence escalated quickly, with "mounted policemen in groups of three, four, and five [riding] on to the sidewalks and charg[ing] straight into the crowds." After two hours of clashes, fourteen people were sent to the hospital, and many more suffered from scrapes and bruises. By late afternoon, eight women and twenty-three men had been arrested, and the streets were quiet.[13] The rally had been sponsored by the Communist Party, which had begun to attract scores of city residents into its Unemployed Councils. Daily papers suggested that the majority of unemployed men and women participating in the protests were innocent and upstanding citizens, although dangerously vulnerable to corruption by the less deserving—this time communist agitators.[14]

This coverage suggested that few demonstrators signed onto the demand for "work or wages" but dismissed the communists' claim that dissatisfied unemployed men and women were becoming an increasingly visible and organized presence that would disrupt business as usual if their needs were not met. The newspaper reports about the protests, like those about the unemployed more generally, portrayed their subjects as white men. In fact, only one article about the March 6 protest in the daily papers mentioned African Americans at all. The article, printed in the *Detroit Evening Times*, indicated that one of the arrestees, William Smith, was "a negro who has been jobless and homeless." He was the only one whose race or ethnicity was explicitly mentioned by the newspapers.[15] This representation foreshadowed a shift in both coverage and public discussions about unemployment.

Although journalists generally cast white men as the sympathetic face of unemployment, African Americans in Detroit were more consistently financially devastated by the crisis than any other single group.[16] The saying "the last hired and first fired" was devastatingly accurate for black workers in the Depression. Downward occupational pressure meant that white workers began to push African Americans out of jobs at the "bottom of the employment hierarchy" that had previously been defined as too laborious or demeaning and poorly paid for them to take. By 1933, John Dancy, executive secretary of the Detroit Urban League, explained that many jobs "that through tradition have been thought of in the light of Negro jobs, colored people are losing. Such jobs as waiters in hotels, bellmen, barbers, boot-blacks, porters, janitors in stores and apartment houses have been taken from Negroes. Whites have supplanted them." Dancy also reported that jobs that were not necessarily marked as exclusively African American, but that had been a source of employment for black Detroiters, were also being lost by black workers. "One store here," he explained, "has dismissed all of its colored help and replaced them with whites."[17]

This trend cut across almost all forms of black employment. White women who could not find factory work turned to household service jobs to make ends meet, displacing black domestic workers. Many middle- and working-class families who had employed domestic workers during the 1920s saw hiring household workers as a luxury they could not afford during the Depression, shrinking the number of available positions. Furthermore, wages for domestic workers stagnated or dropped to as little as one dollar a day, and unemployment among African American women soared. African American men did not fare better. More than half of all black male skilled and semiskilled workers lost their jobs between 1930 and 1936.[18] Job placements for men and women made through the DUL illustrate the extreme effects of economic retraction on African American workers. In 1925, the league found employment for more than 3,500 women, mostly as domestic workers, and for almost 1,500 men. The organization also convinced four companies—Packard, Lincoln, Murray Body, and Dodge—to create whole "new departments for colored men."[19] By 1931, the DUL's placement numbers had plummeted to only 764 women and 318 men—but many of these jobs were part-time and temporary, not much better than total unemployment.[20] Despite media coverage of unemployment as a problem for sympathetic white men at risk of corruption by the undeserving poor, in reality unemployment was a much more severe problem for African Americans than for whites.

The Negro Advisory Committee, Discrimination, and the Limits of Racial Liberal Ideology

Frank Murphy's mayoral administration welcomed African Americans into the emerging welfare state as recipients of aid and, on a limited basis, as participants in producing public institutions. However, African Americans' most important concerns—about discrimination and full access to local citizenship—were often sidelined, illustrating their ambiguous relationship to the liberal government.[21] Rather than downplaying relief and unemployment as previous mayors had done, Murphy drew attention to them, and to the committees and policies created to address them. Consequently, relief rolls grew significantly during his mayoral campaign and after his election.[22] In his first action after he became mayor, Murphy set up the Mayor's Unemployment Committee (MUC) to register the unemployed, produce support for his relief programs, and help coordinate private and public welfare into a coherent, citywide program. The Common Council granted the committee $35,000 to cover its "overhead and working expenses" for its first six months, a minuscule sum for the task it was assigned, but enough to begin its project. The committee was separated into divisions, including a relief committee, an "employment regularization" committee, a committee that worked with employment agencies, one that dealt with publicity, another that managed public works projects, one that provided legal aid, and one for overseeing the state's relationship to African Americans, the Colored Advisory Committee, which African Americans called the Negro Advisory Committee (NAC).

African Americans were the only ethnic or racial group that had their own committee, which means that Murphy recognized the division between white and black as a social distinction with important political consequences. Murphy's choice to create the NAC suggests that he was making a conscious effort to draw black leaders into his government and to address African American concerns explicitly. The NAC, the only MUC subcommittee that was not responsible for administering a government program, was designed to "act as the voice of the local colored people in making suggestions, requests or recommendations to the Mayor's Unemployment Committee." However, the official explanation of its goals illustrates that its purpose was conflicted. It was designed both to monitor discrimination in the administration of relief and to quell what it identified as unfounded fears on the part of African Americans that they were experiencing discrimination. A report on the organization and activities of the MUC explained:

> The colored people have been anxious to assist in the work of the Committee and desire to have representation in the relief and unemployment activities, etc. Misunderstandings and unfounded claims of discrimination are avoided or eliminated by clearing all such questions through the Colored Advisory Committee, which makes reports, and offers suggestions and recommendations to the General Committee.[23]

African Americans on the committee thus received an unprecedented voice in city government at the same time that, among their principal responsibilities, they were encouraged to subdue criticism of discrimination.

Detroit's liberal Depression-era government articulated egalitarian ideals that would become integral to New Deal racial liberalism. These included an explicit commitment to care for the needy, regardless of race or nationality, as well as an effort to work with African American leaders on strategies for addressing black concerns. However, city leaders also developed a stance toward African Americans that presaged another side of the New Deal state. While they used the liberal language of equal opportunity to distinguish themselves from the conservatives whose explicit commitment to racism they disdained, their programs both allowed for the sustenance of existing racial stratification and frequently denied the legitimacy of black concerns about discrimination. Liberal architects of the local welfare state were certainly constrained by pressure from conservatives, but as close attention to their practices illustrates, they sustained their own reservations about designing programs that would target African Americans as recipients of aid. They were also suspicious of black claims about discrimination. Furthermore, while some white liberals were able to see that individual African Americans were the targets of discrimination, few recognized racism as an institution that structured African American access to resources, and many cast African Americans' disproportionate poverty as an indication of a problem internal to blacks themselves.

This simultaneous recognition that discrimination could be a problem and the dismissal of its seriousness were part of the Murphy administration's approach to managing demands African Americans made for fair treatment. For example, Elva Forncrook of the Mayor's Unemployment Committee dismissed John Dancy's concerns about three African American clerical workers in her office. Dancy, the executive secretary of the Detroit Urban League, complained that the black women were not being paid, while white women in the same office were. Forncrook responded indifferently. The black women, she explained, had not asked for compensation, which is why they were not receiving it. Forncrook did not attempt to contradict Dancy's suspicion that the black women were the only unpaid clerical staff, nor did she offer to begin to pay them.[24]

G. Hall Roosevelt, head of the Mayor's Unemployment Committee and a prominent white liberal in the city, was even more dismissive about discrimination against African Americans. When the Reverend D. W. Wade, president of the Civilization and Information Club, complained that African Americans were having difficulty accessing relief, Roosevelt calmly explained that the NAC was investigating all reports of discrimination against African Americans, but none was proving to have merit. "No such discrimination," Roosevelt declared, "is being practiced." Roosevelt graciously urged Wade to call "any specific cases to our attention" but quickly reasserted that there was a minimal likelihood that they would discover anything more than "minor instances of such discrimination." Cynically, Roosevelt concluded that he was "as anxious as you to see that all people are treated with the same degree of attention."[25] Like Blain's declaration of his interest in caring for African Americans, this closing remark represented Roosevelt's effort to sidestep critique. He pronounced his commitment to race neutrality at the same time that he dismissed the possibility that African Americans faced discrimination.

R. A. Phillips, the mayor's assistant, agreed with Forncrook and Roosevelt that discrimination was not a significant problem. He also expressed clear antipathy toward African Americans seeking relief. Phillips explained to G. Hall Roosevelt that he was frustrated by the deluge of requests coming from African Americans who "daily congregate in the mayor's outer office, seeking immediate relief, jobs, clothing, etc." In a dramatic illustration of his revulsion, he claimed to have seen vermin crawling on the clothes of an African American woman. He described her as "typical of those who stop in this office," suggesting that poor African Americans were dirty, unable to take care of themselves, and likely to spread their filth onto anyone who came into contact with them, since insects could jump from black bodies onto white ones. Philips concluded that segregating services for white and black recipients was the best way to quell African American complaints of ill-treatment. "It might be wise," he advised, "to set up a relief organization to divorce whites from colored. In this way, those colored organizations who are now deluging this office with their letters of complaints regarding treatment of their race and discrimination against them when given relief from the Welfare Department, would be silenced."[26] This internal letter sustained a different tone than Roosevelt's exchange with Wade, an African American activist. Forncrook, Roosevelt, and Phillips were strategic about how they expressed their concerns and reservations about African Americans, black protest, and segregation. Ultimately, their actions and correspondence illustrate that they were frustrated by African American demands for equality, interested in segregation as a solution to racial tensions, and unable to recognize discrimination as a systematic problem. These attitudes were as much part of white liberals' racial ideas as were their proclamations about racial tolerance, understanding, and neutrality. White leaders' actions suggested that African

American deficiencies, *not* government racism, determined the logical limits of state largesse. In this period, northern racial liberalism came to define the gap between explicit promises that state aid would be administered fairly and the actuality of racially differential access to resources.

Murphy's limited commitment to racial equality was mirrored in the contradiction between his proclamations about building a new political order and his limited implementation of changes in urban governance that aligned well with his rhetoric. His appointments to the MUC and his maintenance of fiscally conservative policies when dealing with nonrelief spending show how little his administration would veer from the priorities of the existing political, economic, and racial hierarchies. Murphy announced that his appointments represented "a true cross-section of the city's life," including "representatives of the business, social service, labor, racial, and church groups."[27] However, his MUC appointments more accurately reflected the city's power structure than a cross section of its population. Most of Murphy's appointees had substantial wealth and considerable political connections.[28] Only one factory worker served on the committee, and not a single unemployed person. Interestingly, the factory worker was African American and was one of the few black people to serve on the MUC who was not also on the Negro Advisory Committee.

While Murphy expressed a commitment to liberalism on a philosophical level, his appointments betrayed his belief that governments could be run effectively only by elite experts, even when their priorities were both conservative and antirelief. For example, Murphy tapped G. Hall Roosevelt to head the MUC and serve as the city controller. Roosevelt, a prominent local banker, was also a former General Electric executive. While he was an influential member of the Democratic Party, he supported fiscal conservatism and pushed, alongside other bankers, for the city to prioritize repaying its loans over relief expenditures. His sister was Eleanor Roosevelt, which made him brother-in-law to New York governor and soon-to-be-president Franklin D. Roosevelt. All of the men Murphy picked to sit on the MUC's three-person board of trustees, which oversaw the committee's budget, were bankers. Prominent businessmen served as chairpeople for MUC committees, including men from the Michigan Manufacturers Association and the local Employers' Association, as well as other bankers.[29] All but three of his major appointees were connected to banks or corporations "notoriously hostile to liberalism of any sort."[30] In response to criticism, Murphy explained that he would have been glad to pick liberals as his assistants, but he "found few of them qualified for the positions to be filled."[31] Murphy sought votes from the working class but relied on and looked to local power leaders to govern, a decision he made because he genuinely believed in those aspects of conservatives' vision that prophesied problems if business interests were challenged too boldly.

White liberals' ambivalence about challenging existing hierarchies was reflected in their approach to racial liberalism. While they defended the downtrodden, liberals did not use the state to substantially reorganize urban power along economic lines. Instead, they expanded access to some state resources beyond their traditional recipients at the same time that they left many existing economic hierarchies unchallenged and thus intact. Similarly, although liberals defended the rights of African Americans and promoted race-neutral language, they did not use government institutions to reorganize power along racial lines. They celebrated their defense of universal access to state programs—in contrast to the racial exclusion they rejected—but did not design strategies that were oriented toward reversing existing racial inequalities, thereby leaving them intact as well.

Those men and women who disagreed with Murphy's interest in expanding the welfare state continued to attack him and his programs, even though he worked hard to appease them. They implied that Murphy's policies favored the city's undeserving poor at the expense of the hardworking. Conservatives conjured images of contemptible men and women exploiting an overly generous and easily defraudable system. All of their stock characters had a damnable or deviant quality that excluded them from sympathy: sexuality, family organization, citizenship, politics, criminal histories, or blackness. Like these other figures' reliance on state aid, conservatives cast African Americans' need for assistance as an intractable cultural deficiency, neither the product of hard times nor an effect of discrimination. They claimed to be defending all of Detroit's residents, including upstanding African Americans, against excess and dishonesty. At the same time, they sustained a cynically race-neutral rhetoric, mostly avoiding the explicitly racist language of organizations like the KKK. Conservatives' attacks on the

MUC focused on labor issues, the power of workers' organizations, and proposed regulations for industry. None of these concerns was solely connected to the city's black residents, but race played a central if not always explicit role in debates over Murphy's liberal policies.

Over conservatives' objections, the relief budget expanded to unprecedented proportions in the first few months of Murphy's tenure as mayor. In December 1930, Murphy's third full month in office, relief expenditures soared to $1.65 million per month, and the DPW served almost 40,000 families. While some residents may have decided to apply for relief because Murphy promoted government programs, most were driven to the DPW by the state of the economy. Factory employment hit an eight-year low that month. Detroit was unique in its continuing generosity to those residents who qualified for relief. In 1930, its total relief expenditures outpaced all other cities in the country except for New York, which spent less than twice as much as Detroit even though its population was more than four times as large.[32]

Over the same period, tensions between liberals and conservatives on the MUC grew. While all parties involved stressed that they were working to address the needs of the unemployed and help manage the mounting crisis, divisions surfaced between representatives from banks and employers' groups on the one hand, and labor and social service organizations on the other. Labor groups complained that industrialists were trying to use the committee as a placement service designed to hire nonunion workers at less than prevailing rates in the skilled trades. Businesspeople, conversely, objected to labor representatives' ideas about regulating industry, arguing that they could make the best decisions without government or labor groups' interference. They had little interest in discussing unemployment in a public forum, revealing their wage rates, explaining their hiring practices, or opening their books to scrutiny. These tensions culminated in December 1930, as the relief budget expanded, and only three months after the MUC was established. Frank X. Martel, the head of the Detroit Federation of Labor and a member of the advisory committee, proposed a resolution calling for a five-day workweek. Labor delegates and social service representatives supported the measure, which passed since they held a majority on the advisory committee. In a dramatic show of disgust, conservatives walked out of the meeting. In response, Murphy appointed five new publicly antiunion industrial leaders to the committee, declaring that "labor is not going to use me in an attempt to organize Detroit."[33]

A thinly veiled attack on the MUC and the city's liberal leadership, linking the expansion of city services to undeserving African Americans, appeared in the conservative *Detroit News* just a few days after business leaders walked out of the MUC. The article, a condescending portrait of Alex G. W. Rivers, an African American messenger for Mayor Murphy and the MUC, suggested that there were sinister connections between African Americans and the committee—a damning claim at a moment when it looked to some observers like liberals might wind up in complete control of the committee. The piece provided a viciously sarcastic and patronizing portrait of Rivers. The reporter, Clifford Epstein, was ostensibly attempting to elicit Rivers's thoughts about the state of the economy. His language mimicked the style that reporters used when interviewing important and busy city leaders, all the while making it abundantly clear that this was meant ironically. "Mr. Rivers," Epstein mocked, "caught on the wing on one of his numerous daily excursions between the Mayor's office and the headquarters of the Unemployment Committee, consented to grant a short interview on the aspects of the times."[34] Rivers's self-perception, the reader understood, was both overblown and laughable.[35]

Epstein suggested that Murphy and the MUC were building a political machine designed to grant African Americans favors that would dangerously shift the balance of racial power from white toward black and that were not even needed by black people themselves. Rivers, for example, had been well-off before he started working for the city. He was the personal assistant to Ty Cobb, a famously racist baseball player for the Detroit Tigers.[36] The comments that Epstein attributed to Rivers read like a primer in how to pique white anxieties about African Americans. All of Rivers's quotes, which were written in dialect, gave the impression that he was ambitious and politically savvy, and that he, like other African Americans, saw Murphy's mayoralty as a source of political opportunity. For example, Rivers explained that "when Mis' Murphy done got himself dat Mayor's job, Ah says to mahself, 'Aleck, dere's de man fo' yo' to hitch yo' wagon to. Dere's de basket for' yo' eggs.'" Epstein's minstrelized caricature of Rivers suggested that African Americans were freeloaders rather than victims of the Depression, interested in the unemployment committee to receive political favors, not because they were in need of support. Epstein also sent a message to African Americans. Do not try to gain more municipal power, he suggested, because your reward would be humiliation. The *News* included two photographs of Rivers, one captioned "Alex, Messenger," and the other "Alex, Mascot."

Local Citizenship and Transients

Epstein's racist portrait of Alex Rivers illustrates how conservatives linked relief efforts and the expansion of the local government to African Americans and to the disruption of the city's racial balance of power. Conservatives like Epstein and Blain used inflammatory representations of African Americans profiting from state largesse in order to attack liberal programs and undermine the notion that an expansive welfare state was in everyone's best interest. Liberals, meanwhile, had their own motives for depicting African Americans in less than flattering ways. Liberals, unlike conservatives, wanted to build a more robust welfare system and a larger local government. However, they were decidedly *not* interested in building a socialist state or in promoting any policies that might radically redistribute wealth or upend the racial order of things. Liberals were interested in saving capitalism, in part by keeping the class system intact. That system—in the United States in general and Detroit in particular—was a deeply racialized one. Maintaining capitalism thus meant, in part, maintaining racial inequalities. While conservatives used African Americans to represent the dangers of a state-sponsored welfare system, liberals used representations of African Americans to mark the limits of their willingness to implement change. Such representations allowed liberals to make claims about how they could expand the state without producing the kind of radical racial equality that many feared would undermine the structures of local power.[37]

In the beginning of the Great Depression, Detroit's liberals and city managers expressed these concerns through the language of residency. This seemingly race-neutral language masked implicit links they made between dependency, transience, and African Americans on the one hand, and residency, citizenship, and white Detroiters on the other.

White city leaders did not call African American claims to *American* citizenship into question. Rather, they implicitly denied black assertions that African Americans' *local* residency was legitimate and long-term, and that black Detroiters thus deserved the rights and resources conferred on local citizens. Welfare workers articulated concerns about nonresidents taking up city resources that should be reserved for "Detroit citizens." Murphy's assistant, R. A. Phillips, for example, wondered whether "most of our charitable cases which are receiving city aid" were not from out of town, "making it hard for the Detroit citizens of long standing and deserving of aid to receive quick and immediate relief."[38] These concerns about transients informed decisions about city resources from the start of the Depression.

Concerns about literal citizenship animated anti-immigrant feeling in Detroit during this period, inspiring Michigan's 1931 Alien Registration Act and other measures.[39] However, state and industrial practices of the early 1930s also helped racialize distinctions between local residents and "transients" regardless of citizenship. Hysteria about Mexican Americans taking jobs and resources from rightful white locals, for example, was reinforced by the federal government's deportation of a huge portion of Detroit's Mexican-descended residents, many of whom were American citizens.[40] Department of Public Welfare policies and practices also helped reinforce the idea that whites were the city's most valued and legitimate residents. The department's policy mandated that a person receiving relief had to have been a Detroit resident for at least a year. If she had not, the DPW would provide carfare or other means of transportation to return her to her place of legal residence. These policies were originally instituted in the 1920s, when controversies over their racially disparate implementation initially emerged. However, they became newly visible and politically important during the Depression. Under this system, long-term, foreign-born, noncitizen residents were eligible for relief, but native-born, citizen families from outside Detroit were not.[41] DPW officials were so committed to this approach that they appealed to the state legislature to increase the time required to establish legal residence in Michigan so that Detroit did not have to provide for so many members of the "transient population." Under current laws, the DPW protested, people who had "come here during peak periods of employment and who have been able to maintain themselves for the year" were taking relief away from longtime residents.[42]

This concern about transients had particularly important consequences for African American relief recipients and for local ideas about the relationship between blackness, dependency, and permanence. By the 1930s, the term "transient" was already racially laden; through the 1920s, white journalists, social workers, and city officials cast all African Americans as recent migrants and outsiders in the city's life. Two-thirds of African Americans living in Detroit in 1930 had indeed arrived since 1920, but migration slowed down considerably by 1928. By 1931, very few African Americans failed to meet the DPW residency requirement. Still, journalists and city managers consistently linked African Americans to migration and the South. An article in the *Free Press* in April 1931, for example, referred to African Americans as "permanent transients" and described the city's largest African American enclave as the area "in which most of the so-called 'transient' families are located."[43] Meanwhile, whites—from the South, from rural areas in Michigan and the Midwest, and from other countries—though they represented 85 percent of in-migrants to Detroit over the course of the 1920s, were much less likely to be identified as "transients." White migrants escaped this moniker because they blended into white city life. They did not face the structural obstacles to employment that African American migrants did, and they integrated easily into established white neighborhoods based on class, not migration status. African Americans, conversely, lived in segregated areas with high-majority African American populations, which were high-majority migrant.[44] Black leaders also contributed to concerns about non-Detroiters coming to the city looking for handouts. African American leader John Dancy, who was a member of the MUC's Publicity Committee and head of the Detroit Urban League, explained that he was working to tell the world that "Detroit was only taking care of her own." He was not attempting to connect African Americans to dependency and knew that very few African Americans moved north once the Depression began. But he was reinforcing the notion that transients did not have a legitimate hold on local resources.[45]

The sense that African Americans were "outsiders" served to intensify suspicion of their reliance on city relief. Soaring unemployment among African Americans meant that blacks were overrepresented on the relief rolls.[46] Once Murphy took office, the disproportionately high numbers of African Americans on relief became more noticeable. Murphy's unemployment committee began to place relief recipients on "jobs created for the purpose of relieving unemployment," mostly as common laborers in various city departments. According to the employment manager of the MUC, nearly half of the men sent out to work in these jobs were African American. Dancy doubted that the numbers were so high, based on what he saw "on the street," but he did confirm that a "goodly portion of the men sent out have been Negroes." City relief workers were very visible as recipients, since they worked on public projects located outdoors or in municipal buildings and spaces. Many white Detroit residents concluded that African Americans were benefiting disproportionately from the work program. The real explanation for the demographics of relief workers—the massive occupational discrimination that left so many African Americans unemployed in the first place—was far less visible. Though plenty of white workers took advantage of city relief, the high proportion of African Americans in this group helped bring the charge of "freeloading" upon them. The very use of city relief to which they were entitled as city residents served to make African American Detroiters seem even more divided from whites, cast not as citizens but as local dependents.[47]

Trends in personnel policies among industrialists throughout the city also encouraged a division between Detroit citizens (figured as white) and transients (figured as African American). Plants conducting layoffs reserved jobs for white men with seniority, and African Americans with seniority frequently lost their jobs to white men with less time in the same plant. Meanwhile, industrial employers with all-white workforces generally hired new workers from the pool that had already been employed in their plants, cutting black workers out of industrial employment.[48] These practices helped mark all African Americans as "transients" who were less rooted in their jobs and without a legitimate claim to employment. Foremen's and personnel managers' consistent decision to lay off black workers first and rehire them last meant that African Americans were visibly excluded from industrial work in ways that other city residents were not.

Frank Murphy's policies and pronouncements helped reinforce this divide. In 1931, he proclaimed that "Detroit should be for Detroit business men and Detroit workmen first." He announced a new requirement that public employees had to live in the city and declared that city contracts would be awarded to Detroit-based firms as long as he was mayor. Although he reneged on his plan to contract exclusively with local companies due to pressures to economize, Murphy's protectionist impulses articulated and reinforced the social and cultural divide emerging between Detroit citizens and others. The public works committee of the MUC, designed to study avenues to expand public improvements and employ a "maximum number" of men on city projects, also helped enforce this distinction. Its "typical activities," an MUC report explained in January 1931, included "the investigating of reports that contractors on public jobs hire out-of-town workmen and persuading such employers to hire only Detroit residents."[49] Ultimately, local citizenship acquired a new political resonance during the first part of the Depression that helped mark distinctions between legitimate, white, Detroit citizens and transients, a category that became linked to African Americans. Detroiters, this logic implied, may be down on their luck, but they had been contributing members of society before the crash; transients did not have access to resources because they had not previously contributed to the city. Preexisting ideas about white and African American access to local resources were thus reinforced and reshaped by these new political identities: the working white resident and the undeserving transient, most likely to be African American.

"Taxpayers," Race, and Citizenship

In the early 1930s, local citizenship came to be intertwined with another heavily racialized identity—that of the "taxpayer." This designation grew, in part, out of Detroit's financial crisis, exacerbated by the Depression but originally caused by the city's disastrous and debt-producing overdevelopment of the previous decade.[50] Under pressure from real estate developers, Detroit had annexed a massive amount of land, almost tripling in physical size between 1916 and 1930.[51] Realtors joined forces with white, middle-class families and with the Detroit

Board of Commerce to push for the city to pave streets, extend sewers, erect electrical lines, and maintain infrastructure in sections owned by developers even before homes were built.[52] African American residents of newly annexed land were far less likely to benefit from this sort of investment; they did not have the political power to win improvements. The Eight Mile–Wyoming district, for example, a destination for African Americans who bought small parcels of land and built their own homes over time, received almost no infrastructure development or city services even after many residents had moved in.[53]

The local government stopped borrowing in 1927, when construction dropped and unemployment rose in a year that foreshadowed the impending crisis. By 1930, the city's debt had climbed to $350 million, but it did not become a major political issue until the Depression hit and the city began to face possible bankruptcy. Detroit held the second-highest per capita debt of the twenty-six "leading cities" of the United States. Unpaid taxes also soared in 1930 to 15 percent of all taxes levied, contributing to these concerns. Calls for fiscal responsibility animated the mayoral campaign of August 1930; all of the candidates (except the Communist Party's Philip Raymond) promised to reduce the city's budget and maintain low taxes.[54] During this time, Detroit residents and city officials began to use the figure of the "taxpayer" to describe local residents who were contributing to the city's resources and who should have a say in how those resources were distributed. Like transients, "taxpayers" were not explicitly defined by race. However, self-identified taxpayers racialized themselves as white and "tax-spenders" as African American in their activism. Ironically, the core of taxpayer activism was rooted in the newly developed, all-white neighborhoods that had sent the city into the red in the first place. Spending on relief never accounted for more than 15 percent of the annual budget, a far smaller portion than debt repayment, which climbed to 45 percent by 1932. But the city's indebtedness due to development was invisible in public discourse, which cast relief as the source of the problem, rather than the pro-growth policies that had benefited Detroit's self-identified white taxpayers.

Detroit's conservatives were more likely to suggest that taxpayers were being overburdened by the city's expanding welfare programs, but liberals also used this language to define the outer limits of their support for the welfare state or to distance themselves from communist advocates of wealth redistribution. In their private communications, city managers in the Murphy administration, including members of the MUC, aptly articulated the social and cultural divide that liberals drew between taxpayers and indigents. They cast taxpayers as the most worthy recipients of aid, linking them to long-time residents and differentiating them from needy "transients." For example, one month after Murphy took office, in October 1930, R. A. Phillips requested advice from G. Hall Roosevelt about how to manage the droves of people who were coming into the mayor's office looking for help. "Please bear in mind," he reminded Roosevelt, "that the majority of cases coming to this office are citizens who have been prosperous tax-payers for years, and in no sense of the word charitable cases."[55] By extension, non-taxpayers were less deserving of state aid, like the African American woman whom Phillips described as crawling with vermin. Liberals formulated a mythic taxpayer who was fiscally conservative, especially about relief, and deeply hostile to any policies that could be cast as state-sponsored wealth redistribution. This allegorical character justified policies oriented toward reining in spending on public relief. The MUC's public works committee, for example, would only make recommendations "with due regard to efficiency, economy, and the prerogatives of tax-payers."[56]

By the spring of 1931, criticisms of the MUC and of relief expenditures began to build. Popular concerns focused on swindlers defrauding the welfare department. One journalist summarized these criticisms succinctly. "Councilmen and others," he declared, were complaining "that many of those obtaining relief from the City are living happily at the taxpayers' expense."[57] Thus, Detroit residents who did not rely on public relief were especially likely to express their concerns about mounting welfare costs in terms of the tax burden it created for them. A DPW report from 1931 defended the agency from accusations that it was giving aid to the undeserving poor, offering a portrait of popular ideas about welfare in its effort to dispel them. The DPW explained that the "Public" had begun to connect its concerns about welfare cheats to anxieties about taxes and public spending. The report explained that "unworthy" recipients were a small minority of those on relief, but that the "Public" had become increasingly focused on this issue. "Stories of those unworthy of relief were widespread," the report explained, and with "the possibility that there would be an inevitable increase in the tax rate if relief expenditures continued, the Public feeling toward relief changed and the attitude that too much assistance was being given became prevalent."[58] As the DPW report illustrates, many of the city's liberal managers supported the expansion of the welfare state and called its critics to task for mischaracterizing and demonizing relief. At the same time, other liberal politicians shared some of the antistate sentiment of their conservative contemporaries. This tension played out as a contradiction that sat at the heart of local liberal governance.

Self-identified taxpayers appealed to the mayor to recognize the connection between relief spending and taxes. These letters portrayed Detroit "taxpayers" as Detroit citizens, and nontaxpayers, including relief recipients and municipal employees, as undeserving parasites. For example, a group of rental property owners described themselves as "taxpayers in the city of Detroit" when they appealed to Mayor Murphy in June 1931 to reimburse them for "housing destitute families and individuals." The letter writers compared themselves favorably to the welfare recipients living in their buildings. "We, the undersigned," they explained, "are not indigent families receiving aid from the welfare under false pretense, but humble taxpayers, some in dire need." For example, they continued, "one of the signers was deprived of past due rent," while her or his tenant was "given a food check, milk tickets, and the rent guaranteed elsewhere." Ultimately, they concluded, their taxes were "helping to support this welfare while we suffer."[59] Unlike these welfare cheats, taxpayers were contributing to civic society. In March 1931, C. C. McGill, secretary of Detroit's Board of Commerce, echoed these ideas. "It is ridiculous," he argued, "to think of spending money that our citizens do not possess." He portrayed city employees as lazy freeloaders and argued that relief recipients should work for their benefits.[60]

The power of the taxpayer in Detroit emerged out of the very real fiscal crisis, but it also came from largely social and cultural beliefs about money and who paid taxes that were intimately connected to ideas about citizenship and race. The vast majority of taxes collected by the city were levied on real estate, which meant that owners of residential and commercial buildings had the most direct contact with tax collectors. The taxpayers' movement portrayed homeowners as the only private citizens in the city who were paying taxes, since they were the ones who handed tangible money over to the government—city income taxes did not begin until 1964. But one could easily argue that renters paid property taxes through their rent. Snow Flake Grigsby, a black activist, made just such a claim. He argued that owners of apartment buildings were not taxpayers at all, since the money they paid in taxes came out of money earned from rent they collected from their tenants.[61] The idea that property owners were the only taxpayers was a powerful fiction that shaped arguments made by "taxpayers" about who was a contributing member of society and who was not. Citizenship, taxpayers suggested, required ownership; renters were not contributing to the city's coffers, and if they came to rely on relief, they were merely dependents who had never really contributed to the city. This ideology largely excluded African Americans as taxpayers because they owned the fewest parcels of private property in the city, but it also excluded the vast majority of whites—more than 80 percent of all city residents were renters. It was also problematic because it misrepresented who was playing the lion's share of the city's taxes. Owners of single-family homes, who became synonymous with "taxpayers" in public discourse, paid one-quarter of all taxes levied by the city between 1929 and 1931. Owners of property worth more than $110,500, which represented only 2 percent of all taxed parcels, paid half of the city's taxes. These larger properties were almost all factories, owned by the city's elite.[62]

By the middle of 1931, when it became clear that the Depression would persist, support for Detroit's comparatively generous welfare benefits began to wane. City officials cut city funding for relief, developed a new prioritization scheme for who could receive benefits, and began kicking families and individuals off of the rolls. Their belt-tightening coincided with an explosion of language about taxpayers' rights, transients, and tax cheats. In April 1931, for example, welfare commissioners substituted food orders for cash payments in an effort to clamp down on cheating and ensure that recipients could not spend city money on anything unnecessary. In July, the Common Council imposed a cap of $600,000 per month on the welfare department, which subsequently kicked 40 percent of families off of the relief rolls.[63] In June 1931, 46,000 families and individuals were on the relief rolls. By the end of that year, only 18,000 remained.[64]

Taxpayers came to play an important role in these decisions. For example, along with its plan to cut relief, the DPW imposed a "stringent program of verification . . . on all families under care." The agency began to require welfare recipients to collect documents verifying their legal residency in Detroit, number of dependents, and need for relief. This evidence had to be corroborated by a "disinterested citizen" and countersigned by a "taxpayer," making "disinterested citizens" and "taxpayers" representatives of the state and suggesting that they were indeed doling out their own money to relief recipients.[65] Murphy also absorbed the language that self-identified taxpayers used to describe the city's fiscal crisis. In his appeal for more federal aid to cities, for example, Murphy described Detroit's "$14,000,000 welfare burden [as having been] borne by 300,000 home-owners, many of them with modest homes and means."[66]

Even backers of Murphy, who supported the liberal expansion of the welfare state, expressed concerns about African Americans' access to public resources and cast black welfare recipients as the antithesis of white taxpayers. Anne M. Conrad, for example, described herself as generally skeptical of reports about welfare cheats, which she saw as efforts to "discredit the administration." She believed in what Murphy was doing, in general, but she simply could not doubt that African Americans were pilfering off of the system. Indeed, her concerns about fraud were specifically focused on black welfare recipients, and she saw it as her duty to report what she had heard to the mayor. A "carload" of "quite well dressed" "colored folks," she explained, were "driving up to a restaurant and paying for their meals with welfare checks." While Conrad supported welfare in principle, she imagined that these African American relief recipients were living well off of taxpayers' hardships. "It is the taxpayers," she argued, who "are scrimping and scraping to make ends meet in order to keep even." Rather than being disproportionately hurt by the Depression, she believed African Americans were unfairly profiting from the state aid they received.[67]

Criticisms of the DPW reached a fever pitch amid a series of scandals and controversies that were widely publicized by opponents of relief. A week after Commissioner Blain's proposal to save money by cutting the Herman Kiefer Hospital's maternity ward, police arrested Alex Lewis, a clerk at the DPW, who had embezzled more than $200,000 from the department. Lewis had been fabulously indiscreet about his new wealth, buying himself two new cars, and house, a boat, and a summer cottage in the space of a few months and bragging about his acquisitions while still working at his low-paying DPW job. Lewis's embezzlement was pounced on by opponents of relief, who had a field day denouncing government corruption and implying that most of the DPW's budget was going straight into the pockets of its employees or into the hands of freeloaders. Even though Lewis was not making a false claim for undeserved relief—he was literally embezzling money—his story was used to raise concerns about undeserving masses of people using loopholes in the government's welfare policies to amass their own little fortunes.[68]

As language about taxpayers proliferated and became more potent in the early 1930s, organizations formed around this identity in Detroit and cities across the country. These groups were closely linked to and funded by local real estate boards, though their populist political rhetoric obscured their connection to elites. They demanded restraint in government spending, attacking financiers and the poor, both of whom they cast as greedy parasites, attempting to profit from taxpayers' hard work. Rather than elected leaders, they suggested, middle-class white taxpayers were the rightful holders of municipal purse strings.[69] Detroit's taxpayer groups got their start organizing against Murphy's reelection in the fall of 1931. The November campaign was a referendum on public funding for welfare, with Murphy's opponent, former police commissioner Harold Emmons, arguing that private charities, rather than the local government, should fund and manage relief. While taxpayers' groups failed to achieve their goal—Murphy won with a two-thirds majority, and his allies took full control of the Common Council—they became players in both local and statewide politics.[70]

These organizations drew implicit links between "taxpayers" and whites, regardless of class. Frederick Wayne, the head of Detroit's Taxpayers' Protective Association, expressed the racism and elitism of local taxpayers' associations at a March 1932 Common Council hearing. Wayne called on the council to reduce property taxes by 25 percent and replace them with sales taxes and a five-dollar poll tax. The poll tax, he explained, could have a dual purpose: it could both raise money for the local government and "eliminate a lot of these group votes." The "large audience" of supporters "wildly cheered" in response to Wayne's proposals. The cheering audience knew that poll taxes were commonly used to disenfranchise blacks in the South since the late nineteenth century. Even if Wayne was not referring *only* to black Detroiters when he celebrated the prospect of eliminating "these groups" from politics, suggesting poll taxes as a device for the disenfranchisement of non-"taxpayers" was a clear reference to white supremacy.[71]

In the spring of 1932, the city's taxpayers' organizations were at the height of their popularity. The Association for Tax Reduction (ATR), an organization designed to coordinate the work of the local taxpayers' groups, began a drive to put a citywide referendum on the ballot designed to limit the budget of the municipal government. Campaigners argued that the proposal would root out "tax-spenders'" grip on local authorities at the same time that it would reduce taxes. ATR leaders distanced themselves from realtors and large property owners in their literature, but this rhetoric was dishonest; the group was funded and run by the Detroit Real Estate Board. Its leaders promoted the idea that everyone would benefit from lower taxes, especially small property owners, and that the city could handle lower taxes because it needed less government.[72] The local referendum failed in August 1932, but a statewide measure designed to cap real estate taxes at 1.5 percent of the taxable value of a property passed a few months later, in November 1932. This was a significant drop in levels of taxation.[73] Taxpayers' associations also launched high-profile campaigns against the city's public employees, characterizing them as horrible tax-spenders. However, relief functioned as an even more important target for their animus. Taxpayer activists, as well as city administrators, marked African Americans as the most extreme dependents in the city, the ones who would never enter into the ranks of the "taxpayer." Liberals and African Americans were the ultimate "tax-spenders."

The last two years of Murphy's administration were characterized by similar struggles over local resources and who had the right to access them, but those resources were never again as generous as they had been in the first year of his tenure. Murphy became increasingly beholden to the financiers he had appointed to his administration, and banks put more pressure on the mayor to restrict spending on social programs while servicing the city’s debt. Once the federal government began to fund relief, interest in tax reform waned. In 1932, the federal government finally provided some resources to cities in the form of food aid, which helped the DPW reduce its costs for food. Public employees’ wages and salaries had been cut significantly since the crisis began but remained a target of taxpayers’ organizations as long as relief was funded at the local level. The city depended on its own resources for almost all its costs through the middle of 1932, but by the end of that summer, relief funds distributed through the Reconstruction Finance Corporation became available to Detroit. The Reconstruction Finance Corporation provided the majority of funds to the welfare department, which spent almost $4 million on relief between July and December 1932.[74]

Racial Liberalism under the New Deal

By the end of 1932, Detroit continued to reel from the Depression, and it was unclear when or whether recovery would come. As the crisis deepened, symptoms of the vast social and economic dislocation became more and more visible across the city. Stores sat boarded up or empty. Previously bustling factories were idled, and formerly lively neighborhoods were devastated by evictions, mortgage foreclosures, and poverty. Men were “sleeping on newspapers—shoes off, washing feet, etc., in the very heart of the City.”[75] Jobless men, “speech-makers,” and “hangers-on” had become a constant presence in most municipal parks and were especially visible in Grand Circus Park, a downtown square that Mayor Murphy had designated one of two “public forums” in the city.[76] Approximately 750,000 people had inadequate food in Detroit in 1932. Four people a day were coming to the Receiving Hospital “too far gone from starvation for their lives to be saved.” In February 1932, firefighters’ salaries were cut drastically, which forced them to discontinue the fifty-eight breadlines they had been running on a volunteer basis since 1929. Fire stations had been having trouble accommodating the demand; 16,000 to 17,000 people had been eating in their soup kitchens and now needed to find new sources of help. In November, Murphy announced that women were “begging alms in the streets like men" and that burglary and larceny had increased dramatically since the year before.[77] Murphy's "victory garden" program had taken off, with more than 2,700 plots growing on twenty-seven fields scattered across the city. These gardens helped feed and occupy hungry and unemployed residents, but they also served as a stark visual reminder of the depths of despair in the city and an indication that Detroit's geography was changing in response to the economic crisis.[78] In January 1933, 40,000 families were on relief in Detroit, and well over 30 percent were African American.[79]

As the Depression deepened, white city leaders continued to explain persistent African American inequality as a product of nonracial characteristics that most—though not all—African Americans shared. They did not attempt to rein in racial discrimination or exclusion, neither of which they saw as their responsibility. Instead, while many sympathized with African American struggles to overcome discrimination, most also saw existing racial hierarchies as too entrenched to challenge. These ideas shaped the local administration of federal programs, which expanded dramatically after the New Deal began in 1933. For example, when the National Recovery Administration (NRA) set codes mandating minimum rates of pay, thereby raising the wages of the lowest-paid workers, employers across the city laid off hundreds of African Americans and replaced them with whites. As jobs that had been held by African Americans became dignified work because of their higher rates of pay, employers chose to protect the hierarchies on which the racially segmented labor market depended rather than raise African Americans' incomes.[80] Local officials refused to interfere with these arrangements, suggesting that they had no authority over private employment, even though the conceit of the NRA was that the state could be involved in setting private sector rates of pay. Indeed, government leaders generally accepted employers' explanations and dismissed black complaints of discrimination as overblown or unfounded. The managers of three hotels laid off more than 1 hundred black workers in response to the NRA codes, arguing that African Americans, many of whom had been there for years, were not "efficient" workers.[81] After appeals from John Dancy to address the problem, city officials remained silent. "It is astonishing," Dancy remarked sneeringly, "how quickly [African American workers] became inefficient after the establishment of the N.R.A.

codes."[82] Other managers explained their decision to replace African Americans with white workers as an effect of public pressure. One at Sears & Roebuck, for example, claimed that "public sentiment" forced him to dismiss three black men from the tire and battery department, even though the store was heavily patronized by black shoppers.[83] Again, NRA administrators made no attempt to forestall his actions or question his motives.

Race-based exclusion from employment remained a problem for African Americans in Detroit under the New Deal. Local administrators of federal programs, for example, seldom hired African American social workers or clericals even though many well-qualified candidates were available and applying for those positions.[84] Only two African Americans worked in the "Social Security or labor and employment service" by August 1937.[85] African Americans also had trouble when they tried to use the U.S. Employment Service (USES), a federal agency that placed unemployed workers into private sector jobs. Interviewers at USES offices tended to "assume that white workers were preferred to Negroes" and refused to send African Americans out for available jobs, even though few employers expressed preferences "regarding color, religion, race, or age." Ninety-eight percent of relief recipients who had found employment in private industry were "members of white races," an extreme underrepresentation of African Americans, since 25 percent of the relief caseload was black.[86] Black advisers—including John Dancy, state senator Charles Diggs, and Mrs. Mamie Bledsoe—pushed state officials to hire black interviewers in USES offices "in order to overcome any race prejudice or attempt at discrimination against the Negro applicant on the part of the staff members," but USES managers did not see their racial practices as problematic.[87] Indeed, white government leaders frequently advised African Americans to mute their complaints of discrimination. At the Conference on Negro Employment Problems in Michigan, Eugene Elliot, superintendent for the state's Department of Public Instruction, counseled African Americans to "restrain themselves even though they may be oppressed [because] the greater gain of simply living up to what we deem to be the American ideal of government will bring lasting results." Speaking at the same conference, Edward Jeffries, who would become mayor of Detroit, advised African Americans to be "less temperamental in relation to alleged discrimination." "I am not so sure," he explained, "that there is as much discrimination as I have many times heard it described."[88]

Most white liberals believed in a robust system of state support for the jobless and in race neutrality. However, they were likely to express concerns about black welfare recipients that mirrored conservative claims about public relief. They held different views of black and white joblessness, representing unemployed African Americans as an unneeded and burdensome surplus and whites as rightful local residents, worthy of aid. As John Dancy explained, "Many . . . white leaders" continued to insist that African Americans were merely transients and pushed for their return to the South "in order to take the relief burden off Detroit."[89] John Ballenger, for example, head of Detroit's Department of Public Welfare and a Democrat, maintained that "the Negro group" presented a "distinct and different picture" than "the native born, white American, . . . the foreign born [or] the alien." While one in twenty-five whites in the city was on relief, a staggering one in nine black residents received welfare. Ballenger saw this predicament as a product of African Americans' position in the local labor market and their recent history of migration to Detroit. African Americans had been called to local industries in the 1920s, he explained. "With the subsequent unemployment," however, "they became a labor reservoir to be maintained publicly until the demand for labor includes them."[90]

Ballenger understood that black workers were "laid off among the first and do not find their opportunity for re-employment until the other labor has been engaged." Rather than condemning this practice as discriminatory, however, he merely described it as standard. Even though whites had constituted more than 85 percent of the city's newcomers during the 1920s, Ballenger did not identify white southerners as a distinct class of welfare recipients. For him, they had shed their status as migrants and integrated successfully into white working-class culture. He did not see unemployed African Americans, conversely, as Detroiters.[91]

While Ballenger supported the public administration of welfare and defended relief recipients against charges that they were content to receive state aid, he cast African Americans, unlike whites, as perversely not humiliated by public handouts.[92] This was Ballenger's effort to carefully separate the worthy from the unworthy poor and define the limits of state aid.[93] At the same time that Ballenger expressed profound ambivalence about black welfare recipients, he oversaw the only local relief agency that hired African Americans in significant numbers. By 1937, thirty-five black caseworkers and investigators worked at the DPW, most of whom managed African American cases, although some oversaw relief recipients, and two supervised both black and white employees.[94] Ballenger's commitments and concerns illustrate that white liberals could simultaneously support welfare, ally themselves with middle-class African Americans seeking public jobs, and participate in demonizing African American welfare recipients as problems. Indeed, administrators of federal programs were unwilling to give African Americans, as a group, the resources they would qualify for as individuals if they were white. Relief officers were concerned that all African Americans would develop an expectation that their community deserved state support. According to this logic, blacks were positioning themselves to unfairly profit from federal largesse.

Conclusion

By the early 1930s, white liberals and conservatives had embraced the language of northern racial liberalism. While implicitly agreeing that baldly racist statements were unacceptable, they still linked dependence and welfare to blackness, at the same time that they tended to dismiss African Americans' concerns about discrimination. Conservatives demonized African Americans, caricaturing them as dependents and chronic freeloaders and decrying their potential to undermine the city's color line. They used this language to attack the expanding welfare state. Liberals were more committed to the principles of racial equality and to building a robust government apparatus. They were far less likely to use racist language in their public discourse, thus distancing themselves from the explicitly condescending language that figures like Alex Blain—the welfare commissioner who used minstrel caricatures to describe black newborn babies in 1931—deployed. They believed in a more expansive welfare state that would better support the needs of indigent residents, a large portion of whom were African Americans. At the same time, however, they made similar connections between African Americans, dependency, and fraud as their conservative counterparts. As relief administrators worked against the popular notion that all recipients of aid were leeching off of the system, they grafted this anxiety onto African Americans specifically. These links helped them define the limits of state largesse, defend themselves against demands for a more comprehensive welfare state, and dismiss African American accusations about discrimination. Ultimately, liberals helped produce a racially bifurcated definition of local citizenship that cast African Americans as culpable for their own poverty and thus less deserving of state resources than their white counterparts.

5

"Let Us Act Funny"

Snow Flake Grigsby and Civil Rights Liberalism in the 1930s

In February 1934, African American movie patrons prevented a white theater owner from firing a black ticket seller by threatening to boycott his cinema. The theater, located in the middle of the city's largest black neighborhood, had a majority–African American clientele. Its owner, unwilling to face a boycott, capitulated to moviegoers' demands within a few hours. "Colored people," he exclaimed, "are getting funny."[1] He thus suggested that the black protesters he encountered were part of a larger movement of African Americans newly willing to participate in collective fights for equal rights. Indeed, during the 1930s, African Americans mounted unprecedented challenges to urban inequality and subordination. Their protests, aimed at exposing and reversing discrimination, threatened the unself-conscious maintenance of the racially unequal status quo.

Fannie Peck, president of the local Housewives' League, had brought the cinema protest to the attention of the *Detroit Tribune*, a black-owned weekly that had just gotten its start. Peck had helped spearhead Detroit's early 1930s boycott movement and was likely to have been involved in the charge against the theater owner. *Tribune* editors celebrated the confrontational approach that moviegoers had adopted in their push to save the ticket seller's job. Ultimately, the editors argued, "getting funny" was exactly what African Americans needed. "If thinking, thinking for ourselves, thinking in our own interests, is going to put us in the category of 'getting funny,' then, we say, let us get funny, let us be funny, let us act funny."[2] This small labor and civil rights victory was significant, of course, for the woman who retained her job. More broadly, it was one of a series of organizing victories spearheaded by black Detroiters that contributed to African Americans' increasing visibility and galvanized a local spirit of protest—an inclination toward "getting funny."

An X-Ray Picture of Detroit

In late 1933, Snow Flake Grigsby published a pamphlet called *An X-Ray Picture of Detroit*. The pamphlet was a scathing condemnation of the extent to which African American Detroiters were excluded from public employment and an indictment of the city's established black leadership for lacking the political will to do anything meaningful about it. A drawing of the famous trio of "hear no evil, see no evil, speak no evil" monkeys appeared on the front cover. The image was a clear expression of Grigsby's disdain for a black leadership that he believed was failing African American Detroiters. Each of the monkeys held a sign identifying the group it represented. The first was "Negro Politicians, Urban League and Medical Society." The second was the "Local Branch NAACP," and the third was the city's "Civic and Christian Leadership." These groups, Grigsby suggested, were reluctant to hear or see the real problems that black residents faced in the city because they were not willing to confront the white leaders in positions of power. Grigsby accused black leaders of focusing their energy on cultivating the goodwill of white industrialists, philanthropists, and politicians, from whom they imagined they could cull favors and support. Because they considered their relationships with powerful whites as too important to jeopardize, Grigsby complained, the city's established black leaders were unwilling to mount overt challenges to discriminatory and segregationist policies or practices. They saw powerful whites as allies, not to be alienated by protest or by overly demanding appeals. Finally, below the monkeys, a caption asked rhetorically, "Is this silence perpetual?"

Grigsby used this pamphlet to announce his departure from the executive committee of the NAACP and to signal a change in the direction of black political engagement. The pamphlet also became a manifesto for his new group, the Civic Rights Committee (CRC), founded to take on fights that the local NAACP would not. The group used the rhetoric of democracy, mass mobilization, and public pressure to reinforce the newly emergent political style of the city's civil rights coalition—one

This image appeared on the cover of Snow Flake Grigsby's *An X-Ray Picture of Detroit*. Image courtesy of the Bentley Historical Library, University of Michigan.

that combined the militance of more radical organizations with a relatively moderate civil rights agenda. Instead of seeing white leaders as their patrons and southern black migrants as an unfortunate lot that needed to change, African Americans interested in the politics of confrontation, like Grigsby, believed that white institutions and compliant black leaders were what needed changing. Respect, he suggested, needed to be wrested out of the hands of the city's white establishment, rather than asked for politely. Grigsby and his allies worked to reshape popular ideas about citizenship, race, and community both within the black community and in the city at large in order to accommodate this new political vision.

Grigsby opened his *X-Ray Picture* with three claims about Detroit's African American residents:

1. That we are American citizens;
2. That we are entitled to the same consideration of all American citizens, regardless of race or color;
3. That we are taxpayers, directly or indirectly, as other American citizens.

He thus inverted the cultural, political, and racial meanings that white conservatives attributed to the concept of the "taxpayer" in Detroit, eliding taxpayer with citizenship. Rather than defining a small set of property owners whose rights to citizenship outpaced all others', Grigsby argued that the term "taxpayer" described all citizens and that each one of them deserved equal rights, resources, and opportunities. He urged black Detroiters to reject the notion that they were not taxpayers "unless they [paid] directly on real estate," an idea that "some white men have tried to make Negroes believe." Any renter, he explained, was a taxpayer, and because black residents paid "higher rent for inferior places," they carried a disproportionately high tax burden. Furthermore, he explained, the racial implications of the term "taxpayer"—the idea that taxpayers were white and nontaxpayers were not—were grossly misleading because more than 80 percent of all Detroit residents were renters, including the majority of native-born whites.[3]

Grigsby used statistical evidence about the prevalence of discrimination to draw attention to the gap between white liberal ideas and northern realities. White racial liberals painted a picture of northern discrimination as a relatively minor problem that affected individual African Americans when they confronted uniquely hostile whites. Grigsby used his numbers to undermine this sensibility and called on white leaders to rectify the structures that were producing segregation, discrimination, and black poverty. The first half of *An X-Ray Picture* was an exhaustive list of facts and figures demonstrating that African Americans held less than 10 percent of the jobs to which they were entitled according to their representation in the population. African Americans deserved 1,361 municipal jobs but held only 115. As a result, they had been denied $20 million in wages since 1923.[4] Grigsby focused on public employment because, he argued, African Americans deserved the same proportion of city jobs as their numbers in the city—7.6 percent.

The second half of the pamphlet was an indictment of the black elite for its disinterest in mobilizing African Americans to respond to these problems. Grigsby argued that the local NAACP was practically useless, with its low membership and its general inactivity. Furthermore, he claimed, black leaders had failed to organize black voters or adequately support black political candidates. "Our Negro political leaders, ministers, and particularly our Local Branch of the N.A.A.C.P. should bow their heads in shame for not putting on a constructive program," he argued. "Do we have the moral courage to take a definite stand, or is it easier to be a jelly-fish?"

African American Civil Rights Liberalism

African American political organizing in Detroit underwent a shift during the 1930s. Civil rights activists moved from cautious political engagement to more direct confrontation in their struggles for equality. Established black leaders had seen alliances with wealthy and powerful white men as the root of their political power since early in the century. A "new crowd" of activists emerged during the Depression that looked to public exposure, community organizing, and mass protest as better and more effective strategies. Led principally by recent southern migrants, these mostly younger activists pushed established organizations toward a more grassroots style and built their own political organizations.[5] In Detroit, this shift was both ambivalent and uneven. For many people, these two strategies for addressing African Americans' concerns—patronage politics and mass organizing—were not necessarily contradictory practices. In fact, what some black residents experienced as profound and irresolvable ideological differences, many others saw as complementary political approaches. For example, many people who supported Communist Party (CP) organizations, which used grassroots tactics and were oriented toward overthrowing capitalism, were also members of groups with radically different political goals, like the NAACP, or one of Detroit's many popular black nationalist organizations.

Detroit's civil rights coalition activists ultimately forged a popular front–style politics that accommodated strategies from a range of perspectives, including grassroots fights against white domination, efforts to push established leaders to "do the right thing," established connections with the city's wealthy, and efforts to build separate African American economic and business networks. This political coalition—rooted in a truce between groups with divergent beliefs about integration, black nationalism, capitalism, and communism—helped shape civil rights activism and northern racial liberalism in the city and defined the terms of the debate that black Detroiters engaged. As a group, they settled on a strategy that included alliances with white leaders as well as grassroots fights against white domination, segregation, and discrimination. Black Detroiters sustained alliances across generational and political divides at the same time that they engaged in sometimes bitter disagreements about how to fight for equality. Members of the "new" and "old" crowds both worked with and criticized white leaders. In Detroit, an informal civil rights coalition emerged that integrated mass action alongside a range of strategies designed to push white leaders to respond to black concerns.

African American civil rights liberals stood at the center of this spectrum. They participated in both ad hoc and ongoing protest organizations that emerged in the middle to late 1930s. Their activism relied on the premise that black activists could push white liberals to enact policies and develop practices designed to undermine racial inequality. These groups focused on exposing the contradictions between city leaders' ostensible commitment to justice and the deep inequalities that actually shaped race and class relations in Detroit. This interest in exposure was not new—black civil rights groups had worked to draw attention to racism and discrimination for generations. However, by the middle of the Depression, black civil rights liberals linked exposure with protest politics more and more consistently.

Black protest, alongside African Americans' growing political power in the electoral sphere, contributed to the formation of northern racial liberalism because it forced white leaders to address black concerns rather than simply ignoring them. White liberals saw themselves as having a strong commitment to racial equality in the political sphere. However, their use of racial liberal discourse could be quite cynical, since their support for black equality was often narrow. African American activists insisted that white city leaders recognize racial discrimination, inequality, and segregation as urgent urban problems. They called for a reorganization of institutions and urban power relations that would undermine white supremacy. But white liberals resisted this pressure, and even those who enthusiastically embraced the language of northern racial liberalism saw this approach as neither politically viable nor desirable. Their commitment to black rights did not extend as far as their black constituents believed it should.

Detroit's African American civil rights activists took white liberals' pronouncements about their commitment to race neutrality seriously. They did not, however maintain a naive faith in these proclamations, nor did they believe that white Detroit leaders would make the fight for racial equality a priority. Instead, they consistently worked to highlight the contradictions that animated northern racial liberalism at the same time that they saw northern racial liberal ideology as an available discourse they could use to support their claims within the city's political sphere. Black activists helped bolster the sense that racial liberalism was both politically relevant and well accepted in the city by pressuring white liberals to live up to their promises. They engaged in a range of battles for social, economic, and racial justice that drew on both radical and liberal forms of protest.

Over the course of the 1930s, middle-class, working-class, and unemployed black Detroiters made more consistent and successful demands on the growing and increasingly liberal state, using new strategies to fight for the promises of full urban citizenship. As the government grew larger and provided more benefits like relief, Detroit's black residents were more likely to engage in fights for equal access to state resources and for support from public institutions. In other words, as they gained more access to the public sector, African Americans pushed harder and more successfully for that access to be on equal footing with whites.

Compared with African American leaders in other northern cities, Detroit's black middle class was more politically conservative, more reserved about the promises of unionization, and more consistently Republican, a party affiliation that many sustained well into the 1930s. These positions reflected the political conservatism and widespread hostility toward unions among Detroit's broader elite. Wealthy white businesspeople, especially those connected to the automobile industry, maintained significant influence in local government. Detroit was famous for being an "open shop" town—industrialists were extremely successful at quashing union drives and keeping labor organizers out of their plants.[6] Henry Ford's patronage and his support for African American institutions, especially churches, combined with his aggressive hostility to unions, further encouraged black middle-class leaders to reject organized labor. Finally, predominantly white unions made little effort to recruit black members before the mid-1930s, frequently discriminated against African Americans, and maintained segregated locals. Some working-class African Americans were active union members, and others sustained a general interest in the principles of union organizing, but it was not until the late 1930s that African Americans came to align themselves more consistently with labor than with business interests.

More conventional black leaders focused on building alliances with whites. They believed that upstanding individuals could draw concessions from specific white leaders in exchange for favors, but nonelite blacks had little to offer, would be dismissed as troublemakers, and would undermine middle-class leaders' relationships with power brokers. They were interested in opening the doors of political power to educated and economically stable African Americans who were being shut out by virtue of their race. Socialists and communists, conversely, believed it was the masses—or the black working class—that should take over the reins of municipal power from the existing elite. Leftists imagined a radically democratic city structured by equality rather than capitalism and its attendant hierarchies. These activists participated in popular front politics both in their urban civil rights activism and within unions.[7] In spite of their ideological differences, however, members of these two groups, and those who held political positions between them, often worked together in the 1930s and ultimately helped change the center of black political discourse.

Civil rights liberals worked with and stood between these two camps. They embraced confrontational politics and believed that black protest was the only way to win real citizenship. They reasoned that a confrontational approach could deliver results because white leaders, as self-proclaimed upholders of fairness and equality, and as racial liberals, positioned themselves as caring about injustice and racism. Exposing racism, airing black complaints, and articulating indignation about inequality could and should move white leaders to take action. Ultimately, supporters of this approach believed that their cause was righteous and that their goals were politically possible, even if unlikely, within the current urban terrain. They saw white leaders as susceptible to mass-based pressure because racial liberalism was an important element of white liberal politics, even if it was often far weaker than black activists would have liked. For advocates of black protest, racial liberalism was an existing tenet of political discourse in Detroit. It was incumbent upon white city leaders to respond to black concerns in order to live up to their understanding of themselves. This assessment may have been more idealistic than realistic. But that idealism itself was an important difference and was based on the growing political importance of racial liberalism.

Rather than a comprehensive social history of African American protest in Detroit, this chapter examines civil rights liberals and considers their dialogue with white officials and established African American leaders. It will not closely examine black nationalist organizations, which, by the 1930s, had attracted many members in Detroit and were quite active in the city. These groups built businesses and organizations in both the formal and informal economies that were oriented exclusively toward the city's black residents and largely divorced from the public and private institutions of the larger city. Since the First Great Migration, black Detroiters had joined organizations that promoted economic self-help and black nationalism, like the Universal Negro Improvement Association, Spiritualist and Sanctified storefront churches, and the Nation of Islam, in very high numbers.[8] In 1922, Detroit boasted the second-largest UNIA chapter in the world, which had more than 5,000 members and could attract up to 15,000 to its meetings and parades. By the middle of the 1930s, the Nation of Islam had between 5,000 and 8,000 followers. These organizations worked toward building alternative African American institutions and encouraged their members to reject integration and disengage from urban whites. However, the overlap between nationalist and nonnationalist strategies for improving the lives of black Detroiters was far more significant in practice than it was in theory. For example, very few black Detroiters criticized the idea that African Americans should support black businesses, a key element of nationalist rhetoric. At the same time, only the most orthodox followers of economic nationalism rejected the idea that expanded access to state resources would benefit all African Americans, especially when federal money began to be channeled toward some nationalist priorities, like job training.

The work of the Detroit Housewives' League, founded in 1930 by Fannie Peck, as well as its brother organization, the Booker T. Washington Trade Association, provide local examples of nationalist organizations that embraced this syncretic approach. The Housewives' League promoted black businesses by organizing African American women to shop in black-owned stores and buy products made by black companies. This tactic was a two-pronged strategy designed to both support black entrepreneurs and create jobs for unemployed African American women and men who, the group reasoned, would work in positions created by the expansion of black business. The Housewives' League also offered black women tips on economizing as a way to help manage their limited resources.[9] While the group's principal work stressed economic nationalism, its members also engaged in fights to access state resources and battle discrimination in spaces that were not exclusively black. For example, the group proposed rent-control legislation as part of its platform, something that would affect all Detroiters. Its members also participated in boycotts of white businesses that refused to hire black workers. As the example of the Housewives' League illustrates, many Detroiters oriented toward economic nationalism simultaneously engaged in fights for racial equality without seeing a contradiction between these tactics. Furthermore, it illustrates that black nationalist organizations played an important role in emerging black protest movements that engaged white leaders and residents because they contributed to and reinforced a culture of institution building among the city's black residents.

Ultimately, the shift from patronage politics to confrontation was both ambivalent and uneven in Detroit. For many people, these two strategies for addressing African Americans' concerns were not necessarily contradictory impulses. In fact, what some black residents experienced as profound and irresolvable ideological differences, many others saw as political strategies that were complementary or, at least, that could be pursued simultaneously. Many people supported organizations like the Communist Party that used grassroots and street-level tactics to agitate for changes that would overthrow the current distribution of power and resources at the same time that they were members of the local NAACP, a group that resisted confrontation as a model for its own activism well into the middle of the decade. A number of ideologically contradictory political ideas could and did make sense to community members at the same time. This suggests that many black residents believed that the struggle for full local citizenship could be, and in fact needed to be, fought on multiple fronts. Political diversity was a central element shaping black civil rights coalition politics of the 1930s.

This change in orientation was built on a new set of assumptions about urban politics and racial liberalism. More conventional black leaders, who believed that building private and quiet alliances with white liberals was a more effective way to gain access to political power, sustained a less robust sense of the ability of African Americans to force compliance from the urban establishment. Whites in positions of power, they reasoned, would dismiss black protesters because white leaders did not care about racial inequality or black suffering. Individuals could draw concessions from specific white leaders in exchange for favors, but groups of nonelite blacks had little to offer and would be dismissed as troublemakers. Activists who embraced confrontational politics believed that black protest was the only way to win real citizenship for African Americans in the urban North. They reasoned that a confrontational approach to white leaders could deliver results because white leaders, as self-proclaimed upholders of fairness and equality, and as racial liberals, positioned themselves as caring about injustice and racism. Exposing racism, airing black complaints, and articulating indignation about inequality could and should move white leaders to take action. Ultimately, supporters of this approach believed that their cause was righteous and that their goals were politically possible, even if unlikely, within the current urban terrain. They saw white leaders as susceptible to mass-based pressure because racial liberalism was an important element of white liberal politics, even if it was often far weaker than black activists would have liked. For advocates of black protest, racial liberalism was an existing tenet of political discourse in Detroit. It was incumbent upon white city leaders to respond to black concerns in order to live up to their understanding of themselves. This assessment may have been more idealistic than realistic. But that idealism itself was an important difference and was based on the growing political importance of racial liberalism.

The New Politics of Confrontation

Middle-class African Americans who used the language of civil rights rather than reform or uplift to explain their activism developed their comparatively confrontational political style in Detroit in the 1920s. Not all black Detroiters felt comfortable challenging the institutional discrimination or exclusion that they encountered. However, those who did protest unfair treatment were acting on a community understanding, particularly common among economically stable black Detroiters by the late 1920s, that black residents shared ownership of Detroit's public resources with other residents. Thus, those women and men who challenged discrimination were publicly expressing the indignation shared by many African Americans.[10] This sense of permanence and ownership was built on the small but growing political power of middle-class African Americans. Although this power had been won through patronage-style politics, it empowered residents to make more clear demands on the state because it raised their expectations about progress. Seemingly small victories, such as the creation of the Mayor's Interracial Committee in 1926, helped more black residents identify the city government as a possible, though often reluctant, ally in the push for social and political equality. These victories created a generation of black residents who expected progress to continue.

Snow Flake Grigsby was emblematic of this new group of activists. Like the vast majority of African Americans living in Detroit in the 1930s, Grigsby was a migrant. He was born in Chatsville, South Carolina, in 1899 during a rare snowstorm (after which he was named) and moved north in 1923. Grigsby expected to find new forms of equality in Detroit and was disappointed when he immediately encountered discrimination.[11] Rather than give up on his vision of the urban North, however, he fought to make the city live up to his initial expectations. From the beginning, he was interested in taking white leaders to task for failing to abide by their articulated commitment to urban racial equality. By 1927, he was superintendent of the Sunday school at St. John's Presbyterian Church and used his position to organize a public speaker series, "Let's Know the Negro in Detroit." Ostensibly, Grigsby invited white city and civic leaders, including government officials and businesspeople, to give African American audiences their "unbiased views of the colored people." These popular forums, at least one of which attracted more than 2,000 people, were actually designed as an opportunity for African Americans to put white leaders on the spot, expose some of the contradictions between their rhetoric and their practices, and pressure them to extend more resources, opportunities, and access to African American Detroiters.[12] Grigsby took this spirit with him into all aspects of his life. In the late 1920s, he enrolled as a pharmacy student at the Detroit Institute of Technology (DIT), where he won his first fight against institutional discrimination. Grigsby had been required to take physical education at the African American branch of the YMCA rather joining his classmates at the Y's central branch. The school and the Y ultimately allowed him to join his classmates at the central branch but not "without a fight"; Grigsby took the case to a lawyer before the DIT or the YMCA would take him seriously.[13]

Grigsby graduated from the DIT in 1930, but he could not find a job as a pharmacist. Like many African Americans with professional degrees, he turned to public employment and found work as a clerk at the central post office, one of the few public institutions in Detroit that employed a significant number of black workers. As federal employees, postal workers did not have to take the city's civil service exam, which excluded almost all African Americans from municipal jobs. Grigsby was active in his union, the National Alliance of Postal Workers.

After he began working at the post office, Grigsby maintained his interest in fighting discrimination. He joined the executive committee of the local NAACP in 1931 and initiated a campaign against Detroit City College for its decision to rent space for swimming classes at a whites-only pool. Grigsby persuaded Walter White, head of the national NAACP, to speak at City College and raise the issue in his lecture. He also convinced L. C. Blount, secretary of the Detroit branch, to participate in negotiations with the school's dean. In his campaign, Grigsby placed considerable emphasis on the fact that City College was a *public* institution, arguing that African Americans maintained the same rights to city resources as all other municipal residents. In fact, Grigsby informed the dean that he would take the case to court "because the money used to pay for the pool was tax payer money." He thus suggested that African Americans were full citizens of Detroit, entitled to rights accorded to all other "tax payers."[14]

Grigsby's first two fights against institutional discrimination, at DIT and City College, were remarkably similar. In both cases, Grigsby based his strategy on the premise that racial liberalism was an accepted political stance among the city's elite. In other words, he relied on the notion that the political parameters within which Detroit's upper classes functioned included the view that enforcing racial equality was the morally appropriate choice. He approached the white men in charge of these two academic institutions as if they believed that discrimination and segregation were wrong and would do what they could to rectify inequality once they saw it was occurring. In his effort to put pressure on the two colleges, Grigsby thus appealed to administrators' sense of decency and fair play. Furthermore, because City College was a public institution, his campaign against segregation in its swimming classes included an additional element of faith in the inherent race neutrality of urban public institutions, a theme that he would continue to stress as the decade progressed. Each case was also a response to the exclusion of black students from athletic education within an otherwise integrated school program. These acts of segregation emphasized and reinforced the notion that intimate physical proximity between African Americans and whites was inappropriate.

Less than two months after he raised the issue, City College capitulated to Grigsby's demands and opened its swimming classes to black students. The negotiations ended well. Dean Coffey agreed to put his commitment in writing and, in a gesture of goodwill, accepted Grigsby's invitation to address congregants at St. John's Presbyterian Church, where Grigsby served as president. However, this victory also exposed a rift between Grigsby's political and civil rights goals and those of the "old guard," as illustrated by Grigsby's disagreement with the Reverend Robert L. Bradby, of the Second Baptist Church. After City College agreed to integrate its physical education classes, Bradby sent a telegram to black churches around the city claiming that Edward H. Williams, a white school inspector who was running for city council, was responsible for the change in policy. Williams, Bradby claimed, had "always been our friend" and deserved black votes in the upcoming election. When Grigsby heard about Bradby's recommendation, he was incensed: not only had Williams *not* participated in the campaign to desegregate the swimming classes, but he had refused appeals for help and had evaded the issue, explaining that he would not take a stand until after the election. Furthermore, Bradby declined to recognize the role of the local NAACP even though he had been the branch's president and was serving as an officer at the time. Grigsby demanded a retraction and apology from Bradby, but to no avail. Bradby remained unremorseful, and, to Grigsby's dismay, the local branch was on Bradby's side.[15]

Grigsby's frustration with Bradby points to a fundamental rift between the two men's political styles and their two competing approaches to the struggle for civil rights. Bradby maintained clear loyalties to white politicians and self-consciously, even cynically, used his position as an African American leader to promote those connections. His decision to urge black congregants to vote for Williams indicates that he saw black votes as his to leverage as he saw fit. Bradby's endorsement reflected his belief that African Americans would benefit from their connections to white politicians, even when those politicians were unwilling to fight for equality. In the 1930s, Bradby continued to maintain his interest in closely affiliating himself with white industrialists like Henry Ford. Bradby was interested in preserving a close relationship to those institutions and people—industrialists and politicians—that he identified as powerful, something that he believed was possible only if African Americans demonstrated their obliging and unqualified political loyalty.

Grigsby was offended by Bradby's opportunism.[16] He did not believe that a white politician who had been unwilling to support a campaign against discrimination should be assisted by African Americans in a citywide election, let alone given credit for the victory. Rather than proximity to industrialists and Republicans, Grigsby put his faith in liberalism. He maintained a reserved confidence that the people in power would capitulate to his demands once they were presented with the "facts and figures." Furthermore, he reasoned, if city leaders failed to make the right choice, activists could appeal to the courts, which also professed a commitment to race neutrality.

The Declining Hold of Patronage Politics

This shift in emphasis from patronage politics to confrontation was accelerated in the 1930s by a dramatic drop in migration as well as the declining fortunes of black reform institutions. Since the First Great Migration began, Detroit's most established black leaders had embraced reform and respectability as the cornerstone of their vision for uplifting the race. This "old crowd" believed that migrants' unfamiliarity with the North, lack of appropriate mores, and poor social comportment brought undue suspicion upon all African Americans. Their vision for reducing discrimination and ultimately producing the conditions that would allow for racial integration was the successful assimilation of black southerners into northern culture. This idea was severely undermined when southern migrants stopped arriving in large numbers, but racism remained.[17] Furthermore, the economic downturn also helped weaken the authority of uplift ideology by undercutting its central local institutions. By the early 1930s, black-run reform programs cut back their services significantly. Churches and social agencies ended programs they had been running since the 1910s, and some closed their doors altogether.[18] In 1933, the Sophie Wright Settlement, the Franklin Street Settlement, and the Delray Institute "were on the verge of closing" and were running as "simply skeleton organizations."[19] The Detroit Urban League was also hard hit by the Depression. In 1930, the Employers' Association, which had paid the salary of the DUL's job placement officer for fifteen years, withdrew its support for the position. By 1933, the league could pay neither its bills nor its employees for more than two months. That summer, it laid off a third of its already shrunken staff, leaving the organization with five employees, including its director.[20] The DUL began to recover in the middle of the decade, but its 1930 budget of $20,000 was only half that size by 1936.[21]

At the same time that the finances of black-run social services plummeted, the local government began to provide more resources to city residents, including African Americans. Indeed, welfare and the growing state became avenues through which African Americans made new demands on the city government and new claims to permanence. Black Detroiters began to depend on the state to meet more of their needs once the Depression began. For example, fifty of the black families who received aid from Detroit's Department of Public Welfare in 1930, relied on city services they had not previously used. Parents in this group took their babies to public health clinics set up by the city in 1930. Others used expanding state resources for less dire reasons: black boys and girls took theater, dancing, and other recreational classes through the Department of Public Welfare, which also offered night school for adults. Users of these programs continued to struggle with poverty. Ten of these fifty families lost their apartments and moved in with relatives.

Seven families, "of very high grade type," took in roomers, and seven others took their children out of school so they could work to supplement the family income.[22]

Beginning in 1933, the New Deal expanded these types of programs, helping black residents see the state as a potential, if not always consistent, ally and resource. It provided new services to African Americans through the alphabet soup of public agencies and through private social service organizations, which it began to fund. The Detroit Urban League benefited from this alliance. The DUL, whose resources had contracted significantly since the start of the Depression, began to work in partnership with local New Deal administrators, running programs on contract for the state. The Works Progress Administration (WPA), for example, funded the Urban League to run a series of "practice houses" designed to train young men and women in household service.[23] African American women used these houses as a "base for activism and social mobility."[24] This creative use of the practice houses indicates that black women felt comfortable using state resources to their own advantage, rather than acting as passive recipients of often-condescending programs.[25] Before the New Deal, black Detroiters had such limited opportunities to procure resources from the government that they developed few expectations about what the state could do for them. At the same time that the Depression drained the coffers of traditional reform organizations, public agencies, with white liberals at their helm, began to offer more resources to African Americans. This new dynamic led to a movement on the part of black residents toward the state as a way of bringing resources into their communities. This turn both fostered and was fostered by a new kind of activism oriented toward mass mobilization.

African Americans' expanding access to more conventional political power also pushed many away from private patronage and toward the state as a potential resource, ally, and site to build political strength. The growth in black electoral organization, the successes of African American politicians, and a shift from predominantly Republican to predominantly Democratic voting patterns all contributed to this change.[26] African Americans had just begun to win local elections in the beginning of the Depression. In April 1929, Cecil L. Rowlette, a black lawyer who was tied to the Republican Party and who served on the board of directors of the Detroit Urban League, was a candidate for Recorder's Court judge. Although he lost the election, his citywide candidacy meant that Detroiters saw an African American lawyer positioning himself as a person with enough political clout to participate in the electoral process as a candidate for a judgeship.[27] That year, the city council appropriated $30,000 to build a community center "in the heart of the Negro district," an award that indicated African Americans were able to procure some city resources from elected officials.[28] In 1930, black Republican Charles Roxborough won a state senate seat, and by 1932, sixteen African American candidates were running in the primaries for county, state, and federal positions, three of whom won spots in the general election, including Dr. Ossian Sweet.[29] None of the three won his bid for office, including Roxborough, who was not reelected. Charles Mahoney faced antiblack propaganda, but the three lost because they were all Republicans running against Democrats, who were swept into office on Franklin Roosevelt's coattails.[30]

African Americans' turn to the Democratic Party also helped expand their access to political appointments and elected officials. In 1932, fewer than one-third of Detroit's black voters cast their ballot for Roosevelt, but by 1936 that proportion had inverted. This turn was the result of a national shift among African Americans, but it was also a product of local organizing. In 1928, mortician Charles Diggs, who would go on to become a state senator, joined the Democratic Party. A few years later, he organized the Michigan Democratic League, an African American political club. By the next year, the group boasted 8,000 members statewide, the vast majority of whom lived in Detroit.

Because Detroit never had powerful political machines and local elections were nonpartisan, few opportunities had existed for African Americans to win public employment or political authority through party organizations. Local elections were nonpartisan, and the civil service exam excluded most African Americans from city jobs. However, political parties were significant at the county and state levels. The Democratic machine started to produce jobs for African American party activists in the early 1930s, from stenographer, a position held by Helen Bryant, to Charles Diggs's first major political appointment as deputy parole commissioner.[31] Democrats were also far more likely than Republicans to hire African Americans. Wayne County sheriff and

Democrat Henry Behrendt, for example, hired three times more African American deputies in 1930 than any Republican had before him, even though black Republicans had long-standing party organizations.[32] In his 1935 report to the Earhart Foundation titled *The Negro Voters in Detroit*, Thomas Solomon celebrated the positive effects that the ascendancy of the Democrats in the state government had for black voters. He explained that Michigan's Democratic governor, William Comstock, who had entered office in 1933, had dispensed more patronage jobs to African American supporters in a single year than the Republicans had for the previous eighty years, including a handful of higher-level positions. Joseph Coles, a black realtor who had become an active Democrat in the 1920s, would have agreed with Solomon's assessment. Coles remembered that political appointments of African Americans had been unheard of before Comstock took office. In 1934, Comstock appointed African American lawyer Harold Bledsoe as assistant attorney general of Michigan. Democrats' appointments of African Americans to high-profile positions pushed Republicans to do the same. In 1935, after a Republican retook the governorship, Charles Roxborough was appointed to replace Bledsoe, and in 1939 Charles Mahoney became state labor commissioner. Democrats still far outpaced Republicans in their willingness to hand out jobs and their support for black candidates. In 1936, Charles Diggs, a black Democrat, won a state senate seat with help from African American and white party organizations. The growing power of Democrats on the state and national levels had a positive effect on African American party activists. The electoral successes of African Americans and the expanded political power that they experienced after their turn toward the Democratic Party helped reshape black civil rights institutions, like the local branch of the NAACP.[33]

Established black leaders also faced considerable pressure from radical groups to change their political approach. Black communists, whose numbers had been quite small before the Depression, garnered new interest from African Americans as the economic system fell apart.[34] While the majority of black residents never joined CP-affiliated groups, many supported Left-led actions. Black interest in the Communist Party was rooted in the neighborhood-based activism it sponsored through its Unemployed Councils and in its advocacy for the nine black defendants in the Scottsboro case. The CP's Unemployed Councils brought residents together to fight for local resources and for state protection from the ravages of the Depression. They were most successful in their reverse eviction campaigns. Squads of council members helped families move back into their apartments after being evicted. This practice stalled and sometimes even forestalled evictions, allowing people time to amass enough resources to pay rent or move. Early in the decade, reverse evictions were common in Detroit's black east side; sometimes four or five happened simultaneously on the same block.[35] The Party amassed a high profile among African Americans as a result of its campaign. "Left-wingers," black Democrat Joseph Coles remembered, "made pretty good gains back in those days. . . . I wouldn't say that the majority of Negroes went along [with the communists], but there was a substantial following."[36] Black communists and radicals also set up soapboxes in Paradise Valley and spoke in Grand Circus Park, among the city's other leftists. Communists frequented employment agencies, recruiting members and sympathizers into its League of Struggle for Negro Rights (LSNR).[37]

The most public struggle between the Communist Party and the NAACP was the Scottsboro case, which brought attention to the ongoing public debate about their divergent political styles.[38] In Scottsboro, Alabama, in 1931, nine young black men were arrested and charged with raping two white women on a freight train. Although the state's evidence was weak, the defendants were tried, convicted, and sentenced to death within two weeks. The NAACP did not comment on the case or offer to defend the men when the news first broke. The association was concerned about allying itself with defendants who had been hoboing and whose respectability was in doubt. The Communist Party, however, jumped to their defense soon after the men were convicted, dispatching attorneys to Alabama to handle the appeal. Meanwhile, the Party pushed the Scottsboro case into the national limelight, organizing community meetings and fund-raising parties across the country. Once word of Communist involvement reached the NAACP, national leaders reconsidered their original stance and attempted to wrest control of the case from the CP.[39]

On the national level, a bitter fight emerged between the two organizations over who would defend the men on trial and how to best agitate on their behalf outside of the courtroom. Although these tensions emerged in Detroit, many local residents and organizations were indifferent to the ideological debates that produced animosity between the NAACP's more moderate political approach and the communists' insistence on confrontation. They saw both organizations' strategies as different parts of the complicated and seemingly interminable struggle against racism. Indeed, concern for the Scottsboro defendants frequently trumped the ideological rifts that divided the two groups. Detroit's Scottsboro organization, for example, was politically diverse, "a cross-section of Detroit citizens." Dr. Ossian Sweet, a Republican famous for his criminal trial in the mid-1920s, headed the committee, which included the Reverend William H. Peck, head of the Booker T. Washington Trade Association, and Joseph Billups, a member of the CP. These three men clearly held politically diverse views, but each of them was committed to the Scottsboro trial and was able to work with Communists whether or not they toed a CP line.[40] Thus, clashes between political styles did not necessarily separate working-class and middle-class people, even as radical activists called their politics "working-class." Although political strategies were certainly connected to ideas about class, political divisions did not fall neatly along class lines, and the animosity between the NAACP and the CP was not as divisive in Detroit as it was in other cities.[41]

Another example of an alliance between African American leftists and more moderate black leaders in the early 1930s occurred after the Ford Hunger March of 1932. The march, sponsored by an alliance of Unemployed Councils, was an extremely significant event for black Detroiters, many of whom walked in it. Marchers called for unemployment insurance from the state and from private industry. They targeted the Ford Motor Company, which had been a symbol of prosperity through the 1920s but was not offering any assistance to its laid-off workers or contributing to Detroit's Department of Public Welfare—the company was located in Dearborn, its own municipality, and was thus exempt from taxation by Detroit, even though most of its workers lived within the confines of the city. When marchers arrived at Ford's River Rouge plant, they were attacked by the police and by the company's security guards, who shot into the crowd. Four white protesters were shot dead at the site, and one African American man, Curtis Williams, died of his wounds a week later. The enormous funeral procession for the four white men brought thousands of people back out onto the streets five days after the original march. However, when Williams died, the cemetery refused to bury his body alongside the graves of the other slain men.

Joseph Billups, a member of the CP, paired up with Charles Diggs, a prominent black Democrat and future state senator, to push the city to force the cemetery to accept Williams's body. This alliance across political convictions was typical of Detroit's civil rights coalition during the 1930s. After little response from the city, Billups and Diggs threatened to bury Williams in Grand Circus Park, a square near downtown. They organized a large funeral procession that marched to Grand Circus Park with Williams's casket, picks, and shovels. During the march to the park, word came down that Billups and Diggs finally won their battle. The cemetery agreed to cremate Williams's body, averting a clash between marchers and the police. Ultimately, Billups spread Williams's ashes over the Ford River Rouge plant.[42]

Established middle-class civil rights leaders and groups ultimately responded to these pressures. Those men and women who were most clearly poised to step into the next generation of traditional leadership were particularly affected. They supported and even organized mass action without subscribing to the radicalism of the Left. However, they continued to face indifference, resistance, and sometimes even hostility from more established black leaders.

Detroit's NAACP

Over the course of the 1930s, the local NAACP, like most branches in the urban North, both grew significantly and changed its focus from legal defense toward an effort to activate members. The rising popularity of Left-oriented mass politics coincided with a period of disorganization and scant activity on the part of Detroit's NAACP. The branch's dormancy reflected its leaders' neglect, but it also mirrored their political priorities. Branch leaders, including the Reverend Bradby and Moses Walker, both of whom served as president in the early 1930s, were African American professionals who saw their positions at the helm of the NAACP as prestigious and strategic—for them as individuals and for African American Detroit. While poor and working-class people certainly belonged to the association, the NAACP membership list also included members of the city's educated African Americans, as well as whites who saw themselves as black peoples' allies. Branch leaders thus saw themselves as managers of an important network whose very existence stood as an emblem of race advancement. In their minds, their leadership of the NAACP augmented their prestige at the same time that it offered them a platform from which they could negotiate with white leaders and defend African Americans against discrimination. Their program reflected this sensibility: they provided legal defense to city residents who approached them, especially middle-class African Americans who fought for access to homeownership, but they actively resisted efforts to build the local NAACP into a community-based group. For them, mass-based organizing against systemic discrimination was a different kind of political project, one that would undermine their ability to engage white leaders as distinguished representatives of the race.[43] Aside from a few well-attended meetings that featured prominent local or national speakers, the branch had little visibility in the early 1930s. By 1932, membership had waned significantly, the branch forwarded little dues money to the national organization, and local officers would not respond to letters from national staff people.[44] While the branch grew to more than 2,000 members in 1926, when it was defending Ossian Sweet, by 1933 that number had dropped to 550.[45]

Some African American Detroiters pushed to change the local organization. In 1928, Lucile Owen was so aggravated by the branch's "moribund condition" that she organized a women's auxiliary. Arthur Randall, an executive committee member, complained with frustration that the branch had failed to do much of anything in 1930—it had not developed its membership, "electrif[ied] the masses," raised adequate funds, or even held regular business meetings.[46] National officers also pushed branch leaders to turn the organization into an active group. Finally, they found an ally in Snow Flake Grigsby, who joined the local executive committee in 1931.[47] Grigsby hoped that the NAACP would provide him with an institutional platform from which he could launch the kind of protest-oriented civil rights activism he had already been engaging. After a year on the committee, he was frustrated and developed an agenda designed to breathe new life into the organization. He wanted the branch to establish a legal redress committee, expand its membership, and, most important, make clear demands for African American inclusion on the city government. He wanted to see the NAACP push for the promotion of at least one black garbage worker to a supervisory position, the placement of black interns and nurses at municipal hospitals, and the dismissal of two white police officers who had willfully ignored a cry for help from an African American resident.[48] Ultimately, Grigsby pushed to expand and democratize the local association.

NAACP leaders were not interested in reorienting the work of the branch, and Grigsby's platform fell on deaf ears. Furious, Grigsby complained that branch leaders were "using the office for personal advancement rather than for the good of the people." Grigsby began to organize the association on his own. He pulled together a meeting that attracted 800 people aimed at advertising the NAACP's national work and recruiting new members.[49] Frank Murphy was the speaker. National officers appealed to local executive committee members to support Grigsby, but branch leaders were loath to cede control over the association or allow Grigsby access to its membership lists. Nonetheless, Grigsby, supported by the national office, ran the 1933 membership campaign relatively independently of the local officers.[50]

Grigsby's vision for the branch was quite different than that of its established leaders. He believed that the association needed to wage clear, aggressive, and uncompromising protest in order to remain relevant. "If the N.A.A.C.P. Officials challenge various individuals and Department heads in our City and institutions," he explained, "we get a greater response from the citizens to support the branch." In other words, the cautious strategy of the branch's leadership, crafted with an eye toward maintaining status among the black middle class and approbation from white elites, was only hurting the organization. He suggested that black leaders who backed down in the face of white resistance in order to preserve their legitimacy would lose respect and support among the city's African Americans.[51]

Grigsby also took African American professionals and other members of the black middle class to task for their lack of interest in the NAACP. Only 10 percent of the city's 175 black attorneys, doctors, and dentists and 15 percent of the 400 black federal employees were members of the branch. Grigsby was particularly dismayed that so few local ministers belonged, since the program of the NAACP was, in his mind, "to make Christianity practical." He cynically concluded that their lack of interest reflected their indifference to anything "that does not put something in their coffers." Grigsby thus extended his critique of the association's local leadership to members of the black middle class who were not willing to fight for the rights of the community.[52] Grigsby also argued that African Americans who were complicit in the exploitation of other black people should not be safe from criticism or protest. For example, he attacked black doctors for defending substandard hospitals and proclaimed that it was his duty as a member of the NAACP executive committee "to see that no institution or person goes unchallenged that infringes on Negroes' rights in any form."[53]

Although Grigsby attacked the middle class for its failure to take an interest in the NAACP, he was not calling for the working class to take the reins of leadership from the city's professionals. Grigsby was not interested in challenging the premise that members of the black middle class were the rightful leaders of the race.[54] Rather, he was angry because the people he believed should have been mounting legal and political campaigns against discrimination were instead, from his perspective, unwilling to risk their own success in order to fight for the greater good of the race.

For Grigsby, the NAACP of the early 1930s was a platform from which to articulate his frustration with Detroit's black leadership partly because the national association was engaging in the kind of fights Grigsby found worthy and using tactics that made sense to him. Other NAACP branches were frustrated by the gradualist and traditional approaches of the national association in this period—annoyed by its anticommunism and its episodic hostility toward unions.[55] Grigsby, conversely, used the activism of the national office to push for more militance on the local level and to stress the importance of building the local chapter in Detroit. Militancy, for Grigsby, was about shifting black politics from a reliance on white patronage as the source of power, to the mobilization of the city's black residents. Grigsby also pushed for black economic concerns to remain front and center within struggles for civil rights, although he was not interested in reimagining what the urban economy looked like in the way that communists were. Instead, his economic ideas were more in line with the economic nationalism of groups like the Housewives' League, the Booker T. Washington Trade Association, and the local UNIA. Grigsby worked to ensure that fights for good jobs, especially in the public sphere, remained at the forefront of civil rights struggles. Rather than prioritizing the interests of the elite, Grigsby's ideas about the common welfare of Detroit's African Americans respected the concerns of working-class and poor community members as well.

By the summer of 1933, Grigsby had earned a reputation among African American Detroiters for his work with, and in spite of, the local NAACP. He also began to deliver lectures to black audiences across the city to promote the association and to air his grievances, publicly denouncing those people "who call[ed] themselves Negro leaders" for being "lethargic stooges." Grigsby became one of the most popular African American speakers among Detroit's black residents. Indeed, his popularity rivaled that of Detroit's most high-profile preachers. Frustrated by the inaction of conventional black leaders, Grigsby continued to mount his own campaigns against discrimination. That fall, he launched an attack on the abysmal treatment that black patients were receiving at the Bethesda Tuberculosis Hospital, an overcrowded and underfunded municipal facility for African Americans. He blamed these problems on "Uncle Tom Negro leaders who had no guts" because they were not willing to confront either white city officials or the black doctors who ran the hospital. These black administrators, Grigsby suggested, would not demand better facilities for their patients because they did not want to disrupt the arrangement with the city that allowed them to maintain control of the facility. After a few months of negotiations, the DPW made a commitment to admit black TB patients to the Herman Kiefer Hospital, integrate other public hospitals, and hire black doctors, nurses, and staff across the system.[56]

Snow Flake Grigsby's Civic Rights Committee

Snow Flake Grigsby assumed that racial liberalism was a relevant element of urban political discourse—so relevant that he could use it to his own advantage in his organizing. Indeed, civil rights liberalism in Detroit was animated by the assumption that white liberals could be persuaded to live up to the ideals they propounded, even though they

Snow Flake Grigsby. Image courtesy of the Burton Historical Collection, Detroit Public Library.

were clearly unlikely to do so. Grigsby thus accepted northern white leaders' positioning of themselves in opposition to southern racists. At the same time, he strategically exploited the gap between how white liberals saw themselves and the realities of African Americans' experiences. He believed that exposing racism and inequality and then vocally protesting against their maintenance was the best strategy for winning concessions from white city leaders.

Grigsby and his cohort recognized that white liberals were susceptible to protest because they valued their identities as upholders of race neutrality and urban fairness. He relied on these elements of their political vision. More conventional leaders did not share this sensibility.

For them, African Americans were only relevant to white leaders in their role as power brokers—they saw themselves as traders of votes for patronage. Grigsby and his cohort used the growing strength of racial liberalism among the city's white leaders to develop their political style. They also relied on African Americans' growing electoral strength but conceived of that power as leverage for expanding rights rather than something that could be exchanged for favors like monetary support for a church or social agency. Grigsby and the Civic Rights Committee publicly attacked advocates of patronage-style politics for their lack of vision. In so doing, they strengthened the power and relevance of northern racial liberalism, with mixed consequences for African Americans.

After two years on the executive committee and a failed bid for the branch's presidency, Snow Flake Grigsby grew tired of fighting against Detroit's moribund NAACP and finally gave up his efforts to reshape the organization.[57] He founded the CRC as a new platform for his activism and used it to focus his energy on expanding black access to public jobs and resources. The CRC's principal objective was to push African Americans to use their collective strength to fight against the discrimination that kept them economically subordinate. The rhetorical question "What are you going to do about it?" appeared on the cover of the committee's first pamphlet, which reprinted employment figures from *An X-Ray Picture*. This question stood as a challenge to black Detroiters to take action and as an attack on more conventional black leaders for failing to mobilize black political power. Indeed, although there were almost 80,000 eligible African American voters in the city, slightly more than 25,000 were registered, and only 8,000 had voted in the last election.[58]

The CRC encouraged African Americans from across the class divide to vote, sign petitions, attend lectures, join protest organizations, and remain educated and indignant about how discrimination affected their lives. This outrage marks an important difference between Grigsby's political style and the approach of more established black leaders. No black Detroiter could have been surprised at the news that discrimination had shut off municipal employment to African Americans. But Grigsby's assertion that this discrimination constituted a profound and egregious violation of basic civil rights—that it had nothing to do with black ability, comportment, respectability, or talent—and that average black residents could change these conditions by joining together and asserting their political power was a departure from the message of established black leaders. For the CRC, rectifying the city's discriminatory practices and pushing African Americans to use their vote strategically were part of a larger campaign to redefine urban citizenship and to reshape what it meant, politically, to be black in Detroit. Grigsby encouraged black residents, even working-class and poor African Americans, to see themselves as politically organizable, rather than as politically dominated, and as legitimately threatening to the status quo. The CRC did not align itself with either political party. Instead, its leaders consistently argued that black voters would lend support to candidates who expanded access to public jobs for African Americans. This focus on employment certainly challenged endemic white supremacy, and the CRC was uncompromising when it came to black exclusion, but theirs was a liberal approach to civil rights activism. Unlike communist or anticapitalist demands, the CRC was not calling for the reorganization of urban power, the mass redistribution of wealth, or a profound change to the city's economy.

In order to reorient the relationship between African American Detroiters and city politics, the CRC held frequent public forums, sponsoring debates and lectures by black and white speakers. These meetings were extremely popular and often attended by hundreds of people. They were an important part of the committee's push to get African American Detroiters to see themselves as civic participants. Their aim was to draw average residents into political conversations and confrontations, and to challenge the notion that elites held a monopoly on engaged citizenship. As they negotiated with public officials, CRC leaders drew on this support to position themselves as influencers of black public opinion. Rather than presenting audiences with clear-cut answers, the CRC worked to cultivate civic engagement by encouraging average citizens to challenge black leaders with questions. For example, in February 1934, the committee sponsored a presentation that featured three influential African Americans, the Reverend R. L. Bradby, Charles Roxborough, the Republican state senator who had recently lost his seat, and attorney Charles Mahoney, all of whom were invited to speak on the topic "The Greatest Need of the Negro in Detroit." After their short talks, the

Reverend William H. Peck, a member of the CRC's board of directors and head of the Booker T. Washington Trade Association, responded to their proposals, opening up questions about effective political engagement and inviting participants to make decisions of their own.[59]

Grigsby and the CRC believed that white liberals' embrace of race neutrality was politically meaningless unless it was accompanied by access to jobs and the wealth that came with them. Its 1934 forum featuring Frank Cody, the superintendent of Detroit's public schools, provided a clear illustration of this political idea. In his address, Cody pledged that he would not permit segregated schools in Detroit, which, he explained, were being covertly introduced in other cities. However, this promise did not deter criticism or scrutiny. "It's not worth anything," Grigsby declared, "to be able to go in one of your finest places and sit down to eat, if you don't have the price of a meal."[60] Cody was asked "many pointed questions, some of which were apparently difficult to answer." For example, audience members wanted to know why the word "black" was written on the school cards of African American students, why so few black teachers were employed in the system, and why it was so difficult for African Americans to get even unskilled jobs from the Board of Education. Grigsby and CRC activists posed many of these questions, but even if less activist-oriented attendees were not comfortable confronting Cody head-on, they watched other black men and women verbally challenge a white public official who had already promised to uphold integration.[61]

Grigsby saw CRC forums as opportunities for citizens to engage directly with speakers, white or black. For example, the committee invited Lloyd Loomis, a white city prosecutor, to address a mass meeting. The *Tribune* reported that "many questions" were being asked of the CRC when it announced the event, since the courts often treated blacks unfairly and employed no African Americans. A few weeks before Loomis's talk, a black man who had been arrested for robbing a white girl with a knife and stealing $4 was placed under a $100,000 bond. Meanwhile, after attempting to assault an African American girl in her home, a white traffic officer was released on a $1,000 personal bond. Grigsby responded to these concerns with skepticism about Loomis's aims and with an invitation to residents to come and challenge the prosecutor's sincerity. If Loomis's decision to speak at a CRC forum was a "political move," Grigsby explained, "Mr. Loomis will have a lot of questioning to answer."[62]

Grigsby's commitment to fighting for the expansion of state resources for African Americans, and for a more robust welfare state in general, was probably also shaped by his wife's experiences as a social worker for the city's Department of Public Welfare. Eliza Grigsby, who held a master's degree in social work, trained volunteer social workers to help manage the city's caseload. In 1934, she traveled to Atlanta, Georgia, for six weeks to run a training program at the Atlanta School of Social Work, sponsored by the Federal Emergency Relief Agency, for African American women from southern states.[63] Eliza Grigsby was not on the board of the Civic Rights Committee, but, like her husband, she was clearly interested in how and in what manner the state could and would help African Americans.

The CRC worked hard to expand the power of the black vote and, in so doing, demonstrate the political importance of black voters. Indeed, it was vitally important to the growth of Detroit's black electorate. The CRC maintained a policy of endorsing candidates based on their records of service to African Americans rather than their party affiliations. African Americans, the committee believed, had more hope of asserting their power outside of political parties than as a subordinate part of integrated political machines. This electoral independence, Grigsby explained in a public meeting attended by more than a thousand people, meant that politicians would not be able to take black votes for granted.[64] Furthermore, Grigsby and the CRC were willing to ally themselves with activists with a broad range of political convictions. For example, Grigsby spoke to the Nat Turner Club, an African American chapter of the Communist Party, on the "Tragedy of White Christianity as Applied to Negroes."[65]

Grigsby frequently drew attention to the difference between his new, confrontational approach to civic engagement and what he saw as the ineffective political style of established black leaders. He reserved his staunchest criticism for those men and women who used their positions at the head of African American organizations to advance their own needs rather than working toward civil rights for all black residents. In his well-attended lectures, he expressed his animosity toward their orientation, accusing them of undermining fights to "secure economic justice for the Negro."[66] For example, in a typical lecture at the black YMCA attended by 300, Grigsby declared that ministers' "false leadership" and their inability to understand poor African Americans' concerns hampered their effectiveness. He lauded "the awakening of the younger generation" and also denounced white public officials for failing "to play fair with their constituents." Grigsby called on white circuit court and Recorder's Court judges to assign more cases to black lawyers and also "charged some of the colored lawyers with attempting to block the investigation launched by the committee," in an effort to protect their relationships with judges, even though they received so little in exchange for their loyalty.[67]

Grigsby came into conflict with established middle-class black leaders who were reticent to go too far in their criticisms of men whom they considered white patrons. John Dancy, of the Detroit Urban League, was particularly cautious. He did not want the DUL to be publicly associated with actions or campaigns that could be seen as controversial. He was particularly averse to alienating powerful white men or women with what he identified as overly antagonistic tactics. For example, his initial response to a case of discrimination at the University of Michigan, and his subsequent anger about how it was ultimately handled, demonstrated that he believed that the most effective way to rectify discrimination was through private channels of patronage. In the spring of 1934, Dancy agreed to help Jean Blackwell secure a place in Martha Cook, the women's dormitory. Blackwell, an African American student at the University of Michigan, had applied early for a spot in the dorm and met the academic qualifications for admittance but was denied a room. Dancy agreed to speak to his contacts at the university, but by the middle of August nothing had happened. Frustrated, Blackwell's mother, Sarah Blackwell, approached the CRC and began to publicize the case. Grigsby wrote a letter to Alice Lloyd, the university's dean of women, demanding a place for Jean at Martha Cook. After Lloyd refused, Grigsby appealed to the governor for help, stressing the fact that the university was a public institution and that Lloyd's decision violated Michigan's Civil Rights Act.[68]

Dancy was furious about this turn of events. He was especially incensed by a Negro Associated Press article, reprinted in black weeklies across the country, in which Sarah Blackwell accused him of having done nothing for her daughter. In a letter to a friend at Baltimore's Urban League, he wrote that he had "had the right people interested in this case—bosom friends of the administration at the University," but that he would no longer pursue his leads. He explained that he was "very much surprised that Mrs. Blackwell should resort to such tactics," indicating that he did not agree with her decision to take the case to the CRC or to expose his connection to the issue. In fact, Dancy suggested, bringing the issue out into the public jeopardized his ability to work behind the scenes, especially since he had made the appeal "on personal grounds." He was also leery about associating the Urban League or his name with the Blackwell issue; he believed that the league could only be hurt if it or he was associated with this type of pressure campaign.[69] He believed that public strategies for confronting discrimination were appropriate as long as they maintained a clear connection to the NAACP or to other protest organizations. He was willing to work quietly for the Blackwells, but once the case became public, he believed that it became "purely a National Advancement Association job" and did not want his name associated with the debate.[70] This case also demonstrates that the Blackwells, a comfortably middle-class family that could afford to send their daughter to the University of Michigan during the height of the Depression, chose to use a far more confrontational political style than the norms of middle-class respectability might have dictated in a previous moment. It underlines the relatively broad acceptance that protest politics and the political styles of activists like Grigsby had achieved among the city's middle class.

In 1937, Grigsby published another pamphlet, whose title clearly exposed his antipathy toward the weakness of current leaders. In *White Hypocrisy and Black Lethargy*, Grigsby took black leaders to task for not having done enough to address the problems that black Detroiters faced. He accused them of being "too afraid to go out into the deep where things are rough" and called on them to take a more confrontational stance toward city leaders. Finally, he concluded, "If the Negroes are going to solve the problem that confronts them in Detroit and in America today, we must move . . . into a realm of friction. . . . The Negro will never take his place as a respectable citizen until he learns to serve notice to everyone that he is willing to fight for his rightful place in the Sun."[71]

The CRC fought to open jobs for black workers—from professionals to unskilled laborers—in branches of the city government as well as private companies. Over the course of the decade, Grigsby and the CRC became known for forcing the Detroit Board of Education, Detroit Edison, Detroit Receiving Hospital, the U.S. Postal Service in Detroit, and the Detroit Fire Department to hire and promote African Americans.[72] The CRC used tactics that ranged from relatively conventional efforts to negotiate with existing organizations, to electoral campaigns, to the pressure of flooding an agency with applicants. Its efforts to open more positions to black firefighters and end segregation in firehouses were typical of how the CRC fought its battles. The CRC used a range of strategies to address the problem. A group of prominent black citizens met with representatives from the Firemen's Union to express concerns about their support for segregation in firehouses and discrimination against black applicants interested in becoming firefighters. The CRC also organized African Americans to vote against an amendment to the city's charter that would allow the Fire Department to uphold segregation. Grigsby also petitioned the Common Council to subpoena the city's fire commissioners and hold hearings to investigate Fire Department practices. The Common Council rejected this appeal numerous times, in spite of Grigsby's threats to advertise its disinterest to the city's black voters.[73]

Finally, the CRC organized a weeklong campaign designed to pressure the city to open up its hiring process. This campaign is a clear example of Grigsby and the CRC's central strategy of first closely monitoring a problem to expose how racial inequality worked, and then using this exposure, alongside mass organizing—in this case getting black men to apply for jobs as firefighters en masse—and electoral pressure to push white leaders to do the right thing. In early May 1938, the CRC called on African American men between eighteen and twenty-seven years of age to apply to the Fire Department during the first week of the month. The CRC provided a private physician to examine black applicants during that week and had special observers watch the oral examinations of black candidates. A small article on the front page of the *Detroit Tribune* announced the call and encouraged all black clergy to draw attention to the campaign from their pulpits the Sunday before in an effort to widely publicize the campaign and get as many men to apply as possible. This kind of diligent observation was one way that Grigsby used racial liberalism as a tool in his campaigns. It was exposure—something that was relevant only in the face of an urban-wide discourse, at least outwardly accepted despite severe limits by the city's white leaders, that suggested that the state *should* be more equitable—that Grigsby used to his advantage.[74]

Grigsby was a tireless organizer and networker. Throughout the decade, he and the CRC worked to expose racial discrimination and used their research, alongside diverse forms of political pressure, to push local institutions to hire more black workers and end discrimination and segregation. Grigsby maintained a high profile in Detroit's black neighborhoods. The city's black weeklies, the *Detroit Tribune* and the *Michigan Chronicle*, both ran articles on their front pages referring to Grigsby or the CRC at least once a month between 1934 and 1939. Grigsby attracted large audiences to hear reports about the CRC's work, and toward the end of the decade, he was elected "Negro Citizen of the Year" by a community-wide poll.[75] In 1939, after the U.S. Congress passed a bill disallowing federal employees from participating in political activism, Grigsby was forced to resign from the CRC. He did, however, remain active in the National Alliance of Postal Workers, an all-black union of postal workers.

Protest Politics

Activist groups linked to the city's informal civil rights coalition fought a range of battles for social, economic, and racial justice that drew on radical and liberal forms of protest and helped bolster racial liberalism in the city. Civil rights struggles in Detroit during the 1930s were often organized around the principle that protest could help relieve inequality because protesters would expose the fundamental contradiction between liberal discourse and urban realities. Rent strikers, for example, drew attention to race-based exploitation and the enormous gap between their ability to pay high rents and landlords' monthly earnings. One group, the Renters and Consumers League, organized working-class black and white Detroiters to fight against rent "gouging" and the exploitation of tenants. In the summer of 1937, activists in Detroit, inspired by a series of successful rent strikes in Pontiac, formed the organization with ties to the United Automobile Workers–Congress of Industrial Organizations (UAW-CIO), the Communist Party, and activist black ministers.[76] The league called on tenants to organize neighborhood rent strikes as a strategy to pull down the cost of housing and push landlords to take care of buildings that were crumbling into disrepair. Rents in black neighborhoods had skyrocketed since 1936, when the city began to tear down a large area it had deemed a slum to make room for an all-black public housing project. The Renters and Consumers League organized both black and white renters to testify at an open meeting of the Common Council in July 1937 to air their concerns and demand rent subsidies from the city.[77] In early August, the group held an organizing meeting that attracted more than 200 participants. Speaking to an enthusiastic crowd, the Reverend Horace White, an African American, proclaimed that black and white tenants needed to stick together if they wanted to beat back exploitative rents. After raising the rents of black tenants, he explained, "landlords tell the white people if they don't pay high rents, they'll evict the white tenants and put Negroes in."[78]

Over the next year, more than 200 black families participated in at least three successful rent strikes across the city that used this language to explain their actions.[79] In one apartment building, forty-two tenants stopped paying rent when their landlord asked for increases. In three years, as the building went from a majority-white to majority-black tenancy, the strikers' spokesperson explained, rents had been raised from seven to twelve dollars, and the final increase, to thirteen dollars, had driven the tenants out on strike. The landlord was making $2,000 per month on the building, which was sitting in disrepair. The landlord relented quickly on the rent demands, but protesters continued pushing to get their needs met. Tenants asked for a signed agreement holding rent at the lower levels, which the landlord resisted. They also pushed for laundry facilities in the basement, decorations in the hallways, and new furniture to replace old and broken furnishings.[80]

Groups like the Civic Rights Committee and the Renters and Consumers League found an eager audience among Detroit's African Americans in the late 1930s. Angela Dillard demonstrates that the Detroit's "labor–civil rights community . . . began to develop a more stable organizational infrastructure" during this time. The UAW and its

Negro Organizing Committee, the National Negro Congress, the Communist Party and its "various front groups," and the Conference for the Protection of Civil Rights all fought against racial discrimination and for workers' rights.[81] The approach of these groups helped push more mainstream organizations, like the local NAACP, toward a more activist stance.

By the end of the decade, Detroit's NAACP had became more confrontational in its approach to protest than it had been in the early 1930s. Different leaders headed the organization, but their influence alone did not create the new political culture. The national association had begun to push the Detroit branch toward a more confrontational style as well. National officers believed that the best strategy for managing discrimination was to collect and publicize anecdotal and statistical information that exposed injustices faced by African Americans and use it to put pressure on local officials, an approach that fit neatly with Grigsby's strategies.[82] As August Meier and John Bracey have explained, the association worked "to reach the conscience of America," a goal that was based on the liberal premise that compassionate white Americans would see racism as a travesty of justice once they truly understood its impact on their fellow citizens. NAACP officers and activists were not naive; they did not believe that this task was an easy one or that white Americans would automatically understand the meanings of prejudice, even if it was presented to them clearly. However, they continued to accept this liberal tenet as an ideal and maintained faith in its framework as the most appropriate way to approach the struggle for equality.[83]

Organizations like the Civic Rights Committee posed a threat to the prominence of the NAACP locally because they appealed to the same group of people that NAACP leaders saw as their principal audience.[84] National officers believed that local leaders were not doing enough to ensure that the NAACP remained in the spotlight. William Pickens lamented that the CRC was doing such a good job working on NAACP-like campaigns that Snow Flake "Grigsby's organization is going ahead doing work that [the] NAACP should do."[85] Pickens complained that local leaders were working to preserve their control over the association. Unlike Chicago's NAACP, which participated in the fight to push the national association toward the left, Detroit's branch was reticent about change. The national office was not attempting to push Detroit's branch toward radicalism. On the contrary, it shared the branch leaders' concerns about being associated with an excessively confrontational political style. The association's most influential leaders worked self-consciously to uphold its moderate posture within the field of protest, in spite of the fact that NAACP activists on the left, especially those with communist, socialist, or labor-based sympathies, were pushing the association to support union organizing and, more generally, to change its tactical approach.

By the end of the decade, a new middle-class black leadership that embraced civil rights liberalism, sustained closer ties to the concerns of working-class Detroiters, and was more open to coalitions with Left-oriented groups took the reins of power at the local NAACP. The association's work against police brutality offers an example of the shift in black political culture toward protest politics, which helped bolster racial liberalism in the city as a whole. Police brutality had been an NAACP issue in the 1920s, but the association's approach shifted over the 1930s to one that was more confrontational and based more in efforts to organize protests, petitions, and meetings for many members of the community rather than simply sending a group of middle-class black leaders to negotiate with white men in positions of power.

Brutality and neglect had characterized most black residents' experiences with the city's police force for decades, and officers consistently acted with impunity. Some contemporary observers believed that relations between African Americans and the police deteriorated significantly in the mid-1920s, around the time of the Sweet case. In 1926 alone, police officers shot and killed fourteen African Americans.[86] The next year, in a widely publicized case, a white police officer shot and killed a black man while he was holding his hands in the air.[87] The NAACP successfully pressured the prosecutor to issue a warrant for the officer's arrest, but the policeman was charged with manslaughter, released on bail, and ultimately found not guilty of murder.[88] This was not an isolated incident. Just a week later, for example, a white police officer threatened to murder two black men who had been accused of crimes the officer could not prove and feared for their safety based on precedents of violence in similar situations.[89]

During the Depression, activists monitored and protested police brutality more assiduously and consistently than they had in the past. In the early 1930s, the League of Struggle for Negro Rights, a Communist Party organization, took the lead on issues of police brutality, and the NAACP did not work with it. When James Porter was shot to death by a policeman in his home, the LSNR provided its headquarters for Porter's body to lie in state and turned his funeral into a political meeting. Funeral attendees elected fifteen people to approach the police commissioner and mayor with a list of demands. Five thousand people attended a protest meeting in Grand Circus Park, indicating broad community interest in this issue and outrage over the killing of Porter.[90]

By the end of the decade, black outrage against police brutality reached a fevered pitch, and the NAACP began to participate more actively in protests against these violations of African Americans' rights. In fact, fighting police brutality jumped to the forefront of the association's activities and became the most important issue for negotiations with white city officials by the end of the 1930s. In July 1938, NAACP leaders successfully pressured Mayor Richard Reading to open a probe of police brutality at the Canfield station, a precinct in the city's largest black neighborhood. J. J. McClendon, president of Detroit's NAACP—which had once again become the largest branch in the nation in 1939, with 6,000 members—headed a committee of black community leaders designed to address the chronic lack of accountability for police officers who abused African American residents. A July 1939 meeting sponsored by this group at the AME Bethel Church attracted 3,000 people. The speaker, African American attorney Charles Houston, from Washington, DC, called police brutality the "second stage of lynching."[91] The NAACP's renewed activism against police brutality signaled its willingness to work in coalition with leftist organizations, since struggles against police brutality linked racial justice to the left wing of the labor movement. The NAACP, for example, worked with the Civil Rights Federation, a coalition of labor and leftist organizations from across the city and state, which took a lead in organizing against police brutality. The federation recorded and publicized incidents of police harassment of African Americans as well as welfare recipients, leftists, labor activists, protesters, and strikers.[92] The NAACP also joined a coalition of leftist groups in an organization called the Committee to End Police Brutality, which McClendon chaired. Collecting more than 21,000 signatures, the group presented a petition to the Common Council in September 1939, asking for the ouster of the city's police commissioner, Heinrich Pickert. The council refused to fire Pickert, and in answer to the committee's request to investigate 100 instances of "brutal treatment of citizens," Mayor Reading responded that only two officers' actions warranted further investigation because the others had not employed too much force.[93]

Conclusion

As African Americans became more assertive and confrontational in their fight for racial equality, white leaders responded by taking black concerns more seriously and addressing black demands more readily. Thus, struggles for equality and survival during the 1930s reshaped African Americans' orientation toward white city leaders, changed how those white leaders managed their relationships with African Americans, and shifted how white leaders thought about racial equality. White leaders' increasing embrace of racial liberalism was thus rooted in their responses to black residents' demands. This dynamic can be difficult to see for a few reasons. First of all, white liberals tended to describe their racial liberalism as a product of their unusually expansive tolerance rather than a response to African American demands, as Frank Murphy did in his speech on the "races question." Second, white leaders frequently ascribed little importance to their interactions with black residents. For example, black organizations saved numerous examples of correspondence with white city leaders that do not appear in those leaders' papers. Finally, white daily newspapers rarely covered black protest. Together, these practices make it difficult to trace how a specific protest or a specific action may have affected white leaders generally or white liberals specifically. However, a close examination of black protest, how it developed over the decade of the 1930s, what kinds of strategies black activists deployed, and how blacks understood their relationships with white city leaders sheds light on this understudied dynamic.

By the end of the 1920s, uplift ideology, patronage politics, and the reform institutions that had shaped the ideological and institutional centers of black political life throughout the 1910s and the early 1920s had already begun to lose their political authority among black Detroiters. The dominance of patronage, uplift, and reform as solutions to political and economic problems suffered a further blow during the Depression. Ultimately they maintained their importance as cultural and social discourses throughout the decade, but most African Americans interested in civil rights activism moved away from these ideas. Instead, economically based arguments about how to improve the fortunes of the black community and change the racially defined relations of power in the city took on new political importance and informed the outlook of new organizations while reshaping the approach of some established groups, like the NAACP. Rather than self-help and philanthropy as models for attaining equality, the language of civil rights and demands on the state for full citizenship began to be articulated more clearly and consistently during the Great Depression.[94] This changing perception included the beliefs that the city, state, and federal governments could become dependable allies and that public sector leaders needed to rely on black voters. These ideas helped promote the turn among African Americans toward civil rights coalition politics because they contributed to the reduction in importance of private patronage and cultivated the sense that mobilizing African Americans as an electorate could be a viable political strategy.

The city's labor movement also relied on the growing liberalism of local and statewide leaders. In 1937, Frank Murphy was elected governor of Michigan, a victory for liberalism that helped encourage the state's labor movement as well as black activism. Detroit's African American civil rights activists owed a great deal to the labor movement for supporting their work.[95] This dynamic became increasingly important in the second half of the decade, after the Wagner Act gave workers significantly more protection to form unions. The UAW-CIO, along with other unions, began to organize and then win recognition in plants and workplaces across the city. The labor movement gave a significant number of African American activists organizational training, which they also used to mobilize support and build movements outside of labor unions. African Americans active in their own unions or involved in labor politics, like Snow Flake Grigsby, frequently stood at the forefront of struggles against segregation and discrimination in nonunion settings. Predominantly white unions became allies in specific campaigns for black rights in the city, or they worked on related issues simultaneously, sometimes coordinating their efforts closely and other times working quite independently from civil rights groups. The dynamic presence of the labor movement in Detroit, in a more general sense, helped to produce a culture of protest that supported the work of black activists. The next chapter turns from the urban political sphere to a discussion of how race and black activism shaped debates about labor and interracial unionism.

6

Northern Racial Liberalism and Detroit's Labor Movement

In a hotly contested mayoral election in November 1937, Richard Reading beat Patrick O'Brien in what turned into a referendum on the power of the Congress of Industrial Organizations (CIO) in Detroit. Reading, who railed against what he called the "Communist dominated" CIO, was a friend to business and hostile to New Deal programs. He promised to clamp down on welfare cheats and support the law-and-order police department, which was notoriously antagonistic and aggressively brutal toward both union activists and African Americans. Although the elections were officially nonpartisan, Reading was clearly aligned with the Republican Party. O'Brien, aligned with pro-labor Democrats, headed a group of five other candidates who were running for the city's Common Council and called themselves the "Labor Slate." Their platform included a commitment to end discrimination against African Americans in city jobs and to fire the police chief, who had been unresponsive to complaints about his officers' conduct. However, black voters were suspicious of the CIO. In this election, most supported Reading, who swept into victory with majorities in most precincts, including predominantly black neighborhoods.[1]

Few African Americans were willing to vote for a CIO-backed candidate for mayor in 1937, even though O'Brien expressed his interest in working against racial discrimination. Many more black voters supported the future mayor, whose political platform seemed to conflict with some of the major goals and priorities of black residents—like his clear support for a police department that was brutalizing African Americans. Detroit's more conservative black leaders, who endorsed the Republican-aligned ticket, helped sway black voters toward Reading.[2] The city's African American, pro-labor civil rights activists campaigned for O'Brien, but their minority voices failed to generate widespread support among black voters, and Reading won by large margins in African American neighborhoods.[3]

African American voters' skepticism about O'Brien was rooted in their experiences with white liberal supporters of racial liberalism who made claims about racial justice but failed to deliver on their promises. It also emerged from their responses to the city's Left, its predominantly white labor movement, and the CIO, all of which promoted interracial organizing but did not did so consistently. Finally, it came out of African American voters' doubts about the labor movement's ability to mobilize real political or social power, and whether an alliance with labor would strengthen or weaken African American access to influence, jobs, and resources.

O'Brien, the Labor Slate, and the African American activists who supported them were unable to demonstrate to black voters that an alliance with the CIO and a break from established business interests would work in African Americans' favor. Joseph Coles and Wilfred Newman, two African American Democrats active in the O'Brien campaign, printed 1,000 copies of a circular directed at black voters the week before the election. The pamphlet highlighted the Labor Slate's civil rights planks and described the CIO as a "Godsend" for unskilled black workers. It also included editorials warning that a Reading administration would bring "police terror," poor housing, and high rents, while O'Brien, a Democrat aligned with the New Deal, could secure "financial assistance from Lansing and Washington."[4] Furthermore, Labor Slate candidates appeared frequently at campaign stops in black neighborhoods. However, black newspaper editors, most of whom supported Reading, were loath to cover the O'Brien campaign and instead celebrated Reading as fair-minded.

While these voting results appear decisive—African Americans rejected a liberal CIO-backed candidate in 1937 in favor of a conservative, business-aligned candidate—the choice here between liberals and conservatives was ambiguous rather than straightforward. Black support for Reading in the 1937 election was possible because Reading, like other Republican politicians, had been influenced by the discourse of racial liberalism and used race-neutral language to describe his goals and principles. In an interview with Ulysses Boykin, a black Republican who had been appointed to a job by Reading when he was city clerk,

Reading described himself as interested in upholding the state and federal constitutions and "all of the obligations which guarantee equal representation to all regardless of race color or creed." While he supported a police department with a racist record and was interested in cutting public programs that benefited African Americans, he explained these commitments in terms of his support for "law and order" and fiscal caution.[5] Thus, African Americans in 1937 were not rejecting O'Brien's antiracism in favor of a candidate who used explicitly racist epithets, or whose supporters were organizing a racist whisper campaign as Charles Bowles's supporters had in 1929.

African Americans aligned with the labor movement were skeptical of Reading's weak commitment to black residents' concerns. Charles Berry, for example, secretary of the Civic Rights Committee, asked Reading whether he would fire the police commissioner, hire more black police officers, or include more African Americans on city commissions. Reading sidestepped these questions with race-neutral language; he pledged to ensure that all police officers and appointees met "basic qualifications" but did not agree to hire or appoint African Americans, specifically.[6]

Although some of the African Americans who campaigned most aggressively for Reading were decidedly antiunion—like Willis Ward and Donald Marshall, Ford Motor Company's personnel agents for African Americans—most of Detroit's black Republicans also enthusiastically endorsed Maurice Sugar, a radical labor lawyer who was running for the Common Council on O'Brien's Labor Slate.[7] The *Detroit Tribune*, a black weekly that retained clear allegiances to the Republican Party and consistently endorsed Republican-aligned local candidates, regularly ran positive news articles on its front pages detailing the work of black radicals and labor activists and lauding their victories. Sugar, a Jewish, left-wing lawyer closely aligned with the industrial labor movement, defended sit-down strikers and worked as counsel for the UAW.

Sugar worked closely with the city's pro-labor black civil rights activists and was famous among African Americans for defending James Victory in 1934.[8] Victory had been accused of slashing a white woman and stealing her purse. He had an excellent alibi but was framed by police and demonized by one of the city's daily newspapers. The *Detroit Times* used the case to argue that increasing and rampant criminality justified support for the police department's use of aggressive tactics—which were principally directed toward union activists and African Americans. Without explicitly claiming that African Americans were to blame for urban crime and disorder, the *Times* used Victory to strongly suggest this link. African Americans organized Victory defense committees and participated in letter-writing campaigns to support the defendant. Sugar recast Victory as honest, hardworking, and subject to discriminatory abuse. His team, which included two black lawyers, won a verdict of not guilty from an all-white jury, and Sugar came to be widely praised among African Americans. The *Detroit Tribune* covered the case in great detail, celebrating Sugar's win and attributing Victory's win to the work of the International Labor Defense and the League of Struggle for Negro Rights, both of which were Communist Party organizations.[9] The *Tribune*'s seemingly contradictory endorsements reflected its multiple commitments—to the Republican Party and fiscal conservatism, and to white activists who were strongly committed to the struggle for racial justice.

African Americans' rejection of O'Brien was a product of the CIO's uneven record of racial inclusion, which was starkly illustrated in a well-covered incident of discrimination less than one week before the election. At the end of October 1937, four African Americans were turned away from a UAW-CIO dance sponsored by the welfare committee of a Chrysler local. Members of the Michigan branch of the National Negro Congress (NNC) organized a series of meetings to respond to the incident. The NNC had been working closely with the UAW and consistently promoted industrial union organizing among African Americans. The organizations had cosponsored a two-day "industrial and economic" conference in August. The local issued an apology a few days later and restructured its committees, adding a black member to each one in an effort to ensure fairness. While the local union responded quickly to NNC organizers' concerns, the incident confirmed skeptics' assertions that the CIO's rhetoric about interracial organizing and its commitment to black equality could be superficial in practice. Furthermore, NNC complaints about the CIO's weak commitment to interracial unionism were given significant coverage in black weeklies, with a front-page story in the *Detroit Tribune* just days before the election.[10]

Like other white liberal leaders in Detroit, CIO leaders practiced northern racial liberalism. They used racially progressive language to describe their commitments, but they also failed to build institutions that lived up to their rhetorical convictions. Their interest in allying with African Americans and in fighting for interracial unionism seemed instrumental from the perspective of black voters. Maurice Sugar, however, received support from a range of African American voters because he had demonstrated, through his activism, that his interest in racial justice was more than rhetorical. He had developed real alliances with African Americans in the fight to defend James Victory. Unlike Sugar, white liberal union leaders and leftists often developed an approach to racial justice that mirrored the northern racial liberalism of their counterparts in urban politics. This contributed to and reinforced the importance of racial liberalism in the labor movement and in the city at large. African Americans saw the predominantly white labor movement's explicit commitment to interracial union organizing as a superficial beginning. By the end of the 1930s, black workers and residents sustained a reasonable expectation that white leaders interested in their support would use language about racial equality when they addressed a black audience. They were looking for something more: white allies committed to the fight for racial justice who used clearly and consistently inclusive practices in their own work.

Occupational Segregation

Occupational segregation between African American and white workers increased during the first half of the Depression, which was due, in part, to white employers' consistent practice of dismissing black workers before laying off whites. The aggregate loss of jobs in Detroit industries is a stark illustration of this phenomenon. Between 1929 and 1933, more than 70 percent of black industrial workers lost their jobs, while a little more than 50 percent of white workers in the same industries lost theirs. The proportion of African Americans in industrial jobs fell from almost 7 percent, which was approximately the same as the proportion of African Americans in the city's population, to less than 4 percent over the same years.[11] The National Industrial Recovery Act of 1933 (NIRA) amplified this trend. Instead of raising black workers' pay, after the federal government mandated higher wages for a range of positions, white employers frequently fired black workers and replaced them with whites. John Dancy, head of the local Urban League, saw white employers' practices as evidence of an explicitly racialized way of thinking. He argued that white employers were thinking "in terms of [their] own" kind. These businesspeople believed that white men and women should hold jobs that paid decent wages before African Americans. They were happy to employ African Americans when they were able to pay minimally.[12]

African American women and men frequently appealed to industrial leaders, either as individuals or as spokespeople for the race, to hire more, or any, black workers. The cordial letters that they received back from these companies exemplify white employers' evasiveness and illustrate the slipperiness of a racist practice that was veiled under the sheen of northern racial liberalism. In one typical exchange between the Michigan Democratic League, a group of African American Democrats, and the Stroh Brewing Company, Stroh's politely explained that the company did not foresee any openings for black workers. The brewery planned to "take care" of its former employees before it would consider hiring anyone new.[13] Until the early 1930s, letter writing, cordial appeals, and face-to-face meetings with employers were the most common forms of action taken by African Americans in their quest to secure wider access to employment for black workers. These were the tactics used by the Urban League, as well as countless other organizations and individuals. However, in 1933, Dancy explained that the new wave of firings in response to the passage of the NIRA was "causing an increasing amount of unrest." In fact, Dancy wondered why more black residents were not involved with radical movements that offered clear critiques of the New Deal. "Is it not a wonder," he asked rhetorically, "that Negroes do not more quickly subscribe to the radical movement that offers at least an imaginary surcease from this form of discrimination?"[14]

Black residents and workers frequently used tactics that were not connected to established labor unions in order to push for integration in the workplace. For example, in Pontiac in 1933, a group called the Independent Club successfully pressured the district manager of a Kroger grocery store to hire a black clerk. Kroger stood in the heart of Pontiac's largest black neighborhood, and more than 90 percent of its customers were African American. The Independent Club began its campaign by appealing to the store's managers, but after six weeks of negotiations, the club failed to win a commitment from Kroger to hire any black workers. Frustrated, club members called a boycott and began to canvass the neighborhood to drum up support. The boycott lasted for only three hours, after which store managers relented and agreed to hire a black clerk and "groom [him] for the managing of it."[15] African Americans also formed community-based labor organizations designed to address the needs of black workers and coordinate their relationships with unions. In October 1933, four months after the NIRA was passed, a group of black Detroiters got together to form the National Federation of Negro Labor. The group argued that job discrimination and hostility from white unions had left black workers in an unenviable position. However, it proclaimed, African Americans still needed a *labor* organization to effectively fight for their rights as workers.[16]

Over the course of the 1930s, African American activists formed many similar organizations to fight for occupational integration, some of which dispersed after a single issue was addressed and others of which continued on through the decade. More established groups, like Snow Flake Grigsby's Civic Rights Committee, saw job discrimination as a main target for their activism. As the decade wore on, most of these organizations developed increasingly confrontational political styles. Boycotts and other actions designed to have an economic impact on discriminatory employers became more and more popular. As Dancy elliptically observed, discrimination clearly hurt black residents, but it also encouraged them to fight more aggressively for their rights.

African Americans used a range of strategies to address employment discrimination and develop an alternate vision of racial justice in the workplace. Some organized their own, predominantly black unions. Others became interested in the Left—rejecting the political approach of what they saw as an ineffective black leadership. A few hundred African Americans in Detroit joined communist or socialist organizations, the largest proportion of whom became members of the Communist Party. A far larger group of black residents, which numbered in the thousands, joined or supported Left-led organizations such as Unemployed Councils. These men and women helped or supported reverse evictions, participated in protests, or became interested in left-leaning labor organizations, which promoted interracial unionism. Still others shied away from the Left and unions altogether, suspicious of the extent of white leftists' and unionists' commitment to inclusion and racial justice. Finally, some African Americans became involved or allied with the predominantly white labor movement. Interracial unionism, like northern racial liberalism, was a conflicted and inconsistent promise for racial justice coming from leaders of the predominantly white Left and the white union movement.

Predominantly Black Unions and the National Alliance of Postal Employees

When white unionists talked about "labor activism" during the 1930s, they were referring to struggles over wages, the pace of production, union recognition, and a host of other issues that pit the needs of workers against the accumulation of profits and power. For them, discrimination in hiring was a civil rights issue rather than a labor issue. African Americans would not have made this distinction. Conversely, most would have described access to jobs as one of the most important labor issues that they confronted. They saw occupational segregation and discrimination as community, civil rights, and labor concerns.[17] African American workers had experience with unions and collective action before they encountered the CIO in the mid-1930s. Some participated in the Communist Party or were active in the Auto Worker's Union (AWU) in the 1920s.[18]

Black union members in majority-black unions represented a small portion of the overall black workforce, but their visibility far outstripped their numbers. Before the late 1930s, most black union members worked in nonindustrial jobs, as musicians, barbers, or government workers. Musicians and barbers, among others, belonged to segregated locals that maintained separate organizations for black workers, who were excluded from membership in white locals. Other black workers belonged to predominantly black unions that were not officially segregated but reflected the occupational segregation that shaped the city's labor market. For example, the union for the city's garbage workers, while not formally segregated, was predominantly black, since 98 percent of Detroit's 610 garbage workers were African American.

Most of the black union members who belonged to majority-white unions before the middle of the 1930s worked in the skilled trades as electricians, brick masons, plasterers, or printers. However, very few black men belonged to these unions, since African Americans were rarely permitted to become apprentices, and when they were, they were only allowed to apprentice to other black workers. Even though it was very difficult to break into the union as a black brick mason, the masons held a strong antidiscrimination policy for their members. They sent out mixed-race groups to jobs all over the city and penalized employers for turning away black workers who had been dispatched from the union hall to fill a job.[19] Little solid evidence remains of smaller-scale union drives or of organizing efforts designed to pull workers together to fight collectively for improved conditions. However, traces of this activity do linger and indicate that black workers used collective organizing as a tool to assert their rights and to fight for their interests. One example of this activity was the mention of an "organization of domestic workers in Detroit" in 1934.[20]

Few records from segregated or predominantly black locals have made their way into public archives, and records from majority-white locals in Detroit that were not affiliated with the CIO include few explicit references to African Americans or to race before the beginning of explicitly interracial campaigns. However, black workers and issues relating to race were significant players in the union movement before the CIO began its push toward interracial organizing. The black press is one of the few sources available for examining the experiences of black workers in predominantly black unions in the urban North before they encountered the industrial drives of the middle to late 1930s. Black newspapers frequently covered the activities of predominantly black unions, reporting on their meetings, conventions, and negotiations with their predominantly white counterparts. The papers rarely covered work-based disputes, like negotiations with managers, or went into detail about workers' grievances on the job. Members of predominantly black unions were newsworthy partly because their members maintained a high level of visibility within black community institutions.

The National Alliance of Postal Employees (NAPE) was the largest and most visible majority-black union in Detroit. Its local chapter was founded in 1927 "for the purpose of protecting and advancing the cause of the Negro worker in the postal service."[21] Founded in Tennessee in 1915, by the early 1930s, NAPE had grown into a national union with 28,000 members, and branches all over the country. NAPE activists worked to organize and build their union at the same time that they fought to represent and advocate for black postal workers. The two other national postal unions that were active in Detroit excluded black workers from their ranks.[22] The growth of NAPE coincided with the growth of black workers in federal jobs in Detroit and across the country. Unlike cities like Chicago and New York, where machine politics offered African Americans a limited entrée into municipal public employment, black workers had little access to other public employment in Detroit.

Detroit's black weeklies consistently covered NAPE, reporting on local, regional, and national meetings and frequently praising the work of the organization.[23] Detroit's NAPE activists made no distinction between their fight to protect their rights as workers and their struggle to win battles against racism and discrimination in the city. For example, in April 1934, union activists pushed the issue of restaurant discrimination into the courts because their members were having trouble finding a place to eat lunch. That month, the federal government had opened a new building downtown to serve as the city's main post office, its federal courthouse, and its customs office. The building opened in April and did not include a cafeteria. Before the move, postal workers had patronized the federally run cafeteria, which was not segregated. This proved to be an enormous problem for black workers, since restaurants and cafeterias in the area maintained segregated seating and refused to serve black workers who would not comply with their strictures. Black men and women who worked in the area before the new federal building opened had been patronizing these restaurants and accepting segregated seating without complaint. The influx of many more black workers in the area meant that available accommodations were no longer adequate. This practical problem—that black postal workers had no place to eat lunch—combined with the alliance's commitment to fighting against discrimination propelled NAPE activists to protest against the offending restaurants. Six postal clerks, including the union's president, J. J. Anderson, brought their case to the city's prosecutor, who warned local restaurant owners that if they continued to discriminate against black patrons, warrants would be issued against them. The Michigan Civil Rights Act of 1865 outlawed some discrimination in public accommodations. Activists were using this law to support their effort to integrate the cafeteria.[24]

NAPE activists saw their fight against restaurant discrimination as part of a larger civic dispute over the place of African Americans in the increasingly interracial city. Even after the warning, white restaurant owners in the area were quite aggressive about asserting their prerogative to either maintain segregated seating or refuse service to black patrons. For example, one restaurant owner asked two black postal workers when they broke for lunch and, beginning the following day, closed his restaurant during the time that overlapped with their lunch hour. Black postal workers were not deterred by these tactics and continued to demand service in areas designated whites-only and at the times they could break for lunch. The alliance also maintained pressure on the prosecutor's office, which finally issued a warrant for the arrest of John Peterson, one of the restaurant owners, who denied the accusation that his segregation policies stood in violation of the Michigan Civil Rights Act. Ultimately, three cases were brought against Peterson, who was found guilty of violating the act. However, the judge gave Peterson a suspended sentence and declared that the local NAACP should monitor the problem, making it clear that he did not believe it was the state's responsibility to uphold antidiscrimination laws. NAPE activists were disappointed with this outcome.[25]

The alliance's fight against discrimination gave the organization power and visibility that the group's white counterparts could not ignore. A few days after the alliance began to publicize its case against local restaurants, the all-white local of the National Federation of Post Office Clerks (NFPOC), a union affiliated with the American Federation of Labor, finally agreed to meet with a committee of activists from NAPE. The meeting was designed to "bring about a more amicable relation between the two organizations, and to break down the color barrier which has kept the white and colored clerks estranged."[26] Soon thereafter, the postal clerks' union invited African Americans to join their group. By 1937, 100 of the predominantly white local's 1,100 members were African American. In fact, that November, Snow Flake Grigsby was elected first vice president of Detroit's NFPOC and became the union's delegate to the Wayne County Federation of Labor. Grigsby defeated two white opponents in his bid for office.[27]

NAPE activists were interested in joining the NFPOC, but they did not relinquish their own organization, and they were unwilling to settle for second-class membership in the predominantly white group. For example, a few weeks after the NFPOC met with the alliance, the post office social committee invited NAPE members to form an all-black orchestra for post office functions. Alliance members saw this invitation as an insult, since they had been working to open up the NFPOC band and glee club to black workers who were interested in performing. NAPE thus rejected the offer to form an orchestra until the other music groups stopped discriminating, refusing to settle for Jim Crow status and reserving their right to continue pushing for integration.[28] NAPE activists also remained suspicious of white politicians, a few of whom visited alliance meetings to court their votes. NAPE member Thomas Solomon warned black workers to be wary of these visits, since newly elected officials rarely displayed "tangible evidence" of their support for African Americans. For example, he complained in the *Detroit Tribune*, elected officials had failed to give "Negroes employment in the cafeteria at [the] Roosevelt Park" post office.[29]

Readers of the city's black weeklies, the *Detroit Tribune* and the *Michigan Chronicle*, would have associated black unions with struggles in the workplace, but they would have also connected them to fights against discrimination and for civil rights more generally. These organizations stood alongside groups like the Civic Rights Committee, which was also oriented toward labor issues, and the NAACP, which became more interested in labor struggles as the decade wore on. Black unions were frequently in the news for their fights to ensure equal access to employment and accommodations. Furthermore, black postal workers who were active in the alliance were also relatively prominent citizens within the black community; a number were leaders in civil rights organizations or held positions on their boards of directors. Snow Flake Grigsby, head of the CRC, was the most well-known example in Detroit. Thomas Solomon, who was on the board of the CRC, was also a postal worker.

Solomon was the lead plaintiff in the restaurant discrimination case and also was in the news because he challenged the president of Detroit's NAPE in the local's elections soon after the restaurant discrimination case went to court—an election that was covered by the *Tribune*.[30]

Among black Detroiters, postal workers were recognized as members of a well-respected and celebrated laboring class. They were men and women who often were very well educated and held relatively well-paying working-class jobs. They fit comfortably into the cultures created by African American organizations that were dominated by black business owners and professionals. Many of them had trained to become professionals, but discrimination prevented them from finding jobs in their chosen fields, and instead they ended up working in the post office. Grigsby, for example, held a pharmacy degree. Thomas Solomon had a bachelor's degree and was working on his PhD in political science at the University of Michigan. In 1934, he won a fellowship from the Earhart Foundation and completed his degree in 1939, all while working at the post office. His dissertation, "The Participation of Negroes in Detroit Elections," focused on black voting patterns in Detroit. Solomon was also active in other community organizations. He was a member of the Boys' Work Committee of the YMCA and a student member of the Nacirema Club. Solomon was also a member of the local chapter of the Alpha Phi Alpha fraternity.[31]

In 1935, Thomas Solomon ran for president of NAPE local in a race that mirrored the struggles for power within the black political sphere. Solomon argued that black postal workers needed to be more proactive about demanding their rights, and that they needed to approach overtures from white union leaders with caution. He lost to J. J. Anderson, who was interested in maintaining a less confrontational posture toward both the post office and white unions. Like other political struggles within the black community, this election pitted two men against each other who were well educated and maintained at least semielite status among other African Americans. Their differences lay in their ideas about the direction of leadership. In other words, neither man was calling for a radical departure from the existing model for attaining their goals—one that put a well-educated man at the helm of a struggle over community rights and power. Rather, they disagreed about how and whether it was politically expeditious to mobilize a constituency of less privileged community members in order to fight for equality, or whether it was more advisable to appeal to white leaders, in this case of unions, to achieve those goals.[32]

Few black postal workers trusted that their concerns would be addressed adequately as members of the Post Office Clerk's union, and so they continued to maintain an active NAPE chapter even after a majority signed up with the white union. In 1937, Detroit's NAPE began a cooperative buying club, inviting members to buy food in bulk and share the savings among them. The branch continued its cultural programming, sponsoring a concert at the YWCA and women's auxiliary, even though the alliance had female members.[33] In the summer of 1937, alliance activists appealed to national NAACP leaders to help them pressure managers at Detroit's post office to promote black workers. Ten black clerks and carriers had been recommended to the local postmaster, but none was promoted into any of the six supervisory positions filled that year.[34] NAPE activists, while calling for a robust labor movement in support of the organizing that was taking place around Detroit, also provided an explicit critique of what they saw as the most common approach to interracial organizing. In an editorial in the local's newsletter, one writer asserted that "most white fellow workers . . . have a great desire to help uplift the Negro and to help him better his condition." However, he explained, these white workers held a condescending attitude toward their black colleagues. They "feel gratified in thinking that they have helped uplift an inferior creature." The article differentiated this approach from one that "regarded the Negro worker solely as a man or woman placed under similar circumstances. . . . They regard him as a man [or woman], possibly superior in intellect, or inferior in intellect. This class is very small."[35] By 1939, no African American postal worker held a job as a foreman or at a post office window in Detroit, but NAPE continued to press for more fair promotion policies, as well as sponsor other activities, like a benefit dance for the group.[36]

Detroit's Communist Party

The Communist Party and other leftist organizations were visible and influential in Detroit's labor movement and in the city at large. They helped to shape labor-based and municipal debates about race and about African Americans and, by extension, the meanings of racial liberalism in Detroit. By aligning themselves with fights for racial equality and against "white chauvinism," the CP and other radicals helped support and publicize African Americans' claims about the negative consequences of discrimination and the positive social effects of interracial cooperation and robust racial equality—in both private and public spaces. This was a position that separated their ideas about race from the notions of equality promoted by northern racial liberals, most of whom did not advocate social integration. At the same time, however, white communists' and leftists' commitment to interracial organizing and racial justice was uneven.

Although radicals did succeed in getting some white workers and some African Americans to align themselves with the Left, their ideas about race, labor, and capitalism were not widely accepted by the city's mainstream. However, their influence remained important and affected the discourse of racial liberalism for two reasons. First, white and black communists and socialists, alongside other African Americans, produced rhetoric about interracial organizing and about building an interracial city that was ultimately taken up by white liberal leaders. Second, northern racial liberals deliberately cast their ideas in opposition to those of radicals. They self-consciously rejected radicals' claim that racial and class inequalities were intertwined. Instead, they carefully separated their vision of what racial equality should look like from an analysis that criticized capitalism, private property, and other forms of institutional and class inequalities that shaped northern cities. In contrast to communist ideas about racial justice, northern racial liberals held a vision of urban peace and racial equality that relied on the sustenance of most existing relations of power.

The first predominantly white organization to promote interracial union activism was the Communist Party, which started to recruit African Americans in the late 1920s.[37] The CP's advocacy of racial equality influenced some white residents' ideas about African Americans and interracialism by encouraging them to connect their struggles to the fight for racial equality. The coincidence of the Communist Party's mass appeal to employed and unemployed people in Detroit and of its national, concerted campaign to integrate the Party and to fight against "white chauvinism"—its term for racism—meant that many whites in

Detroit were exposed to the CP line on racial equality. Not all white communists or communist sympathizers took these dictates to heart, although the CP's ideas about interracial unionism became influential in the local labor movement by the middle of the 1930s and thus affected white and black city residents.[38]

The Party cast interracial unity as revolutionary, and African Americans functioned as a powerful symbol, representing the most oppressed and revolutionary class of American workers, employed or unemployed.[39] As part of its effort to recruit more black members, Detroit's Trade Union Unity League and the AWU cosponsored an "Inter-racial Proletarian Cabaret" at the New Workers Home. The New Workers Home was located in a neighborhood that was becoming increasingly integrated, on the east side of the city, directly north of Paradise Valley, Detroit's largest black district. Detroit's CP also held an interracial mass meeting at the end of 1929, designed to "lay the basis for building a branch of the American Negro Labor Congress" (ANLC), one of the first labor organizations in the city to take an exclusive interest in black workers and African American unionism. In 1930, the ANLC met with some success, appealing to more African Americans than the few who organized it. It sponsored a lecture by Otto Huiswood, the head of the National Negro Department of the CP, and held a number of meetings in black neighborhoods focused on "solidarity with the Negro workers of Haiti," which had been occupied by the United States since 1915. These meetings ultimately attracted twelve new black members to Detroit's CP.[40]

The CP and African American communists in Detroit argued that it was crucial to organize and recruit black workers into unions and Party activities in the industrial North. In an article in the *Daily Worker* about organizing the "Negro masses" in Detroit, Robert Woods emphasized the importance of recruiting black members to the Party and stressed the importance of supporting interracial relationships. African Americans were the "most exploited section of th[e] working class," he explained, and had "shown their readiness to carry on a militant fight against . . . intense economic and racial discrimination." As such, they were central players in the fight to overthrow capitalism and build a more just and equitable society. White chauvinism, he argued, was a bourgeois and reactionary tendency that undermined the Party's effort to win the support of the majority of workers.[41]

The CP explicitly encouraged interracial dating among its members. In his article, Woods addressed one of the central, and often unarticulated, anxieties of white workers: miscegenation. He dismissed the idea that sexual relations between white women and black men were inherently problematic and instead came out in favor of interracial relationships. "When the well-known question 'What would you do if a Negro wanted to marry your sister?' is asked," he explains, "we must not only state that we would not resent it, but that we welcome such inter-racial marriages, as a step towards breaking down the capitalist instilled antagonisms between the different sections of the working class."[42] According to Jacob Spolansky, an informant paid by industrialists to infiltrate communist circles in Detroit, the CP lured in black members with "inducements in the form of social recognition." In his testimony to the House of Representatives, which was investigating communist propaganda in 1930, he suggested with clear horror that white communists would attract black workers to their cause by demonstrating their interest in racial equality. Furthermore, Spolansky reported with alarm, African Americans would be shown "where white people freely intermingled with the colored men and women." The Party's commitment to racial equality and to social integration challenged ideas commonly held by white Detroit residents about racial propriety.[43]

The Party's interest in recruiting black members, its militant stance against white chauvinism, its recognition of discrimination in hiring, and its denouncement of poor working conditions, pay, and living standards faced by African Americans all reflect the Communist Party line. However, while African Americans held an important symbolic and ideological place in CP thought, real African Americans often confronted prejudice and hostility from CP members and sympathizers. Campaigns to recruit more African American Party members and to condemn what the Party called "white chauvinism" did not eliminate racism. For example, Al Goetz, president of the AWU, would not admit black workers into an event at the Graystone Ballroom in 1929, which frequently held events for African Americans. No one in the Detroit branch challenged his decision, with some members openly supporting him.[44] The next year, one woman, Mrs. Estrin, attempted to prevent a group of African Americans from attending a Communist Party meeting at the Jewish Workers Club, even though they had been assigned to a "nucleus" that was meeting there. Implying that her petit bourgeois status accounted for her racist behavior, the *Daily Worker* reproached Mrs. Estrin for her actions, explaining that she was not a worker but merely "the wife of the owner of a tailor shop." While the Jewish Workers placed her on probation and claimed to "sharply condemn her actions," members of the club were not unanimous in their criticisms, and at least two defended her.[45]

Black Detroiters continued to be interested in the CP. Shelton Tappes, a black activist who became very involved with the UAW, believed that the CP helped black workers see the importance of organizing. His father and uncles, he explained, were antiunion because of the discriminatory policies of the AFL, but they "responded to the Unemployment Council, and other organizations which called for the workers to get together and do something about their problems."[46] Indeed, during the Depression, as black political allegiances were shifting away from patronage politics and white business leaders, even relatively mainstream African American Detroiters became interested in alliances with the CP. A 1934 editorial in the Republican-affiliated *Detroit Tribune* endorsed the Party's growing influence, concluding that communism could help bring about "the 'New Deal' that the American people are determined to get."[47] Another *Tribune* editorial concluded that communism was far better than "the race hatred and injustice of the average 100 per cent white American citizens who think Negroes are footballs to be kicked around at will."[48]

The CP's advocacy for racial equality helped shape some white residents' ideas about African Americans and interracialism by encouraging them to connect their own struggles against unemployment to the fight for racial equality. Not all white communists or communist sympathizers took these dictates to heart, but the CP's ideas about interracial unionism became influential in the local labor movement by the middle of the 1930s and thus clearly had an effect on many city residents.

Majority-White Unions and Black Ambivalence about the Labor Movement

A small portion of African Americans affiliated themselves with the labor movement before the late 1930s, including men and women with experience in predominantly black unions like NAPE, as well as a cadre of black leftists. These activists provided African American Detroiters with models for labor organizing that considered black civil rights concerns. They also sustained relationships with predominantly white labor and leftist organizations like the Communist Party and the Civil Rights Federation, which maintained visible connections to struggles for racial justice. Indeed, black residents' attitudes toward unions were affected by the growing popularity of a more confrontational political style among African Americans over the course of the 1930s, as well as gradual shifts among a range of black leaders toward the labor movement. They were also reshaped by the increasing importance of industrial organizing within the labor movement. At the same time that black activists and their supporters were pushing unions to fight against discrimination, the national labor movement began to shift from a commitment to craft-based organizing to industrial unionism.

By the mid-1930s, African Americans in Detroit held a broad range of opinions about unions. Most saw the city's majority-white unions as institutions that actively discriminated against black workers. Their wariness was rooted in experience with these organizations and their activists. The American Federation of Labor, for example, had a history of supporting segregation both nationally and locally, and in the beginning of the Depression it was notorious among African Americans for its racism. Almost all of Detroit's AFL locals were segregated, and some colluded with employers to retain whites-only workplaces. At one plant, white AFL-affiliated activists signaled their willingness to accommodate, if not abet, their employers' exclusion of African Americans when they refused to fight for their black coworkers' jobs after they won a wage increase. Together, a group of white and black AFL-affiliated workers walked out of their plant in a strike over wages. The next day, employers invited the whites to return to the plant at higher pay but fired the black workers who had participated in the action, replacing them with whites who had not previously been at the plant. Rather than continuing to fight for the black jobs, white workers saw the outcome of their action as a victory. Whether or not they conspired with management to segregate the workplace, their actions illustrated that their black coworkers' continuing employment was a low priority for them.[49]

Frequently, black workers complained that AFL craft unions would take their dues but fail to send them out on jobs. In one instance, the union officials actually returned a black workers' dues when he tried to join the organization. The only black mechanic at the city garage, George Collier, was asked by a white coworker to join the Detroit Municipal Club to help fight against an impending wage cut. A few weeks after he paid his two-dollar membership fee, Collier received a letter from the club, which explained that the bylaws did not permit him to belong to the union, and a refund of his money.[50] Some specific locals were frequent targets of African American complaints about discrimination. Black workers accused the AFL-affiliated Brewers' Union, for example, of pressuring the Goebel Brewing Company to fire its black workers and replace them with whites. While white union officials denied the accusation, they remained unwilling to open their ranks to their African American coworkers, indicating that they supported segregation, even if they were not, in this instance, pushing for the elimination of black jobs.[51] In 1935, the national AFL confirmed its disinterest in racial equality by participating in a successful campaign against the inclusion of antidiscrimination language in the Wagner Act, the law that guaranteed workers' right to organize trade unions, improved their protections against antiunion retaliation, and required employers to engage in collective bargaining.[52]

While AFL craft unions unapologetically supported segregation, changes in the federation that began in the early 1930s saw a growing proportion of activists embracing interracial unionism. The 1933 passage of the National Industrial Recovery Act, which guaranteed the right of workers to organize independent unions and collectively bargain with their employers, inspired strike waves in Minneapolis, San Francisco, Toledo, and other cities. These victories left few permanent organizations in their wake, but they empowered leaders of large, industrially based unions to push the AFL to take an interest in unskilled workers. John Lewis, head of the United Mine Workers, emerged as a leader of this "rank-and-file" movement.[53] Rather than representing workers who shared a common trade, industrial unions aimed to organize all workers in a single industry into the same union, including unskilled laborers. Advocates of industrial organizing were also promoters of interracial organization. They saw racism as a management tool to divide workers, although their actual interest in organizing workers of color was uneven at best.[54]

Inspired by the 1935 Wagner Act, leaders of eight large industrial unions formed the Committee for Industrial Organization, with John Lewis as its president. Originally designed to remain within the framework of the AFL, the CIO began its drive to bring unorganized workers into the federation. AFL leaders, however, remained hostile to the CIO, denouncing it as divisive and ultimately damaging to the labor movement.[55] In Detroit, AFL craft unions tried to obstruct autoworkers' attempts to build an industrial union, but the federation capitulated in 1935 and chartered the United Automobile Workers. By 1936, relations between the AFL and the CIO had grown strained. The UAW soon joined the CIO and invited the independent unions to merge into its ranks. In November 1936, the AFL expelled all CIO-affiliated unions from its federation.[56]

The UAW's and CIO's public positions on racial integration and discrimination, as well as the practices they implemented to either hinder or facilitate equality between white and black workers, varied enormously.[57] These inconsistencies were as important as the public positions of the internationals when considering how African Americans understood and interacted with unions, and how all Detroiters came to understand interracial organizing. There was certainly a small cadre of prominent and vocal antiunion African American leaders in Detroit, including Donald Marshall, Ford's personnel manager for African American workers, and the Reverend Robert Bradby, who had a close relationship to the Ford Motor Company. Indeed, many African Americans' concerns about majority-white unions' racism were accompanied by misgivings about whether black workers would benefit from organizing against white employers, particularly Henry Ford, who employed a large number of African Americans, positioned himself as a friend to black Detroit, and was extremely antiunion.[58] However, the debate among African Americans about unionization was quite robust and included high-profile defenders of both unionization and the UAW.

These included state senator Charles Diggs, as well as the Reverends Horace White and Charles Hill, members of the Civic Rights Committee and activists in the local National Negro Congress.

Black newspapers' coverage of union drives through the 1930s also illustrates this range of support for unionization. Typically, the *Detroit Tribune* was supportive of unionization for black workers at the same time that its writers expressed concerns about racism within existing unions, as well as a political allegiance with the city's Republicans. In 1934, the *Tribune* concluded that black workers had reason to be suspicious of the AFL, but that "the time has arrived when all wage-earners should be organized. . . . Whether Negro workers join the American Federation of labor or not, self preservation demands that we organize and learn to bargain collectively."[59]

While African Americans remained suspicious of white unions, many black workers and leaders in the industrial North believed that unionization had the potential to undermine some of the most egregious elements of class inequality, a project that would benefit black workers as well as white. Beginning in the middle of the 1930s, high-profile black organizations in northern cities began to lend their support more consistently to the labor movement. For example, in 1934, when asked to provide 500 strikebreakers to undermine an elevator operators' work stoppage, the New York Urban League refused and instead issued a press release supporting the strikers. Lester Granger, of the National Urban League, came to speak in Detroit the following year to promote the national league workers' councils as a step toward joining "the ranks of organized labor."[60] National civil rights organizations also pressured unions to reject segregation. The national NAACP, for example, conducted a letter-writing campaign urging white labor leaders to reconsider discriminatory policies. The San Francisco branch allied with black longshoremen to demand that the AFL end its segregated practices and begin to admit black workers into unions as equals. Rather than dismissing unions, these protests clearly demonstrated African Americans' interest in reforming the labor movement in order to create space for black workers inside of it.[61]

Black activists also pushed for a commitment to interracial organizing from inside of the labor movement. A. Philip Randolph, head of the Brotherhood of Sleeping Car Porters, had brought the brotherhood into the AFL in 1929, and since then had been working to reshape the federation's racial practices and policies. Every year, he would come to the AFL national convention with proposals designed to open up the union and force its affiliates to accept black workers as full and equal members. In 1934, as the NAACP and other black activists protested outside of the convention, Randolph introduced a resolution to convention delegates. His proposal called for the AFL to expel affiliate unions that were maintaining a "color bar"—through either their policies or their practices—and for the federation to appoint a committee to investigate the current state of the organization of black workers. Convention delegates refused to support Randolph's more substantive demand, to expel unions for practicing discrimination, and even refused to go on record against "color bars." They did, however, agree to authorize the formation of a committee to investigate discrimination.[62]

Even though protesters' victories were sometimes partial, incremental, or even superficial, these combined actions had an effect on labor leaders. William Green, president of the AFL, promised NAACP leaders that he would eliminate discrimination against African American applicants for union membership. At the same time, however, he denied that general discrimination against African Americans existed within the AFL and expressed disappointment that black workers were not more interested in unions. Although Green's response demonstrates that he maintained little real interest in doing anything about discrimination, it does show that he believed he needed to pay attention to black protest and, if nothing else, contain African Americans' demands.[63] Although disappointing, responses like these helped African Americans believe that change within unions was possible in the same way that they saw the New Deal as something they could help shape. Many union leaders, like New Deal liberals, were beginning to believe that they *had* to respond to African Americans' demands in order to contain their protests. Even if their initial responses were dismissive, the fact that they were beginning to respond more consistently was heartening and encouraged more protest. The AFL was slow to convene the special committee, but it finally did so in July 1935, after pressure from Randolph and activists in the rank-and-file caucus. The committee heard testimony from a number of prominent black leaders. Charles Houston of the NAACP argued that the federation needed to address and remedy de facto discrimination as well as de jure exclusion of black workers from AFL unions. A. Philip Randolph urged the committee to hold hearings in cities across the country, and a group of black workers "gave concrete personal experience of their fight to become affiliated with local unions." Ultimately, the African American witnesses cautioned, unless it opened its doors to black workers, the AFL would find "this class of workers going into other labor bodies."[64]

African Americans and Unionization in the Automobile Industry

Debates among African Americans about joining predominantly white unions took on a new urgency at the end of 1936 when unions started to win significant victories in Detroit and other industrial areas. What had seemed like academic questions about whether African Americans should ally with white unionists in the industrial union movement became far more immediate concerns for black factory workers. African Americans made complicated decisions about unionization that were most frequently driven by an assessment of the local situation, rather than a larger ideological commitment to unionization. Thus a racially liberal approach—one in which white labor leaders touted racial equality in principle but failed to struggle for racial justice in practice—was ineffective. African Americans did not ally themselves with whites who touted their commitment to black workers without standing up for African American rights, especially when blacks' positions as workers were consistently more vulnerable than whites'. Furthermore, once it became clear that the union movement would ultimately win recognition across the auto industry, African Americans' assessment of the situation changed, and alliances with white unionists began to make a new kind of sense.

By the end of 1936, the UAW had had few significant victories, but in late November, strikers at Midland Steel initiated the first sit-down strike in Detroit. The strike took place just three weeks after the elections that swept Roosevelt back into office and made Frank Murphy, a pro-labor New Deal candidate, governor of Michigan. Midland Steel, an enormous foundry that produced pressed-steel auto bodies for Ford, Chrysler, and other companies, had employed only African Americans through 1933. However, like other workplaces across the city, the complexion of its employees lightened along with the NRA codes. One-third of Midland workers were African American, and the plant was unusually integrated; black and white men worked side by side in a broad range of job categories.[65]

The Midland strike was characterized by interracial cooperation. Black and white workers stayed in the plant in proportionately equal numbers, and Oscar Oden, a black assembler, was elected to the strike committee. Two hundred white women also worked in the plant, but they left the factory during the sit-down "to avoid any scandals." Instead, they established a strike kitchen in the nearby Slovak Hall and organized committees to talk to strikers' wives about what was happening. African American women—wives of strikers and other volunteers—worked alongside white women, cooking meals and taking them up to strikers. Labor activists across the city rallied behind the Midland workers, who demanded the recognition of the UAW-CIO as their union, a raise of ten cents an hour, a forty-five-hour week with overtime pay for extra hours, and the end of piecework. After eight days, shortages forced Chrysler, Ford, and Briggs Manufacturing to idle 72,000 workers, and Midland Steel settled, with workers winning their most important demands. For the first time in the city's history, workers won important concessions from a major automobile company and won union recognition at an auto plant. These victories were only possible because of the interracial organizing that preceded them, something that was visible to activists and participants, including thousands of autoworkers from throughout the city who came by the strike headquarters at Slovak Hall to lend a hand during the sit-down.[66]

Even though the Midland win rested on interracial organizing, which helped produce solidarity between black and white workers, this aspect of the strike was frequently overlooked. Coverage of the event by mainstream white newspapers and by the UAW itself did not point out the interracial quality of the strike in explanations of the action's significance.[67] This missed opportunity points to the episodic and utilitarian nature of most white UAW leaders' interest in interracial organizing. When necessary, they publicized their interest in organizing black workers, but interracial solidarity stood at the tops of their agendas only when it mattered for white demands. African American workers were not particularly active in subsequent sit-down strikes. A minority of black workers participated in the wave of sit-downs that hit Detroit and southeast Michigan in the months following the Midland strike. These included a series of actions in plants and other work sites across Detroit, as well as the Flint sit-down strikes, where the UAW won recognition from General Motors. During these clashes, according to Roy Wilkins, editor of the NAACP's *Crisis* magazine and assistant secretary of the organization, most black workers were "hanging back asking the usual question: 'Will the union give us a square deal and a chance at some of the good jobs?'"[68]

By the spring of 1937, sit-down strikers had won recognition from a majority of automobile companies with plants in Detroit. The Ford Motor Company, however, resisted unionization, and the UAW was not strong enough at the company to stage a strike. African American workers engaged each other in spirited debates about whether allying with the UAW would offer them important benefits, like union leaders promised, or whether it would hurt their ability to sustain access to good jobs. One often-articulated concern was that union seniority policies would help cement racist practices that shut African Americans out of the industry's best jobs. The Ford Motor Company's unusually aggressive and violent Service Department intimidated both black and white workers, scaring some away from affiliation with the union. Beginning in January 1937, after dramatic UAW wins in sit-downs across the region, the Service Department began to hire black armed guards as part of a company strategy to ensure black rejection of unionization. The UAW also turned more aggressively toward the recruitment of black workers, who represented 12 percent of the workforce, or almost 10,000 workers in 1937. Black workers at Ford were unusually integrated at the River Rouge plant, although the majority still held the dirtiest jobs in the factory's overheated foundries. Both the company and the union expended resources designed to cultivate the allegiance of black workers. In April 1937, the union hired its first full-time, paid "Race organizer," Paul Kirk, an autoworker with ties to the Communist Party. By the summer, the union had six paid black organizers, all of whom reported to a newly devised Sub-committee for Organization of the Negro, a group of activist black members established soon after Kirk was hired.[69]

In the summer of 1937, the national NAACP held its convention in Detroit. Roy Wilkins spearheaded a campaign to get the convention to endorse the UAW organizing drive at Ford and invited union leaders to speak about the importance of black participation in the industrial union movement. Speakers included Homer Martin, president of the UAW-CIO, and Paul Kirk. Both spoke passionately about the importance of joining the union and argued that African American workers would benefit from affiliation. Martin was "heartily applauded" during his speech. Others, like John Davis, head of the National Negro Congress, also endorsed the union at the convention. While the convention did decide to come out in support of the UAW, prominent black local ministers railed against this alliance. William Pickens, a minister and head of the local NAACP, and others preached against the UAW and Homer Martin from his pulpit the subsequent Sunday.[70]

The first major attempt to unionize Ford failed by the middle of 1938. The union had not built enough strength to stage a sit-down strike, and the "Roosevelt recession" led to layoffs and slowdowns in the factory that soured an already harsh climate for organizing. Internal fighting within the UAW also derailed the organizing drive and drew resources away from the campaign to bring black workers into the union. Debates among African Americans about the benefits and pitfalls of black Ford workers joining the UAW continued, and Ford's black allies supported the company's efforts to squelch interest in unionization. In January 1938, for example, no "large [African American] church in the city" was willing to allow the Civic Rights Committee or the West Side Improvement Association to use their space because speakers sponsored by those groups promoted union organizing among black workers and supported the CIO. The speakers the churches banned included Mordecai Johnson, president of Howard University and a supporter of unionization, and the Reverend Horace A. White, who had backed O'Brien and the Labor Slate in the recent election, and was already active in a UAW-CIO organizing drive at Ford.[71] However, the heated antiunion rhetoric that had characterized some black leaders' responses to the organizing campaign at Ford were considerably less audible two years later. In the intervening time, the leadership of the local NAACP changed hands. Dr. James McClendon replaced Rev. Pickens, a Ford minister, as president of the branch at the end of 1937. While not closely aligned with the UAW or the CIO, McClendon rebuilt the NAACP into a far more activist organization that had a close alliance with labor-oriented groups like the Civil Rights Federation, especially in its work against police brutality.

Black efforts to push the UAW and the CIO to respond to black workers' concerns in job sites around the city had also begun to receive more coverage in Detroit's African American newspapers than anti-union missives. One such example, covered in the *Detroit Tribune* in May 1938, involved the local NAACP campaign to save the job of Curtis Hardy, a black driver who had worked for Family Creamery for three years. When the Detroit Creamery bought out the Family Creamery, the new company fired Hardy, and the CIO union to which Hardy belonged failed to do anything about it. The NAACP pushed the creamery and the union to remedy the clear case of discrimination and specifically took the union to task for not having "carried out or lived up to its principles of fairness and justice to all races regardless of color."[72] While this story certainly provided bad press for the CIO, unlike long-standing claims about Ford, there was no suggestion that black workers would be better off allying with the company than the union, since the company was certainly not protecting their rights either. The UAW and its Negro Organizing Committee, the National Negro Congress, the Communist Party, and the Conference for the Protection of Civil Rights, which would become the Civil Rights Federation, all fought against racial discrimination and for workers' rights.[73] Some of these groups were principally African American, like the NNC, but others, like the Civil Rights Federation, had a predominantly white membership.

Supporters of industrial unionization also received more coverage in the black press than they had previously. The *Michigan Chronicle* vocally supported industrial organizing, publishing op-eds which predicted that autoworkers would soon win a union at Ford and appealing to African Americans to be on the right side of history. While certainly reserved in its praise for the CIO, the *Chronicle* stressed that an alliance with labor was the best choice for black workers, since unions seemed well positioned to win important battles over the long term: "We have seen at least some recognition of black labor, some recognition of its plight and some recognition of its capacity on the part of those who seem destined to lead the great body of American workers in the next few years."[74] The National Negro Congress held its statewide convention at the African American branch of the YWCA, in the heart of Detroit's largest black neighborhood, in June 1938.[75] Protests involving relief workers and public employees, as well as black organizing within the UAW, were all consistently covered in the city's black newspapers by the end of the decade. These actions illustrate the broad support for unions and labor-based activism among African Americans, in spite of clear reservations about the limits of predominantly white unions to address and fight for black workers' concerns. Protests against changes in WPA jobs, for example, brought a parade of nearly 15,000 marchers down Detroit's main thoroughfare in July 1939. State senator Charles Diggs, an African American, as well as R. J. Thomas, president of the UAW-CIO, and other local union leaders spoke at the rally, which included 1,500 African Americans.[76] The NAACP also fought alongside the State, County, and Municipal Workers of America against a new DPW policy prohibiting black social workers from managing the cases of white relief recipients.[77]

After the failed Ford drive of 1937–1938, the next major union battle in Detroit to bring black workers high visibility in the local labor movement was a dispute at Chrysler's Dodge Main plant at the end of 1939. The company had locked out its workers after a slowdown action in October. At the end of November, after stalled negotiations and in an effort to break the power of the union, the company, in alliance with a splinter group of conservative unionists, sponsored a "back to work" campaign. Chrysler specifically recruited black workers to return to their jobs, and in response the UAW-CIO called a strike so these workers would be crossing a picket line. Of the 22,000 workers employed in the plant, 1,700 were African American, the majority of whom remained neutral in the labor dispute. On Friday, November 24, sixty strikebreakers, the vast majority of whom were African American, entered the plant, and six were injured by UAW-CIO picketers. Police arrested twenty-two protesters. R. J. Thomas accused the company of stirring up racial tensions in a deliberate effort to start a race riot, get the governor to call in the National Guard to quell the racially based disturbance, and thereby defeat the union. A range of black leaders agreed with Thomas that racial tensions might explode into a large-scale conflict. They lined up with the union to discourage African

Americans from returning to work and picketers from hurting the men who would try to enter the plant the following workday. On Sunday, thousands of black parishioners received circulars signed by the Reverend Horace White, the Reverend Charles A. Hill, state senator Charles Diggs, and Louis Martin urging them to reject the back-to-work movement and stand with the union. No prominent African Americans, including none of the conservative Ford ministers, publicly lined up behind the back-to-work movement. Of the 205 workers who crossed the picket line the next day, 181 were African American. Black leaders, including Horace White, attempted to dissuade African Americans from entering the plant. Thomas, alongside union officials, White, and other black leaders, distributed pamphlets to picketers urging them to protest peacefully and not to be provoked by a company effort to spark violence. Protesters largely complied with these appeals and allowed the majority-black group of strikebreakers into the plant without violence. The strike was resolved later that day, so it is unclear whether this standoff would have been sustainable.[78] Like other labor struggles of the 1930s in Detroit, racial politics of the Chrysler strike were both complicated and ambivalent. The strike cannot be fully characterized by interracial cooperation, which was present to some degree. Nor can it be explained as an example of total racial animosity, even though tensions between black and white workers based on race and on their relationships to the work stoppage were certainly elements of the conflict.

The union drive at Ford Motor Company, which ultimately won recognition for the UAW at the last of the Big Three automobile companies in 1941, was possible because a majority of Ford's black workers agreed to remain neutral vis-à-vis the organizing drive. In 1941, black workers helped fight for and win recognition for the UAW-CIO in Ford's enormous River Rouge complex. A majority of Detroit's black residents supported the union drive, but it was not a foregone conclusion that African Americans would favor the UAW over the company. The Ford Motor Company had been celebrated as a valuable friend to African Americans for years. Ford had waged an intensive antiunion campaign. The company's antiunion tactics included both implicit and explicit threats to abandon its investment in African American institutions if black workers threw their support behind the union.[79] Some African Americans were extremely active in the campaign. Black activists gained important organizing experience, and the victory strengthened "the leftist labor–civil rights community" of the city.[80] Black and white members of this coalition contributed to citywide debates about the meanings of race, about the roles that African Americans should play in Detroit, and about the dynamics of interracial spaces and interactions. African Americans active in labor struggles, alongside some of their white allies, promoted racial justice, interracial cooperation, and a robust form of social, economic, and political equality. They also promoted a class-based analysis of racial inequality that considered how bosses used racism as a tool to advance their class interests over the interests of workers.

The predominantly white labor movement in Detroit provided models for understanding interracial engagement that were profoundly ambivalent. Its leaders celebrated the idea of racial inclusion at the same time that, in practice, unions often sustained racial hierarchies and contributed to the maintenance of white privilege. The union movement in Detroit provided a site where interracial cooperation and inclusion were visible, but the limits of that cooperation were always a central part of the story. It provided a model for how to produce urban racial interactions that was self-consciously more inclusive than previous approaches.

The CIO's commitment to interracial organizing was one of the dynamics that contributed to and reinforced the importance of racial liberalism in the labor movement and in the city at large. CIO activists' belief in the need for cooperation between black and white workers and their use of race-specific language to promote that vision meant that they were more racially progressive than most mainstream leaders and politicians. However, by the end of the 1930s, few established political leaders or organizations used white supremacist or racist language in public settings. A majority of liberal and conservative politicians and labor leaders were using race-neutral language to describe their ideas, whether they supported liberal programs that benefited African Americans or a police force that was consistently brutalizing black residents. This meant that liberals' and labor activists' use of nonracist language was not unique.

The popularity of northern racial liberal discourse among the city's white leaders meant that the CIO's explicit commitment to interracial union organizing was a superficial beginning from the perspective of African Americans. By the end of the 1930s, black workers and residents sustained a reasonable expectation that white leaders interested in their support would use language about racial equality when they addressed a black audience. They were looking for something more: white allies committed to the fight for racial justice who used clearly and consistently inclusive practices in their own work. Liberals' and labor activists' commitment to black rights and equality was inconsistent, at best. The UAW-CIO, for example, used the language of interracial organizing to describe its push to persuade African Americans to join its campaigns, but this meant different things in different contexts. Indeed, black activists involved in the union movement frequently criticized their leaders for sustaining a weak commitment to black concerns. For example, in 1939, Joseph Billups, one of the UAW's African American organizers, pulled together a group of black union activists in order to develop proposals aimed at changing the practices of the CIO and ending discrimination in auto factories. The conferees resolved that union officials needed to better "understand that problems of Negroes must be dealt with as such and apart from those problems of the regular membership." They also listed black workers' grievances in area plants and suggested that the union needed to work harder to address these concerns if it wanted to hold itself up as a champion of interracial organizing. These included differentials in pay between white and black workers doing the same type of work, sometimes in the same department; discrimination against African Americans in opportunities for apprenticeships; and departmental seniority rights, giving African Americans seniority only in their segregated departments.[81]

Although CIO leaders celebrated their union as an institution that stood on the front lines in the fight for integration and African American rights, some of its members were unwilling to comply even with its antisegregationist policies. African Americans had extensive experience, by the end of the 1930s, with groups and individuals that touted their commitment to black rights without upholding these promises. Thus, they were skeptical of rhetoric that seemed to speak to their interests but that left racial hierarchies in place. In the next chapter I will return to a discussion of city politics and examine debates about race, slum clearance, and low-income housing during the 1930s.

7

"Better Housing Makes Better Citizens"

Slum Clearance and Low-Cost Housing

On a warm Saturday morning in October 1938, fifty black families moved into their brand-new apartments in the Brewster Homes. Brewster, which was built exclusively for African American occupancy, was one of two federally funded housing projects to open in Detroit that day. Most of its tenants would pay higher rent than they had for their previous apartments, but they were attracted to the housing project because of its promises of cleanliness and stability, alongside central heat, private bathrooms, electric stoves, new plumbing, and other modern amenities.

Parkside Homes, an all-white project, opened its doors to considerably more fanfare than Brewster. Early in the morning, Mayor Richard Reading greeted its first tenants, Mr. and Mrs. Walter J. Martin. The mayor arrived, shook Mr. Martin's hand, and handed him the key to his new apartment, as journalists and photographers from the daily newspapers recorded the ceremony. Reading thus invited the male head of this white working-class family to take possession of a clean, new apartment and, in the process, become a full member of civic society. He granted legitimacy to the claim that upstanding members of the white working-class had the right to possess public resources and occupy city space, as long as they conformed to the prescriptions set by the housing project, one of which was segregation.[1] Later in the day, the mayor headed over to Brewster and took a tour of the site led by George Isabell, the African American manager of the apartments who had been an important Reading supporter in the last election. It is entirely possible, and even likely, that Reading shook hands with some of Brewster's new tenants—he had won large majorities among the city's black voters in the previous election, less than a year before. However, Brewster residents saw less fanfare than their white counterparts across the city.[2]

Like the mayor, the *Detroit News* focused its attention on Parkside. In an article describing the day and optimistically celebrating the potential of the new projects, the paper profiled three families moving into the whites-only project with "tears in their eyes." These white tenants, the paper explained, would be watched as "the living evidence for and against the Washington theory that 'better housing makes better citizens.'"[3] This interest in Parkside in lieu of Brewster was a departure from the last five years of newspaper coverage. The area on which Brewster had been built and the black residents it had displaced were at the center of a years-long debate about slum clearance, low-cost housing, and the politics of race in Detroit. Representations of African Americans as dependents—crippled and infantilized by unemployment, poverty, and reliance on the state—had characterized this coverage. These images suggested that urban racial inclusion was troubled by the inherent inferiorities of African Americans rather than limits imposed on equality by upholders of segregation and discrimination. At the same time, stories about the projects cast white urban leaders as the protectors of black rights and equality.

Although Reading neglected to hand a key to a black tenant in front of reporters, this had no material impact on Brewster residents; they had no problem getting into their apartments, and probably had other things on their minds—like how to arrange the living room furniture. However, the distinction that Reading drew between African American families, who were invited to become residents of housing projects, and white families, who were being made into better citizens through their new, federally funded apartments, was significant. By the end of the 1930s, northern racial liberalism had become the language through which the city's white establishment explained its relationship to African Americans. Although Reading did not align himself with the New Deal or with liberalism per se, his embrace of northern racial liberalism is evidence of the extent to which the ideology had been accepted within the urban political sphere. In this instance, and in the case of most federally funded need-based programs in the urban North during the 1930s, African American residents of Detroit received the relatively robust benefits afforded by the New Deal state. The Parkside

The *Detroit News* published this image of an African American family settling into their new apartment on October 14, 1938, a few days after the Brewster Homes opened. Image courtesy of the Walter P. Reuther Archives of Labor and Urban Affairs, Wayne State University.

and Brewster Homes had about the same number of units—around 725—which means that black Detroiters, who represented 7 percent of the city's population, were receiving proportionately more federal assistance in low-income housing than whites. In this instance, segregation did not deprive black citizens of public resources as much as it shaped the way in which those resources were administered, received, and understood.

Reading was a conservative, but administrators of Detroit's slum clearance and low-income housing programs were liberals who used federal aid to build a new kind of city, one that they envisioned as more democratic and egalitarian that previous urban forms. While they saw themselves as allies of African Americans, who would receive invaluable state resources from the housing program, their vision meant the removal of the poorest black residents from the city's downtown district, as well as the expansion and formalization of residential segregation. White liberals built a New Deal coalition that included African Americans as recipients of resources but upheld both segregation and discriminatory ideas about black people.

At the same time, black leaders and residents embraced the federal government's claim that "better housing makes better citizens" and fought for full access to *both* of these promises. Black Detroiters refused to settle for resources alone and insisted on fighting for the noneconomic elements of citizenship, including political autonomy and the right to live, eat, and work anywhere in the city on equal ground with whites. Black residents' ideas about what they needed shaped the resources that they received from the state. Finally, black activists across the social and political spectrum imagined and described a vision of urban America that transcended the promises of the New Deal.

The "Project" of Housing Projects, Slum Clearance, and Low-Cost Housing

The word "project" in the phrase "housing project" referred as much to the project of making good citizens as it did to the task of building and maintaining the physical environment in which those citizens would live. Working-class nuclear families, housing officials suggested, would be elevated to full citizenship because they would live in clean and spacious apartments designed to accommodate the needs of modern Americans.[4] Public administrators were interested in uplifting white as well as black working-class families. However, for them, the project of producing better citizens was connected to white, not black, tenants of the new buildings in subtle yet clear terms. This distinction between housing all members of the American working class, making "better citizens" out of white families and state recipients out of black residents, began well before publicly funded housing programs opened their doors. From the beginning, decisions about the two housing projects were dependent on the racial identities of their future residents. The first black housing project was sited on top of a densely populated African American neighborhood that administrators identified as a slum area. Existing housing was torn down to make room for the new apartments. The first white housing project, conversely, was built on land that was not previously occupied.

In 1933, the National Industrial Recovery Act created the Public Works Administration (PWA), whose Housing Division began to solicit proposals from cities for public works projects designed to clear away dilapidated neighborhoods and replace them with federally built apartments for working-class families. The Detroit City Plan Commission was the first local agency to win approval for its project. Detroit's proposal, which the PWA lauded as exemplary, was to demolish up to forty square blocks of buildings in the heart of the city's largest black neighborhood and build segregated, low-cost housing exclusively for black residents on the cleared site. The previous summer, the commission had hired relief workers, more than half of whom were African American, to survey all of the city's oldest and poorest neighborhoods to determine which areas should be targeted for clearance. Surveyors collected statistics about the part of the city that stood within an area bounded by Grand Boulevard, a street that looped around the center of town. These seventeen square miles still housed a large proportion of the city's population but had been losing residents and businesses as people moved into outlying areas and suburbs, either to be closer to the factories where they worked or to retreat into newer residential districts.[5]

Planning commissioners settled on what they called "the East Side Blighted Area" for clearance because, they explained, "it was known to be the worst section of the city." This "blighted area" overlapped almost entirely with the black east side, or Black Bottom; most of its blocks were more than three-fourths black, and 65 percent of the city's black residents lived there.[6] Many houses in this "blighted" area were quite run-down. Landlords, the vast majority of whom were white, rented to black tenants who had few choices about where they could live because of intense residential segregation. Knowing this, landlords allowed buildings to deteriorate to the point of ruin and often refused to complete basic maintenance and upkeep. Many apartments did not have running water or private bathroom facilities. The northern part of the area, in contrast, was quite well maintained and boasted a high proportion of home ownership, but because it was also majority black, it was included in the area targeted for clearance, as was Hastings Street, the city's largest black commercial strip. Although some Hastings Street storefronts were run-down, profitable businesses remained. In fact, one of the problems that ultimately held up the slum clearance project was that the city was hesitant to pay the assessed valuation for storefronts on the street, a number of which were quite valuable because of the businesses they contained as well as the buildings they occupied. The condemnation of the entire black east side as a slum was not, in fact, an accurate reflection of the whole neighborhood but rather an assessment of its "blackness."

The swath of land identified by the planning commission as a slum was three-fifths of a mile wide from east to west and more than three miles long. The first fifteen-block section targeted for clearance had the highest proportion of black residents; more than 96 percent of the 800 families who lived there were African American. Ten black families owned their own homes, and eleven white families did. One-third of the black families were on welfare, while only 8 percent of the white families were.[7] Residents displaced by the slum clearance would not be eligible for the low-income housing that would be built on the site. Josephine Gomon, director of Detroit's Housing Commission, explained that the federally funded apartments were "being put up for the benefit of industrious, low-income families, not necessarily for the people now living in the slum areas."[8]

The area targeted to be demolished first included a high proportion of single men and women, as well as couples without children. Commissioners concluded that black families with children had moved out of the district and into nearby neighborhoods because of the prevalence of crime. If the project of public housing was, in part, to build better citizens, New Deal administrators saw African American adult men and women living outside of the bounds of nuclear families as outside of the bounds of full urban citizenship as well. While the average family size in the city was 4.4 people, it was only 2.8 among families in the "blighted area."[9] Very few families that were large enough to qualify for the housing project would have been able to move into it either, since they would not have been able to afford it. Rent in the new apartments would far exceed what residents of the area had been paying. Designers and supporters of slum clearance project thus suggested that the way to eliminate blight and reduce poverty in Detroit was to remove the poorest African Americans from the center of the city. Commissioners understood their decision to flatten a large proportion of Black Bottom as something that would be good for Detroit's African American community. Many of the city's African Americans agreed. By replacing slums with low-cost housing, commissioners believed, they would help uplift and beautify the majority-black area. For them, the key to urban renewal was the removal of these undesirable elements, replacing them with a clean built environment that housed the best kind of working-class African Americans.

Detroit's city planners started with the assumption that public housing would be segregated. While segregation seemed like the natural choice to housing commissioners, it was not the one available. The PWA's Housing Division required that new projects sustain existing neighborhood racial geographies, but this included the possibility of building low-income housing in mixed areas and offering the same proportion of apartments to each race represented in the district. Of the fifty projects constructed by the PWA during the New Deal, five were built for mixed-race occupancy, including one in South Carolina and one in Kentucky. While these two integrated projects represent a small proportion of all public housing built, their presence in the Upper South indicates that segregation in Detroit was the outcome of a local plan with a northern base that was nationally supported and even encouraged.[10] Detroit's housing commissioners explained their decision to choose to build segregated projects as a way to forestall anticipated criticism from public housing opponents, like the Detroit Board of Realtors, which staunchly opposed government-funded housing as well as residential racial integration.

The second major difference between city officials' ideas about housing working-class whites and working-class blacks centered on the location of the new apartment buildings. Apartments for African Americans would be built on land already occupied by black residents, while apartments for whites were to be built on unoccupied land that would not have to be cleared. The slum clearance project was partly predicated on the idea that African Americans had the right to live only in neighborhoods that they already occupied. Detroit had huge swaths of vacant land in the mid-1930s, but commissioners did not consider building a black project in an area that was not already black. This meant that they thought of unoccupied land as white, and that they wanted to contain African Americans in existing black neighborhoods and forestall their spread into other areas of the city.

Maintaining Residential Segregation

In November 1933, with the plans for the Brewster project approved, Detroit received a low-interest loan of $3 million from the PWA and a promise of $27 million more to come. Mayor John Smith, who was serving out the end of Frank Murphy's term in office, set up a Housing Commission to oversee and manage this project and future state-funded slum clearance and housing programs. Smith appointed five private citizens to serve as commissioners, all of whom were Democrats interested in housing: one "real estate man," a doctor who was "sociologically inclined," the president of the Women's Study Club, the manager of a local radio station, and a "publisher of labor papers" who was also "comptroller of the Unemployed Citizens League." The five were all white, even though the city's plans would have the most immediate impact on African Americans, and black residents pushed Smith to appoint at least one black commissioner. Smith, who had been mayor during the Ossian Sweet trial, saw himself as an ally of African Americans, but he was unwilling to appoint a black member to the Housing Commission.[11]

Upon Smith's recommendation, commissioners hired Josephine Gomon to direct the commission and oversee its daily operations. Gomon, one of the city's most vocal supporters of slum clearance and low-cost housing, believed that the success or failure of the project "as far as public opinion is concerned" would be based on how well it maintained residential segregation. She felt "a personal responsibility . . . that the character of no neighborhood in Detroit will be changed as a result of this shifting of population."[12] Successful relocation, she explained, meant moving African American residents out of the cleared area and into other black neighborhoods. Thus, she believed that the only way that African Americans would be able to get the resources they deserved was through a program that encouraged, rather than undermined, the increasing residential segregation of the city.

Josephine Gomon, right, and Eleanor Roosevelt during the opening of the Detroit slum clearance project, September 9, 1935. Image courtesy of the Bentley Historical Library, University of Michigan.

Josephine Gomon was a northern racial liberal with a genuine interest in the welfare of black residents. She believed that the state could participate in providing a more equal playing field for African Americans in northern cities, and she worked to ensure they received public resources. By the middle of the 1930s, she was one of the city's most prominent liberals. She first became active in local politics in the 1920s when she helped found Planned Parenthood and became president of Detroit's chapter, a position that brought her into close contact with black and white social service providers.[13] Like many of Detroit's prominent white liberals, Gomon was comfortably middle-class and circulated in a largely segregated world of educated white professionals. She majored in engineering in college and taught math and physics before she had children with her husband, an engineer and businessperson. Her most important political connection was to Frank Murphy, with whom she became close friends when they were both undergraduates at the University of Michigan. Gomon, a Democrat and opponent of Prohibition, sustained close ties some of the city's prominent politicians, including the liberal Republican senator James Couzens, with whom she kept up a correspondence.[14]

Gomon was an enthusiastic supporter of racial tolerance and African American inclusion, which she saw as centrally important to her politics and as a marker of her true commitment to liberalism. For example, she was quite active in the Sweet defense. A regular fixture in the courtroom during the trials, she became close friends with Sweet's attorney, Clarence Darrow.[15] African Americans, Darrow claimed, would recognize her as someone who "has a thorough understanding of the negro, has no race prejudice, and they could rely upon her as they could on few people."[16] In the late 1920s, as Gomon and Murphy worked to build a liberal political core in Detroit, they saw African American inclusion as an element of their politics. In 1929, for example, Gomon organized a club for Detroiters interested in the *Nation*, a liberal magazine with a national circulation, and invited white and black liberals to attend events. One enthusiast described the club's interracial dinners as a "crystallizing point for liberal opinion."[17] Like the white urban liberals with whom she organized, Gomon embraced the language of race neutrality, invited African Americans into the liberal coalitions she was building, and won respect from black activists.

In 1930, Gomon worked on Murphy's campaign for mayor. When he won office, she became his executive secretary, chaired the Mayor's Unemployment Committee, helped the administration establish its emergency relief programs, and developed plans to apply for money for slum clearance and low-cost housing from the federal housing program.[18] Gomon built connections with black leaders and visibility among politically engaged Africans. For example, when she ran for Common Council in 1933, John Dancy, the executive secretary of Detroit's Urban League, enthusiastically supported her candidacy and spoke highly of her interest in black Detroiters. In November 1934, Gomon called on Dancy for advice about how to manage "some problems facing the Housing Commission" and invited him to a private meeting to discuss her concerns.

As head of the Housing Commission, Gomon was well respected by black leaders for hiring both skilled and unskilled black workers into a range of different jobs and for making sure they received fair wages. She spoke at the "Economic Life of the Negro" conference in 1934 at the Lucy Thurman YWCA, highlighting the role of the Housing Commission in hiring otherwise unemployed African Americans.[19] Gomon saw direct engagement in battles over residential segregation as something that would weaken, rather than strengthen, her legitimacy and, by extension, her program. For her, tolerating segregation and understanding it as a necessary evil that would allow resources to flow to an underresourced community were not the same as promoting it. Thus, she believed in race neutrality at the same time that she helped implement segregation because she saw this Faustian bargain as the only option. For her, African Americans' ability to access urban resources was a move toward racial equality. Addressing segregation simultaneously could undermine those success and thus jeopardize the allocation of resources to black people. Gomon believed that if she focused more energy on fighting for integration, she would lose her political leverage and thereby exhaust her ability to help African Americans in housing altogether.

White liberals' unwillingness to take on segregation—even though it was rooted in their fears that disrupting the racial order would undermine their ability to extend benefits to blacks or to build a more just state—had important political and ideological consequences. Northern racial liberals distinguished between the material needs of African Americans on one hand and their needs for autonomy, respect, and meaningful political power on the other. They understood and sometimes fought enthusiastically for a more equitable distribution of state resources, but they simultaneously shied away from a confrontation with the culture of racism that helped shape these material inequalities. In spite of their best intentions, this approach meant that white liberals were inviting African Americans into the New Deal coalition as passive recipients of state resources, relegated to separate quarters and isolated in the city's increasingly segregated neighborhoods. Black Detroiters certainly appreciated the benefits they received from government programs, but many remained unsatisfied with the implicit terms of the agreement.

Northern racial liberals' tolerance of segregation and their simultaneous embrace of race-neutral discourse were rooted in a theory of race which assumed that white racism was destined to decline over time as Detroit became progressively more modern and cosmopolitan.[20] For them, racism was a premodern and southern practice that northern cities would shed as they developed. Thus, they believed that they could win segregated resources for African American residents without contributing to the maintenance of racial disparities, since those disparities were in the process of eroding.

Detroit's public officials saw the slum clearance and low-cost housing programs as a social intervention as well as a physical change in the city's geography. In other words, by clearing African American "slums" and then building new segregated housing, they would be creating an environment that would produce a different sort of sociability than the one currently practiced by the city's poorest black residents. Harold Ickes, head of the national PWA, praised Detroit's plan as being one of the best "from a social standpoint." The project, he explained, was "designed to eliminate uneconomic and unsocial conditions" and to build "a group unit conducive to neighborliness," all of which would happen in a space where African Americans would be the only residents. He suggested that the "slum" conditions that were being cleared away had contributed to African Americans' "uneconomic" habits. Ickes, in other words, like the project's local designers, saw poverty as an effect of black residents' inability to occupy space correctly or to adopt proper urban modes of interaction, an analysis that implicitly rejected capitalism or racism as building blocks for poverty. Furthermore, rather than casting segregation as a problem that might limit economic opportunities or isolate and exclude African Americans, Ickes and local planners saw residential segregation as part of their solution for existing racial inequalities.[21]

The Slow Pace of Slum Clearance

The slum clearance project ended up moving very slowly f of reasons, many of which were connected to issues that an debates about the New Deal and about the growth of state power. Some property owners refused to sell their buildings at the "market prices" set by the government and used slum clearance as an opportunity to challenge the state's power to compel "private" citizens to relinquish their property. Furthermore, the city was hesitant to pay the assessed valuation for Hastings Street storefronts. In April 1934, the PWA stepped in and began to condemn buildings so that the city could take possession of them. This plan was far from popular among realtors and businesspeople, who complained that it was an unfair government intervention into the free market.[22] A member of the Detroit Housing Commission, who was a self-described "real estate man," resigned from his post in protest. Other property owners, complaining that the project was "unadulterated socialism," fought the condemnation proceedings in court. The final approval for the slum clearance project came in October 1934 when the PWA granted Detroit $6.6 million in loans to raze the first area and build new housing. The project promised to provide 2,000 unemployed men with jobs and ultimately house 1,400 families.[23]

Even though the men, women, and children displaced from the cleared area would not be able to live in the new federal housing, the Housing Commission devoted few resources to help them find new apartments. A few months before demolition began, commissioners hired relief workers to help residents and businesses relocate to other black neighborhoods. However, commissioners did not offer these displaced people or businesses any financial assistance in their relocation. It proved very difficult to find housing for displaced tenants, since vacancies in black areas were already extremely low. By the end of 1935, the number of residents living in the area to be torn down had decreased from a little under 1,000 to 343. Gomon appealed to the federal government for help, explaining that it was becoming more and more difficult to find housing for displaced tenants, since vacancies in black areas were already low and decreasing rapidly. Generally, however, she was satisfied with the progress of relocation and particularly pleased that she had received no complaints from "the general property owners in the city," who were happy that "neighborhood preservation," a euphemism for segregation, had been maintained. Although, she admitted, black residents had been "subjected to a good deal of inconvenience and hardship," Gomon was pleased because they were "very cooperative" about moving.[24]

While Gomon was satisfied with the pace of relocation and with her success in maintaining residential segregation, others were furious because the clearance program was proving enormously disruptive and damaging to so many already destitute residents. Karen Dash, for example, the director of a social service agency in Detroit, called the relocation program a farce. Relocated residents, she complained, were living in far worse conditions than they had been subject to before they moved. Furthermore, she explained, these black residents were treated very poorly by the welfare workers and relocation officers responsible for helping them. For example, although legally they had thirty days to move, a welfare officer in the area explained that tenants were told they had from five days to two weeks to get out of their apartments. Furthermore, there was simply no housing available at the prices residents of the "blighted area" had been paying. Many evicted families were "doubling up" to afford new apartments. "Any slum-clearance project," Dash complained, "which does not improve the condition of those who suffer from filthy, unsanitary housing is a fake."[25]

The maintenance of residential segregation and the clearing away of black-occupied slums were higher priorities for the Housing Commission than improving living conditions for all black residents. Detroit officials could have built the housing projects before they cleared the neighborhood. The PWA had no policies against building low-cost housing on vacant land. However, housing commissioners were not willing to allow African Americans to move into areas that were not already occupied by black residents, even outlying sections of the city that were barely populated. They believed, instead, that the only way they could build housing for black residents was to tear down an existing black neighborhood and rebuild on the cleared site.

The slum clearance project drew white and black Detroiters' interest, support, and animosity from the beginning. White residents sustained a range of responses to the project, depending on their political position and their ideas about African Americans. A vocal minority were against the projects altogether. These residents drew clear links between poverty, unworthiness, African Americans, and the state. They usually complained that black residents in the slum district were unworthy of state resources and, more broadly, that the government should not be involved in the housing market. J. W. Barbey, for example, expressed his concerns about the state helping the "unworthy" poor. He complained that the federal housing policy appeared to be "restoring prosperity to the thrifty as well as the unthrifty," which, he suggested, was a misguided goal. Sophia Kelleher, a landlord who claimed to have "experience" with "the people down in the slum district," made more explicit connections between her concerns about the clearance project and her assertion that African Americans in the area were "very near all Welfare Suckers." She advised Mayor Couzens not to cater to "them Southern Negroes" because, she suggested, they were unworthy of help from the state and were "accustomed to living in shaks" anyway. By marking black residents as "Southern," she cast them as transients and illegitimate recipients of local resources.[26]

Other white residents expressed misgivings about the slum clearance project because they were concerned that clearing the area would force displaced African American residents to push past the boundaries separating black from white neighborhoods. W. H. Chapman, a local businessman, complained to the mayor that "if the people now living in the above district were to be put out, they would move into other districts and cause a further decrease in property values wherever they might go." John W. Chandler, secretary and general manager of the Central District Protective Association, believed that if small numbers of African Americans moved into his rather exclusive neighborhood, which was close to the slum district, the area would be almost immediately "swallowed up in the so-called 'black belt.'" "I won't waste paper telling you what happens!" he exclaimed to the mayor. These complaints provide a clear example of how discourses about African Americans and race shaped some white Detroiters' understanding of the slum clearance project.[27]

Taxpayer organizations had lost a lot of ground in the city since the summer of 1932.[28] However, white Detroiters opposed to public works projects and to welfare continued to describe themselves as "taxpayers" when they made claims about why the city should not extend resources to its poor black residents. In fact, a majority of the people who wrote letters to the mayor protesting the slum clearance or the construction of low-income housing either identified themselves as taxpayers in the first sentence of their letters or wrote "taxpayer" under their signature as if to formally identify themselves and clarify their relationship to city resources. Guy W. Buck, for example, was disturbed at the prospect that taxpayer money would be directed toward the housing project because, he suggested, the people to be housed would quickly turn the newly renovated area back into a slum. He asked Mayor Couzens to show "the TAXPAYERS of Detroit, Why the Appartment Buildings to be erected in the SLUM distrect, Will Not Become A POOR HOUSE . . . which the Government and the TAXPAYERS have to support." A group that identified itself as "a number of taxpayers" agreed with Buck's assessment. "If we are to judge by some welfare tenants," it complained, "these new structures would be in the same disreputable condition (in a very short time) that the old ones are." Even though the federal government was sponsoring the slum clearance project, this group argued, because the majority of people in the district were "welfare tenants," local taxpayers would be paying the rent. Therefore, it reasoned, taxpayers had the right to express their concerns and ultimately stop what they saw as an egregious waste of money. While this argument was based on erroneous claims—the majority of slum area residents were not, in fact, welfare recipients, and the federal government had already taken on a large proportion of the relief bill—it shows that these white "taxpayers" saw themselves as exclusive owners of city resources. Buck suggested that the district would make "A GOOD PARK," indicating that he was not opposed to using public resources to clear the area but was opposed to expending money on its current residents.[29]

Even though these men and women did not mention race when they protested the slum clearance project, "taxpayers" had far less to say about the Parkside Homes, the low-cost housing planned for white occupancy. In 1935, the Housing Commission won approval for a new project to be built on the far east side, close to the exclusive, all-white Grosse Pointe suburbs. The Common Council voted down the plan, on the grounds that low-income housing should not be located in previously "unblighted" districts because it would be an "unwarranted, unfair and unsound invasion" of those areas. Couzens vetoed their decision, but he assured the council that "neighborhood preservation" would be upheld, explaining that the new housing would be for white tenants and reconfirming that the slum-cleared site would house only African Americans. Couzens's assurance quelled the council's concerns, and its members began to support the new project. Their reaction to the original proposal for the white housing project—a proposal that did not include explicit language about race—and their change of heart when Couzens promised to uphold segregation indicate that their concern that low-cost housing was an "unsound invasion" into nonblighted areas was about race.[30]

The Parkside Homes attracted far less public acrimony. Furthermore, complaints about this project, which generally came from realtors, took on a different tone than those directed toward the slum clearance project and the future Brewster Homes. Those people who did complain about Parkside tended to express concerns about publicly funded housing being an incursion into the free market, rather than an incursion into a previously intact—meaning white—neighborhood. Thomas Danahey, head of the Detroit Real Estate Board, for example, opposed Parkside because he saw it as an "economically unsound invasion of the field of competition with private enterprise." His concern was that government-funded housing projects would undermine the revival of the building industry. Private interests, he believed, would be undersold by publicly subsidized projects.[31] Those people who did suggest that Parkside might lead to neighborhood decline connected that decline to the possibility of future residential integration, even though the project was going to be all white. For example, the Eastern Detroit Real Estate Board argued that since "the federal government cannot restrict against race, color or creed, we fear that the ultimate results of this question can only lead to rack and ruin of any good community."[32]

White men and women who supported the housing project did not write letters to the mayor or the Housing Commission, so it is difficult to explore their opinions. However, some of the coverage of the slum clearance project in Detroit's daily papers offers some insight. Reporters often encouraged white residents to consider the structural reasons that African Americans lived in the worst neighborhoods. They offered sympathetic, if condescending, accounts of why the area was so run-down and the barriers its residents faced to full employment or better housing.[33]

Black Responses to Slum Clearance and Low-Cost Housing

African Americans responded to the proposed slum clearance and low-cost housing projects with a mixture of hope and caution. In August 1933, Theodore Barnes, a regular columnist in one of the city's black weeklies, was enthusiastic about the good things that could come out of these federal programs, but he maintained skepticism about the commitment of city officials. He argued that the housing projects could help remove "one of [the] excuses for discrimination" and even help unite African Americans across class who, he believed, were divided by a "social gulf" between residents of the "slum district" and those living in "what they term 'better' residential" areas. He ultimately concluded, however, that the only way the program could work would be if black Detroiters remained vigilant about ensuring that their rights were respected and pushed hard to make sure the government lived up to its promises.[34]

A few months later, *Detroit Tribune* editors welcomed the slum clearance and low-cost housing projects with the same ambivalence and caution as Barnes. They proclaimed that the project would be "a great social and civic benefit to Detroit" because "it is calculated to remove many of the unwholesome environments that breed crime, disease, and corruption among the unfortunate." They were also pleased because it would create thousands of relief jobs for Detroit residents. However, they cautioned, the project would only truly benefit the city "if put into effect without racial discrimination." *Tribune* editors thus made it clear that public housing would not be acceptable alone. The city would have to adopt a housing policy that was not racially discriminatory in order to satisfy black residents.[35]

This skepticism about the government's commitment to African Americans did not challenge some of the fundamental assumptions that shaped the housing projects. For example, middle-class black observers generally agreed that slum clearance was a beneficial plan for African Americans, even if it would deeply inconvenience some black residents.

Karen Ferguson demonstrates that members of the black middle class in Atlanta supported and helped enforce some of the condescending dictates of public housing policy. However, their enthusiasm for slum clearance was always rooted in their excitement about new federally funded housing.[36] Black activists had yet to coin the term "Negro removal" to describe slum clearance, a phrase they would begin to use in the 1940s. By then, two things had changed. First, black residents had more experience with slum clearance and its problems, and second, the city began to propose clearance projects for "urban renewal" more frequently than for low-income housing. Beginning after the Second World War, it had become more apparent that clearance often meant the removal of black neighborhoods without any promises of benefits for African Americans who were displaced.

African Americans had been working to get the state to respond to their concerns about poor housing since the 1910s, when the First Great Migration sparked a severe housing shortage among black workers and residents. Although black neighborhoods grew significantly during the 1920s, formal and informal restrictions confining black occupancy to limited areas became more clearly codified, and Detroit's neighborhoods grew more segregated over the decade. Black residents consistently paid higher rents to live in shabbier buildings than whites, and they inhabited some of the most dilapidated housing stock in the city.

African Americans received public housing from the state during the 1930s because they had been struggling for residential integration and equality in housing for years. Black efforts to move into white neighborhoods had elicited violent reaction from white residents since the First World War, but African Americans persisted in their fight to live wherever they pleased. This effort to win residential integration, one house at a time, failed to open up white neighborhoods to black occupancy, but it did have a distinct and important effect on city politics and on the resources that would become available to African Americans. These actions put pressure on city officials to address the crisis in black housing. Ironically, black Detroiters won resources from the state as part of public officials' efforts to maintain residential segregation and contain African Americans' efforts to integrate white neighborhoods surrounding the black east side, but they would not have received public housing from the state if they had not persisted in their fight against segregation.

Throngs of people came to see Eleanor Roosevelt at the slum clearance demolition ceremony on September 9, 1935. Image courtesy of the Walter P. Reuther Archives of Labor and Urban Affairs, Wayne State University.

Although the slum clearance project clearly made life difficult for residents of the area, it remained popular among the black community. When Eleanor Roosevelt came to Detroit in the fall of 1935 to kick off the first demolition for the project, African Americans thronged to the ceremony to see her and to welcome the new project.[37] The promise of public housing was quite appealing, but these promises did not stop black residents from fighting for better accommodations in their current apartments, even if they lived in the designated "blighted area." A few days before Mrs. Roosevelt arrived in Detroit to launch the clearance project, Mrs. Mattie Smouthers filed a suit against her landlord for $50,000 in damages. Smouthers had fallen off of the back porch of her second-story apartment in the "down-town East side section" after the railing gave way. Her lawyer, William Banks, an African American, announced that her building was "one of many similar buildings . . . owned by landlords who charge high rents for property which can be rented only to poverty-stricken people, who happened to be members of the colored group. . . . In my opinion, it might better conditions for occupants of dilapidated buildings in this locality if a few more similar suits were filed."[38]

In contrast to white racial liberals, African Americans were unlikely to separate their struggle for material resources from their fight to gain full citizenship or to push for residential, occupational, and educational integration. In fact, black activists made it clear that they would not be satisfied with second-class status even when they were receiving benefits from the state. For example, although black residents were enthusiastic about slum clearance, they remained concerned about African American employment on the project. Gomon had hired black workers to help with relocation, but activists complained that no African Americans worked in positions of authority or leadership on the project, even though black men and women with both higher education

This image of the Brewster Homes, which appeared in the *Detroit News* on December 1, 1936, represents the area as having been scrubbed clean by slum clearance and whitened by the new housing project. Image courtesy of the Walter P. Reuther Archives of Labor and Urban Affairs, Wayne State University.

and experience in social services had applied for these jobs. Dancy described the six African Americans he recommended to Gomon as "college trained individuals belonging in Detroit and in need of work." Even though black men and women had been able to secure relief jobs on equal footing with white workers, black activists and residents were not content with a lack of discrimination in just one area of the program. Instead, they demanded full equality. Gomon reported that black residents had been "subjected to a good deal of inconvenience and hardship" during relocation but remained "very cooperative" about moving.[39]

Similarly, in October 1937, editors at the *Detroit Tribune* worried aloud about the consequences of state-sanctioned segregation in the new housing projects. The paper's editors concluded that African Americans would be better off if they accepted the housing at the same time that they fought for integration.[40] Federally sponsored segregation was particularly pernicious because it was actually far easier to enforce than the combination of formal and informal strictures that upheld residential segregation in the city. Privately enforced segregation relied on individuals to comply with their dictates, and often whites failed to do so either because they did not abide by segregation or because they prioritized other interests over upholding divisions between black and white residents. For example, black "pioneers," middle-class men and women who bought houses in white neighborhoods, bought their houses from whites who chose not to comply with segregation.

The willingness to accept state resources and simultaneously reject second-class citizenship was not merely rhetorical. Black activists and journalists were offering a different vision of what urban citizenship meant. This was part of a change within the black political sphere during the 1930s. Over the course of the decade, black Detroiters across the social spectrum began to make more consistent and more successful demands on the state at the same time that they used new political strategies to fight for the less material promises of full urban citizenship. At the same time that discourses about welfare and poverty were getting more attached to African Americans in a distinctly negative way, welfare and state programs were becoming avenues through which black activists made new demands on the city government. New Deal programs helped strengthen the orientation of black activists toward the state. Indeed, the ideological underpinnings of the New Deal reinforced African American demands for something more abstract—full equality. Black Detroiters did not see the housing project as the end of their worries about affordable and livable homes and instead retained a commitment to continue fighting for full access to local resources.

Although they disagreed with the original decision to segregate Detroit's publicly financed housing projects, black leaders and activists pushed city officials to live up to their promise that segregation would not hinder African Americans' ability to access equality in the city. Ironically, in the urban North, because of the power of northern racial liberalism and its celebration of colorblindness, explicit, state-sponsored segregation made black appeals for the race-specific allocation of resources and power easier to make and win than they were in contexts where segregation and inequality were tolerated but implicit. For example, Mayor Reading did not appoint a black housing commissioner, even after repeated requests from influential African American leaders, but he did choose an African American man, a realtor named George Isabell, to manage the Brewster Homes.[41] Reading could justify his unwillingness to include a black representative on the Housing Commission in the ideological terms of northern racial liberalism. First of all, he reasoned, judicious white leaders would govern in a colorblind manner, and second, the appointment of an African American commissioner could elicit hostility from less enlightened whites and undermine the commission's good intentions. These implicit claims were more difficult to sustain when dealing with a state-crafted, all-black institution like the Brewster Homes, which was cast by its developers as a social project, not simply a physical space. Because Detroit's black social service agencies and other all-black city institutions were run by African Americans, it made the most sense for a segregated housing facility to be set up in a similar manner. Isabell's appointment was an important victory for African Americans that was possible because Brewster was built as a segregated facility.

Race-specific claims about the allocation of resources to African Americans continued to animate debates about the occupancy of the Brewster stores and jobs in the housing project. In April 1938, six months before the projects would open, the new secretary of the Housing Commission, Carl Braidt, spoke at a regular meeting of the

Noonday Luncheon Club. His audience, a group of mostly middle-class black businesspeople and professionals, questioned him about the twenty stores in the Brewster projects. Members of the luncheon club made it clear that they wanted the Housing Commission to give preference to African American merchants, especially because black businesspeople were not permitted to bid for storefront space in Parkside, the whites-only project.[42]

Demands for an all-black staff at Brewster were far less subdued. Activists established the Afro-American Institute in order to negotiate with local authorities and push the city to hire black workers to staff the Brewster Homes. The institute's name marked its agenda as racially specific. Its organizers rejected the languages of rights, advancement, or uplift and instead called on black residents to organize as "Afro-Americans" for exclusive access to the project's jobs and to run its stores. They began to negotiate with the Housing Commission in the summer of 1938, but when negotiations reached a stalemate, the institute began to picket the project and circulated a petition among African Americans to support their agenda. A crowd of picketers and spectators convened in front of the project and began a daily protest. Volunteers collected hundreds of signatures on the petition. Facing considerable pressure from the black community, and a Housing Commission that supported the plan, Reading bowed to black demands and endorsed a plan to relax civil service requirements and hire an all-black staff to work at Brewster. However, the Common Council vetoed this proposal. Even though they did not win this battle before the projects opened, black residents continued to fight for an all-black staff and guarantees that black merchants would have priority in Brewster's storefronts.[43]

Ultimately, in Detroit during the 1930s, both white racial liberals *and* black residents were testing the federal promise that "better housing makes better citizens." However, they began with two conflicting assumptions and two different sets of goals. Housing commissioners asserted that urban residents could be formed into "better citizens" if they started off with jobs, the resources to pay moderate rent, and, perhaps most important, whiteness. African American Detroiters, conversely, emphasized the universality of the claims being made by the New Deal state and pushed city leaders to live up to those promises. White liberals built the New Deal coalition on the premise that African

Americans could and should have access to public resources. However, they simultaneously relegated black urban residents to secondary roles in the urban sphere. Black activists, however, fought to ensure their right to participate as full, active citizens. They also struggled to build a more just and more equal metropolitan order instead of accepting their role as passive voters who simply supported white leaders for granting them needed resources.

Conclusion

In 1940 and 1941, "pressure groups, in and about the City of Detroit, particularly those representing the colored elements," were pushing government officials to open an additional Civilian Conservation Corps (CCC) camp for African Americans in Michigan. The CCC, a New Deal program, provided work relief to young men between the ages of seventeen and twenty-three. It ran racially segregated camps in rural areas across the country. In Michigan, the CCC focused on reforestation. Youths planted trees, fought forest fires, diked flooding riverbanks, strung telephone wire, laid down truck trails and roads, and built bridges and fire towers. According to H. J. Rigterink, supervisor of Michigan's CCC program, black pressure groups had pushed Detroit's Department of Public Welfare to advocate for another African American CCC camp. African Americans in Detroit, Rigterink explained to his superiors in Washington, DC, had become "more and more insistent." Indeed, they had organized three conferences on "negro problems" between November 1940 and February 1941, each of which passed resolutions supporting a new black camp. Although Rigterink was sympathetic to African Americans' demands, he explained that the CCC regional supervisor was unwilling to consider them. These "pressure groups" achieved at least one symbolic victory. They got Detroit's welfare commissioners to back their plan and pass their own resolution recommending a new camp for black youths.[1]

Rigterink identified black activist demands as the impetus for the DPW's request for another camp, but G. R. Harris, superintendent of the DPW, made no mention of this pressure in his communication with Rigterink. Instead, Harris framed his request as a response to the deep mismatch between need and available resources. Harris had only five white youths interested in the CCC and was finding it impossible to fill the white quota of more than 100 slots, even after aggressive recruiting. Conversely, 100 African Americans were attempting to secure positions in the CCC, even though the DPW had made no concerted effort to attract black applicants. The department had 75 percent more interest than the "colored" quotas allowed, which had capped black recruits at fewer than 60. These skewed numbers, Harris explained, were an effect of the recent recovery. White men were finding jobs in "National Defense production"; African American youths were shut out of these positions, and the number of blacks interested in the CCC remained steady.[2]

Rigterink knew that Harris was responding to pressure from black activists because the two had discussed the issue in person. However, in his letter to Rigterink, Harris represented African Americans as a *social* problem rather than a *political* problem. He did not mention the black activist groups that Rigterink was describing, organizations that were using conventional political strategies, like passing resolutions and holding conferences, to push for expanded access to resources. Instead, he cast African Americans as unorganized and apolitical—a threat to urban peace because of their potential for criminality, *not* because of their ability to organize politically. Indeed, Harris framed government leaders' interest in another black CCC camp as part of their larger effort to manage African American youths and by extension all African Americans, since, he suggested, unemployed black youths posed a threat to urban peace. "The social problem of unemployed colored youth in an industrial city such as Detroit," he explained, was "very serious." Harris implied that black youths without jobs disrupted the social fabric and were likely to be criminally inclined. Harris was not appealing to CCC administrators' compassion for the hardships faced by African Americans. Instead, he suggested that black Detroiters were a problem for the political establishment because of their disruptive, illegitimate, and antisocial behaviors, *not* because of their organized, activist citizenship. Thus, at the same time that Harris was being pushed by black activists to respond to their demands, he dismissed black activism as politically unimportant, drawing attention away from the power of political mobilization and onto African Americans, especially black youths, as a potentially explosive urban problem that needed to be resolved through careful state management. Furthermore, he suggested that white liberals should support his approach, since it served their governing goals. "The advantage of CCC enrollment for these youths," he explained, "is something we all agree upon."[3]

Charles Taylor, assistant director of the CCC in Washington, DC, denied Harris's request for more slots for African Americans and justified his decision with the contradictory logic of northern racial liberalism. He refused to acknowledge that racism shaped black Detroiters' employment experiences. Already, he explained, more than 7 percent of CCC enrollees in Michigan were African American, while the black population of the state was merely 3.5 percent. Thus, he concluded, "Michigan has set aside an adequate share of CCC vacancies for colored applicants." Like other liberals, Taylor focused on the seemingly high proportion of resources going to African Americans and implied that black Michiganders were benefiting from more public generosity than others. He thus dismissed the notion that a more accurate measure of racial justice would be to consider whether African Americans facing economic hardship were receiving the same level of benefits as poor whites facing similar difficulties. Furthermore, he explained, the mismatch that Harris was describing was even more acute in the American South. In other words, while individual African Americans in Detroit *may* have been receiving inadequate benefits (something that Taylor was unwilling to acknowledge), they were better off than blacks in the South, who were far less represented in their states' CCC programs. Taylor turned down Harris's request for more CCC positions by both denying that blacks faced discrimination in the North and simultaneously suggesting that if they did, their problems were insignificant compared with the hardships faced by African Americans in the South, and thus unworthy of being addressed. Indeed, white northern liberals defined their racial views against those of their southern colleagues, whom they consistently cast as more racist.[4]

Like other northern racial liberals, Taylor cast himself and his agency as defenders of African Americans even as he denied a request to improve their level of benefits. He underlined what he saw as his agency's disproportionate generosity toward African Americans in Michigan and its ostensible concerns about the *real* discrimination faced by African Americans in the South. Taylor also communicated that he was willing to seriously consider the problem presented: he concluded his letter by thanking Harris for alerting him to "the matter" and by suggesting that it was not closed but "merely deferred for the present." Ultimately, however, Taylor was unwilling to expend political capital delivering resources to African Americans. Instead of admitting more blacks into the CCC, his agency allowed the racial status quo to stand.[5]

This ensemble of three letters is unusual because it exposes how black activism was affecting white liberal decision making while at the same time revealing how white racial liberals rendered black activism invisible. Like Harris, Taylor did not mention the "pressure groups" that Rigterink described. Indeed, very few white racial liberals wrote explicitly about black activism, and fewer still addressed its impact on their thinking, choices, or conclusions. In their public speeches and their private communications, white liberals were far more likely to portray black Detroiters as disorganized, ineffectual, and threatening elements of an "urban problem" than they were to represent African Americans as serious political actors. This remained true even when those white liberals themselves were confronted by organized pressure groups and felt compelled to respond to black demands. White liberals certainly communicated with African American leaders of political organizations, but their relationships with these groups did not disrupt their limited portrait of blacks' political roles in the city, a portrait designed to undercut the power of organized black political action.

White liberals' consistent silence about black activism was a symptom of their ideological position. They both rendered black activism invisible and represented African Americans as socially troublesome, inclined to criminality, disorganized, and potentially mob-like. This helped white liberals dismiss black complaints about the contradiction that stood at the heart of northern racial liberal practices—that white liberals laid the foundation for their legitimacy on their commitment to justice, liberty, and equality at the same time that they sustained a high tolerance for black inequality. If African Americans were unable to make legitimate claims on the state as full political actors, then white liberals did not need to respond to their concerns or be compelled to address evidence that racial stratification characterized the city.

Black liberals fought hard to win recognition as legitimate political actors, although many also formed alliances with radicals who rejected the notion that appeals to white liberals' sense of justice may be effective political tools.[6] Indeed, a new culture of black protest that emerged alongside northern racial liberalism helped push white leaders to address African Americans' concerns. While those leaders did far less than black activists would have liked—few proposed solutions that might threaten white power or supremacy in the city—some took small steps toward remedying the most egregious manifestations of racism. White leaders who embraced northern racial liberalism imagined a very limited role for state intervention in racial matters at the same time that they promoted the idea that northern cities needed to be built on the foundation of political racial equality. They were careful to line themselves up against discrimination yet were unwilling to offer real remedies for the concerns African Americans were articulating. Ironically, the complicated range of activities that represented black civil rights coalition protest politics helped to underline and support the growing strength of racial liberalism in Detroit. As white leaders devised new strategies for managing and contain the growing African American population, black activists, conversely, worked to build a city that prioritized justice and equality over the maintenance of segregation.

From Northern Racial Liberalism to Race Relations

Soon after the end of the Second World War, "race relations" became the language through which seemingly well-intentioned white liberals managed African American complaints about structural inequalities. State actors helped to produce and sustain racial inequality at the same time that they said they were producing institutions designed to improve race relations or even extend new resources to African Americans and other people of color in cities. Rather than being a structural problem, white liberals cast racial discrimination as something rooted in cultural misunderstanding and irrational prejudice, which, once eradicated, would cleanse the nation and render racial difference irrelevant. A critical assessment of liberal efforts to both respond to and contain black activism in the immediate post–World War II period sheds light on contemporary colorblind practices. Politicians across the mainstream political spectrum limit racial justice and sustain racial inequality under the cover of caring about discrimination. Detroit's Commission on Community Relations is a window into these kinds of practices.

As cities expanded and became more racially diverse, liberal leaders produced both governmental and nongovernmental agencies that ostensibly addressed racial inequality but were actually a cover for managing and containing black protest and African American political participation. These institutions were circumscribed by a contradictory set of assumptions. First, they rejected the notion that racial inequality was systemic or that it emerged out of political or economic systems of power. Instead, they assumed that racism was cultural and that the eradication of individual prejudice was the foundation upon which equality could be built. Indeed, white liberals predicted, inequality would melt away in the face of tolerance, empathy, and productive intergroup dialogue.[7] At the same time that they built their agendas around this rosy forecast, white liberals sustained the contradictory belief that racism was intractable, since, they claimed, prejudice was a constitutive element of human nature and the urge to separate into racially distinct communities—and thus segregate—was essentially innate.

This set of assumptions meant that institutions that were supposed to address "racial problems" head-on remained weak, with few affirmative powers and a limited mandate. These institutions drew attention away from structural and economic inequalities and focused instead on avoiding conflict. Detroit's Commission on Community Relations, for example, a typical government agency in a postwar northern city, was charged with a narrow set of responsibilities, many of which were advisory. The commission was originally formed by the mayor in response to Detroit's 1943 race riots—the longest, deadliest, and most costly race riots in a U.S. city up until that point. At first, the commission was called the Mayor's Interracial Committee and was made up of an advisory board of agency heads and prominent private citizens, three of whom were African American, as well as three staff members to do the work. It was charged with studying the recent race riots, making recommendations about how to avoid future clashes, and pushing city departments to improve municipal services for black residents. This original mandate fell far short of a commitment from the city government to work on building a more racially just metropolis. The agency was designed to quell racial conflicts with the aim of upholding the current urban order and saving the city from the negative economic and political consequences of discord. It was decidedly *not* an effort to reorganize municipal resources or power along more racially just lines.

Even on its own modest terms, the Commission on Community Relations remained small, underfunded, and less powerful than its mandate would require. Compared with other city departments, it employed few staff members and sustained a small budget. In 1953, for example, nine people worked for the agency, which had no independent powers of enforcement at its disposal. Its budget was $65,000, all but $5,000 of which went to salaries, rent, and office supplies.[8] The agency continued to conduct research, push other city departments to eliminate discrimination, and sponsor "tension-reducing programs" for both residents and city officials designed to "increase mutual understanding" among Detroiters.[9] Similar agencies sprouted up across the urban North in the early postwar period either in response to local racial conflicts or modeled after institutions like the one built in Detroit.

From the perspective of the city government, Detroit's Commission on Community Relations can be understood as something of a public relations stunt. City administrators used it to stave off criticism and co-opt African American and white progressives who were critical of their records on racial justice. Mayor Edward Jeffries, for example, the person who established the commission, was openly contemptuous of black complaints about discrimination. In a speech at a 1940 conference on "Negro Employment Problems," Jeffries dismissed African American concerns about discrimination as unwarranted—rooted in a pessimistic disposition rather than a realistic understanding of how race and power functioned in the city. "I am not so sure," he announced, "that there is as much discrimination as I have many times heard it described." Indeed, in his mind, African Americans were hypersensitive and would actually be "materially aid[ed] and assist[ed]" by being "less *temperamental* in relation to alleged discrimination."[10]

Jeffries's short speech reads like a contemporary primer for a colorblind racist. He argued that African Americans who believed that discrimination shaped their lives were really just vain and shortsighted. To illustrate his point, he told a condescending story about an African American "gentleman" who thought that prejudice had hurt his chances of success on a civil service exam. Jeffries explained, quite simply, that there was no evidence of discrimination in this case, since other African

Americans had passed the test. The real problem, according to Jeffries, was that this man could not admit that "anybody could be mentally better equipped" than him.

In another familiar move, Jeffries suggested that current complaints about discrimination were overblown, since the present—1940—stood at the pinnacle of centuries of racial progress. He argued that "the prejudices that now exist between nationalities and between races" were far worse 100 years earlier. Furthermore, because progress was inevitable, and Americans were only becoming more tolerant and accepting with time, fights for racial justice were unnecessary. Finally, typical of his counterparts today, Jeffries cynically closed with a celebration of his own commitment to racial equality. He vowed to "cooperate . . . with a wholesome, progressive program for the assistance of the Negro or . . . any other group and for *all the people* within the community." By supporting "all the people," he implied that African Americans' concerns were not unique and thus once again suggested that complaints about racial discrimination were overblown and invalid.

While Jeffries sounds like a conservative in today's terms, it is important to understand that he was actually a pro-government, pro-growth liberal. In the short speech I have described here, he also argued that the government was "theoretically and practically . . . the only single agency which is big enough or all-inclusive enough to create an environment which will eventually make for Utopia." In his view, building a larger and more robust state was the best way to address unemployment, encourage urban growth, and foster prosperity. Indeed, for pro-growth liberals like Jeffries, the state's job was to promote commerce and create wealth by securing urban order, organizing expansion, and creating opportunities for capital investment. As a liberal, Jeffries believed that the government should provide social services and extend some care to the most disadvantaged urban residents, but neither at the expense of order or growth nor as a challenge to existing relations of power.

As the original architects of Detroit's Commission on Community Relations, members of the Jeffries administration designed the agency to help sustain urban order. However, many of the men and women who got involved with the commission, as staff people, members of its advisory board, or participants in its programs, sustained a different understanding of its mandate. First, they saw the commission's formation as a victory. African Americans had been calling for the local government to be more responsive to their claims for many years, and black liberals, especially, believed it was a step in the right direction. Indeed, many saw the commission as a new location from which they could push for more substantive change and a more robust state response to their concerns.

While the commission was not designed to alter racial relations of power in a meaningful way, this state project—intended to contain and depoliticize claims about discrimination—did have unintended positive effects on the citywide struggle for racial justice. For example, as the first permanent governmental body to record and collect information about racial discrimination in Detroit, the commission lent official legitimacy to these claims, even though it took no specific actions to remedy them. Indeed, complaints about discrimination flooded its offices for years, even after complainants clearly knew that their problems would simply be recorded. The commission used this information in its "Community Barometer," a measure it kept of "public attitudes" designed to "predict social behavior" and prevent future race riots.[11] By ferreting out potential conflict, agency heads believed, the commission could prevent problems before they started. However, activists (and now historians) used this rich body of evidence for their own purposes—to expose structural urban inequality and work toward building racial justice.

Activists who engaged in Commission on Community Relations programs, even those who seemed most co-opted by it, often participated in struggles outside of their work with the state. Beulah Whitby, for example, a prominent, well-educated, and well-connected African American woman, was assistant director of the commission from 1943 to 1962 and did help to lend legitimacy to the agency. However, she was not fully contained by its parameters. Whitby participated in the fight for state and city Fair Employment Practices Commissions in the late 1940s. This struggle for local fair employment commissions brought together left-wing activists alongside their more liberal counterparts, although red-baiting and liberals' hostility toward Communist Party and National Negro Congress activists ultimately split and weakened the movement.[12] Furthermore, it is important to remember that municipal employment was one of the few professional avenues open to members of the educated African American elite. A final unintended consequence of the Commission on Community Relations is that it helped to foster and sustain the networks upon which struggles for civil rights and racial equality depended.

While liberals used the Commission to limit African Americans' access to municipal power, conservatives saw it as supporting struggles for racial justice and attacked it accordingly. In 1953, a federation of Home Owner Civic and Improvement Associations attempted to place a referendum on the ballot that would overturn the city ordinance that established the Commission on Community Relations. The group was a federation of white neighborhood homeowners' councils that was notorious for its often-violent defense of segregation and white residential exclusivity.[13]

Ultimately, understanding the dynamics of northern racial liberalism in Detroit in the interwar years—as well as its postwar extension, race relations management—helps to explain the seeming racial contradictions embedded in mainstream political discourse today. Even as conservatives position themselves against liberals, both use liberal ideas about liberty, democracy, and equality to promote their projects and describe their governing sensibilities. Both of them take on positions that have a disproportionately negative impact on low-income people of color, even as they use the language of equality to justify their actions. To take a recent example, in April 2011, President Barack Obama supported the Republican effort to raise the age of Social Security eligibility—a proposal that will have a disproportionately negative effect on poor people of color if passed. However, he claimed that this policy would be good for Americans because it would relieve them of the debt they would incur by supporting the elderly in a more robust fashion.[14] Politicians across the political spectrum are participating in a political economic system that is draining welfare institutions of state support and privatizing public-owned resources—a tool for the massive extension of exploitation and markets into both new and old arenas. These strategies do not actually shrink the state. Instead, they promote capitalist projects and help amplify wealth and racial inequalities. Liberals have historically claimed that part of their project is to remedy capitalism's most grotesque manifestations of inequality. However, they are simultaneously interested in using the state to promote urban growth and expansion. Their efforts to resolve the contradictions that emerge out of these conflicted commitments have allowed them to pioneer many of the strategies that conservatives use today—casting themselves as allied with "the downtrodden," to use a term from the 1930s, but simultaneously working to sustain and extend deep inequalities. Liberals' persistent rejection of leftist ideas about the reorganization of power and wealth shapes how they resolve these contradictions. Even as the political center moves to the right, these logics of northern racial liberalism still hold.

NOTES

NOTES TO THE INTRODUCTION

1. Willing to Give Up Home as a Gesture to First Lady," July 1935, Clippings/Scrapbooks in Josephine Gomon Papers, Bentley Historical Library, University of Michigan, Ann Arbor (hereafter Bentley).
2. "'First Lady' Starts a Housing Project," *New York Times*, September 10, 1935; "First Lady Dooms Slum," *Detroit News*, September 10, 1935; Cook, *Eleanor Roosevelt*.
3. Perry to Reading, May 9, 1938; Isabell to Reading, July 25, 1938; Peck to Reading, July 28, 1938; Bradt to Danahey, n.d., Mayor's Papers (hereafter MP) 1938, Box 6, Folder "Housing Commission (2)," Burton Historical Collection, Detroit Public Library (hereafter Burton).
4. See Pascoe, *What Comes Naturally*.
5. Bonilla-Silva, *Racism without Racists*; Carr, *"Colorblind" Racism*; Collins, *Black Sexual Politics*; Wang, *Discrimination by Default*; Wise, *Colorblind*. P. J. Kellogg has examined how white liberals thought about race from the late 1930s to the early 1950s. He argues that "race was not so much a problem to be solved as a diversion to be avoided. When [they] noticed the plight of black people at all, they tended to picture them not as victims of the exclusions of caste, but as the archetype of the dispossessed Southern poor." Kellogg, "Northern Liberals and Black America," 3.
6. Justice John Roberts explained the Supreme Court's 2013 rejection of the preclearance requirement for specific states in the Voting Rights Act. "Things," he claimed, "have changed dramatically." *Shelby County v. Holder*; Gary Younge, "On the Voting Rights Act: The Colour-Blind Have Been Led by the Blind," *Guardian*, June 25, 2013; Horowitz, *Hating Whitey*.
7. Some scholars examine how the prewar world contributed to these ideas. In his study of the "idea of black criminality," Khalil Gibran Muhammad argues that the urban North was "a crucial site for the production of modern ideas about race" during the interwar years. Muhammad, *Condemnation of Blackness*.
8. McGerr, *A Fierce Discontent*.
9. See Lasch-Quinn, *Black Neighbors*; Kunzel, *Fallen Women, Problem Girls*.
10. Woodward, *The Strange Career of Jim Crow*; Hale, *Making Whiteness*.
11. Harvey, *The Condition of Postmodernity*; Smith, *Making the Modern*.

12. Tuttle, *Race Riot.*
13. Cazenave, *The Urban Racial State.*
14. Storm to Mayor, March 4, 1935, MP 1935, Box 6, Folder "Interracial," Burton.
15. Secretary to the Mayor to Russell, March 13, 1935, MP 1935, Box 6, Folder "Interracial."
16. Russell to Couzens, March 22, 1935, MP 1935, Box 6, Folder "Interracial," emphasis in original.
17. Ibid.
18. For a discussion of African Americans and the New Deal, see Argersinger, *Toward a New Deal in Baltimore*; Brown, *Race, Money and the American Welfare State*; Katznelson, *When Affirmative Action Was White*; Lieberman, *Shifting the Color Line*; Mink, *The Wages of Motherhood*; Quadagno, *The Transformation of Old Age Security*; Sitkoff, *A New Deal for Blacks*; Weiss, *Farewell to the Party of Lincoln.*
19. R. Rothman, "Detroit Elects a Liberal," *Nation* 131, no. 3406 (October 15, 1930): 400–401; "Engel Outlines Constructive Platform in Opening Campaign," *Detroit Free Press*, August 28, 1930; Frank Murphy, Campaign Address, August 1930, Frank Murphy Papers (hereafter FM), Reel 141, Bentley.
20. Franz Boas, "What Is Race?," *Nation* 120, no. 3108 (January 28, 1925): 89. See Barkan, *The Retreat of Scientific Racism*; Guglielmo, *White on Arrival*; Guterl, *The Color of Race in America*; Ross, *The Origins of American Social Science.*
21. Frank Murphy, speech on the "races question," n.d., FM, Reel 141.
22. See Cohen, *The Reconstruction of American Liberalism.*
23. Beth Bates, Angela Dillard, Richard Thomas, and Victoria Wolcott provide rich portraits of black-led struggles for racial justice during this period. Thomas, *Life for Us Is What We Make It*; Wolcott, *Remaking Respectability*; Dillard, *Faith in the City*; Bates, *The Making of Black Detroit in the Age of Henry Ford.*
24. Dillard, *Faith in the City.*
25. Burchell, Gordon, and Miller, *The Foucault Effect.*
26. Freund, *Colored Property*; HoSang *Racial Propositions*; Sugrue, *The Origins of the Urban Crisis.* Carol Horton argues that some liberalisms included elements of racial egalitarianism before the 1950s, but none of these sustained significant political traction until the rise of the mainstream civil rights movement. Horton, *Race and the Making of American Liberalism.* David Carroll Cochran emphasizes the popularity of colorblind discourse across the mainstream political spectrum and argues that conservatives and liberals alike have come to embrace its tenets. Cochran, *The Color of Freedom.* Jacqueline Dowd Hall argues that the conservative movement reinvented itself in the 1970s, distanced itself from "old-fashioned racism," and embraced the ideal of *formal* equality. Hall shows that the New Right positioned itself as inheritor of the civil rights legacy. Hall, "The Long Civil Rights Movement and the Political Uses of the Past." Amy Ansell similarly argues that the New Right developed a distinctive language about race that challenges what she identifies as the "liberal consensus" that emerged after World War II.

Ansell, *New Right, New Racism*. Some scholars root the origins of domestic racial liberalism in U.S. responses to international politics, first against fascism and then as a Cold War strategy to draw postcolonial activists toward the U.S. sphere. Winant, *The World Is a Ghetto*; Gerstle, *American Crucible*; Dudziak, *Cold War Civil Rights*.

27. David Harvey demonstrates that the urban form requires hierarchy. Harvey, "The Right to the City."
28. Examples of this approach include Lemann, *The Promised Land*; Fine, *Violence in the Model City*. For a treatment of the First Great Migration that avoids this pitfall, see Wilkerson, *The Warmth of Other Suns*.
29. Two edited collections have examined northern exceptionalism in the postwar world: Lassiter and Crespino, *The Myth of Southern Exceptionalism*; Theoharis and Woodard, *Freedom North*; see also Countryman, *Up South*; Purnell, *Fighting Jim Crow in the County of Kings*.
30. Peggy Pascoe is also interested in this dynamic in the early twentieth century. Pascoe, "Miscegenation Law, Court Cases, and Ideologies of 'Race' in Twentieth-Century America."
31. Brown, *Race, Money and the American Welfare State*; Katznelson, *When Affirmative Action Was White*; Lieberman, *Shifting the Color Line*; Quadagno, "Welfare Capitalism and the Social Security Act of 1935"; Wilder, *A Covenant with Color*.
32. Poole, *The Segregated Origins of Social Security*.
33. Leach, "Against the Notion of a 'New Racism.'"
34. Hirsch, *Making the Second Ghetto*; Thomas, *Redevelopment and Race*; Self, *American Babylon*.
35. Sugrue, *The Origins of the Urban Crisis*.
36. Carter, *From George Wallace to Newt Gingrich*; Countryman, *Up South*; Freund, *Colored Property*; Wolfinger, *Philadelphia Divided*.
37. Herron, *AfterCulture*.
38. *Korematsu v. United States*.
39. "Gloster B. Current, 84, Leader Who Helped Steer N.A.A.C.P.," *New York Times*, July 9, 1997.
40. Sugrue, *The Origins of the Urban Crisis*; Thompson, *Whose Detroit?*
41. Sugrue, *The Origins of the Urban Crisis*.

NOTES TO CHAPTER 1

1. "Detroit N.A.A.C.P. Stops Injustice to Immigrants," *Detroit Leader*, June 7, 1918.
2. Ibid.
3. "Board of Health and Urban League Co-operate to Improve Health Conditions," c. 1918, Detroit Urban League Papers (hereafter DUL), Box 1, Folder 10, Bentley Historical Library, University of Michigan, Ann Arbor (hereafter Bentley).
4. "Detroit N.A.A.C.P. Stops Injustice to Immigrants."
5. Forrester B. Washington, *The Negro in Detroit: A Survey of the Conditions of a Negro Group in a Northern Industrial Center during the War Prosperity Period, 1920*

(Detroit, 1920), Burton Historical Collection, Detroit Public Library (hereafter Burton); Finkelman, "The Promise of Equality and the Limits of Law"; Katzman, *Before the Ghetto*.

6. Foner, *Free Soil, Free Labor, Free Men*.
7. Peebles, "Fannie Richards and the Integration of the Detroit Public Schools."
8. Finkelman, "The Promise of Equality and the Limits of Law"; Katzman, *Before the Ghetto*.
9. Katzman, *Before the Ghetto*, 198–204.
10. McGerr, *A Fierce Discontent*.
11. Katzman, *Before the Ghetto*; Joseph Billups, interviewed with Roberta Billups by Herbert Hill and Shelton Tappes, Detroit, October 27, 1967, Blacks in the Labor Movement Oral History Project (hereafter BLM), Archives of Labor and Urban Affairs, Wayne State University, Detroit (hereafter ALUA).
12. "Mob Fiendishly Tortures Aged, Inoffensive Negro," *Detroit News*, August 17, 1908.
13. "Assault on White Woman Precipitates Rioting and Bloodshed," *Detroit News*, April 16, 1908.
14. "Posse Goes for Negro, May Lynch Assaulter," *Detroit News*, April 16, 1908.
15. "Refugees in Decatur Seek to Organize Negroes for Fight," "Negro Kills Himself to Avoid Capture by Possee," "Mob Attacks Jail to Lynch Negro Assailant of Women," *Detroit News*, April 16, 1908.
16. "Blacks and Whites Shouldn't Amalgamate," *Detroit News*, April 16, 1908.
17. "Detroit Fights 'Birth of a Nation,'" *Chicago Defender*, January 1, 1916; "Mayor Revokes Theater License," *Chicago Defender*, January 8, 1916.
18. "Supreme Court Rules Out 'Birth of a Nation,'" *Chicago Defender*, December 4, 1915; Butler, "*The Birth of a Nation* (1915)."
19. Albert F. Ross, "Detroit Citizens Overcome by Lethargy," *Chicago Defender*, October 23, 1915.
20. "Must Bar Children from 'Birth of Nation,'" "Folly Is Closed, License Revoked by Mayor's Order," *Detroit News*, December 27, 1915.
21. "Mayor Revokes Theater License," *Chicago Defender*, January 8, 1916; "'*Birth of a Nation* Is Damnable'—Gov. Ferris," *Chicago Defender*, February 19, 1916.
22. "The Mob's Tendency Might Be Restrained," *Detroit News*, August 18, 1908.
23. Campbell J. Gibson and Emily Lennon, "Historical Census Statistics on the Foreign-Born Population of the United States, 1850–1990," February 1999, Population Working Division Paper no. 29; U.S. Bureau of the Census, "Detroit's Population, 1850–1940," UAW-CIO Research Papers, Box 9, Folder 24, ALUA.
24. Washington, *The Negro in Detroit*; Brown, *Racial Conflict and Violence in the Labor Market*; U.S. Bureau of the Census, "Detroit's Population, 1850–1940."
25. Scott, "Additional Letters of Negro Migrants," 461.
26. "Detroit Branch of N.A.A.C.P. Wins Victory," *Detroit Leader*, May 24, 1918.
27. Kennedy, *The Negro Peasant Turns Cityward*; Detroit Urban League, "Conditions among Newcomers in Detroit," Spring 1918, DUL, Box 1, Folder "General Files

and Correspondence 1918"; Detroit Bureau of Governmental Research, "The Negro Population of Detroit," in *The Negro in Detroit*, 3.

28. Murage, "Making Migrants an Asset."
29. Jacobson, *Whiteness of a Different Color*; Guglielmo, *White on Arrival.*
30. Washington, *The Negro in Detroit*; Murage, "Making Migrants an Asset."
31. Pascoe, "Miscegenation Law, Court Cases, and Ideologies of 'Race' in Twentieth-Century America."
32. Zunz, *The Changing Face of Inequality.*
33. Ibid.
34. Meyer, *The Five Dollar Day*; Hooker, "Ford's Sociology Department and the Americanization Campaign and the Manufacture of Popular Culture among Assembly Line Workers"; Lewchuck, "Fordism and the Moving Assembly Line"; May, "The Historical Problem of the Family Wage"; Harvey, *The Condition of Postmodernity.*
35. Stanley, *From Bondage to Contract.*
36. Gregory, *The Southern Diaspora.*
37. Maloney, "Personnel Policy and Racial Inequality in the Pre–World War II North."
38. Washington, *The Negro in Detroit*; Kennedy, *The Negro Peasant Turns Cityward,* 74–75, 90.
39. Martin, *Detroit and the Great Migration.*
40. "Housing, 1919," DUL, Box 1, Folder "General Files and Correspondence 1919."
41. Spero and Harris, *The Black Worker*, 142; Washington, *The Negro in Detroit.*
42. "Housing, 1919," DUL, Box 1, Folder "General Files and Correspondence 1919"; Brown, *Racial Conflict and Violence in the Labor Market.*
43. Spero and Harris, *The Black Worker*; Brown, *Racial Conflict and Violence in the Labor Market.*
44. Pascoe, "Miscegenation Law, Court Cases, and Ideologies of 'Race' in Twentieth-Century America," 48.
45. Flanagan, *Seeing with Their Hearts*; McGerr, *A Fierce Discontent.*
46. Drews, "A History of the Detroit Board of Health."
47. Quoted in Fragnoli, *The Transformation of Reform*, 19.
48. Peterson, *American Automobile Workers*; Paxton, "The Trend of Reorganization in City Government"; Fragnoli, *The Transformation of Reform.*
49. Fragnoli, *The Transformation of Reform.*
50. Detroit's industries were unusually large-scale and bureaucratic. Sullivan, " 'On the Dole,' " 19.
51. Lovett, *Detroit Rules Itself.* Lovett was the publicity director for a successful state prohibition campaign, which passed by referendum in Michigan in November 1916. "Vote on Prohibition," 1928, Harry Ross Papers, Box 8, Folder "Election 1928," ALUA.
52. Lovett, *Detroit Rules Itself*, 20–22.
53. Fragnoli, *The Transformation of Reform*, 159–167.

54. Zunz, *The Changing Face of Inequality.*
55. Ibid.; Levine, *Internal Combustion*, 50.
56. Zunz, *The Changing Face of Inequality*, 158; Haynes, *Negro New-comers in Detroit, Michigan*, 10.
57. City of Detroit Housing Commission, *Housing in Detroit*; Secretary to the Members of the Detroit Board of Commerce, August 9, 1920, Detroit Board of Commerce Papers, Bentley.
58. Detroit Bureau of Governmental Research, "Population," in *The Negro in Detroit*, 4.
59. "In order to provide you an adequate picture . . . ," c. 1930, DUL, Box 1, Folder 30.
60. Quoted in Detroit Bureau of Governmental Research, "Population," in *The Negro in Detroit*, 4.
61. Rice, "Residential Segregation by Law, 1910–1917"; Vose, *Caucasians Only*; Clark and Perlman, *Prejudice and Property.*
62. Sugrue, *The Origins of the Urban Crisis.*
63. Detroit Bureau of Governmental Research, "Housing," in *The Negro in Detroit*, 42, 46.
64. Ibid.
65. Ibid.; Forrester B. Washington, Description of Harper Ave. Forced Eviction, August 25, 1917, DUL, Box 1, Folder "General Files and Correspondence 1917."
66. Wolcott, *Remaking Respectability.*
67. Dillard, *Faith in the City*; Thomas, *Life for Us Is What We Make It*; Meier and Rudwick, *Black Detroit and the Rise of the UAW.*
68. Bates, *The Making of Black Detroit in the Age of Henry Ford.*
69. Meyer, *The Five Dollar Day*; May, "The Historical Problem of the Family Wage."
70. Murage, "Organizational History of the Detroit Urban League"; Murage, "Making Migrants an Asset."
71. "Request for May Appropriations," January 1918, James Couzens Papers, Box 123, Folder "Detroit Community Fund," Library of Congress; Wolcott, *Remaking Respectability*, 49.
72. "Detroit Urban League," DUL, Box 1, Folder 1: "General Files and Correspondence undated."
73. Spero and Harris, *The Black Worker*, 140.
74. Memo, November 20, 1918, DUL, Box 1, Folder "General Files and Correspondence 1918"; Memo, October 30, 1918, DUL, Box 1, Folder "General Files and Correspondence 1918."
75. "Plans for Colored Welfare Workers in Industrial Plants," October 26, 1918, DUL, Box 1, Folder "General Files and Correspondence 1918"; Peterson, "Black Automobile Workers in Detroit," 178; Bailer, "Negro Labor in the Automobile Industry"; Bates, *The Making of Black Detroit in the Age of Henry Ford.*
76. Forrester Washington, "A Program of Work for the Assimilation of Negro Migrants into Northern Cities," December 17, 1917, DUL, Box 1, Folder "General Files and Correspondence 1917."

77. Haynes, *Negro New-comers in Detroit, Michigan*, 10; Birney Smith, interview by Jim Keeney and Roberta McBride, June 15, 1969, BLM.
78. Washington, *The Negro in Detroit*; Gregory, *The Southern Diaspora*.
79. Press release, October 9, 1917, DUL, Box 1, Folder "General Files and Correspondence 1917."
80. *Crisis* 4 (July 12, 1912): 125.
81. "Detroit Branch of NAACP Wins Victory," *Detroit Leader*, May 24, 1918, Papers of the National Association for the Advancement of Colored People (hereafter NAACP), Part 12, Series C, Reel 11.
82. Ibid.
83. Warren to Shillady, July 22, 1918, NAACP, Part 12, Series C, Reel 11; Secretary to Villard, June 20, 1918, NAACP, Part 12, Series C, Reel 11.
84. J. F. Johnson, "Report for the Branch Bulletin from the Detroit, Mich. Branch," July 16, 1920, NAACP, Part 12, Series C, Reel 11.
85. "N.A.A.C.P. Secures Ending of Jim Crow Cars in Detroit," September 3, 1920, NAACP, Part 12, Series C, Reel 11.
86. Detroit Branch National Association for the Advancement of Colored People, "Bulletin Number One," September 13, 1920, NAACP, Part 12, Series C, Reel 11.
87. "Report from the Detroit Branch of the N.A.A.C.P.," *Michigan State News*, April 21, 1921, NAACP, Part 12, Series C, Reel 11.

NOTES TO CHAPTER 2

1. "Riot Curb Demanded by Mayor," *Detroit Times*, September 13, 1925.
2. White, "Reviving the Ku Klux Klan."
3. Ibid.
4. Nash to Couzens, June 16, 1925, James Couzens Papers (hereafter JCP), Box 144, Folder "Income Taxes," Library of Congress (hereafter LOC); "Received for 2180 Shares of Stock," n.d., JCP, Box 144, Folder "Income Taxes."
5. Couzens to Gentlemen, May 10, 1921, Papers of the National Association for the Advancement of Colored People (hereafter NAACP), Part I, Box C-264, Folder "James Couzens (KKK)," LOC.
6. Gregory, *The Southern Diaspora*.
7. Detroit Bureau of Governmental Research, "Welfare," in *The Negro in Detroit*, 2.
8. Couzens to Gentlemen, May 10, 1921.
9. Couzens to White, June 20, 1921, NAACP, Part I, Box: C-264, Folder "James Couzens (KKK)."
10. Couzens to White, May 17, 1921, NAACP, Part I, Box: C-264, Folder "James Couzens (KKK)."
11. White to Washington, May 26, 1921, NAACP, Part I, Box: C-264, Folder "James Couzens (KKK)."
12. Washington to White, June 3, 1921, NAACP, Part I, Box: C-264, Folder "James Couzens (KKK)."
13. Boyle, *Arc of Justice*; Finkelman, "The Promise of Equality and the Limits of Law."

14. McGerr, *A Fierce Discontent.*
15. Wolcott, *Remaking Respectability*; Baldwin, *Chicago's New Negroes*; Chapman, *Prove It on Me.*
16. Wolcott, *Remaking Respectability.*
17. McGerr, *A Fierce Discontent*, 201.
18. Quoted in Bates, *The Making of Black Detroit in the Age of Henry Ford*, 71.
19. Murage, "Making Migrants an Asset"; Martin, *Detroit and the Great Migration.*
20. Detroit Bureau of Governmental Research, "Welfare," in *The Negro in Detroit*, 2.
21. Conot, *American Odyssey.*
22. Josephine Gomon, "Judge Jeffries," n.d., Josephine Gomon Papers, Box 9, Folder "Miscellaneous Regarding City Politics in Detroit before Murphy Mayoralty," Bentley.
23. George Cantor, "Detroit History (and Legends) Seen through the Eyes of Jo Gomon," *Detroit*, March 12, 1972.
24. Fine, *Frank Murphy.*
25. McLaughlin, "Reconsidering the East St Louis Race Riot of 1917"; Rudwick, *Race Riot in East St. Louis*; Tuttle, *Race Riot.*
26. Solomon, *The Negro Voters in Detroit*, 123.
27. Boykin, *Handbook on the Detroit Negro.*
28. Jackson, *The Ku Klux Klan in the City*; Babson et al., *Working Detroit.*
29. Fragnoli, *The Transformation of Reform.*
30. Secretary to Bradby, July 22, 1925, NAACP, Part 12, Series C, Reel 12.
31. Cecil B. Rowlette and W. Hayes McKinney, "People vs. Flita Mathis, Defendant," State of Michigan Case Report, Legal Redress Committee, and "Detroit N.A.A.C.P. Wins Three Cases for Colored People," both in NAACP, Part 12, Series C, Reel 12; Detroit Bureau of Governmental Research, "Housing," in *The Negro in Detroit*, 38; "Argument of Clarence Darrow," *The People v. Ossian Sweet*, 42, 58.
32. *The People v. Ossian Sweet*; Weinberg, *A Man's Home, a Man's Castle*; Boyle, *Arc of Justice.*
33. Farrell, *Clarence Darrow.*
34. Boyle, *Arc of Justice*, 180.
35. David E. Lilienthal, "Has the Negro the Right to Self-Defense?," *Nation* 121, no. 3155 (December 23, 1925): 724–725.
36. "Argument of Clarence Darrow," *The People v. Ossian Sweet*, 35.
37. Cooley, "Moving On Out"; Womak, " 'To Die Like a Man or Live Like a Coward.' "
38. *The People v. Ossian Sweet*; *Pittsburgh Courier*, September 19, 1925.
39. "Sweet Case to Be Ended This Week," *Pittsburgh Courier*, May 15, 1926.
40. "Argument of Clarence Darrow," *The People v. Ossian Sweet.*
41. "Mrs. Sweet Tells Tragic Story of Lonely Hours in Detroit Jail as She Waited, Helpless, for Aid," *Pittsburgh Courier*, November 7, 1925; "Sweet Case to Be Ended This Week," *Pittsburgh Courier*, May 15, 1926; *The People v. Ossian Sweet.*

42. "Courtroom Stormed as Case Opens," *Pittsburgh Courier*, November 7, 1925.
43. Ibid.
44. "Action of Sweet Jury Is Flayed," *Pittsburgh Courier*, December 5, 1925.
45. "Membership and Money to National Office," December 14, 1926, NAACP, Detroit, Michigan, 1917–1939, Part 12, Series C, Reel 12. *The Negro in Detroit* reported that the branch had 3,386 members in 1926. Detroit Bureau of Governmental Research, "Community Organization," in *The Negro in Detroit*.
46. Johnson to Friend, November 16, 1925, Detroit Urban League Papers (hereafter DUL), Box 1, Folder 15, Bentley.
47. Reverend Joseph Homes, Chairman, John Dancy, Secretary, and Linnie M. Cloud, Secretary, to "All Fraternal Organizations," November 11, 1925, DUL, Box 1, Folder "General Files and Correspondence Jan–June, 1925"; invoice, November 17, 1925, DUL, Box 1, Folder "General Files and Correspondence Jan–June, 1925."
48. Quoted in Fleming, "The Right to Self-Defense."
49. Bergman to Murphy, June 3, 1931, Mayor's Papers (hereafter MP) 1931, Box 9, Folder "Welfare (3)," Burton Historical Collection, Detroit Public Library (hereafter Burton).
50. "Riot Curb Demanded by Mayor," *Detroit Times*, September 13, 1925; "T. W. McGregor Heads Inter-racial Board," *Detroit Free Press*, September 16, 1925.
51. "Riot Curb Demanded by Mayor."
52. "2D Smith Quits Race for Mayor," *Detroit Times*, September 10, 1925.
53. "Riot Curb Demanded by Mayor."
54. "T. W. McGregor Heads Inter-racial Board."
55. Chicago Commission on Race Relations, *The Negro in Chicago*.
56. Kennedy, *The Negro Peasant Turns Cityward*, 224.
57. Chicago Commission on Race Relations, *The Negro in Chicago*, xvii.
58. Sherman, "The Harding Administration and the Negro."
59. Drake and Cayton, *Black Metropolis*.
60. By 1919, 27 percent of the men served by the McGregor Institute were African American. Washington, *The Negro in Detroit*; McGregor, *Toward a Philosophy of Inner Life*.
61. Niebuhr to Lodge, January 18, 1928, MP 1928, Box 2, Folder "Interracial Commission 1928."
62. Detroit Bureau of Governmental Research, "Introduction," in *The Negro in Detroit*, 1926, 12, DPL.
63. Niebuhr to Lodge, January 18, 1928.
64. Detroit Bureau of Governmental Research, *The Negro in Detroit*.
65. Detroit Bureau of Governmental Research, "Introduction," in *The Negro in Detroit*, 13.
66. Ibid., 12. Also see Fragnoli, *The Transformation of Reform*, 286–284; "$10,000 Appropriated for Negro Survey of Detroit, Is Sequel to Sweet Trial," *Pittsburgh Courier*, July 10, 1926.
67. Scott, *Contempt and Pity*, 44.

68. See Holloway, *Confronting the Veil.*
69. Greenstone, *A Report on the Politics of Detroit*, 15.
70. Mayor's Committee on Race Relations, "Report of the Mayor's Committee on Race Relations," 3.
71. Ibid., 3.
72. Ibid., 3.
73. Ibid., 3.
74. Ibid., 5.
75. Ibid., 7.
76. Dancy to North, May 4, 1928, DUL, Box 1, Folder 23.

NOTES TO CHAPTER 3

1. "Detroiters Give an Interesting Bit of Information on Race Relations," *Pittsburgh Courier*, March 5, 1927.
2. For a discussion of gradualism and white liberals, see King, *Letter from the Birmingham Jail.*
3. Josephine Gomon, "Early Family History," in Josephine Gomon Papers (hereafter JG), Box 8, Folder "Draft Biography: Early Family History to Big Four Campaign," Bentley Historical Library, University of Michigan, Ann Arbor (hereafter Bentley).
4. Frank Murphy, Speech on the "races question," 1920s, n.d., Frank Murphy Papers (hereafter FM), Reel 141, Bentley.
5. Ibid.
6. Ibid.
7. Brown, *Regulating Aversion.*
8. Pascoe, *What Comes Naturally.*
9. Wolcott, *Remaking Respectability.*
10. Quoted in Fleming, "The Right to Self-Defense."
11. Detroit Bureau of Governmental Research, "Negro Crime," in *The Negro in Detroit*, 19–21.
12. The *Detroit Times* praised him for not releasing anyone on bail. "Politics by the Observer," *Detroit Times*, September 5, 1930.
13. Detroit Bureau of Governmental Research, "Negro Crime," in *The Negro in Detroit*, 20.
14. Ibid., 18; Detroit Bureau of Governmental Research, "The Negro Population of Detroit," in *The Negro in Detroit*, 5.
15. "Police Commission Head Addresses Citizens," *Pittsburgh Courier*, October 29, 1927.
16. Detroit Bureau of Governmental Research, "Negro Crime," in *The Negro in Detroit*, 19–20.
17. For a discussion of case histories, see Kunzel, *Fallen Women, Problem Girls*; Gordon, "Social Insurance and Public Assistance"; Tice, *Tales of Wayward Girls and Immoral Women.*

18. See Muhammad, *Condemnation of Blackness.*
19. Fellows, "Detroit's Crime Clinic."
20. Ibid.
21. Frank Murphy, "Only the Helpless Hang," *Detroit Times*, February 1, 1927.
22. Zunz, *The Changing Face of Inequality.*
23. Detroit Bureau of Governmental Research, "The Negro Population of Detroit," in *The Negro in Detroit*, 10–13; Katzman, *Before the Ghetto*; Zunz, *The Changing Face of Inequality*; Wolcott, "The Culture of the Informal Economy."
24. McKinney to National Association for the Advancement of Colored People, February 13, 1928, Papers of the National Association for the Advancement of Colored People (hereafter NAACP), Part 12, Series C, Reel 12; McKinney to Lodge, February 9, 1928, Mayor's Papers (hereafter MP) 1928, Box 2, Folder "Interracial Commission, 1928," Burton Historical Collection, Detroit Public Library (hereafter Burton); W. Hayes McKinney, "Report of the Legal Redress Committee," 1928, NAACP, Part 12, Series C, Reel 12.
25. While the popularity of the UNIA waned considerably after the arrest of Marcus Garvey, it could still boast a following in Detroit, which hosted its annual meetings in 1926. Smaller nationalist groups also continued to promote independent black economic development. "Serious Situation Brewing in U.N.I.A.," *New York Amsterdam News*, March 31, 1926; also see Wolcott, *Remaking Respectability.*
26. Detroit's police force had 2,848 officers in 1926, with 14 African American officers (0.5 percent), an unusually low proportion compared with other northern cities. "Table Showing Use of Colored Police in Ten American Cities," 1926, Detroit Urban League Papers, Box 1, Folder 15.
27. Eastmond to Bagnall, May 23, 1927, NAACP, Part 12, Series C, Reel 12.
28. W. Hayes McKinney, "Petition of Dewey Adams and Annie Mae Adams for Ample Police Protection," February 1928, NAACP, Part 12, Series C, Reel 12; McKinney to Lodge, January 13, 1928, and February 9, 1928, MP 1928, Box 2, Folder "Interracial Commission, 1928"; G. D. Howard, "Trouble between Races Is Feared in Detroit," *Pittsburgh Courier*, February 18, 1928; "Sweet Case Recalled as Mob of 300 Tries to Rout Rich Detroit Family," *Pittsburgh Courier*, January 21, 1928; McKinney to NAACP, February 13, 1928, NAACP, Part 12, Series C, Reel 12; McKinney to Lodge, April 16, 1928; W. Hayes McKinney, "Report of the Legal Redress Committee," 1928, NAACP, Part 12, Series C, Reel 12; R. L. Polk & Company, *Polk's Detroit City Directory.*
29. McKinney to Lodge, April 16, 1928, MP 1928, Box 2, Folder "Interracial Commission, 1928"; McKinney, "Report of the Legal Redress Committee."
30. "Detroiters Fight over Jim Crow Decision, Repetition of Sweet Case Is Imminent," *Pittsburgh Courier*, December 15, 1928.
31. "White Black Exams in Detroit Now," *Baltimore Afro-American*, November 17, 1928.
32. "Police Commission Head Addresses Citizens"; "Police Head Scores 'Crackers' on Detroit Force," November 12, 1927, *Pittsburgh Courier.*

33. "Police Head Scores 'Crackers' on Detroit Force."
34. Ibid.
35. Ibid.
36. "Kelly Miller Says," *Baltimore Afro-American*, August 7, 1926.
37. "Mayor Smith Welcomes Joint Annual Meeting of Eastern and Western Colored Leagues," *New York Amsterdam News*, January 19, 1927.
38. "Charge Unfair Tactics in Registration," *Pittsburgh Courier*, October 29, 1927; "Race Councilmanic Candidate Active," *Pittsburgh Courier*, September 17, 1927.
39. "Detroit Nominates a State Senator," *Afro-American*, September 20, 1930.
40. "Detroiters Banquet New City Leader: New Council Member Pledges Aid," *Chicago Defender*, December 31, 1927.
41. "Detroit Attorney Refuses to Join Democratic Ranks," *Pittsburgh Courier*, September 29, 1928; "The Great Conspiracy," *Pittsburgh Courier*, November 23, 1929; Floyd J. Calvin, "U. S. Poston Will Speak in Chicago and Detroit," *Pittsburgh Courier*, November 29, 1930; Weiss, *Farewell to the Party of Lincoln*.
42. Detroit's NAACP recruited 2,145 members and forwarded $1,000 to the national office in the beginning of 1927. Eastmond to Bagnall, December 14, 1926, NAACP, Part 12, Series C, Reel 12; "An Awakening in Detroit," *St. Louis Argus*, January 28, 1927.
43. Black to Hall, March 7, 1939, NAACP, Part 12, Series C, Reel 12.
44. White to Bradby, January 25, 1927, NAACP, Part 12, Series C, Reel 12; White to Bradby, February 1, 1927, NAACP, Part 12, Series C, Reel 12.
45. M. L. Walker et al., "Subject: Final Call for Co-operation in 1930," January 1930, NAACP, Part 12, Series C, Reel 12; "Mayor Murphy of Detroit Launches NAACP Drive," October 24, 1930, NAACP, Part 12, Series C, Reel 12; Dancy to Pickens, November 4, 1930, NAACP, Part 12, Series C, Reel 12; Director of Branches to Blount, November 7, 1930, NAACP, Part 12, Series C, Reel 12.
46. Thomas, *Life for Us Is What We Make It*, 230.
47. "The Up and Coming Mr. Bowles," *Detroit Saturday Night*, November 9, 1929.
48. "A Myth Is Exploded: Bowles, Touted as Civic Savior, Fails in Test," *Detroit News*, September 10, 1930; "Reduce Taxes!!! How? Elect Charles Bowles Mayor," 1929, Carl May Weideman Papers, Scrapbook, 1929–1931, Bentley.
49. "Walker Comes Out for Smith," *Detroit Free Press*, October 25, 1929.
50. "Walker Denies Aid to Bowles," *Detroit Free Press*, October 28, 1929.
51. Ibid.
52. One journalist called Bowles's campaign "one of the smoothest working political organizations ever seen in Detroit." "Smith Facing 'Whisper' Crew," *Detroit Free Press*, October 29, 1929; "Race Question Is Brought Up," *Detroit Free Press*, November 4, 1929.
53. The *Detroit Free Press* refers to the paper as a "Negro paper . . . published on Oct 13, [1929]"; "A Myth Is Exploded."
54. Detroit annexed 60 square miles of land in the early 1920s, increasing its

total size by 43 percent to 140 square miles. Detroit Bureau of Governmental Research, *Accumulated Social and Economic Statistics for Detroit.*

55. "Calls Opponent 'Oily Politician,'" *Detroit News*, November 1, 1929. The Twenty-Second Ward Republican Club had "helped to establish the new ward as an important factor in the political life of the city." "22nd Ward Republican Club Officers," *Detroit Free Press*, January 19, 1930; "Smith Talks in 22nd Ward," *Detroit News*, November 2, 1929.
56. "All Charter Amendments Are Rejected by Voters," *Detroit Free Press*, November 6, 1929.
57. "The Up and Coming Mr. Bowles," *Detroit Saturday Night*, November 9, 1929.
58. "Bowles Asks Explanations," *Detroit News*, October 28, 1929.
59. "Smith Tells of 'Roorback,'" *Detroit Free Press*, October 27, 1929.
60. Zanbervis to Weideman, n.d., Scrapbook, 1929–1931, Carl Weideman Papers (hereafter CW); "Calls Bowles Mud-Slinger," *Detroit News*, October 29, 1929.
61. "All Charter Amendments Are Rejected by Voters," *Detroit Free Press*, November 6, 1929.
62. Monroe et al., *The City of Detroit, Michigan*; "Cary Appoints Managers for Ouster Drive," *Detroit Free Press*, July 10, 1930.
63. "School Pupils Greet Smith," *Detroit Free Press*, October 17, 1929.
64. "Calls Bowles Mud-Slinger."
65. Solomon, *The Negro Voters in Detroit*, 88.
66. "Smith Facing 'Whisper' Crew."
67. Larry to Jo, November 11, 1929, JG, Box 1, Folder "Correspondence, 1929"; untitled speech, JG, Box 1, Folder "Correspondence, 1928."
68. Zanbervis to Weideman, n.d., CW, Scrapbook, 1929–1931; *Onlooker* 10, no. 20, January 25, 1930, CW, Scrapbook, 1929–1931.
69. "Bowles Goes in Today Facing Record Deficit," *Detroit Free Press*, January 14, 1930; "City's Bonded Debt," April 8, 1932, FM, Reel 141; Detroit Bureau of Governmental Research, *Accumulated Social and Economic Statistics for Detroit*; "Gunmen Must Be Driven Out," *Detroit Free Press*, January 15, 1930; and "Would Lop 4 Millions in Salaries," *Detroit Free Press*, January 23, 1930.
70. Quoted in Sullivan, "'On the Dole,'" 42–43.
71. Council of Social Agencies, "A Brief Summary of Historical and Current Data on the Detroit Department of Public Welfare," Bentley; Department of Public Welfare, *The Department of Public Welfare, 1930–1940* (Detroit, 1940), Bentley.
72. "A Myth Is Exploded"; Haber, "Fluctuations in Employment in Detroit Factories," 151; Brown, *Public Relief*; Council of Social Agencies, "A Brief Summary of Historical and Current Data on the Detroit Department of Public Welfare"; Department of Public Welfare, *The Department of Public Welfare, 1930–1940*, 8.
73. "Gunmen Must Be Driven Out"; "Bowles Goes in Today Facing Record Deficit"; "Would Lop 4 Millions in Salaries."
74. Fragnoli, *The Transformation of Reform*, 343–348; "Will Direct Recall Campaign,"

Detroit Free Press, July 10, 1930; "120,863 Vote 'Yes' and 89,907 'No' in Recall Contest," *Detroit Free Press*, July 23, 1930.

75. Fine, *Frank Murphy*, 171–177.
76. "Decision Due Tuesday on Candidacy," *Detroit Times*, August 17, 1930; Mayor's Unemployment Committee, "Depression Study Based on Survey of 1400 families," Detroit, 1932, Joe Brown Papers, Archives of Labor and Urban Affairs, Wayne State University, Detroit.
77. "Decision Due Tuesday of Candidacy," *Detroit Times*, August 17, 1930; "Engel Outlines Constructive Platform in Opening Campaign," *Detroit Free Press*, August 28, 1930, "Murphy Tells Peril of Tacks," *Detroit Free Press*, September 1, 1930; Frank Murphy, Campaign Address, August 1930, FM, Reel 141.
78. Quoted in Howard, *Mr. Justice Murphy*, 30; Joseph Coles, interview by Jim Keeney and Roberta McBride, July 8, 1970, Blacks in the Labor Movement Oral History Project, Archives of Labor and Urban Affairs, Wayne State University, Detroit; "2,000 Enlist in Murphy Campaign," *Detroit Times*, August 13, 1930; Fine, *Frank Murphy*, 211.
79. George Cantor, "Detroit History (and Legends) Seen through the Eyes of Jo Gomon," *Detroit*, March 12, 1972.

NOTES TO CHAPTER 4

1. "Economy Cuts Mothers' Beds: Welfare Department Proposes Curtailment in Care for City's Indigent," *Detroit Free Press*, June 2, 1931; Detroit Bureau of Governmental Research, *The Herman Kiefer Hospital of Detroit*.
2. Blain to Williams, June 24, 1931, Mayor's Papers (hereafter MP) 1931, Box 9, Folder "Welfare (3)," Burton Historical Collection, Detroit Public Library.
3. Blassingille to Murphy, June 3, 1931, MP 1931, Box 9, Folder "Welfare (3)."
4. Roxborough to Murphy, June 2, 1931, MP 1931, Box 9, Folder "Welfare (3)."
5. Blain to Williams, June 24, 1931.
6. Harris to Blain, June 3, 1931, MP 1931, Box 9, Folder "Welfare (3)."
7. Bergman to Murphy, June 3, 1931, MP 1931, Box 9, Folder "Welfare (3)."
8. "Economy Cuts Mothers' Beds."
9. Minutes of Special Meeting of the Welfare Commission, July 8, 1931, MP 1931, Box 9, Folder "Welfare (3)."
10. Detroit Bureau of Governmental Research, *The Herman Kiefer Hospital of Detroit*.
11. Detroit Urban League Board Minutes, September 12, 1929, Detroit Urban League Papers (hereafter DUL), Box 11, Folder 10, Bentley Historical Library, University of Michigan, Ann Arbor (hereafter Bentley); Haber, "Fluctuations in Employment in Detroit Factories"; U.S. Bureau of the Census, "Detroit's Population, 1850–1940," UAW-CIO Research Papers, Box 9, Folder 24, Archives of Labor and Urban Affairs, Wayne State University, Detroit (hereafter ALUA); "Automobile Plants Reopen after 3-Week Shutdown," *Detroit Free Press*, August 3, 1930; "Drought Hits Budget," *Detroit Times*, August 8, 1930.

12. William C. Richards, "Boy Fights Poverty, Tragedy, Stays 'Clean,'" *Detroit Free Press*, January 21, 1930.
13. Caroline Parker to the Editor, *Nation*, April 30, 1930; "Twenty-Two Are Injured as Police Clash with Mob during Demonstration," *Detroit Free Press*, March 7, 1930; "Scenes as Police Fought Milling Thousands in Red Riot," *Detroit Evening Times*, March 7, 1930; "Crowds Jam Campus to See Communist Demonstration," *Detroit Free Press*, March 7, 1930.
14. "Police Called Brutal by Woman at Red Hearing," *Detroit Times*, March 7, 1930; "5 Women, Men Tried in Riots," *Detroit Free Press*, March 8, 1930.
15. "18 Held in Mob Battle Face Federal Investigation," *Detroit Evening Times*, March 7, 1930.
16. See Bates, *The Making of Black Detroit in the Age of Henry Ford*; Dancy, *Sand against the Wind*; Dillard, *Faith in the City*; Meier and Rudwick, *Black Detroit and the Rise of the UAW*; Moon, *Untold Tales, Unsung Heroes*; Thomas, *Life for Us Is What We Make It*; Wolcott, *Remaking Respectability*; Sterner, *The Negro's Share*; Weaver, *Negro Labor*; Sitkoff, *A New Deal for Blacks*; Kirby, *Black Americans in the Roosevelt Era*.
17. Dancy to Nicholson, January 28, 1933, DUL, Box 2, Folder 25; Dancy to Washington, January 26, 1933, DUL, Box 2, Folder 25.
18. Dancy to Mays, February 27, 1930, DUL, Box 1, Folder 31; Helmbold, "Downward Occupational Mobility during the Great Depression"; Women's Bureau, *Women at Work*; Weaver, *Negro Labor*, 9; Shelton Tappes, interview by Jack W. Skeels, July 12, 1961, "Unionization of the Auto Industry" Oral History Project (hereafter UAI), ALUA.
19. Annual Report of the Detroit Urban League for 1925, March 1, 1926, DUL, Box 11, Folder 8; "Approximate Number of Negroes in Detroit Industries," November 21, 1925, DUL, Box 1, Folder 15; Dancy to Hill, March 1, 1928, DUL, Box 1, Folder 23; Annual Report for the Detroit Urban League for 1928, January 1929, DUL, Box 11, Folder 10.
20. "Employment," January 7, 1931, DUL, Box 2, Folder 9; "Employment—Mr. Jones," 1932, DUL, Box 2, Folder 8.
21. George Cantor, "Detroit History (and Legends) Seen through the Eyes of Jo Gomon," *Detroit*, March 12, 1972.
22. Norton, "The Relief Crisis in Detroit."
23. Mayor's Unemployment Committee, "Organization Activities and Program of the Mayor's Unemployment Committee," January 31, 1931, DUL, Box 9, Folder 12, 8; "Mayor's Unemployment Committee, Appointed by Hon. Frank Murphy, Mayor of Detroit," DUL, Box 9, Folder 12.
24. Forncrook to Dancy, October 19, 1930, DUL, Box 9, Folder 11.
25. Roosevelt to Wade, n.d., DUL, Box 9, Folder 11.
26. Phillips to Roosevelt, October 22, 1930, Josephine Gomon Papers (hereafter JG), Box 1, Folder "Correspondence, 1930–1935," Bentley.

27. Mayor's Unemployment Committee, "Organization Activities and Program of the Mayor's Unemployment Committee."
28. Sullivan, "'On the Dole,'" 52.
29. "Mayor's Unemployment Committee, Appointed by Hon. Frank Murphy, Mayor of Detroit."
30. Hallgren, "Detroit's Liberal Mayor."
31. Ibid.
32. Haber, "Fluctuations in Employment in Detroit Factories"; Geddes, *Trends in Relief Expenditures*, 7–8.
33. "Help for Jobless Delayed in Detroit: Plans Go Askew," *New York Times*, December 14, 1930; Klug, "Labor Market Politics in Detroit."
34. Clifford Epstein, "Business Really Too Good Says One Alex G. W. Rivers," *Detroit News*, December 11, 1930.
35. Ibid.
36. Bak, *Ty Cobb*.
37. See Foner, "Why Is There No Socialism in the United States?"
38. Phillips to Roosevelt, October 22, 1930, JG, Box 1, Folder "Correspondence, 1930–1935"; Dancy to Payne, October 28, 1930, DUL, Box 2, Folder 5.
39. Garland, *After They Closed the Gates*.
40. Vargas, *Proletarians of the North*; Klug, "Labor Market Politics in Detroit."
41. Department of Public Welfare, *The Department of Public Welfare, 1930–1940*, 18.
42. Department of Public Welfare, *Report of the Relief and Social Service Division of the Department of Public Welfare*, c. 1931, MP 1931, Box 9, 1931, Folder "Welfare (3)."
43. "April to Show Dole Decrease," *Detroit Free Press*, April 26, 1931.
44. Gregory, *The Southern Diaspora*.
45. Dancy to Nelson, December 18, 1930, DUL, Box 2, Folder 7.
46. Detroit Bureau of Governmental Research, "Welfare," in *The Negro in Detroit*, 2.
47. Dancy to Nicholson, January 28, 1933, DUL, Box 2, Folder 25.
48. One sociologist, who would go on to become a state relief administrator, observed that many unemployed people had left the city when they heard this news, as "evidenced by vacant dwellings, vacant rooming houses, removal of gas and electric meters and similar facts." Landers and Tharp, *Administration and Financing of Public Relief*, 2; Haber, "Fluctuations in Employment in Detroit Factories," 149–150. See García, *Mexicans in the Midwest*.
49. Fine, *Frank Murphy*, 267; Mayor's Unemployment Committee, "Organization Activities and Program of the Mayor's Unemployment Committee."
50. Woodworth, "The Detroit Money Market," 3.
51. Detroit Bureau of Governmental Research, *Accumulated Social and Economic Statistics for Detroit*, 3.
52. Frank Murphy, speech on "Detroit's Financial Condition," 1932, Frank Murphy Papers (hereafter FM), Reel 97, Bentley.

53. Wiese, *Places of Their Own.*
54. Frank Murphy, "Campaign Address," August 1930, FM, Reel 97; "Engel Outlines Constructive Platform in Opening Campaign," *Detroit Free Press*, August 28, 1930; "Employment Issue Put to Fore," *Detroit Times*, September 1, 1930.
55. Phillips to Roosevelt, October 22, 1930; "Organization Activities and Program of the Mayor's Unemployment Committee."
56. Department of Public Welfare, *Report of the Relief and Social Service Division of the Department of Public Welfare.*
57. "April to Show Dole Decrease," *Detroit News*, April 26, 1931.
58. Department of Public Welfare, *Report of the Relief and Social Service Division of the Department of Public Welfare.*
59. Petitioners to Mayor Frank Murphy, June 13, 1931, MP 1931, Box 9, Folder "Welfare (3).
60. C. C. McGill, "Text of Radio Talk over Station WXYZ at 6:00 P.M. March 15, 1931," FM, Reel 97.
61. Grigsby and Berry to Mayor, August 20, 1935, MP 1935, Box 6, Folder "Interracial"; "Petition to Appoint Dr. Remus G. Robinson to the Position as Surgeon at Receiving Hospital," n.d., MP 1935, Box 6, Folder "Interracial."
62. Tickton, *An Analysis of Tax Delinquency*. Furthermore, by the early 1930s, many of the city's homeowners were having trouble staying in their houses. Young, *A Study of the Problems of the Distressed Home Owner of Detroit.*
63. Sullivan, "'On the Dole,'" 68; "Plan to Cut Entire Dole Threatens," *Detroit Free Press*, July 3, 1931; Minutes of Special Meeting of the Welfare Commission, July 8, 1931, and July 17, 1931, MP 1931, Box 9, Folder "Welfare (3)."
64. Norton, "The Relief Crisis in Detroit," 4; Minutes of Special Meeting of the Welfare Commission, July 8, 1931, and July 17, 1931"; Whalen to the Public Welfare Commission, August 20, 1931, MP 1931, Box 9, Folder "Welfare (3)."
65. Whalen to the Public Welfare Commission.
66. Gladys H. Kelsey, "Detroit Faces Need of Government Aid," *New York Times*, August 30, 1931.
67. Conrad to Murphy, June 25, 1931, MP 1931, Box 9, Folder "Welfare (3)."
68. "Detroit Welfare Fund Is Robbed of $213,000," *New York Times*, June 10, 1931, "Ask for Parole for Lewis," *Detroit News*, November 8, 1937.
69. See Beito, *Taxpayers in Revolt.*
70. Gladys H. Kelsey, "Detroit's Election Study in Sociology," *New York Times*, November 8, 1931.
71. Landers and Tharp, *Administration and Financing of Public Relief*, 6.
72. Ibid.; "Budget Limitation Sought in Detroit," *New York Times*, July 9, 1932; Beito, *Taxpayers in Revolt*, 24–26; Fine, *Frank Murphy.*
73. "Taxes and Expense Lower in Michigan," *New York Times*, August 21, 1932; "Two States Limit Taxes on Realty," *New York Times*, December 11, 1932; Sullivan, "'On the Dole,'" 128; "Subject: Detroit's Fiscal Problem," June 6, 1932, FM, Reel 141.

74. Norton, "The Relief Crisis in Detroit," 7.
75. Kenyon to Murphy, August 28, 1931, JG, Box 1, Folder "Correspondence 1930–1935."
76. Josephine Gomon, interview by Jack W. Skeels, December 22, 1959, UAI. Joseph Billups explained that "Grand Circus Park was full, day and night, and always there was someone up speaking." Joseph Billups, interview by Herbert Hill, Shelton Tappes, and Roberta McBride, October 26, 1967, Blacks in the Labor Movement Oral History Project, ALUA.
77. Claire M. Sanders, Report on Homeless Women, November 1932, United Community Services Central Files (hereafter UCS-CF), Box 111, Folder 1, ALUA; *New Republic*, November 25, 1931, in Joe Brown papers (hereafter JB), ALUA; Box 25, Folder "Unemployment Relief, 1930–1933," ALUA; Joe Brown, "Some Highlights of the Depression in Detroit," JB, Box 25, Folder "Unemployment Relief, 1930–1933."
78. Henry A. Johnson, "Report of the Detroit Thrift Gardens Which Helped 4,369 Families in 1931," January 22, 1932, 6, FM, Reel 97; Sullivan, "'On the Dole.'"
79. Dancy to Washington, January 1933, DUL, Box 2, Folder 25.
80. John C. Dancy, "The Negro in the Recovery Program," July 1934, DUL, Box 3, Folder 8.
81. Untitled report, June 1934, DUL, Box 3, Folder 8.
82. National Urban League, "Urban League Fights Evasion of NRA," August 12, 1933, DUL, Box 2, Folder 32; "Seventeen Workers Replaced under New Hotel Code," *Detroit Tribune*, December 2, 1933; Department of Public Welfare, "Report on Families on the Relief Rolls in Detroit," April 1934, DUL, Box 8, Folder 16; Dancy to Weaver, April 23, 1934, DUL, Box 3, Folder 5; Dancy to White, March 15, 1935, and March 29, 1935, DUL, Box 3, Folder 16; Dancy, "The Negro in the Recovery Program."
83. "Colored Employees Fired from Sears Roebuck Store," *Detroit Tribune*, June 17, 1933; "Firing Negroes and Hiring Whites," *Detroit Tribune*, June 17, 1933.
84. Walker to Lenhardt, August 21, 1933, Papers of the National Association for the Advancement of Colored People (hereafter NAACP), Part 12, Series C, Reel 12.
85. Dancy to Jackson, August 18, 1937, DUL, Box 4, Folder "Executive Files Aug 1937."
86. "Haber Reveals Goal of Relief," *Detroit News*, November 8, 1934.
87. "Conference in the Office of the Michigan State Employment Service to Discuss the Problem of the Negro Unemployment and Suggest Methods to Increase Negro Placements," November 20, 1937, NAACP, Part 12, Series C, Reel 10.
88. "Conference Findings Committee on Negro Employment Problems [in Michigan]," October 10, 1940, NAACP, Part 12, Series C, Reel 15; "Findings, Report, and Recommendations of the Michigan State Conference on Employment Problems of the Negro, October 8, 1940," NAACP, Part 12, Series C, Reel 15, 21–22.
89. Dancy, "The Negro in the Recovery Program."
90. "Few Families Here Have Welfare Habit," *Detroit News*, August 26, 1935.
91. Gregory, *The Southern Diaspora*.

92. "Report on the Organized Services Being Rendered in the Field of Family Service and Relief," April 11, 1935, UCS-CF, Box 163, Folder 12.
93. Department of Public Welfare, City of Detroit, Statistical Division, "Color," August 30, 1937, JB, Box 25, Folder "Unemployment Relief, 1934–1937."
94. Dancy to Barnett, March 3, 1938, DUL, Box 4, Folder "General Files and Correspondence March 1938."

NOTES TO CHAPTER 5

1. "Colored People Are Getting Funny," *Detroit Tribune*, February 10, 1934.
2. Ibid.
3. Snow Flake Grigsby, *An X-Ray Picture of Detroit*, Detroit, December 1933, NAACP, Part 12, Series C, Reel 12.
4. Ibid.
5. Bates, "A New Crowd Challenges the Agenda of the Old Guard in the NAACP."
6. Meier and Rudwick, *Black Detroit and the Rise of the UAW*; Bates, *The Making of Black Detroit in the Age of Henry Ford.*
7. See Dillard, *Faith in the City*.
8. Wolcott, *Remaking Respectability*.
9. "Detroit Housewives' League," *Detroit Tribune*, August 7, 1937; Wolcott, *Remaking Respectability*; Thomas, *Life for Us Is What We Make It.*
10. Wolcott, *Remaking Respectability*; Dillard, *Faith in the City*; Thomas, *Life for Us Is What We Make It.*
11. Snow Flake Grigsby, interview by Roberta McBride, March 12, 1967, Blacks in the Labor Movement Oral History Project (hereafter BLM), Archives of Labor and Urban Affairs, Wayne State University, Detroit (hereafter ALUA), 1.
12. "Police Head Scores 'Crackers' on Detroit Force," *Pittsburgh Courier*, November 12, 1927.
13. Grigsby interview, March 12, 1967.
14. "Discrimination in Swimming Pool at Colleges of the City of Detroit Is Discontinued," *People's News* (Detroit), November 15, 1931; Press Release, "Detroit City College Admits Negroes to Swimming Classes after Struggle," December 4, 1931, NAACP, Part 12, Series C, Reel 12; Blount to Grigsby, November 10, 1931, NAACP, Part 12, Series C, Reel 12; "Detroit College Finally Opens Pool to Negroes," *Pittsburgh Courier*, December 12, 1931.
15. Grigsby to Bradby, November 5, 1931, NAACP, Part 12, Series C, Reel 12; Grigsby to White, November 16, 1931, NAACP, Part 12, Series C, Reel 12.
16. Birney Smith, a black realtor who was active in the formation of the Detroit Urban League during the 1910s, also called Bradby an opportunist. Birney Smith, interview by Jim Keeney and Roberta McBride, June 15, 1969, BLM.
17. Dancy to Platt, July 22, 1937, Detroit Urban League Papers (hereafter DUL), Box 4, Folder "Executive Files, July 1937," Bentley Historical Library, University of Michigan, Ann Arbor (hereafter Bentley); Dancy to Tennis, September 11, 1937, DUL, Box 4, Folder "General Files and Correspondence September 1937."

18. Dancy to White, March 9, 1932, DUL, Box 2, Folder 19.
19. Dancy to Fassitt, May 22, 1933, DUL, Box 2, Folder 29.
20. Dancy to Finch, March 23, 1933, DUL, Box 2, Folder 27; "Detroit Urban League: Employees Being Retained by the Agency," 1933, DUL, Box 2, Folder 24; Dodge to Dancy, March 7, 1938; Dancy to Jones, March 2, 1933, DUL, Box 2, Folder 27.
21. Dancy to Wright and McCard, February 4, 1932, DUL, Box 2, Folder 18; Dancy to Hill, April 15, 1936, DUL, Box 3, Folder 24.
22. Dancy to Hill, April 18, 1933, DUL, Box 2, Folder 28.
23. Wolcott, *Remaking Respectability*; Joseph Billups, interviewed with Roberta Billups by Herbert Hill and Shelton Tappes, Detroit, October 27, 1967, BLM.
24. Wolcott, *Remaking Respectability*, 234.
25. Joseph Billups interview, October 27, 1967.
26. Weis, *Farewell to the Party of Lincoln*; Kirby, *Black Americans in the Roosevelt Era*.
27. Dancy to Holsey, September 18, 1929, DUL, Box 1, Folder 28.
28. Dancy to Thompson, May 8, 1931, DUL, Box 2, Folder 12; Dancy to Webster, May 25, 1938, DUL, Box 4, Folder 17; Dancy to Silvers, March 8, 1938, DUL, Box 4, Folder "General Files and Correspondence March 1938."
29. "Detroit Nominates a State Senator," *Baltimore Afro-American*, September 20, 1930; "Many File for Offices in Detroit," *Baltimore Afro-American*, August 6, 1932; "Negro Atty Nominated for House," *Atlanta Daily World*, September 22, 1932.
30. "Voters Want Mahoney for Congressman," *Chicago Defender*, October 1, 1932, "Sen. Roxborough and Running Mates Lose Detroit Election," *Chicago Defender*, November 19, 1932.
31. Clifford Mitchell, "Progressiveness of Democratic Leaders in Michigan Lauded," *Pittsburgh Courier*, September 2, 1933.
32. "Detroit Citizens Boosting Sheriff Behrendt Campaign," *Pittsburgh Courier*, August 20, 1932.
33. Bunche, *The Political Status of the Negro in the Age of FDR*, 586; Solomon, "Participation of Negroes in Detroit Elections"; "Negro Demo Gets Highest Michigan Job," *Atlanta Daily World*, August 5, 1934; "Roxborough Named Asst Attorney General," *Chicago Defender*, February 2, 1935; "Mahoney Gets $5,000 Post in Michigan," *Chicago Defender*, January 28, 1939; Joseph Coles, interview by Jim Keeney and Roberta McBride, Detroit, July 8, 1970, BLM.
34. See Bates, "A New Crowd Challenges the Agenda of the Old Guard in the NAACP"; Naison, *Communists in Harlem during the Depression*; Gaines, *Uplifting the Race*; Solomon, *The Cry Was Unity*; Haywood, *Black Bolshevik*; Keeran, *The Communist Party and the Auto Worker's Unions*.
35. Joseph Billups interview, October 27, 1967; Dillard, *Faith in the City*; Leab, "United We Eat."
36. Coles, interview, July 8, 1970.
37. Shelton Tappes, interview by Jack W. Skeels, July 12, 1961, UAW Oral History Project.
38. Roberta Billups, an African American member of Detroit's CP at the time,

remembered that the Scottsboro case "aroused the interest of all Negroes." Roberta Billups, interviewed with Joseph Billups by Herbert Hill and Shelton Tappes, October 27, 1967, BLM.

39. Goodman, *Stories of Scottsboro.*
40. "The Scottsboro Defense Fund," NAACP, Part 12, Series C, Reel 12; "N.A.A.C.P. Opens Big Spring Drive," *Detroit Tribune*, April 22, 1933; "Local Physician Heads Defense Fund," *Detroit Tribune*, April 14, 1933; "Scottsboro Groups Elect Officers and Committees," *Detroit Tribune*, June 24, 1933. Other men and women on the committee included a number of doctors and lawyers, many of whom shared last names with NAACP activists or prominent Republicans to whom they may have been related. For example, Dr. R. L. McClendon may have been related to Dr. J. J. McClendon, who would become vice president of the association the next year. Similarly, Dr. Stewart Toodles may have been related to Aaron Toodles, head of the Wolverine Republican Club and owner of the *Detroit Tribune*. Ossian Sweet ran as a Republican for state senator in the Third Senatorial District in 1934. He lost the election. "Roxborough and Dr. Sweet Nominated in Primary Election," September 22, 1934, *Detroit Tribune.*
41. White to Walker, May 29, 1933, NAACP, Part 12, Series C, Reel 12; "N.A.A.C.P. Refutes Charges of Misappropriation of Scottsboro Funds," *Detroit Tribune*, June 17, 1933.
42. Sugar, *The Ford Hunger March.*
43. Pickens to Blount, January 3, 1933, NAACP, Part 12, Series C, Reel 12; memorandum to Pickens and Wilkins, January 21, 1933, NAACP, Part 12, Series C, Reel 12.
44. White to Pickens and Wilkins, January 21, 1933, NAACP, Part 12, Series C, Reel 12.
45. Snow F. Grigsby, "1933 Recommendations for the NAACP Local Branch," January 6, 1933, NAACP, Part 12, Series C, Reel 12.
46. Randall, "Detroit's Branch Report for 1929–1930," 1930, NAACP, Part 12, Series C, Reel 12.
47. Grigsby to White, November 16, 1931, NAACP, Part 12, Series C, Reel 12.
48. Grigsby, "1933 Recommendations for the NAACP Local Branch," January 6, 1933.
49. Grigsby to White, January 19, 1933, NAACP, Part 12, Series C, Reel 12.
50. Ibid.; White to Pickens and Wilkins, January 21, 1933, NAACP, Part 12, Series C, Reel 12; Pickens to Walker, January 23, 1933, NAACP, Part 12, Series C, Reel 12; Grigsby to White, February 8, 1933, NAACP, Part 12, Series C, Reel 12; Wilkins to Blount, March 22, 1933, NAACP, Part 12, Series C, Reel 12; Grigsby to White, March 24, 1933, NAACP, Part 12, Series C, Reel 12.
51. Snow F. Grigsby, "Citizens Respond to the N.A.A.C.P. Program," *Detroit Tribune*, April 14, 1933.
52. "N.A.A.C.P. Seeks Members," *Detroit Tribune*, April 21, 1933; Snow F. Grigsby, "Who Supports the NAACP in Detroit?," *Detroit Independent*, April 22, 1933.
53. Grigsby, "Defends His Position," *Detroit Tribune*, July 1, 1933.
54. Grigsby, "Who Supports the NAACP in Detroit?"

55. Bates, *Pullman Porters and the Rise of Protest Politics in Black America*, 120.
56. Hunter, "'Don't Buy from Where You Can't Work,'" 154–155.
57. Pickens to White, May 20, 1935, NAACP, Part 12, Series C, Reel 12.
58. "Detroit's Civic Rights Committee," January 1934, NAACP, Part 12, Series C, Reel 12.
59. "Civic Rights Group Plans Mass Meeting," *Tribune-Independent*, March 31, 1934.
60. Grigsby interview, March 12, 1967.
61. "Our Local School Problems," *Tribune-Independent*, February 24, 1934.
62. "Is Justice Blind?," *Detroit Tribune*, June 9, 1934; "Loomis Appearance Provokes Discussion," *Detroit Tribune*, June 2, 1934.
63. "Government Secures Local Social Worker," *Michigan Chronicle*, August 4, 1934.
64. "Crowd Packs Church to Hear Grigsby," *Detroit Tribune*, October 10, 1935; Hunter, "'Don't Buy from Where You Can't Work,'" 160; Grigsby interview, March 12, 1967, 6.
65. "Grigsby Reveals Civic Injustice," *Detroit Tribune*, November 2, 1935.
66. "Civic Rights Group to Hold Meeting at the St. Antoine Y," *Tribune-Independent*, September 29, 1934.
67. "Civic Group Head Flays Ministers' False Leadership," *Baltimore Afro-American*, October 6, 1934.
68. "University of Michigan Bars Girl from Martha Cook Dormitory," *Detroit Tribune-Independent*, September 1, 1934; "Governor's Aid Is Asked in U. of M. Dormitory Issue," *Detroit Tribune-Independent*, September 15, 1934; Grigsby to Lloyd, August 25, 1934, NAACP, Part 12, Series C, Reel 12.
69. Dancy to Lewis, September 24, 1934, DUL, Box 3, Folder 10.
70. It is unclear whether Blackwell was admitted to Martha Cook. The record in the Urban League papers falls silent after Dancy washed his hands of the case, and the newspaper did not publish a follow-up story.
71. Grigsby, *White Hypocrisy and Black Lethargy*, 58.
72. On his fight to open positions for African Americans in municipal hospitals, see Grigsby to White, November 17, 1936, 1931, NAACP, Part 12, Series C, Reel 12.
73. Grigsby to Dancy, November 2, 1938, DUL, Box 4, Folder 24; "Grigsby Again Files Petition with Common Council for Fireman," *Detroit Tribune*, December 18, 1937.
74. "Applicants for Job as Fireman to Be Examined," *Detroit Tribune*, April 30, 1938.
75. Hunter, "'Don't Buy from Where You Can't Work,'" 169.
76. In his 1949 memoir, Clayton W. Fountain described the Renters and Consumers League as a Communist Party front organization. Fountain, *Union Guy*, 77.
77. "Hit Rent Gouging, Strong Indictment against Landlords," *Detroit Tribune*, July 31, 1937.
78. "League Lists Rent Strikes on Landlords: Renters League to Stage Parade in Protest," August 7, 1937.
79. "Rent Strikes Staged as Protest against Increases by Landlords," *Detroit Tribune*, November 6, 1937; "Rent Strike Ends as Landlord Settles," *Detroit Tribune*,

November 13, 1937; "Rent Hikers Lose Battle," *Detroit Tribune*, November 13, 1937; "Rent Strikers Settle with Landlord out of Court," *Detroit Tribune*, February 5, 1938; "Tenants Blast Rent Increase," *Detroit Tribune*, November 12, 1938; "Landlords and Tenants in Agreement," *Detroit Tribune*, November 26, 1938.

80. "Renters Start Strike," *Detroit Tribune*, October 16, 1937.
81. Dillard, *Faith in the City*, 79.
82. "Program Suggested for the N.A.A.C.P. Branches," *Detroit Tribune*, October 28, 1933; Bates, "A New Crowd Challenges the Agenda of the Old Guard in the NAACP."
83. Meier and Bracey, "The NAACP as a Reform Movement."
84. Blount to White, April 12, 1934, NAACP, Part 12, Series C, Reel 12.
85. Pickens to White, May 20, 1935, NAACP, Part 12, Series C, Reel 12.
86. Solomon, *The Negro Voters in Detroit*, 10.
87. "Patrolman Slays Man with His 'Hands Up,'" January 14, 1927, NAACP Branch Files, Part 12, Series C, Reel 12.
88. *Detroit People's News*, April 9, 1927, NAACP Branch Files, Part 12, Series C, Reel 12.
89. Assistant Secretary to Bradby, n.d., NAACP Branch Files, Part 12, Series C, Reel 12; "Cop Plans Murder of Colored Boys Says Report," *Detroit Independent*, January 28, 1927.
90. Arthur McPhaul, interview by Norman McRae, April 5, 1970, BLM; "Prosecutor Orders Inquest in Killing by Cop," *Detroit Tribune*, August 19, 1933; "Patrolman Orler Exonerated," *Detroit Tribune*, August 26, 1933; "Mayor Couzens Hears Protest about Police," *Detroit Tribune*, September 2, 1933.
91. "Prosecutor Clashes with N.A.A.C.P. in Fracas over Police Warrant," February 11, 1939, *Detroit Tribune*; "3,000 Join Protest of Brutality," *Atlanta Daily World*, July 31, 1939.
92. "Summary of Lawless and Brutal Acts by Detroit Police, 1938–1939," Folder "Police Brutality 1939," Box 79, Civil Rights Committee Papers (hereafter CRC), ALUA; "On Saturday, May 16th on Theodore Street . . . ," Folder "Political Activity—Shootings, 1936," CRC, Box 79; "Your petitioners state upon information . . . ," Folder "Political Activity—Shootings, 1936," CRC, Box 79.
93. "Present 50 Citations of Brutality," *Michigan Chronicle*, September 2, 1939; "Citizens' Committee Petitions for Removal of Pickert from Post," *Detroit Tribune*, September 8, 1939; "Detroit Hearing Sept. 20 on Pickert Ouster Drive," *Detroit Record*, September 9, 1939.
94. Wolcott, *Remaking Respectability*.
95. Dillard, *Faith in the City*; Babson et al., *Working Detroit*; Thomas, *Life for Us Is What We Make It*.

NOTES TO CHAPTER 6

1. Nelson, "Autoworkers, Electoral Politics, and the Convergence of Class and Race Detroit"; Jones, "Labor and Politics: The Detroit Municipal Election of 1937."

2. "The Election Is Over," *Detroit Tribune*, November 6, 1937.
3. "Expect New Detroit Mayor to Break Up City Jim Crow," *Chicago Defender*, January 1, 1938.
4. "The Campaign Express," Folder "Negro File," Box 11, Maurice Sugar Papers, Archives of Labor and Urban Affairs (hereafter ALUA).
5. "City Clerk Promises Equal Representation," *Atlanta Daily World*, September 2, 1937; "Expect New Detroit Mayor to Break Up City Jim Crow."
6. "Reading," *Detroit Tribune*, September 25, 1937.
7. "The Election Is Over."
8. Johnson, *Maurice Sugar*.
9. "Victory's Life Threatened," *Detroit Tribune Independent*, July 21, 1934; Dillard, *Faith in the City*; Johnson, *Maurice Sugar*.
10. "UAW Jimcrows Workers," *Detroit Tribune*, October 30, 1937.
11. Haber, "Fluctuations in Employment in Detroit Factories"; Dancy to Carlson, November 29, 1929, Detroit Urban League Papers (hereafter DUL), Box 1, Folder 29, Bentley Historical Library, University of Michigan, Ann Arbor (hereafter Bentley); Dancy to Johnson, July 16, 1929, Papers of the National Association for the Advancement of Colored People (hereafter NAACP), Part 12, Series C, Reel 12; Johnson, "Incidence upon the Negroes," 737–738; Dancy to Greene, April 29, 1930, DUL, Box 2, Folder 3.
12. Dancy to Washington, January 26, 1933, DUL, Box 2, Folder 25.
13. Theodore R. Barnes, "The New Deal—Our Beer," *Detroit Tribune*, June 17, 1933.
14. Dancy to Nicholson, January 28, 1933, DUL, Box 2, Folder 25.
15. "Manager Forced to Hire Colored Help," *Detroit Tribune*, May 20, 1933.
16. "Federation of Negro Labor Formed by Detroit Workers," *Detroit Tribune*, October 7, 1933.
17. Ross, "The Negro Worker in the Depression."
18. Cyril Briggs, "Our Negro Work," *Communist*, September 1929, 495–497; "Winning the Negro Masses in Detroit," *Daily Worker*, November 2, 1929; "I Joined Because Communists Lead Both the White and Negro Workers," *Daily Worker*, February 12, 1930.
19. "Monthly Report of the Labor Advisor of the Industrial Relations Department of the National Urban League," March 7, 1932, DUL, Box 2, Folder 19; Dancy to Houchins, September 24, 1929, DUL, Box 1, Folder 28.
20. Dieckmann to Dancy, April 9, 1934, DUL, Box 3, Folder 5.
21. Anderson to Dancy, February 24, 1937, DUL, Box 3, Folder 32.
22. "Postal Group Closes Confab in Toledo, Ohio," *Detroit Tribune*, August 26, 1933.
23. "Postal Alliance to Meet Here in June," *Detroit Tribune*, May 26, 1934; "District Confab of Postal Alliance to Meet in Detroit June 2 and 3," *Detroit Tribune*, June 2, 1934; "Many Attend Dist. Session of Postal Men," *Detroit Tribune*, June 9, 1934; Anderson to Dancy, February 24, 1937; Dancy to Anderson, March 8, 1937, DUL, Box 3, Folder 33.

24. "P.O. Workers Denied Food in Cafeterias," *Detroit Tribune*, May 5, 1934; "Committee of Post Office Workers Push Action," *Detroit Tribune*, May 12, 1934.
25. "Civil Rights Act Violated by Café Man," *Detroit Tribune*, May 19, 1934; "Café Discrimination Case Goes to Probation Dept., " *Detroit Tribune*, May 26, 1934; "Civil Rights Law Violator Guilty; But Freed by Court," *Detroit Tribune*, June 2, 1934.
26. "P.O. Workers Get Together for Harmony," *Detroit Tribune*, May 12, 1934.
27. "Whites Visit Meeting of Local National Alliance of Postal Employees," *Detroit Tribune*, February 9, 1935; "Grigsby Elected Vice President P. O. Federation," *Detroit Tribune*, November 20, 1937.
28. "Local Postal Workers Hold Spirited Meet," *Detroit Tribune*, June 2, 1934
29. "Whites Visit Meeting of Local National Alliance of Postal Employees."
30. "Detroit Branch of NP Elects Officers," *Detroit Tribune*, September 29, 1934.
31. The Nacirema Club was a social club designed to provide wholesome entertainment for young, educated black men and women. Its name was "America" spelled backward. Miles, "Home at Last," 212; Snow Flake Grigsby, interview by Roberta McBride, Detroit, March 12, 1967, Blacks in the Labor Movement Oral History Project (hereafter BLM), ALUA; "Wins Fellowship," *Detroit Tribune*, October 6, 1934; Solomon, "Participation of Negroes in Detroit Elections"; "Nacirema Club Opens to Students," *Detroit Tribune*, October 20, 1934; "Wins Ph.D. from U. Of Michigan after Long, Hard Struggle for an Education," *Chicago Defender*, June 24, 1939.
32. "Detroit Branch of NP Elects Officers," *Detroit Tribune*, September 29, 1934.
33. *Detroit Postal Alliance* 2, no. 6, NAACP, Part 12, Series C, Reel 12.
34. Jones to White, June 21, 1937, NAACP, Part 12, Series C, Reel 12; Marshall to Jones, June 23, 1937, NAACP, Part 12, Series C, Reel 12; White to Houston, June 25, 1937, NAACP, Part 12, Series C, Reel 12; Huston to Blount, June 28, 1937, NAACP, Part 12, Series C, Reel 12.
35. *Detroit Postal Alliance.*
36. "The Strength of Unity," *Detroit Tribune*, n.d., NAACP, Part 12, Series C, Reel 12; McClendon to White, February 24, 1939, NAACP, Part 12, Series C, Reel 12; White to McClendon, February 28, 1939, NAACP, Part 12, Series C, Reel 12.
37. Keeran, *The Communist Party and the Auto Worker's Unions*; *The Trade Union Unity League.*
38. Haywood, *Black Bolshevik*; Solomon, *The Cry Was Unity*; Naison, *Communists in Harlem during the Depression.*
39. "May First and Revolutionary Traditions of Negro Masses," *Daily Worker*, April 29, 1930; Otto Huiswood, "Report to Communist Party Convention," *Daily Worker*, March 9 and 10, 1929; Haywood, *Black Bolshevik*, 317; Cyril Briggs, "Our Negro Work," *Communist*, September 1929.
40. "Worker's Calendar," *Daily Worker*, December 18, 1929; "Worker's Calendar," *Daily Worker*, January 9, 1930; "Worker's Calendar," *Daily Worker*, January 16, 1930; "Negro Toilers Join C. P. at Haiti Meets," *Daily Worker*, December 27, 1929.

41. "Winning the Negro Masses in Detroit," *Daily Worker*, November 2, 1929.
42. Ibid.
43. Spolansky had been hired to spy on communists by a committee of manufacturers, the Employers Association of Detroit, and the National Metal Trades Association. House Special Committee on Communist Activities in the United States, *Investigation of Communist Propaganda*, 194, 120–122.
44. "White Chauvinism and the Right Danger," *Daily Worker*, December 5, 1929.
45. "Root Out White Chauvinism," *Daily Worker*, January 14, 1930; "Fight on White Chauvinism: Party Takes Militant Stand in Detroit," *Daily Worker*, January 16, 1930.
46. Shelton Tappes, interview by Herbert Hill, Detroit, pt. 1, October 27, 1967, BLM.
47. "Communism and Colored America," *Detroit Tribune*, March 10, 1934.
48. "Detroit Workers School Offers Interesting Courses," *Detroit Tribune*, October 24, 1933; "Stop Kicking Us Around," *Detroit Tribune*, April 7, 1934; "Radicals Are Needed," *Detroit Tribune*, April 21, 1934.
49. "Should Negro Labor Organize?," *Detroit Tribune*, February 24, 1934.
50. See Bernstein, *Only One Place of Redress*; "Discrimination Practiced by City Workers," *Detroit Tribune*, August 5, 1933; Dancy to William M. Ashby, January 24, 1936, DUL, Box 3, Folder 21.
51. "Brewers' Unions Says Prejudice Not Cause for Barring of Negro Brewery Workers," *Detroit Tribune*, January 26, 1935.
52. Clark to Dancy, February 13, 1934, DUL, Box 3, Folder 2; Clark to Richberg, February 12, 1934, DUL, Box 3, Folder 2; Program for the National Conference of the Urban League, May 18–20, 1934, DUL, Box 3, Folder 6.
53. Lichtenstein, *Labor's War at Home*; Faue, *Community of Suffering and Struggle*.
54. "A.F.L. Faces Fight on Council Issue," *New York Times*, October 8, 1934; "Vast Changes Face A.F.L. as a New Course Is Charted," *New York Times*, October 21, 1934.
55. "Organize to Push Industrial Unions," *New York Times*, November 10, 1935; "Lewis Quits," *New York Times*, November 24, 1935; "Lewis Drive Urges Industrial Unions," *New York Times*, December 4, 1935; "Green's Views Hit by Printer Chief," *New York Times*, December 4, 1935; "Green Rejects Bid of Lewis Group," *New York Times*, December 8, 1935; "Green Bars Joining Lewis Union Group," *New York Times*, December 11, 1935. For a fuller discussion of the origins of the CIO, see Zieger, *The CIO*; Brody, *Workers in Industrial America*.
56. Keeran, *The Communist Party and the Auto Worker's Unions*, 96–101; Fine, "The Origins of the United Automobile Workers," 258.
57. For debates about the sincerity of the UAW's and CIO's commitment to racial justice, see Goldfield et al., "Scholarly Controversy"; Goldfield, "Race and the CIO"; Hill, "The Problem of Race in American Labor History"; Arnesen, "Up from Exclusion"; Nelson, *Divided We Stand*; Horowitz, *"Negro and White, Unite and Fight!"*; Halpern, *Down on the Killing Floor*.

58. Bates, *The Making of Black Detroit in the Age of Henry Ford.*
59. "Should Negro Labor Organize?," *Detroit Tribune*, February 24, 1934; "An Epidemic of Labor Strikes," *Detroit Tribune*, July 21, 1934.
60. "N.Y. Urban League Refuses to Sanction Negro Strike-breakers," *Detroit Tribune*, November 24, 1934; "Economic Conference Closes," *Detroit Tribune*, October 26, 1935.
61. "AFL Convention in San Francisco Picketed by NAACP," *Detroit Tribune*, October 20, 1934; "Two Quakes Excite Labor Convention," *New York Times*, October 3, 1934; " 'Vertical Unionism Adopted by A.F.L.," *New York Times*, October 12, 1934.
62. Foner, *Organized Labor and the Black Worker*, 205–206. For a discussion of the Brotherhood of Sleeping Car Porters and A. Philip Randolph, see Bates, *Pullman Porters and the Rise of Protest Politics in Black America.*
63. "American Federation of Labor Seeks to End Discrimination," *Detroit Tribune*, October 27, 1934.
64. "Restrictions against Negro Workers Are Scored by Charles H. Houston," *Detroit Tribune*, July 27, 1935.
65. Ernest Marshall, "Employment Figures, 1929–1934," June 1934, DUL, Box 3, Folder 14; Lichtenstein, *Walter Reuther*, 63; Babson et al., *Working Detroit*, 72–73.
66. Dancy to Hill, January 27, 1937, DUL, Box 3, Folder 31; Meier and Rudwick, *Black Detroit and the Rise of the UAW*, 35.
67. "Midland Workers Accept Peace Pact," *New York Times*, December 5, 1936.
68. Roy Wilkins quoted in Meier and Rudwick, *Black Detroit and the Rise of the UAW*, 36; "G. M. Strikers Want Race in Union," *Atlanta Daily World*, February 3, 1937.
69. "Detroit Union Appoints Race Executive," *Chicago Defender*, April 24, 1937; "N.A.A.C.P. Enlivens Detroiters," *New York Amsterdam News*, July 10, 1937; "CIO Tilt Rocks NAACP," *Baltimore Afro-American*, July 10, 1937; Meier and Rudwick, *Black Detroit and the Rise of the UAW*, 39–40.
70. "Pickens Assails UAW Leader," *Detroit Tribune*, July 10, 1937; Meier and Rudwick, *Black Detroit and the Rise of the UAW*, 56–59; Dillard, *Faith in the City*, 101–102.
71. "Tells How Negroes Were Received in U.A.W. Union," *Pittsburgh Courier*, September 25, 1937; "Detroit Awaiting Ford Crisis, Schuyler Finds," *Pittsburgh Courier*, September 4, 1937; "Detroit Churches Close Pulpits to Howard Prexy," *Baltimore Afro-American*, January 15, 1938.
72. "Union Bitterly Assailed for Not Supporting Colored Milk Driver," *Detroit Tribune*, May 14, 1938.
73. Dillard, *Faith in the City*, 79.
74. "Angels of Darkness," *Michigan Chronicle*, January 14, 1939.
75. "Congress to Convene Here," *Detroit Tribune*, June 25, 1938.
76. "Negroes on WPA Storm City Hall," *Michigan Chronicle*, July 15, 1939.
77. "NAACP Assails Department of Public Welfare for Alleged Segregation of Social Workers," *Detroit Tribune*, June 18, 1938.

78. The company denied its involvement in the back-to-work campaign and suggested that it was working to uphold racial justice, saying, "We will not discriminate against our colored employees by closing our plants to them as you suggest." "Racial Issue in Auto Strike Threatens Riot," *Baltimore Afro-American*, December 2, 1939; "C.I.O. Union Calls Chrysler 'Strike,'" *New York Times*, November 26, 1939; "Eight Hurt in Riot at Dodge Factory," *New York Times*, November 25, 1939; "Asks State Guards for Chrysler Men," *New York Times*, November 27, 1939; "Strikers Fear Race Rioting," *New York Amsterdam News*, December 2, 1939. For a discussion of the Chrysler strike, see Meier and Rudwick, *Black Detroit and the Rise of the UAW*, 67–71.
79. See Meier and Rudwick, *Black Detroit and the Rise of the UAW*; Dillard, *Faith in the City;* Thomas, *Life for Us Is What We Make It.*
80. Dillard, *Faith in the City*, 106.
81. "Auto Employees Push Demands," *Atlanta Daily World*, March 11, 1939.

NOTES TO CHAPTER 7

1. "Parkside Has First Family," *Detroit News*, October 15, 1938; "Families Begin Migration to New Housing Projects," *Detroit News*, October 16, 1938.
2. "His Honor Looks Over Project," *Detroit Tribune*, October 22, 1938.
3. Bradt to Reading, August 2, 1938, Mayor's Papers (hereafter MP) 1938, Box 6, Folder "Housing Commission (2)," Burton Historical Collection, Detroit Public Library (hereafter Burton).
4. Wright, *Building the Dream*; Radford, *Modern Housing for America*; Jackson, *Crabgrass Frontier.*
5. City Plan Commission, "Annual Report of the City Plan Commission 1933," MP 1934, Box 1, Folder "City Plan"; "Allots 100 Million for Housing Work," *New York Times*, November 22, 1933.
6. Solomon, "Participation of Negroes in Detroit Elections."
7. City Plan Commission, "Annual Report of the City Plan Commission 1933"; Blucher to Couzens, January 16, 1934, MP 1934, Box 1, Folder "City Plan Commission."
8. Sullivan, "'On the Dole,'" 189; Dash, "Slum-Clearance Farce," 412.
9. City Plan Commission, "Annual Report of the City Plan Commission 1933."
10. Radford, *Modern Housing for America*, 100–101.
11. "Slum Clearing Board Named," *Detroit News*, November 22, 1933; "Mayor Names Committee on Housing," *Detroit Times*, November 22, 1933; "Slum Cleanup Office Opened by Board," *Detroit Times*, November 23, 1933.
12. Gomon to Couzens and Common Council, December 10, 1934, MP 1934, Box 4, Folder "Housing Commission."
13. Josephine Gomon, "Ann Arbor," n.d., Josephine Gomon Papers (hereafter JG), Box 9, Folder "Ann Arbor—University of Michigan," Bentley Historical Library, University of Michigan, Ann Arbor (hereafter Bentley).

14. Couzens to Gomon, November 22, 1923, JG, Box 1, Folder "Correspondence, 1923"; Couzens to Gomon, September 6, 1924, JG, Box 1, Folder "Correspondence, May–Dec 1924."
15. Darrow to Marckwardt, January 2, 1928, JG, Box 1, Folder "Correspondence, 1928"; Program for "A Dinner Honoring Josephine Gomon," JG, Box 8, Folder "Michigan Women's Hall of Fame, 1983."
16. Darrow to Marckwardt, January 2, 1928.
17. Hendlin to Gomon, February 26, 1929, JG, Box 1, Folder "Correspondence, 1929."
18. Biography of Josephine Gomon in Finding Aid, Josephine Fellows Gomon Papers, Bentley.
19. "'Join Unions,' Speakers Tell Workers at Economic Conference," *Detroit Tribune*, February 24, 1934.
20. Frank Murphy speech on the "races question," n.d., Frank Murphy Papers, Reel 141, Bentley.
21. "Slum Clearing Board Named," *Detroit News*, November 22, 1933.
22. "Detroit Slum Project Proceeds Despite Ruling," *Detroit News*, July 17, 1935.
23. "Drastic Slum Step Approved," *Detroit News*, April 5, 1934; "Fight Detroit Slum Plan," *New York Times*, July 16, 1935; Gladys H. Kelsey, "Detroit Slum Plan to Cost $6,000,000," *New York Times*, October 14, 1934; City Plan Commission, "Annual Report of the City Plan Commission 1933."
24. Gomon to Hackett, March 22, 1935, MP 1935, Box 6, Folder "Housing Commission"; Gomon to Clas, May 23, 1935, MP 1935, Box 6, Folder "Housing Commission." FERA was disbanded at the end of October 1935, and the WPA took over the project in early December 1935. Josephine Gomon, "Report of Relocation Activities, WPA Project, 1913," January 6, 1936, MP 1936, Box 5, Folder "Housing Commission."
25. Dash, "Slum-Clearance Farce," 412.
26. Barbey to Couzens, January 26, 1934, MP 1934, Box 4, Folder "Housing Commission"; Sophia Kelleher to Couzens, March 19, 1934, MP 1934, Box 4, Folder "Housing Commission."
27. Chapman to Couzens, March 21, 1934, MP 1934, Box 4, Folder "Housing Commission"; Chandler to Couzens, February 14, 1934, MP 1934, Box 4, Folder "Housing Commission"; "Property Owners of Detroit Attempt to Draw Color Bar," *Chicago Defender*, September 17, 1932.
28. "Taxes and Expense in Lower Michigan," *New York Times*, August 21, 1932; "Two States Limit Taxes on Realty," *New York Times*, December 11, 1932.
29. Buck to Couzens, March 26, 1934, MP 1934, Box 4, Folder "Housing Commission"; Clarke to Hackett, June 1, 1934, MP 1934, Box 4, Folder "Housing Commission."
30. "Low-Cost Housing Project Killed by Council's Refusal to Close Six Streets in Chandler Park District," *Detroit Free Press*, December 11, 1935; "Housing Plan's

History Stormy," *Detroit Free Press*, December 11, 1935. Sullivan, "'On the Dole,'" 187.

31. Danahey to Couzens, November 6, 1935, MP 1935, Box 6, Folder "Housing Commission."
32. Irwin to Couzens, January 7, 1936, MP 1936, Box 5, Folder "Housing Commission."
33. M. W. Mountjoy, "Find Squatters in Condemned Slum Area," *Detroit News*, November 20, 1933; "Landlords Target of Slum Quiz," *Detroit News*, October 5, 1938; "Slum Cleanup Options Pour into City," *Detroit Times*, November 24, 1933.
34. Theodore R. Barnes, "The New Deal, National Recovery Housing," *Detroit Tribune*, August 19, 1933.
35. "Detroit's Slum Clearance Project," *Detroit Tribune*, November 18, 1933.
36. Ferguson, *Black Politics in New Deal Atlanta*. A national committee of black social work professionals commissioned a study of African American housing complete with recommendations for the future. Charles S. Johnson, of Fisk University, conducted the study, which promoted the razing of condemned housing and the rehabilitation of neighborhoods. Although his conclusions lent support to the idea of slum clearance, they differed from projects like Detroit's because they were far more discriminating about what needed to be "cleared." The committee, chaired by Nannie Helen Burroughs of the National Training School for Women and Girls, included such luminaries as T. Arnold Hill of the National Urban League, Daisy Lampkin of the NAACP, and other prominent African Americans. Johnson, *Negro Housing*.
37. "'First Lady' Starts a Housing Project," *New York Times*, September 10, 1935; "First Lady Dooms Slum," *Detroit News*, September 10, 1935; Cook, *Eleanor Roosevelt*.
38. "Woman Tenant Sues Landlord for $50,000," *Detroit Tribune*, September 7, 1935.
39. Gomon reported that black residents had been "subjected to a good deal of inconvenience and hardship" during relocation but remained "very cooperative" about moving. Josephine Gomon, "Report of Relocation Activities, WPA Project, 1913," January 6, 1936, MP 1936, Box 5, Folder "Housing Commission"; Dancy to Ballenger, January 17, 1934, Folder 1, Box 3, DUL Papers; Dancy to Gomon, January 17, 1934, Folder 1, Box 3, DUL Papers.
40. "The Brewster Housing Project," *Detroit Tribune*, October 23, 1937.
41. "Housing Commission Names George Isabell Manager of the Brewster Housing Project," *Detroit Tribune*, July 1938; "Housing Project Czars," *Detroit News*, October 11, 1938.
42. "The Brewster Housing Project," *Detroit Tribune*, April 30, 1938.
43. Perry to Reading, May 9, 1938, MP 1938, Box 6, Folder "Housing Commission (2)"; Isabell to Reading, July 25, 1938, MP 1938, Box 6, Folder "Housing Commission (2)"; Peck to Reading, July 28, 1938, MP 1938, Box 6, Folder "Housing Commission (2)"; Bradt to Danahey, n.d., MP 1938, Box 6, Folder "Housing Commission (2)."

NOTES TO THE CONCLUSION

1. Rigterink to Persons, March 11, 1941, in "New Deal Agencies and Black America" (hereafter NDABA), Black Studies Research Sources: Microfilms from Major Archival and Manuscript Collections, Reel 9, Schomburg Center for Research in Black Culture, New York Public Library, New York.
2. Harris to Rigterink, March 4, 1941, NDABA, Reel 9.
3. Ibid.
4. Taylor to Harris, April 21, 1941, NDABA, Reel 9.
5. Ibid.
6. Nikhil Singh examines these contradictions in racial liberalism and explores African American activists' strategies for exposing them. Singh, *Black Is a Country*.
7. Brown, *Regulating Aversion*.
8. In 1953, the agency had a budget of $64,739. Beulah T. Whitby, "Transfer Summary from the Mayor's Interracial Committee to the Commission on Community Relations," May 14, 1953, Detroit Commission on Community Relations Papers (hereafter DCCR), Archives of Labor and Urban Affairs, Wayne State University, Detroit (hereafter ALUA).
9. Finding Aid, Detroit Commission on Community Relations/Human Rights Department Collection Records, 1940–1984, ALUA.
10. "Conference Findings Committee on Negro Employment Problems," October 10, 1940, NDABA, Reel 9.
11. B. Whitby, "The Detroit Community Barometer," January 30, 1945, DCCR, Box 9, Folder 14.
12. See Dillard, *Faith in the City*.
13. "Vote Sought on Race Unit," *Detroit News*, April 21, 1953.
14. Tribich, "Social Security Reform in Black and White." Jodi Melamed discusses the connections between racial liberal ideologies of previous decades and their connections to analogous neoliberal strategies. Melamed, "The Spirit of Neoliberalism."

BIBLIOGRAPHY

PRIMARY SOURCES

Boykin, Ulysses W. *Handbook on the Detroit Negro: A Preliminary Edition*. Detroit: Minority Study Associates, 1943.

Brown, Josephine C. *Public Relief, 1929–1939*. New York: Henry Holt, 1940.

Bunche, Ralph J. *The Political Status of the Negro in the Age of FDR*. Chicago: University of Chicago Press, 1940.

Chicago Commission on Race Relations. *The Negro in Chicago: A Study of Race Relations and a Race Riot*. Chicago: University of Chicago Press, 1922.

City of Detroit Housing Commission. *Housing in Detroit: Reviewing the Past, Previewing the Future*. Detroit: City of Detroit Housing Commission, 1943.

Dash, Karen. "Slum-Clearance Farce." *Nation* 142, no. 3691 (April 1, 1936): 410–412.

Detroit Bureau of Governmental Research. *The Negro in Detroit: Report of the Mayor's Committee on Race Relations*. Detroit: Detroit Bureau of Governmental Research, 1926.

———. *The Herman Kiefer Hospital of Detroit: A Study Made at the Request of the Commissioner of Health*. Report of the Detroit Bureau of Governmental Research, no. 122. Detroit: Detroit Bureau of Governmental Research, April 1931.

———. *Accumulated Social and Economic Statistics for Detroit*. Detroit, July 1937.

Detroit Department of Public Welfare. *The Department of Public Welfare, 1930–1940*. Detroit, 1940.

Drake, St. Clair, and Horace Cayton. *Black Metropolis: A Study of Negro Life in a Northern City*. New York: Harcourt, Brace, 1945.

Fellows, J. A. "Detroit's Crime Clinic." *Nation* 130 (May 14, 1930): 568–570.

Fleming, Thomas J. "The Right to Self-Defense." *Crisis* 76 (January 1969): 9–16.

Fountain, Clayton W. *Union Guy*. New York: Viking Press, 1949.

Geddes, Anne E. *Trends in Relief Expenditures, 1910–1935*. Washington, DC: U.S. Government Printing Office, 1937.

Grigsby, Snow F. *White Hypocrisy and Black Lethargy*. Detroit, 1937.

Haber, William. "Fluctuations in Employment in Detroit Factories, 1921–1931." *Journal of the American Statistical Association* 27 (June 1932): 141–152.

Hallgren, Mauritz. "Detroit's Liberal Mayor." *Nation* 132, no. 3436 (May 13, 1931): 526–528.

Haynes, George Edmund. *Negro New-comers in Detroit, Michigan: A Challenge to*

Christian Statesmanship: A Preliminary Survey. New York: Home Missions Council, 1918.
House Special Committee on Communist Activities in the United States. *Investigation of Communist Propaganda: Hearing before a Special Committee to Investigate Communist Activities in the United States of the House of Representatives*. Pt. 4, vol. 1. 71st Cong., 2nd sess., 1930.
Johnson, Charles S. *Negro Housing: Report of the Committee on Negro Housing*. Washington, DC, 1932.
———. "Incidence upon the Negroes." *American Journal of Sociology* 40 (1935): 737–745.
Kennedy, Louise Venable. *The Negro Peasant Turns Cityward: Effects of Recent Migrations to Northern Centers*. 1930. Reprint, College Park, MD: McGrath, 1969.
Korematsu v. United States. 323 U.S. 214 (1944).
Landers, Frank M., and Claude R. Tharp. *Administration and Financing of Public Relief*. Ann Arbor: Bureau of Government, University of Michigan, 1942.
Lovett, William P. *Detroit Rules Itself*. Boston: Gorham Press, 1930.
Mayor's Committee on Race Relations. "Report of the Mayor's Committee on Race Relations: Embodying Findings and Recommendations Based on a Survey of Race Conditions in the City, Undertaken in 1926." *Public Business* 4, no. 3 (March 10, 1927): 1–16.
McGregor, Tracy. *Toward a Philosophy of Inner Life: For Social Workers and Others*. Detroit, 1933.
Monroe, Clarence, et al. *The City of Detroit, Michigan, 1701–1922*. Vol. 4. Detroit: S. J. Clarke, 1922.
Norton, William J. "The Relief Crisis in Detroit." *Social Service Review* 7, no. 1 (1933): 1–10.
Paxton, Edward T. "The Trend of Reorganization in City Government." *Annals of the American Academy of Political and Social Science* 113 (May 1924): 195–201.
The People v. Ossian Sweet in the Recorder's Court of Detroit, Michigan. 1925–1926.
R. L. Polk & Company. *Polk's Detroit City Directory* (Detroit). Vol. 1928–1929.
Ross, Arthur M. "The Negro Worker in the Depression." *Social Forces* 18 (1940): 550–559.
Scott, Emmett J., ed. "Additional Letters of Negro Migrants of 1916–1918." *Journal of Negro History* 4 (1919): 412–465.
Shelby County v. Holder. 557 U. S. 193 (2013).
Solomon, Thomas. *The Negro Voters in Detroit: Report to the Earhart Foundation*. University of Michigan, June 1935.
———. "Participation of Negroes in Detroit Elections." PhD diss., University of Michigan, 1939.
Spero, Sterling D., and Abram L. Harris. *The Black Worker: A Study of the Negro and the Labor Movement*. New York: Columbia University Press, 1931.
Sterner, Richard. *The Negro's Share: A Study of Income, Consumption, Housing and Public Assistance*. New York: Harper and Brothers, 1943.
Tickton, Sidney G. *An Analysis of Tax Delinquency*. Report of the Detroit Bureau

of Governmental Research, no. 128. Detroit: Detroit Bureau of Governmental Research, June 1932.

The Trade Union Unity League: Its Program, Structure, Methods and History. New York: Trade Union Unity League, 1929.

Washington, Forrester B. *The Negro in Detroit: A Survey of the Conditions of a Negro Group in a Northern Industrial Center during the War Prosperity Period, 1920*. Detroit, 1920.

Weaver, Robert C. *Negro Labor: A National Problem*. Port Washington, NY: Kennikat Press, 1946.

White, Walter F. "Reviving the Ku Klux Klan." *Forum*, April 1921, 426–434.

Women's Bureau. *Women at Work: A Century of Industrial Change*. Bulletin of the Women's Bureau, no. 161. Washington, DC: U.S. Government Printing Office, 1939.

Woodworth, George Walter. "The Detroit Money Market." PhD diss., University of Michigan, 1932.

Young, Nelson J. *A Study of the Problems of the Distressed Home Owner of Detroit as Revealed by Applications to the Home Owners' Loan Corporation*. Ann Arbor, MI: Earhart Foundation, 1934.

SECONDARY SOURCES

Ansell, Amy Elizabeth. *New Right, New Racism: Race and Reaction*. New York: NYU Press, 1997.

Argersinger, Jo Ann E. *Toward a New Deal in Baltimore: People and Government in the Great Depression*. Chapel Hill: University of North Carolina Press, 1988.

Arnesen, Eric. "Up from Exclusion: Black and White Workers, Race and the State of Labor History." *Reviews in American History* 26 (1998): 146–174.

Babson, Steve, Ron Alpern, Dave Elsila, and John Revitte. *Working Detroit: The Making of a Union Town*. Detroit: Wayne State University Press, 1984.

Bailer, Lloyd H. "Negro Labor in the Automobile Industry." PhD diss., University of Michigan, 1943.

Bak, Richard. *Ty Cobb: His Tumultuous Life and Times*. Dallas: Taylor Press, 1994.

Baldwin, Davarian L. *Chicago's New Negroes: Modernity, the Great Migration, and Black Urban Life*. Chapel Hill: University of North Carolina Press, 2007.

Barkan, Elazar. *The Retreat of Scientific Racism: Changing Concepts of Race in Britain and the United States between the World Wars*. New York: Cambridge University Press, 1992.

Bates, Beth Tompkins. "A New Crowd Challenges the Agenda of the Old Guard in the NAACP, 1933–1941." *American Historical Review* 102 (1997): 340–387.

———. *Pullman Porters and the Rise of Protest Politics in Black America, 1925–1945*. Chapel Hill: University of North Carolina Press, 2001.

———. *The Making of Black Detroit in the Age of Henry Ford*. Chapel Hill: University of North Carolina Press, 2012.

Beito, David T. *Taxpayers in Revolt: Tax Resistance during the Great Depression*. Chapel Hill: University of North Carolina Press, 1989.

Bernstein, David E. *Only One Place of Redress: African Americans, Labor Regulations and the Courts from Reconstruction to the New Deal.* Durham, NC: Duke University Press, 2001.

Bonilla-Silva, Eduardo. *Racism without Racists: Color-Blind Racism and the Persistence of Racial Inequality in the United States.* Lanham, MD: Rowman and Littlefield, 2003.

Boyle, Kevin. *Arc of Justice: A Saga of Race, Civil Rights, and Murder in the Jazz Age.* New York: Henry Holt, 2004.

Brody, David. *Workers in Industrial America: Essays on the Twentieth Century Struggle.* New York: Oxford University Press, 1993.

Brown, Cliff. *Racial Conflict and Violence in the Labor Market: Roots in the 1919 Steel Strike.* New York: Garland, 1998.

Brown, Michael K. *Race, Money and the American Welfare State.* Ithaca, NY: Cornell University Press, 1999.

Brown, Wendy. *Regulating Aversion.* Princeton, NJ: Princeton University Press, 2006.

Burchell, Graham, Colin Gordon, and Peter Miller, eds. *The Foucault Effect: Studies in Governmentality.* Chicago: University of Chicago Press, 1991.

Butler, Michael. "*The Birth of a Nation* (1915)." In *The Encyclopedia of American Race Riots*, edited by Walter C. Rucker and James N. Upton, 33–36. Westport, CT: Greenwood, 2007.

Carr, Leslie G. *"Colorblind" Racism.* New York: Sage, 1997.

Carter, Dan T. *From George Wallace to Newt Gingrich: Race in the Conservative Counterrevolution, 1963–1994.* Baton Rouge: Louisiana State University Press, 1996.

Cazenave, Noel A. *The Urban Racial State: Managing Race Relations in American Cities.* New York: Rowman and Littlefield, 2011.

Chapman, Erin D. *Prove It on Me: New Negroes, Sex, and Popular Culture in the 1920s.* New York: Oxford University Press, 2012.

Clark, Tom C., and Philip B. Perlman, *Prejudice and Property: An Historic Brief against Racial Covenants.* Washington, DC: Public Affairs Press, 1948.

Cochran, David Carroll. *The Color of Freedom: Race and Contemporary American Liberalism.* Albany: State University of New York Press, 1999.

Cohen, Lizabeth. *Making a New Deal: Industrial Workers in Chicago, 1919–1939.* New York: Cambridge University Press, 1990.

Cohen, Nancy. *The Reconstruction of American Liberalism, 1865–1914.* Chapel Hill: University of North Carolina Press, 2002.

Collins, Patricia Hill. *Black Sexual Politics: African Americans, Gender, and the New Racism.* New York: Routledge, 2004.

Conot, Robert. *American Odyssey: A History of a Great City.* Detroit: Wayne State University Press, 1986.

Cook, Blanche Wiesen. *Eleanor Roosevelt.* Vol. 2, *The Defining Years, 1933–1938.* New York: Penguin, 1999.

Cooley, Will. "Moving On Out: Black Pioneering in Chicago, 1915–1950." *Journal of Urban History* 36 (July 2010): 485–506.

Countryman, Matthew. *Up South: Civil Rights and Black Power in Philadelphia*. University of Pennsylvania Press, 2005.

Dancy, John. *Sand against the Wind: The Memoirs of John C. Dancy*. Detroit: Wayne State University Press, 1966.

Dillard, Angela. *Faith in the City: Preaching Radical Social Change in Detroit*. University of Michigan Press, 2007.

Drews, Richard S. "A History of the Detroit Board of Health." PhD diss., University of Michigan, 1938.

Dudziak, Mary L. *Cold War Civil Rights: Race and the Image of American Democracy*. Princeton, NJ: Princeton University Press, 2002.

Farrell, John A. *Clarence Darrow: Attorney for the Damned*. New York City: Doubleday, 2011.

Faue, Elizabeth. *Community of Suffering and Struggle: Women, Men, and the Labor Movement in Minneapolis, 1915–1945*. Chapel Hill: University of North Carolina Press, 1991.

Ferguson, Karen. *Black Politics in New Deal Atlanta*. Chapel Hill: University of North Carolina Press, 2002.

Fine, Sidney. "The Origins of the United Automobile Workers, 1933–1935." *Journal of Economic History* 18 (1958): 249–282.

———. *Frank Murphy: The Detroit Years*. Ann Arbor: University of Michigan Press, 1975.

———. *Violence in the Model City*. Ann Arbor: University of Michigan Press, 1988.

Finkelman, Paul. "The Promise of Equality and the Limits of Law: From the Civil War to World War II." In *The History of Michigan Law*, edited by Paul Finkelman and Martin J. Hershock, 187–213. Athens: Ohio University Press, 2006.

Flanagan, Maureen A. *Seeing with Their Hearts: Chicago Women and the Vision of the Good City, 1871–1933*. Princeton, NJ: Princeton University Press, 2003.

Foner, Eric. "Why Is There No Socialism in the United States?" *History Workshop* 17 (Spring 1984): 57–80.

———. *Free Soil, Free Labor, Free Men: The Ideology of the Republican Party before the Civil War*. New York: Oxford University Press, 1995.

Foner, Philip S. *Organized Labor and the Black Worker, 1619–1981*. New York: International Publishers, 1981.

Foner, Philip, S., and Herbert Shapiro, eds. *American Communism and Black Americans: A Documentary History, 1930–1934*. Philadelphia: Temple University Press, 1991.

Fragnoli, Raymond Robert. *The Transformation of Reform: Progressivism in Detroit—and After, 1912–1933*. New York: Garland, 1982.

Fraser, Nancy, and Linda Gordon. "A Genealogy of *Dependency*: Tracing a Keyword of the U.S. Welfare State." *Signs* 19 (Winter 1994): 309–336.

Fraser, Steve, and Gary Gerstle, eds. *The Rise and Fall of the New Deal Order, 1930–1980*. Princeton, NJ: Princeton University Press, 1989.

Freund, David. *Colored Property: State Policy and White Racial Politics in Suburban America*. Chicago: University of Chicago Press, 2007.

Gaines, Kevin. *Uplifting the Race: Black Leadership, Politics and Culture in the Twentieth Century*. Chapel Hill: University of North Carolina, 1996.

García, Juan R. *Mexicans in the Midwest, 1900–1932*. Tucson: University of Arizona Press, 2004.

Garland, Libby. *After They Closed the Gates: Jewish Illegal Immigration to the United States, 1921–1965*. Chicago: University of Chicago Press, 2014.

Gerstle, Gary. *American Crucible: Race and Nation in the Twentieth Century*. Princeton, NJ: Princeton University Press, 2002.

Goldfield, Michael. "Race and the CIO: Reply to Critics." *International Labor and Working-Class History* 46 (1994): 142–160.

———. *The Color of Politics: Race and the Mainsprings of American Politics*. New York: New Press, 1997.

Goldfield, Michael, Gary Gerstle, Robert Korstad, Marshall F. Stevenson, and Judith Stein. "Scholarly Controversy: 'Race and the CIO: The Possibilities for Racial Egalitarianism during the 1930s and 1940s.'" *International Labor and Working-Class History* 44 (1993): 1–63.

Goodman, James. *Stories of Scottsboro*. New York: Vintage, 1994.

Gordon, Linda. "Social Insurance and Public Assistance: The Influence of Gender in Welfare Thought in the United States, 1890–1935." *American Historical Review* 97 (February 1992): 19–54.

Greenstone, David. *A Report on the Politics of Detroit*. Cambridge: Joint Center for Urban Studies of MIT and Harvard University, 1961.

Gregory, James N. *The Southern Diaspora: How the Great Migrations of Black and White Southerners Transformed America*. Chapel Hill: University of North Carolina Press, 2005.

Grossman, James R. *Land of Hope: Chicago, Black Southerners, and the Great Migration*. Chicago: University of Chicago Press, 1989.

Guglielmo, Thomas A. *White on Arrival: Italians, Race, Color and Power in Chicago, 1890–1945*. New York: Oxford University Press, 2003.

Guterl, Matthew Pratt. *The Color of Race in America, 1900–1940*. Cambridge, MA: Harvard University Press, 2001.

Hale, Grace Elizabeth. *Making Whiteness: The Culture of Segregation in the South, 1890–1940*. New York: Vintage, 1998.

Hall, Jacqueline Dowd. "The Long Civil Rights Movement and the Political Uses of the Past." *Journal of American History* 91 (March 2005): 1233–1263.

Halpern, Rick. *Down on the Killing Floor: Black and White Workers in Chicago's Packinghouses, 1904–54*. Urbana-Champaign: University of Illinois Press, 1997.

Harvey, David. *The Condition of Postmodernity: An Enquiry into the Origins of Cultural Change*. Cambridge: Blackwell, 1990.

———. "The Right to the City." *New Left Review* 53 (September/October 2008): 23–40.

Haywood, Harry. *Black Bolshevik: Autobiography of an Afro-American Communist*. Chicago: Liberator Press, 1978.

Helmbold, Lois Rita. "Downward Occupational Mobility during the Great Depression:

Urban Black and White Working Class Women." *Labor History* 29 (Spring 1988): 135–172.

Herron, Jerry. *AfterCulture: Detroit and the Humiliation of History*. Detroit: Wayne State University Press, 1993.

Hill, Herbert. "The Problem of Race in American Labor History." *Reviews in American History* 24 (1996): 189–208.

Hirsch, Arnold. *Making the Second Ghetto: Race and Housing in Chicago, 1940–1960*. New York: Cambridge University Press, 1983.

Holloway, Jonathan Scott. *Confronting the Veil: Abram Harris Jr., E. Franklin Frazier, and Ralph Bunche, 1919–1941*. Chapel Hill: University of North Carolina Press, 2002.

Hooker, Clarence. "Ford's Sociology Department and the Americanization Campaign and the Manufacture of Popular Culture among Assembly Line Workers c. 1910–1917." *Journal of American Culture* 20 (1997): 47–53.

Horowitz, David. *Hating Whitey: And Other Progressive Causes*. Dallas: Spence, 1999.

Horowitz, Roger. *"Negro and White, Unite and Fight!": A Social History of Industrial Unionism in Meatpacking, 1930–90*. Urbana-Champaign: University of Illinois Press, 1997.

Horton, Carol A. *Race and the Making of American Liberalism*. New York: Oxford University Press, 2005.

HoSang, Daniel Martinez. *Racial Propositions: Ballot Initiatives and the Making of Postwar California*. Berkeley: University of California Press, 2010.

Howard, J. Woodford, Jr. *Mr. Justice Murphy: A Political Biography*. Princeton, NJ: Princeton University Press, 1968.

Hoyt, Edwin P. *The Palmer Raids, 1919–1920: An Attempt to Suppress Dissent*. New York: Seabury Press, 1969.

Hunter, Gary Jerome. "'Don't Buy from Where You Can't Work': Black Urban Boycott Movements during the Depression, 1929–1941." PhD diss., University of Michigan, 1977.

Ignatiev, Noel. *How the Irish Became White*. New York: Routledge, 1995.

Jackson, John P., Jr., and Nadine M. Weidman. *Race, Racism and Science: Social Impact and Interaction*. New Brunswick, NJ: Rutgers University Press, 2006.

Jackson, Kenneth T. *The Ku Klux Klan in the City, 1915–1930*. New York: Oxford University Press, 1967.

———. *Crabgrass Frontier: The Suburbanization of the United States*. New York: Oxford University Press, 1985.

Jackson, Walter A. *Gunnar Myrdal and America's Conscience: Social Engineering and Racial Liberalism, 1938–1987*. Chapel Hill: University of North Carolina Press, 1990.

Jacobson, Matthew Frye. *Whiteness of a Different Color: European Immigrants and the Alchemy of Race*. Cambridge, MA: Harvard University Press, 1998.

Johnson, Christopher H. *Maurice Sugar: Law, Labor, and the Left in Detroit, 1912–1950*. Detroit: Wayne State University Press, 1988.

Jones, Thomas Lloyd. "Labor and Politics: The Detroit Municipal Election of 1937." PhD diss., University of Michigan, 1999.

Katz, Michael B. *In the Shadow of the Poorhouse: A Social History of Welfare in America*. New York: Basic Books, 1986.

Katzman, David M. *Before the Ghetto: Black Detroit in the Nineteenth Century*. Urbana-Champaign: University of Illinois Press, 1973.

Katznelson, Ira. *When Affirmative Action Was White: An Untold History of Racial Inequality in Twentieth-Century America*. New York: Norton, 2005.

Keeran, Roger. *The Communist Party and the Auto Worker's Unions*. New York: International Publishers, 1980.

Kellogg, P. J. "Northern Liberals and Black America: A History of White Attitudes, 1936–1952." PhD diss., Northwestern University, 1971.

King, Martin Luther, Jr. *Letter from the Birmingham Jail*. San Francisco: HarperSanFrancisco, 1994.

Kirby, John. *Black Americans in the Roosevelt Era: Liberalism and Race*. Knoxville: University of Tennessee Press, 1980.

Klug, Thomas A. "Labor Market Politics in Detroit: The Curious Case of the 'Spolansky Act' of 1931." *Michigan Historical Review* 14 (1988): 1–32.

Kunzel, Regina. *Fallen Women, Problem Girls: Unmarried Mothers and the Professionalization of Social Work, 1890–1945*. New Haven, CT: Yale University Press, 1993.

Lasch-Quinn, Elizabeth. *Black Neighbors: Race and the Limits of Reform in the American Settlement House Movement*. Chapel Hill: University of North Carolina Press, 1993.

Lassiter, Matthew D. *The Silent Majority: Suburban Politics in the Sunbelt South*. Princeton, NJ: Princeton University Press, 2007.

Lassiter, Matthew D., and Joseph Crespino, eds. *The Myth of Southern Exceptionalism*. New York: Oxford University Press, 2009.

Leab, Daniel J. "United We Eat: The Creation of and the Organization of the Unemployed Councils in 1930." *Labor History* 8 (Fall 1967): 300–316.

Leach, Colin Wayne. "Against the Notion of a 'New Racism.'" *Journal of Community and Applied Social Psychology* 15 (2005); 432–445.

Lemann, Nicholas. *The Promised Land: The Great Black Migration and How It Changed America*. New York: Vintage, 1992.

Letwin, Daniel. *The Challenge of Interracial Unionism: Alabama Coal Miners, 1878–1921*. Chapel Hill: University of North Carolina Press, 1998.

Levine, David Allen. *Internal Combustion: The Races in Detroit, 1915–1926*. Westport, CT: Greenwood, 1976.

Lewchuck, Wayne. "Fordism and the Moving Assembly Line: The British and American Experience, 1895–1930." In *On the Line: Essays in the History of Auto Work*, edited by Nelson Lichtenstein and Stephen Meyer, 17–41. Urbana-Champaign: University of Illinois Press, 1989.

Lichtenstein, Nelson. *Labor's War at Home: The CO in World War II*. New York: Cambridge University Press, 1982.

———. *Walter Reuther: The Most Dangerous Man in Detroit*. Urbana-Champaign: University of Illinois Press, 1995.

Lieberman, Robert C. *Shifting the Color Line: Race and the American Welfare State.* Cambridge, MA: Harvard University Press, 1998.

Lorence, James J. *Organizing the Unemployed: Community and Union Activists in the Industrial Heartland.* Albany: State University of New York Press, 1996.

MacLean, Nancy. *Freedom Is Not Enough: The Opening of the American Workplace.* Cambridge, MA: Harvard University Press, 2006.

Maloney, Thomas N. "Personnel Policy and Racial Inequality in the Pre–World War II North." *Journal of Interdisciplinary History* 30 (1999): 235–258.

Marks, Carole. *Farewell, We're Good and Gone: The Great Black Migration.* Bloomington: Indiana University Press, 1989.

Martin, Elizabeth Anne. *Detroit and the Great Migration, 1916–1929.* Ann Arbor: Bentley Historical Library Printing Services, 1993.

May, Martha. "The Historical Problem of the Family Wage: The Ford Motor Company and the Five Dollar Day." In *Unequal Sisters: A Multicultural Reader in U.S. Women's History*, edited by Ellen Carol DuBois and Vicki L. Ruiz, 275–291. New York: Routledge, 1990.

McGerr, Michael. *A Fierce Discontent: The Rise and Fall of the Progressive Movement, 1870–1920.* New York: Oxford University Press, 2003.

McLaughlin, Malcolm. "Reconsidering the East St Louis Race Riot of 1917." *International Review of Social History* 47 (2002): 187–212.

Meier, August, and John H. Bracey Jr. "The NAACP as a Reform Movement, 1909–1965: 'To Reach the Conscience of America.'" *Journal of Southern History* 59 (1993): 3–30.

Meier, August, and Elliot Rudwick. *Black Detroit and the Rise of the UAW.* New York: Oxford University Press, 1979.

Melamed, Jodi. "The Spirit of Neoliberalism: From Racial Liberalism to Neoliberal Multiculturalism." *Social Text* 24, no. 4 89 (2006): 1–24.

Meyer, Stephen. *The Five Dollar Day: Labor, Management, and Social Control in the Ford Motor Company, 1908–1921.* Albany: State University of New York Press, 1981.

Miles, Norman Kenneth. "Home at Last: Urbanization of Black Migrants in Detroit 1916–1929." PhD diss., University of Michigan, 1978.

Mink, Gwendolyn. *The Wages of Motherhood: Inequality in the Welfare State, 1917–1942.* Ithaca, NY: Cornell University Press, 1995.

Moon, Elaine Latzman. *Untold Tales, Unsung Heroes: An Oral History of Detroit's African-American Community, 1918–1967.* Detroit: Wayne State University Press, 1994.

Muhammad, Khalil Gibran. *Condemnation of Blackness: Race, Crime, and the Making of Modern Urban America.* Cambridge, MA: Harvard University Press, 2010.

Murage, Njeru Wa. "Organizational History of the Detroit Urban League, 1916–1960." PhD diss., Michigan State University, 1993.

———. "Making Migrants an Asset: The Detroit Urban League–Employers Alliance in Wartime Detroit, 1916 to 1919," *Michigan Historical Review* 26 (2000): 67–93.

Naison, Mark. *Communists in Harlem during the Depression.* Urbana-Champaign: University of Illinois Press, 1983.

Nelson, Bruce. "Autoworkers, Electoral Politics, and the Convergence of Class and Race Detroit, 1937–1945." In *Organized Labor and American Politics, 1894–1994: The Labor-Liberal Alliance*, edited by Kevin Boyle, 121–158. Albany: State University of New York Press, 1998.

———. *Divided We Stand: American Workers and the Struggle for Black Equality*. Princeton, NJ: Princeton University Press, 2001.

Pascoe, Peggy. "Miscegenation Law, Court Cases, and Ideologies of 'Race' in Twentieth-Century America." *Journal of American History* 83 (1996): 44–69.

———. *What Comes Naturally: Miscegenation Law and the Making of Race in America*. New York: Oxford University Press, 2010.

Peebles, Robin S. "Fannie Richards and the Integration of the Detroit Public Schools." *Michigan Historical Magazine* (1981). www.michigan.gov/dnr/0,4570,7-153-54463_18670_18793-52956--,00.html. Accessed April 21, 2014.

Peterson, Joyce Shaw. "Black Automobile Workers in Detroit, 1910–1930." *Journal of Negro History* 64 (1979): 177–190.

———. *American Automobile Workers, 1900–1933*. Binghamton: State University of New York Press, 1987.

Phillips, Kimberley. *AlabamaNorth: African-American Migrants, Community and Working-Class Activism in Cleveland, 1915–45*. Urbana-Champaign: University of Illinois Press, 1999.

Poole, Mary. *The Segregated Origins of Social Security: African Americans and the Welfare State*. Chapel Hill: University of North Carolina Press, 2006.

Purnell, Brian. *Fighting Jim Crow in the County of Kings: The Congress of Racial Equality in Brooklyn*. Lexington: University Press of Kentucky, 2013.

Quadagno, Jill S. "Welfare Capitalism and the Social Security Act of 1935." *American Sociological Review* 49 (1984): 632–647.

———. *The Transformation of Old Age Security: Class and Politics in the American Welfare State*. Chicago: University of Chicago Press, 1988.

Radford, Gail. *Modern Housing for America: Policy Struggles in the New Deal Era*. Chicago: University of Chicago Press, 1996.

Rice, Roger L. "Residential Segregation by Law, 1910–1917." *Journal of Southern History* 34 (May 1968): 179–199.

Roediger, David. *The Wages of Whiteness: Race and the Making of the American Working Class*. London: Verso, 1991.

Ross, Dorothy. *The Origins of American Social Science*. New York: Cambridge University Press, 1991.

Rudwick, Elliot. *Race Riot in East St. Louis, July 2, 1917*. Urbana-Champaign: University of Illinois Press, 1964.

Scott, Daryl Michael. *Contempt and Pity: Social Policy and the Image of the Damaged Black Psyche, 1880–1996*. Chapel Hill: University of North Carolina Press, 1997.

Self, Robert O. *American Babylon: Race and the Struggle for Postwar Oakland*. Princeton, NJ: Princeton University Press, 2005.

Sherman, Richard B. "The Harding Administration and the Negro: An Opportunity Lost." *Journal of Negro History* 49 (1964): 151–168.

Silber, Nina. *The Romance of Reunion: Northerners and the South, 1865–1900*. Chapel Hill: University of North Carolina Press, 1997.

Singh, Nikhil. *Black Is a Country: Race and the Unfinished Struggle for Democracy*. Cambridge, MA: Harvard University Press, 2005.

Sitkoff, Harvard. *A New Deal for Blacks: The Emergence of Civil Rights as a National Issue: The Depression Decade*. New York: Oxford University Press, 1978.

Smith, Terry. *Making the Modern: Industry, Art, and Design in America*. Chicago: University of Chicago Press, 1994.

Solomon, Mark. *The Cry Was Unity: Communists and African Americans, 1917–1936*. Jackson: University Press of Mississippi, 1998.

Stanley, Amy Dru. *From Bondage to Contract: Wage Labor, Marriage, and the Market in the Age of Slave Emancipation*. New York: Cambridge University Press, 1998.

Sugar, Maurice. *The Ford Hunger March*. Berkeley, CA: Meiklejohn Civil Liberties Institute, 1980.

Sugrue, Thomas. *The Origins of the Urban Crisis: Race and Inequality in Postwar Detroit*. Princeton, NJ: Princeton University Press, 1997.

Sullivan, Martin Edward. "'On the Dole': The Relief Issue in Detroit, 1929–1939." PhD diss., University of Notre Dame, 1974.

Theoharis, Jeanne, and Komozi Woodard, eds. *Freedom North: Black Freedom Struggles Outside the South, 1940–1980*. New York: Palgrave Macmillan, 2003.

Thomas, June Manning. *Redevelopment and Race: Planning a Finer City in Postwar Detroit*. Baltimore: Johns Hopkins University Press, 1997.

Thomas, Richard W. *Life for Us Is What We Make It: Building Black Community in Detroit, 1915–1945*. Bloomington: Indiana University Press, 1992.

Thompson, Heather. *Whose Detroit? Politics, Labor, and Race in a Modern American City*. Ithaca, NY: Cornell University Press, 2001.

Tice, Karen W. *Tales of Wayward Girls and Immoral Women: Case Records and the Professionalization of Social Work*. Urbana-Champaign: University of Illinois Press, 1998.

Tribich, Chloe. "Social Security Reform in Black and White." *City Limits*, April 20, 2011. www.citylimits.org/conversations/139/entitlement-reform. Accessed April 21, 2011.

Tuttle, William M. *Race Riot: Chicago in the Red Summer of 1919*. Urbana-Champaign: University of Illinois Press, 1996.

Vargas, Zaragosa. *Proletarians of the North: A History of Mexican Industrial Workers in Detroit and the Midwest, 1917–1933*. Berkeley: University of California Press, 1999.

Vose, Clement E. *Caucasians Only: The Supreme Court, the NAACP and the Restrictive Covenant Cases*. Berkeley: University of California Press, 1959.

Wang, Lu-In. *Discrimination by Default: How Racism Becomes Routine*. New York: NYU Press, 2006.

Weinberg, Kenneth G. *A Man's Home, a Man's Castle*. New York: McCall, 1971.

Weiss, Nancy J. *Farewell to the Party of Lincoln: Black Politics in the Age of FDR*. Princeton, NJ: Princeton University Press, 1983.

Wiese, Andrew. *Places of Their Own: African American Suburbanization in the 20th Century*. Chicago: University of Chicago Press, 2004.

Wilder, Craig. *A Covenant with Color: Race and Social Power in Brooklyn*. New York: Columbia University Press, 2001.

Wilkerson, Isabel. *The Warmth of Other Suns: The Epic Story of America's Great Migration*. New York: Vintage, 2011.

Winant, Howard. *The World Is a Ghetto: Race and Democracy since World War II*. New York: Basic Books, 2001.

Wise, Tim. *Colorblind: The Rise of Post-racial Politics and the Retreat from Racial Equity*. San Francisco: City Lights, 2010.

Wolcott, Victoria. "The Culture of the Informal Economy: Numbers Runners in Interwar Black Detroit." *Radical History Review* 69 (1997): 46–75.

———. *Remaking Respectability: African American Women in Interwar Detroit*. Chapel Hill: University of North Carolina Press, 2001.

Wolfinger, James. *Philadelphia Divided: Race and Politics in the City of Brotherly Love*. Chapel Hill: University of North Carolina Press, 2007.

Womak, Hajj Malik. "'To Die Like a Man or Live Like a Coward': The Role of Armed Resistance in the 1925 Dr. Sweet Case." Unpublished manuscript, 1998.

Woodward, C. Vann. *The Strange Career of Jim Crow*. New York: Oxford University Press, 1955.

Wright, Gwendolyn. *Building the Dream: A Social History of Housing in America*. Cambridge, MA: MIT Press, 1981.

Zieger, Robert H. *The CIO, 1935–1955*. Chapel Hill: University of North Carolina Press, 1995.

Zunz, Olivier. *The Changing Face of Inequality: Urbanization, Industrial Development and Immigrants in Detroit, 1880–1920*. Chicago: University of Chicago Press, 1982.

INDEX

ABOUT THE AUTHOR

Karen R. Miller is Professor of History at LaGuardia Community College, City University of New York.

CPSIA information can be obtained
at www.ICGtesting.com
Printed in the USA
LVHW041459171119
637608LV00006B/439/P

9 781479 849208